THE LAST COLONIAL MASSACRE

THE LAST COLONIAL MASSACRE

Latin America in the Cold War

GREG GRANDIN

THE UNIVERSITY OF CHICAGO PRESS

Chicago and London

GREG GRANDIN is associate professor of history at New York University and a Guggenheim fellow. He is the author of *The Blood of Guatemala: A History of Race and Nation.*

The University of Chicago Press, Chicago 60637
The University of Chicago Press, Ltd., London

Printed in the United States of America

13 12 11 10 09 08 07 06 05 4 5

ISBN: 0-226-30571-6 (cloth)
ISBN: 0-226-30572-4 (paper)

Library of Congress Cataloging-in-Publication Data

Grandin, Greg, 1962–
The last colonial massacre : Latin America in the Cold War / Greg Grandin.
p. cm.
Includes bibliographical references (p.)
ISBN 0-226-30571-6 (cloth : alk. paper)—
ISBN 0-226-30572-4 (pbk. : alk. paper)
1. Guatemala—history—1945–1985. 2. Guatemala—History—1821–1945. 3. Massacres—Guatemala—Panzâos. 4. Indians of Central America—Guatemala—Government relations. 5. Communism—Guatemala—History—20th century. 6. Insurgency—Guatemala—History—20th century. 7. Social conflict—Guatemala—History—20th century. 8. United States—Relations—Latin America. 9. Latin America—Relations—United States. I. Title.

F1466.5.G73 2004
972.8105'2—DC22

2004000727

♾ The paper used in this publication meets the minimum requirements of the American National Standard for Information Sciences—Permanence of Paper for Printed Library Materials, ANSI Z39.48–1992.

FOR MG

A VICTORY DESCRIBED IN DETAIL IS INDISTINGUISHABLE FROM A DEFEAT.

Jean-Paul Sartre

Contents

Illustrations

MAPS

FIGURES

Preface

SOON AFTER September 11, 2001, the novelist Ariel Dorfman penned a short essay comparing that day to the overthrow of Chilean president Salvador Allende, which took place on September 11, 1973, also a Tuesday. Dorfman, who served in Allende's government, made his point gently. Although the United States sponsored the military forces that ended Latin America's most stable democracy and killed thousands of Chileans, Dorfman took no pleasure in a retribution exacted by, as he put it, the "malignant gods of random history."[1] Instead he insisted that the twin tragedies offered a unique possibility for reparation. An author of works dedicated to the roughly one hundred thousand Latin Americans "disappeared" by Cold War terror, Dorfman recognized immediately the grief and uncertainty in the faces of the relatives walking about the streets of New York in search of their loved ones, carrying their photographs, not knowing whether their loved ones were alive or dead. That pain, broadcast to the nation, forced the whole United States "to look into the abyss of what it means to be desaparecido, with no certainty or funeral possible for those beloved men and women who are missing." In that confusion resided, Dorfman wrote, an opportunity to end the "famous exceptionalism" that has sheltered the United States from the storms of suffering and insecurity that lash at much of the earth, to nurture a new empathetic internationalism, to mend the many wounds, such as those inflicted on that first September 11, still festering in the wreckage of the Cold War. In catastrophe, he wanted to believe, lay a hope for a future that could escape the repetitions of the past that have made the present so shaken and fearful. Dorfman envisioned a response that, in recognizing a shared fate, a universal anguish, would bring about the humanization rather than the militarization of our world.

U.S. exceptionalism, however, is hard wrought. In the decade following the end of the Cold War, with the implosion and repudiation of Soviet totalitarianism, the idea that the United States has a unique mission in the world flared even brighter than before. Liberal democracy was held to have triumphed absolutely, its fulfillment tightly bound to the history and destiny of the United States.

To be sure, there is no shortage of critiques of U.S. Cold War foreign policy, and many of them, such as investigations into its actions in Indonesia and Southeast Asia, have seeped into popular consciousness. Latin America in particular has long been the Achilles' heel in the hard armor of U.S. virtue, and even the most triumphal of Cold War scholars have been forced into moral contortions to explain away U.S. actions that contributed to the torture and murder of hundreds of thousands of individuals.[2] Aside from making visibly disastrous and deadly interventions in Guatemala in 1954, the Dominican Republic in 1965, Chile in 1973, and El Salvador and Nicaragua during the 1980s, the United States has lent quiet and steady financial, material, and moral support for murderous counterinsurgent terror states, directly resulting in the kind of suffering so easily recognized by Dorfman. But the enormity of Stalin's crimes ensures that such sordid histories, no matter how compelling, thorough, or damning, do not disturb the foundation of a worldview committed to the exemplary role of the United States in defending what we now know as democracy.[3]

A post–Cold War redefinition of democracy has reinforced this fundamental faith. In the years following World War II, a widely held belief across the political spectrum understood democracy as entailing both individual liberty and some degree of equality.[4] Such a definition animated the popular front and the New Deal. Even Ho Chi Minh in 1945 and Fidel Castro in 1953 famously drew from the U.S. Declaration of Independence to make their cases for freedom and justice.[5] Yet today many political theorists, historians, and commentators dismiss as a basic philosophical error the notion that Jeffersonian democracy would lead to, and be fulfilled by, socialism.[6] The horrors of the Soviet Union, not to mention those of Vietnam and Cuba, proved to them that political liberalism with its emphasis on legal equality, procedural guarantees, and individual freedom, and socialism with its market regulations and critique of economic inequities, were not, as many had previously argued, mutually reinforcing. Although socialists and liberal democrats have advanced many of the same causes, the twentieth century, according to this new perspective, bloodily demonstrated that the desire for comprehensive equality, for the achievement of an absent unity, for historical meaning in a meaningless modern world will inevitably lead advocates of the socialist idea to elevate ends over means, reject pluralism, and trespass the legal limits set by constitutional protections and individual rights, especially the right to private property. Socialism today is seen not as a sincere and better variant of democracy but rather as a potentially treacherous ideological progeny that needs to be policed and contained.[7] The Cold War substituted the notion that individual freedom would require some form of economic equality and security with a more vigilant definition of democracy—a definition the United States both embodies and swears to defend. As the opening sentence of its 2002 National Security Strategy puts it, the "great struggles of the twentieth century between liberty and totalitarianism ended with a decisive victory for the forces of freedom—and a *single* sustainable model for national success: freedom, democracy, and free enterprise."[8]

Along with the notion that democracy needs a firm hand comes a rehabilitation of empire. In the decade following the Cold War, Washington preached with evangelical optimism the belief that open markets combined with constitutional rule would produce a peaceful, prosperous world. Yet since September 11, 2001, that faith has given way to a more Napoleonic idealism, one that understands that free market democracy is not necessarily part of the "social order of nature" but requires strong institutional restraints—legal if possible, military if necessary.[9] Such opinions do not only emanate from the political right, although that is where they first gestated. They often receive their most impassioned advocacy from many on the liberal-left. In the face of genocide, social rot, terrorism, corruption, and failed states, it is the West's mission, moral obligation even, to finish the task initiated by the old imperialism, a task that national liberation movements were not up to completing. "Empire," as the human rights theorist Michael Ignatieff put it in his somewhat reluctant endorsement of war with Iraq in 2003, is now "the last hope for democracy and stability alike."[10] So the equation "democracy and socialism" gives way to the equation "democracy and empire" with little notice, at least by those who claim to care about social justice, that the definition of democracy today being exported is a shell of its former self.

Latin America, where this definitional transformation was most profound, plays a curious role in current geopolitical debates taking place in the United States. The right sees the region as a success story: following the 1959 Cuban Revolution, the United States, facing an insurgent blend of Marxism and militant nationalism, responded with an effective mix of hard and soft power, neutralized the opposition, and transformed most of the continent's nations into free market allies and their populations into willing consumers of U.S. goods and technology. Emblematic of this success—and key to understanding Washington's current imperial resoluteness—is the 1981 presidential transition from Jimmy Carter to Ronald Reagan. Carter, the story goes, with his liberal hand-wringing, almost lost the Caribbean and Central

America, if not all of Latin America, until Reagan stepped in, brushed aside a chorus of doubters, and threw the full weight of U.S. power toward containing communism, thus liberating Nicaragua, saving El Salvador and Guatemala, and isolating Cuba. Liberals were wrong about Latin America in the 1980s, conservative strategist William Kristol states today in justifying Washington's new hard line.[11] The left of course draws a different lesson. For those who unequivocally oppose military interventions abroad, the sad history of U.S. hemispheric policy is a self-evident confirmation of their position. Others, however, who support some version of the "war on terror" in the name of progressive values, while admitting the base motives and baleful legacy of the United States in the region, argue that the past does not necessarily have to determine the future. And besides, according to this perspective, even if Washington is driven by less than noble purpose, it does not follow that its power could not achieve some good—to stem religious intolerance, for example, or to stop massive human rights abuses and overthrow indefensible dictatorships—in an increasingly volatile and dangerous world.[12]

But more than just providing a moral standard on which to test the sincerity of U.S. claims, the history the Cold War in Latin America, I believe, can help us understand how our world has become so inflamed. It corrects the myopia of those who decline to consider the toll of Cold War success, who refuse to make the connection between nearly a half century of unrelenting war on real or potential revolutionary threats and the militarization, violence, endemic hunger, chronic poverty, rising fundamentalism, and loss of modernist optimism that now grip much of the world.[13] Cold War triumphalists would of course respond by saying that the West's victory merely set the stage for a potential but by no means guaranteed extension of liberal democracy. This book argues the opposite for Latin America: Cold War terror—either executed, patronized, or excused by the United States—fortified illiberal forces, militarized societies, and broke the link between freedom and equality, thus greatly weakening the likelihood of such a fulfillment and making possible the reversal of the gains that had been achieved.

In Latin America, in country after country, the mass peasant and working-class movements that gained ground in the middle of the twentieth century were absolutely indispensable to the advancement of democracy. To the degree that Latin America today may be considered democratic, it was the left, including the Marxist left, that made it so. Empire, rather than fortifying democracy, weakened it. Launched first by domestic elites in the years after World War II and then quickly joined by the United States, the savage crusade, justified under the guise of the Cold War, against Latin American democratic movements had devastating human and political costs. In some countries, such as Uruguay, Brazil, and Chile, national security states carried out a focused, surgically precise repression. Other states, such as Argentina, El Salvador, and Guatemala, let loose a more scattershot horror. In all cases, terror had the effect of, first, radicalizing society to produce febrile political polarization and, second, destroying the more capacious, social understandings of democracy that prevailed in the years around World War II. One important consequence of this terror was the severance of the link between individual dignity and social solidarity, a combination that, as I will argue through the course of this book, was the wellspring of the old left's strength. During the transition to constitutional rule that occurred throughout Central and South America following the Cold War, democracy came to be defined strictly in the astringent terms of personal freedom rather than social security. This redefinition served as the qualification for the free market ideologies and policies that now reign throughout the continent and indeed most of the world. In other words, to make the point as crudely as possible, the conception of democracy now being prescribed as the most effective weapon in the war on terrorism is itself largely, at least in Latin America, a product of terror.

A Note on Interviews and Archives

THIS STUDY is based on over one hundred interviews with more than seventy-five individuals conducted in Guatemala, Mexico, and the United States. Reasons of privacy necessitate the omission or alteration of many names. When names are omitted, citations will include the informant's significance to the study and the month and year the interview took place. At times I have not attributed contextual information or general observations to specific individuals, particularly when the source is referenced in the text itself. I videotaped one interview with Efraín Reyes Maaz and sound-recorded another. The cassettes and transcripts of both are deposited at the Centro de Estudios Urbanos y Regionales at the Universidad de San Carlos, Guatemala's national university.

A few words on the archives I used may be useful to researchers. Researchers wishing to consult the records of the now defunct Instituto Nacional de Transformación Agraria need to request permission from the president of the state agency Fondo de Tierra. This collection of documents, which is now located eighteen kilometers out of Guatemala City on the road to Escuintla, had been previously stored in a warehouse near the airport in Guatemala City, and included the extant documentation related to the 1952–54 Agrarian Reform. The Agrarian Reform files have now been incorporated into the Archivo General de Centro América. The Guatemalan Document Collection at the Library of Congress is a collection of some 35,000 documents related to union, government, and PGT activity and taken from Guatemala following the 1954 overthrow of Arbenz. It is microfilmed on fifty-eight reels. The Partido Guatemalteco de Trabajo Collection at Tulane University is a collection of PGT manifestos, reports, and position papers dating from the late 1950s. The Universidad de San Carlos's Centro de Estudios Urbanos y Regionales also holds PGT documents. Aside from material housed in the Ministerio de Gobernación section of the Archivo General de Centro

América, I had access to papers in the Ministerio's office on Eighteenth Street in downtown Guatemala City. The San Pedro Carchá Municipal Archives is a large collection, in disarray but generally bundled by year, of documents running from the early nineteenth century through the present.

In addition to the archival sources listed in the bibliography, San Pedro Carchá's civil registry, particularly its Libros de cédulas and Libros de defunciones, was also useful, as were the baptismal records of Carchá's Catholic parish, located opposite the municipal building. In Cahabón and Panzós, I also consulted the civil registries and municipal minutes. Pedro Taracena graciously allowed me to research the personal papers of his uncle, Eduardo Taracena de la Cerda, a prominent anti-communist activist. The labor lawyer Antonio Argueta granted me access to a number of important documents pertaining to the Panzós massacre. The Archivo Histórico del Centro de Investigaciones Regionales de Mesoamérica in Antigua contains invaluable press clippings as well as other miscellaneous material. The Robert Alexander Collection located at Rutgers University Library holds Alexander's notes and reflections on nearly every Latin American and Latin Americanist Alexander came across in his half century of scholarship, ranging from presidents to taxi drivers. The Erwin Paul Dieseldorff Collection at Tulane University was also helpful. Newspapers consulted for this study can be found at either Guatemala City's Hemeroteca Nacional or at Antigua's Centro de Investigaciones Regionales de Mesoamérica and unless otherwise indicated are from Guatemala. Many of the declassified United States government documents used in this book can be found in either the National Security Archive, located at George Washington University, or online in the Declassified Documents Reference System, www.ddrs.psmedia.com. Some of the more important documents, especially those pertaining to Operación Limpieza, have been published in my *Denegado en su totalidad.*

INTRODUCTION

The Last Colonial Massacre

AT FIRST GLANCE, the defining feature of the May 29, 1978, Panzós massacre was its persistent ordinariness, its indistinguishability from the hundreds of other indigenous protests and elite reactions that had taken place throughout the course of colonial and republican rule in Guatemala to that day. Early on a Monday morning between five hundred and seven hundred Q'eqchi'-Mayan women, men, and children arrived in the center of Panzós, a languorous river town sitting low in the marshlands of the Polochic Valley. They gathered to present a letter to the mayor announcing an impending visit of a union delegation from the capital to discuss long-standing peasant complaints against local planters.[1] A military detachment that had set up camp in the central plaza three days earlier met the crowd. Survivors insist that the soldiers opened fire preemptively, even with premeditation. Some however say the protesters were the aggressors, banging their machetes together, throwing chili in the eyes of the troops, and demanding the installation of an "Indian king." Others simply report a more prosaic scuffle that led to a tragic overreaction by both sides. At least thirty-five Q'eqchi's, including a number of children, lay murdered and dozens were wounded by the time the shooting stopped. More died in flight, either in the mountains or swept away by the Polochic River. Guatemalans have debated the exact number of victims to this day. Forensic anthropologists exhumed thirty-four skeletal remains in 1997 from a mass grave, but survivors then and now insist that the dead numbered in the hundreds.[2]

Compare this killing with the bloodshed that led to the establishment of Panzós as a municipality over a hundred years earlier: In the early dawn of June 29, 1865, after months of petitions, the "octogenarian" Jorge Yat led hundreds of Q'eqchi'-Mayans into the center of San Pedro Carchá, an indigenous town above Panzós at the high end of the Polochic Valley. As in Panzós a century later, they protested the influence of Ladinos—the term used to identify those Guatemalans not considered Mayan—on the village's administration and economy.[3] As in Panzós in 1978, Q'eqchi's in 1865 appealed to higher authorities to side with them against their enemies, in this case the newly arrived merchants, coffee planters, and priest. Mixing the millenarian with the mundane, they demanded both the expulsion of foreigners and a reduction of taxes. Ladinos, for their part, worked, as they did later in Panzós, to keep all but the most repressive elements of the state out of their jurisdiction. When Yat presented a "note" supposedly given to him by the president, Carchá's priest flew into a rage, yelling that "an insignificant man" like Yat could never have obtained an audience with the president. He struck Yat, which led the protesters to imprison the cleric and a handful of other Ladinos. In response, militiamen from the region's nearby capital marched on Carchá, laid siege to the square, and opened fire, killing eight Q'eqchi's. Others drowned trying to escape or died of injuries in flight. State violence against Q'eqchi's—no Ladinos were injured or killed—hastened an already established migration down the Polochic Valley to the areas that would soon become the municipality of Panzós.

Both killings have all the elementary characteristics of a run-of-the-mill peasant jacquerie or, as Spanish colonial administrators often described Native American dissent, a *motín de indios*, an Indian riot. Suffering the accumulated abuses of provincial elites, Indians appeal to faraway sovereigns. Upon word that the king or the president has ruled on their behalf, men and women gather in the plaza brandishing unspecified "papers" believed to sanction their cause to demand the application of distant dictates. Faced with an angry crowd, local elites or their militia protectors violently overreact, firing into the assembly, conjuring the riot they have long feared.[4]

Yet the 1978 Panzós massacre is distinct in that it represents the passing of such exhausted patterns of protest and reaction, prefiguring more deadly forms of counterinsurgent violence that were soon to come. Throughout the late eighteenth and early nineteenth centuries, the existence of an agricultural frontier muted many of the conflicts and disruptions created by the fast expansion of coffee capitalism, allowing for the settlement of sanctuaries such as Panzós. Yet by the 1970s, the possibility for flight or migration had greatly diminished, forcing peasants to engage more directly the promise of state-administered justice and to confront frontally the immediate agents of their misery. Likewise, the soldiers who guarded the plaza that Monday morning may have been called in by local planters, but they were no sleepy outland militia detachment occasionally roused into action. They were part of Guatemala's new army, steeped in anti-communism and flushed with counterinsurgent training and equipment, the front line in an escalating civil war between a spreading rural insurgency and an increasingly repressive state. Often in the past, outbursts of protest and reaction would result in some sort of reformed reestablishment of the relations of rule, the expression of a kind of postbellum remorse by all involved. Yet in the wake of Panzós, following a brief period of national soul-searching and talk of reform, politics continued to rapidly decompose. Three years later, the military would launch a genocide the enormity of which would make events in Panzós on that May morning seem as ancient as Yat's protest.

Beginning in 1981, the army executed a scorched earth campaign that murdered over one hundred thousand Mayans and completely razed more than four hundred indigenous communities. Anti-communist zeal and racist hatred were refracted through counterinsurgent exactitude. The killings were brutal beyond imagination. Soldiers murdered children by beating them on rocks as their parents watched. They extracted organs and fetuses, amputated genitalia and limbs, committed mass and multiple rapes, and burned some victims alive. In the logic that equated indigenous culture with subversion, army units destroyed ceremonial sites and turned sacred places such as churches and caves into torture chambers. By the time the war ended in 1996, the state had killed two hundred thousand people, disappeared forty thousand, and tortured unknown thousands more.

It would be tempting to see the Panzós massacre as a third-world perversion of the fall of the Bastille, as ushering in not liberty, equality, and fraternity but a kind of postcolonial modernity based on subjugation, exclusion, and terror. According to a number of critical scholars, it is the Enlightenment, particularly its rationalization of repressive techniques, discourses of racial hierarchy, and terror justified in the name of competing ideologies and historical movement, that accounts for the kind of violence that took place in the wake of Panzós. Yet such arguments tend to turn in circles, blaming oppression on a uniformly oppressive modernity rather than on the outcomes of political struggles that shaped our modern world. Nor did the massacre signal the sudden and spontaneous eruption of peasants into the national arena. Guatemala's four-decade-long civil war, one of the bloodiest in twentieth-century American history, is composed of many stories, as many as there are individuals, families, and communities that lived through it, and each story has a different turning point and climax. Rather, this seemingly routine killing, taking place as it did in a remote outpost in a minor country, is emblematic of the power of the Cold War, which fused together multiple, long-evolving individual, national, and international experiences and conflicts.

This book documents the nearly century-long intermittent mobilization leading up to the Panzós massacre, focusing on the lives of a number of

Q'eqchi'-Mayans, mostly members of the Communist Party but not exclusively so. In Guatemala as in many other areas of Latin America, engagement with ideas and practices associated with the left was, for many, a profoundly disruptive, humanizing experience. To say so is not to ratify any claims regarding the essence of human nature but to underscore the oppressive stasis and brutality of a coercive plantation regime, even as the society as a whole found itself in the midst of rapid metamorphosis. Participation in mass politics to demand that the state administer justice provided for many a way to catapult out of daily traps of humiliation and savagery, fashioning a commonsensical understanding of democracy not as procedural constitutionalism but as the felt experience of individual sovereignty and social solidarity. While each chapter of this book highlights particular individuals, the lives are presented not as isolated portraits but rather as part of a wider social landscape that reflects much of what was fought over in the Cold War.

The Guatemalan civil war in all of its cruelty could understandably be considered history in extremis—singular in its viciousness and devastation—except that it so closely parallels and even propels much of the history of Latin America in the second half of the twentieth century. More even than Cuba, this Central American republic has served as a staging ground for the continental Cold War. In October 1944, a revolution sparked by urban protests brought to an end one of the Americas' longest and most repressive dictatorships, ushering in a decade of unprecedented reform, inluding an ambitious land reform. Invigorated by the Allies' impending victory in World War II, the October Revolution, as the newborn government soon came to be called, was one of the brightest stars in a larger, albeit fragile, democratic firmament that took shape throughout Latin America between 1944 and 1946. Ten years later, however, in 1954, Guatemala had the distinction of suffering the United States' first Latin American Cold War intervention, an ambitious operation that drew not just on traditional military, economic, and diplomatic pressure to unseat a freely elected president, Jacobo Arbenz, but on innovative techniques borrowed from mass psychology, media, and advertising as well. Yet although this operation enjoyed a quick success, the October Revolution's afterburn was not so easily put out. Aborted hopes and frustrated reforms created a social democratic vista that inspired successive generations of activists and revolutionaries. In opposition to them, however, stood Guatemala's newly fortified security and intelligence forces. After 1954, all political actions—in defense or defiance of the status quo—divided according to Cold War priorities. Politics quickly spun out of control as efforts to reestablish democratic rule gave way to a four-decade civil war between leftist insurgents and the military.

The overthrow of Arbenz was a decisive step forward in the radicalization of continental politics, signaling as it did the destruction of one of the last, and arguably the most influential, democracies established in the 1944–46 reform cycle. It confirmed growing suspicions among many democrats and nationalists that the United States was less a model to be emulated than a danger to be feared and led to more militant tactics on both sides of the Cold War divide. Che Guevara, who witnessed firsthand the destruction of the October Revolution, repeatedly taunted the United States in his speeches that "Cuba will not be Guatemala." For its part, the United States would try to replicate its 1954 operation seven years later with the disastrous Bay of Pigs invasion. Throughout the next three decades, the United States continued to provide Guatemalan security forces with a steady supply of equipment, training, and financing, even as political repression grew ferocious. Practices rehearsed in Guatemala—such as covert destabilization operations and death squad killings conducted by professionalized intelligence agencies—spread throughout the region in the coming decades. As Washington increasingly came to regret Vietnam as a failure, it continued to count Guatemala as a success. In the 1980s, the final escalation of the superpower conflict turned the country, along with Nicaragua and El Salvador, into one of the Cold War's last killing fields.

The Latin American Cold War began not in 1954, with the defeat of Arbenz, or in 1959, with the triumph of Castro, but in the years following World War II. In 1944, only five Latin American countries —Mexico, Uruguay, Chile, Costa Rica, and Colombia—could nominally call themselves democracies. By 1946, only five—Paraguay, El Salvador, Honduras, Nicaragua, and the Dominican Republic—could not.[5] Dictators toppled throughout Latin America, and governments extended the franchise and legalized unions. To varying degrees in different countries, urbanization, industrialization, and population growth had created an emerging middle class and urban working class that joined with students, intellectuals, and in some cases a militant peasantry. Such coalitions generated both the demands for democratic restructuring and the social power needed to achieve it. Following the war, revitalized labor unions in Mexico, Brazil, Peru, Guatemala, Colombia, Argentina, and Chile led strike waves of unparalleled belligerence. In a number of countries, populist reform parties, many of them organized in the 1920s, came to power, impelled by this increased mobilization. The more democratic elements of liberalism, which since the mid-nineteenth century had functioned primarily as an elite justification of domination and economic modernization, now came to be advanced not just by urban political elites but by mass movements.[6]

While the masses radicalized democracy, a wartime alliance with "bourgeois" classes helped tame the Marxist left. Communist parties throughout the continent jettisoned their revolutionary and anti-imperialist rhetoric to join a larger electoral "popular front" against fascism, in some places serving as partners in ruling coalitions.[7] The domestication of the left, counterintuitively, contributed to the insurgency of the moment. Headed by a newly rehabilitated Stalinist leadership largely neglected by Moscow, Communists emerged during World War II as part of a broader egalitarian consensus that partly muted the fractional struggles, sectarian tactics, and class antagonisms of the prewar years. The sociology of development offered by Marxism, with its emphasis on advancing national capitalism by breaking the "feudal" power of the landed aristocracy, became an evident truth for a broad spectrum of reformers, Communist and non-Communist alike.[8] Throughout the region, governments enacted social welfare programs and sought to achieve economic development through state planning, regulation of capital, and other initiatives that favored the domestic manufacturing sector, while the left, broadly understood, grew in popularity and institutional strength.

This union of a socialized democracy and a democratized socialism produced a powerful threat to the power and privileges of the incumbent order. Democracy, as Leslie Bethell and Ian Roxborough put it in their survey of the postwar period, came to mean a "commitment to popular, more particularly working-class participation in politics, and social and economic improvements for the poorer sections of the population. Democracy increasingly became identified with development and welfare. This was a vision of the Latin American Left, both Communist and non-Communist."[9] The advance of this vision came not just from the power of persuasion but from the pragmatism of politics, as a wide array of reformers believed that the best way to weaken the oligarchy was to empower those under its thrall. The notion that it was the state's responsibility to provide a dignified life and economic justice was so widespread that it became for many synonymous with modernity, which some politicians felt had finally arrived in Latin America. "We are socialists," said Guatemalan president Juan José Arévalo in 1944, "because we live in the twentieth century."[10] Latin America even exported this vision of social citizenship, as a number of the continent's jurists pushed for economic rights to be included in the United Nations' 1948 Universal Declaration of Human

Rights.[11] Inspired by the defeat of fascism yet spared the barbarism that their counterparts lived through in Europe and Asia, intellectuals, artists, and writers elaborated a buoyant cultural modernism that drew from and reinforced this political effervescence.

This is not to suggest that the reformist, nationalist, socialist, and Communist parties that spearheaded the postwar opening were unambiguous defenders of an Enlightenment tradition worth defending. Many of them succumbed to the corruptions and compromises of politics. Because of their allegiance to the Soviet Union, Communist parties, even while they were often the most ardent advocates of democratic reform at home, defended the indefensible abroad. Nationalists in Argentina, Bolivia, and Brazil perilously flirted with fascism. All continued to exclude, subordinate, or not address the concerns of large segments of their national populations, especially women, indigenous peoples, and descendants of African slaves. And oftentimes, predictably, they fought each other with more passion than they fought the oligarchs. Yet in the years after World War II, a wide range of reformist parties and individuals, including Marxists, felt compelled, either because of their own specific vision of modernity or because of sustained pressure from below, to resolve the problem of mass politics and national development by attempting to socialize democracy. But more than this, politics became an immediate experience in the lives of many, and an increasing number of society's most excluded began to sense that the old entitlements no longer held. The meter of daily life quickened as global events came closer and the possibility of progress, previously depicted as lying in the abstract distance, seemed to draw nearer. No matter how moderate claims to social citizenship may appear in light of the militancy of the 1960s and 1970s, they in fact posed a serious threat to the comforts, conventions, and customs of the privileged order, unleashing a "heretical challenge," as historian Daniel James describes Peronism, not so easily contained.[12]

An emerging international political and economic regime greatly shortened the life expectancy of postwar democracies. Following World War II the world divided into contending camps represented by the United States and the Soviet Union, with Latin America clearly falling under the sway of the former. As this global order took shape with the creation of the United Nations, a series of military, cultural, political, and economic treaties, along with the newly created Organization of American States, bound the Americas together, forming a "closed hemisphere" in an increasingly open and interdependent world.[13] Desperate to attract capital investment, domestic elites, many of them committed reformers, offered little resistance to or dissent from the twin goals of U.S. Cold War foreign policy: to halt the spread of

Communism and not only advance capitalism but ensure U.S. dominance within that system.[14]

The years 1947–48 were bad ones for global democracy. The creation of the Central Intelligence Agency, the Truman Doctrine, Taft-Hartley and the National Security Act, the repudiation of Henry Wallace as the legitimate heir to the New Deal, the institutionalization of apartheid, the partition of colonial India, the ideological hardening of the Soviet Union, the Communist coup in Czechoslovakia, and Stalin's betrayal of the partisans in the Greek Civil War are just a few of the omens that dampened the hopes inspired by the defeat of fascism. No wonder Michael Harrington called 1948 the "last year of the 1930s."[15] Events in Latin America were no less ominous as 1947 marked the beginning of a continent-wide reaction. In Peru and Venezuela military coups overthrew elected governments. In countries that maintained the trappings of democracy there was a sharp veer to the right. In Chile in 1947, President Gabriel González Videla carried out a violent assault against striking coal miners and his erstwhile Communist allies, destroying a popular front coalition that had elected three presidents since 1938. Reform parties lost their dynamism, while governments intervened against work stoppages, passed legislation restricting the right to strike, and outlawed or repressed Communist parties. Unions purged militants from their ranks, while labor confederations either fractured or came under government control. By 1954, dictators once again ruled a majority of Latin American countries.

The emerging counterrevolutionary coalition took specific forms in different countries but in general was supported by the rural propertied classes, the military, church hierarchs, and manufacturing and industrial capitalists who previously may have been in favor of reform but now sought political quiescence in order to attract foreign investment.[16] The dual promises of democracy and development, which just a few short years earlier seemed to be intimately linked, were now practically incompatible. In order to create a stable investment climate and absent a Latin American Marshall Plan, local governments cracked down on labor unrest and other forms of popular mobilization, which in many countries had been on a sharp rise since the end of World War II. At the same time, closer political and military relations with the United States steadily strengthened the repressive capabilities of Latin American security forces. Even before the establishment of the CIA in 1947, the FBI began to turn its surveillance away from Nazi and fascist groups toward Communist parties, an abrupt shift from the U.S. wartime alliance with the left against the right. What was convenient in 1944 became unacceptable by 1947. U.S. embassies began to pressure governments to proscribe Communist parties, which, notwithstanding their internal authoritarianism, were often the most forceful advocates of political liberalization. Local interests took advantage of this sea change to launch a reaction aimed at restoring not just their economic authority but the cultures of compliance they presided over. The importance of the intersection between national and international interests to the containment of Latin American democracy cannot be overestimated. In Guatemala, for example, one of the reasons the October Revolution weathered the first years of the conservative counterthrust is that its Communist Party was not formed until 1949 and therefore could not serve as a lightning rod to join local and foreign opposition.

What Louis Pérez argues for Cuba is true for much of Latin America: pushed to their "logical conclusion," the democratic values represented by the United States created a crisis situation in nearly every country across the continent.[17] Castro's evocation of Thomas Paine in his 1953 "History Will Absolve Me" speech captures the inspiration the progressive currents of U.S. history held for Latin American intellectuals and politicians well into the Cold War. The widely reported anecdote that a fourteen-year-old Castro sent Franklin Delano Roosevelt a letter to congratulate him on his 1940 electoral victory (he also asked FDR for a dollar!) likewise highlights the importance the New Deal state held as a model to would-be Latin American reformers. Yet the increasingly heavy hand of the United States in hemispheric and world affairs reawakened anti-imperialist resentments that had lain dormant during the wartime popular front. Even before the overthrow of Arbenz, the exiled Dominican poet Pedro Mir in 1952 lamented the conscription of Walt Whitman's radical exuberance into a more martial campaign: "The ones who defiled his luminous beard and put a gun on his shoulders. . . . Those of you who do not want Walt Whitman, the democrat, but another Whitman, atomic and savage" (a decade later, Mir's poetics would prove prophetic when Walt Whitman Rostow, an advocate of military escalation in Vietnam, became a key advisor to Presidents Kennedy and Johnson).[18] Many Latin American nationalists and democrats thought the United States was using the dawning Cold War as a pretext to roll back democracy and directly related the global chill to domestic repression within the United States. An impressive letter-writing campaign organized by left unions and parties throughout Latin America, for instance, pleaded for the lives of Julius and Ethel Rosenberg and condemned their executions in harsh terms. "Your consent to the assassination of the Rosenbergs," Guatemala's national labor federation telegrammed Eisenhower in 1953, "makes clear the brutal imperialist policy of the United States. American democracy has been buried."[19]

In "Chronicle of 1948 (America)," Chilean poet Pablo Neruda, having recently abandoned his position as a Communist Party senator owing to government repression, surveyed the ruins of failed reform. From his exile in Mexico, he asked, "how will it end . . . this bleak year? . . . This bleak year of rage and rancor, you ask, you ask me how will it end?"

It ended badly. The Cold War unfolded in its own way in each country, yet in many Latin American nations political strategies radicalized and political visions polarized. Despite the setbacks suffered in the late forties, reformers and nationalists worked with some success to reestablish democracies. By 1961, there were again only a handful of Latin American nations that were not, at least nominally, democratic. And once again, many of these new governments attempted to enact tax, land, and political reforms to promote political and economic modernization, now backed up, verbally at least, by the Kennedy administration's Alliance for Progress, which aimed to create a prosperous, stable middle class inoculated against Castroism. Political scientist Victor Alba viewed the period with such hope that he gushed that Latin American militarism would soon wither away.[20] But it did not. At the same time as the United States was promoting modernization, it was also invigorating Latin American militaries and centralized intelligence agencies in an effort to counter real and perceived insurgent threats. Starting in Argentina in 1962, emboldened militaries toppled democratically elected administrations. Guatemala (again) in 1963. Brazil in 1964. Bolivia in 1971. Uruguay and Chile in 1973. When national actors proved insufficient to contain the threat of mass politics, the United States directly intervened, mostly through quiet encouragement and support as in the coups just mentioned, but occasionally with more fanfare, such as when it invaded the Dominican Republic in 1965. Once more the wheel had turned, and by 1976 there were only three nations that could be considered democratic.

While alternations between reform and reaction were nothing new to Latin America, this mid-century rotation was different. It marked a maturation of an evolution in the conditions governing domestic politics that had been under way since at least World War I. Realizing that a simple barracks revolt could not extinguish the seemingly inexhaustible threats to their powers and privileges, those who opposed change sought help. In Argentina and Chile for example, sectors of the oligarchy that had previously disdained mass action began to actively support and participate in fascist movements.[21] Yet in many countries, established institutions representing the landed elites and the Church had to different degrees lost their regenerative vitality. The fight would not be led by the upper classes but by insurgent counterinsurgents—radical Catholics, socially aspiring middle-class soldiers, anti-communist students. Their affective attachment to yet sufficient distance from vested powers, traditions, and hierarchies allowed them to respond to challenges with efficiency and passion. In Guatemala, for example, the crusade against Arbenz was led not by the oligarchy, the military, or even, at least effectively, the Church but by young, militantly anti-communist students, many of them the professionalized urban sons of middling rural planters. They generated among the middle class, workers, peasants, men, and women a popular anti-communist authoritarianism designed to both assuage the insecurity caused by the liberalization of society and counter the expectations of fulfillment advanced by the left. A deepening cultural pessimism across the liberal-conservative spectrum regarding the deficits of democratic suffrage and self-rule reinforced this political and ideological assault, corroding institutional protections and facilitating the turn to state terror.

The state's increasingly beefed up and increasingly ideological repressive capacity greatly restricted the already cramped space for political negotiation, fueling the passing of Latin America's old left, led by socialist, nationalist, or otherwise reformist parties with working-class and at times peasant bases of support, and the development of a more insurgent new left, inspired by Cuba, Algeria, and Vietnam and rooted in the agrarian, and in many cases indigenous, countryside. One particular episode—the subject of chapter 3—encapsulates this transition. After the 1954 overthrow of Arbenz, the strategies of the left divided. A new generation of revolutionaries dismissed the attempts of Guatemala's Communist Party, the Partido Guatemalteco de Trabajo (PGT), which had served as Arbenz's principal advisor, to usher in progressive capitalism as misguided in light of U.S. intervention and irrelevant in the wake of the Cuban Revolution. By the early 1960s, these young leftists came together in a socialist insurgency that would continue for almost four decades. But the PGT, clandestine and persecuted, was still influential. While it allied with the rebels, it did so grudgingly, viewing armed resistance more as a pressure tactic than as a way of taking state power. Many within its leadership, along with other reformers and nationalists, continued to believe that the 1944 revolution could be remade. Responding to the Cuban Revolution in 1959, the United States actively pushed for the creation of a national and Central America–wide counterinsurgency network, upgrading the intelligence system with new weapons, vehicles, and telecommunication equipment. This revamped repressive apparatus was put to a lethal test with the arrival in Guatemala in November 1965 of U.S. security advisor John P. Longan. Summoned to help stem a rise in urban political unrest, Longan worked with an elite squad to quickly gather and coordinate intelligence, analyze information, and conduct rapid raids on the homes and meeting places of suspected subversives. Throughout 1966, the squad conducted a series of captures and assassinations, scoring its most impressive success in March 1966 when, four months after Longan's training, it kidnapped, tortured, and executed as many as thirty people. This operation took place on the eve of the election of a civilian president who repeatedly evoked the legacy of the 1944 October Revolution. Some in the PGT and its allied guerrilla organization, especially those active during the Arbenz period, thought the imminent election of a civilian government provided the possibility to reenter the political arena, and they encouraged their rank and file to cast their vote in his favor. Opposing these plans stood the Guatemalan military and the CIA, which, declassified documents reveal, were nervous about a possible negotiated end to the insurgency and a return of the Communists to legal status and influence. The executions had a toxic effect on Guatemalan politics, shutting down the possibility of peaceful change by physically eliminating those who advocated a return to electoral politics and inaugurating three decades of institutionalized extrajudicial murder.

In a sense this operation—the first systematic wave of collective counterinsurgent "disappearances" in Latin America—offered in one act a repeat performance of Guatemala's democratic decade: reformers and revolutionaries hoping to create the kind of electoral coalitions that brought about the 1944 revolution now confronted a new set of international relations, put in place with the 1954 counterrevolution, that ensured that such alliances could never come to fruition. Following this collective execution, escalating repression destroyed any conceit that 1944 could be recreated. In the 1970s, the PGT passed into irrelevance, overshadowed by a growing Cuban-inspired insurgency intent on overthrowing, not reforming, the state. In one sense, Guatemala's October Revolution ended in 1966, not 1954.

Accelerating rhythms of reform, reaction, and foreign intervention proved to be potent radicalizing catalysts. Many activists, witnessing one democracy after another break on the rocks of an increasingly unyielding anti-Communist global order, chose militant paths.[22] In Guatemala, for example, a young medical doctor named Ernesto Guevara sought asylum in the Argentine embassy following the 1954 U.S.-backed coup. While he awaited safe conduct to Mexico (where he would meet Fidel Castro), he started a lifelong friendship with Ricardo Ramírez, who went on to lead Guatemala's most formidable insurgent movement in the 1970s and 1980s. Both men would cite their 1954 experience as central to their subsequent rejection of reform politics and embrace of armed revolution. Throughout the continent, increasingly virulent reaction forged among the generation of 1960 a "new ideological armour."[23] Young leftists inspired by the 1959 Cuban Revolution and frustrated by the inability of substantive democracy to take root broke with the electoral tactics of their nations' Communist parties and organized rural insurgencies in the hope of following Cuba's road to revolutionary sovereignty. At the same time, Latin American sociologists and economists began to work out a broad, new historical perspective on Latin American history. They argued against both mainstream theories of development and the gradualist goals of orthodox Latin American Communist parties. Their political passions varied, yet many *dependentistas* shared a belief that development would come not through collaboration with a "nationalist" bourgeoisie or through participation in a world system, as many postwar democrats had hoped, but rather through divorcing from that system and establishing autonomous forms of national development. Similar to their New Left counterparts in the United States who led withering attacks on New Deal corporate liberalism and Stalinism, intellectuals and activists of this generation dismissed or ignored the postwar democratic opening. At best the period was seen as a misguided failure; at worst as neutering potentially revolutionary popular movements and aspirations through incorporation into state welfare systems. By 1977 in Guatemala, after decades of government repression, labor leaders reinterpreted the postwar democratic period—the deepest and longest lasting in the hemisphere—to mean that workers must "not trust the state or the parties of the petty bourgeoisie."[24]

Yet government repression did more than just first militarize and then vanquish the left. By the mid-twentieth century, peasant and working-class movements had become the primary carriers of not only democratization—a project Latin American liberals had long since abandoned—but social democratization. They demanded that the state use its power to rein in the abuses of capital. Yet most governments in the years following World War II proved entirely unable to carry out such an undertaking with any consistency. Their sovereignty did not extend into the plantation or the factory. Lacking not only a monopoly of legitimate violence but the necessary capacity for illegitimate repression to counter seemingly inextinguishable mass mobilizations, security forces imported from the United States (as well as from South Africa, Israel, and France) new repressive technologies to nationalize violence. In Guatemala, this nationalized terror entailed the direct incorporation of independent death squads into military structures as well as an increasingly visible performance of what previously had been quotidian, private acts, such as rape, torture, and murder. The ever more ritualistic nature of repression served as a public display of the military's sovereignty, legitimate or otherwise. The 1981–83 genocidal campaign was designed to counter what strategists deemed the "closed," castelike isolation of indigenous communities, identified as the reason for the supposed collective susceptibility of Mayans to communism.[25] As Héctor Gramajo, one of the young colonels who designed the genocide, put it, "we brought government to the village."[26] Government repression then in a way was both a backlash against the ongoing legacy of postwar democracy and its perverse fulfillment—the hope of a postwar social democratic state mutated into the grotesquerie of a counterinsurgent terror regime.

With a few important exceptions such as Costa Rica, Mexico, and Ecuador, state- and elite-orchestrated preventive and punitive terror was key to ushering in neoliberalism in Latin America.[27] The prerequisite for the rapid economic restructuring that took place throughout the Americas beginning full throttle in the 1980s—lowering tariffs, deregulating capital streams, reducing government social spending, weakening labor protections—had as much to do with the destruction of mass movements as it did with the rise of new financial elites invested in global markets. The threat of mid-century social movements was that they provided a venue in which self and solidarity could be imagined as existing in sustaining relation to one another through collective politics that looked toward the state to dispense justice. Latin American democracy as an ideal and a practice was always more participatory and egalitarian than it was procedural and individualistic. In many countries, Cold War terror changed that, imposing a more restrictive model, one that defined individualism as economic self-interest and advanced it through free market policies. While some regimes, such as Argentina and to a lesser extent Chile, deployed a more explicit antimodernist rhetoric than others—criticizing, for instance, the soullessness of liberalism—there was no attempt to dissolve a plurality of individuals into a totalitarian state or ideology. Instead, counterinsurgent governments installed a kind of mild Hobbesian authoritarianism. They redefined the state not as the fulfiller of individual aspirations but as an enforcer that made the pursuit of self-interest possible by policing the boundaries, defined now by the overlapping metaphors of religion, nation, and family, in which individualism operated. The Chilean dictator Augusto Pinochet, for example, was skilled at weaving together the enticements of individualism and the restraints of authority. He could condemn the spiritual bankruptcy of secular liberalism because it leaves humans alone in a meaningless world while at the same time affirming Chile's pride in being "one of the first countries in the world to abolish slavery."[28] The appeal of such a vision resonated, accounting for the popularity Pinochet enjoys among certain sectors of the Chilean population. As one of his supporters puts it, "I believe in freedom; I like freedom, and as a result, I think that the more freedom you have the more you grow to respect it. But sometimes democratic regimes suffer from too much freedom . . . we must preserve freedom, but with restrictions."[29]

Once security forces contained popular movements and established stability, governments furthered this "profound transformation of consciousness"—as the head of the Argentine junta Jorge Videla, mimicking language associated with the New Left, understood his mission—through consumerism and, for those who submitted, individual liberties.[30] New products flooded national markets, leading to an erosion of working-class, citizen, and other collective identities.[31] In Chile, according to sociologist Tomás Moulian, a society "in which solidarity and community were highly valued was transformed into a bourgeois culture based exclusively on competitive individualism. . . . Individual survival strategies completely absorb each person's energies, and there are no aspirations other than those based on individual interests."[32] During the return to constitutional rule of most Latin American countries in the 1980s and 1990s, political leaders and advisors dissuaded parties from mobilizing their supporters, encouraging them to adopt a more "modern" political style based on passive representation and elite negotiations.[33]

In the aftermath of failed revolutions and unimaginable government repression, some scholars now lament the rise of Latin America's Cuba-fired left, seeing it as interrupting an evolutionary social democracy. Their contrition is confirmed by the perversion of Peru's Shining Path, which embraced with a vengeance the New Left's "will to act" while disavowing its humanism, and by the increasingly pointless and ideologically bankrupt guerrilla war in Colombia. The militancy of Latin American politics in the years after 1960 often is presented as little more than a bad decision taken by a handful of romantic revolutionaries—a decision that provoked Latin American militaries to let loose their repression.[34] Now that the Cold War is over and the flames sparked by Cuba are doused, the left can get back "on the right track" as part of a general democratic renewal.[35] Such an interpretation reverberates with a more pervasive recoil from the extremes of the 1960s, even on the part of those who continue to advocate some form of wealth redistribution. Richard Rorty, for example, believes that the left, after the awfulness of the twentieth century, needs to purge incendiary language and visions from its lexicon, words such as "capitalism," "bourgeois culture," and "socialism."[36] Ignoring provocative social violence, critics condemn New Left radicalism as the meaningless spawn of a politics that, owing to its arrogance or absolutism, ran amuck.

Those who try to isolate democracy from conflict or to blame revolutionary violence on the utopian visions of the left usually underestimate the entrenched and intransigent nature of the forces allied against a more equitable distribution of resources and power. Geoff Eley's description of Europe's twentieth-century democratic achievement is perhaps even more true of Latin America's, considering that the economic situation in the Americas was far less propitious:

> Let there be no mistake: democracy is not "given" or "granted." It requires *conflict,* namely, courageous challenges to authority, risk-taking and reckless exemplary acts, ethical witnessing, violent confrontations, and general crises in which the given sociopolitical order breaks down. In Europe, democracy did not result from natural evolution or economic prosperity. It certainly did not emerge as an inevitable byproduct of individualism or the market. It developed because masses of people organized collectively to demand it.[37]

In Latin America, obstacles toward the achievement of even the most minimal approximation of democratic reform persisted not only in the visible institutions of government bureaucracies, courts, militaries, land tenure, and labor relations but in the closed quarters of family, sex, and community. What is today understood as democracy was achieved by individuals engaged in a myriad of small yet pitched struggles that strained such hierarchical, private, and steadfastly obdurate relations of domination and control. Secular ideologies of nationalism, socialism, Marxism, and communism—those dangerous scions of liberalism—did motivate and give solace to people's lives. But this gift did not merely satisfy an abstract or innate desire for meaning in an increasingly uncertain world, as some theorists would now dismiss the appeal of socialism and communism. Rather, by providing the fuel and steel needed to contest the terms of nearly intolerable conditions, it combined the stuff of mundane survival with the more sublime advance of democracy. In the decades following World War II, the left in nearly every country lost its bid to take over the state and restructure the economy, but it did force a transformation of power relations that allowed broader participation in politics, culture, and society. Panzós was not a "colonial" massacre in the technical sense since it took place well into the second century of independent rule. Yet it was part of a larger epic assault on the private fiefdoms of social control that simultaneously came under siege and were emboldened with the spread of commodified social relations and the extension of state power throughout Latin America.

What follows is an attempt to understand how Q'eqchi'-Mayan activists cultivated their sense of self-understanding in struggle for a fairer world and how the frustration and ultimate destruction of their ideals affected not only those few who survived but a wider post–World War II history. While successive chapters build a narrative starting in the late nineteenth century that culminates with the 1978 Panzós massacre, each explores in depth intimate, often physical dimensions of social transformation. While on one level the Cold War was a struggle over mass utopias—ideological visions of how to organize society and its accoutrements—what gave that struggle its transcendental force was the politicization and internationalization of everyday life and familiar encounters.[38] Politics took on a startling immanence, manifesting itself, as we shall see, in the internal realms of sexuality, faith, ethics, and exile.

All the lives under consideration here, despite providing a diversity of experiences, highlight the formative power of politics to shape human expectations. This, I think, should be a central element of any definition of the Cold War. It was not only an event (what diplomatic historians usually call superpower rivalry) or a cause (as in the Cold War did this or that to this or that country) but also an intensified phase of a larger conflict, an "international civil war" not only between the United States and the Soviet Union or between capitalism and communism but between different views of the shape that social citizenship would take.[39] The spread of capitalism in its raw version in the third world created a dramatic torsion between the anticipation of development and equality and the reality of exclusion and exploitation. This tension was acute in Latin America, where Catholic humanism, liberal nationalism, Native American conceptions of justice, conservative defense of collective rights, socialism, and in some countries the radicalism of militant working-class immigrants combined in different proportions to produce an extraordinarily insurgent twentieth century.

CHAPTER ONE

A Seditious Life

He is mysterious in the smallest of things.

Jean-Paul Sartre

ALTHOUGH WE ARE cautioned against reading history backward, against taking a certain event as inevitable in light of previous occurrences, it would violate the historical imagination not to think of José Angel Icó's life as anticipating, even generating, the hopes and fears that would overrun Latin America during the Cold War. Icó died on November 15, 1950, the day after Jacobo Arbenz was officially declared the winner of Guatemala's presidential elections.[1] His nephew remembers that Icó "stayed alive to see Arbenz take power; he campaigned for him from his sickbed."[2] That he perhaps held death long enough at bay to witness Arbenz's victory testifies to the inseparable union of Icó's life and his politics: "He was married to politics," says his niece, and, in a way, he spent most of his adult life waiting for Arbenz.

Icó was born in 1875 in Chitaña, a small village of about thirty families a few kilometers outside the town of San Pedro Carchá, in the highland department of Alta Verapaz, to peasant parents privileged enough to be spared the worst of what coffee had wrought.[3] Dominga Coc Delgado gave birth to José Angel, the third of five children, in August at an especially bountiful moment. It was the beginning of the corn harvest in the year that her husband, Tomás Icó, along with other men in the village, gained title to over a thousand acres of land.[4] Icó inherited part of his father's land and as late as 1925 had registered as the owner of a farm on which over eighty Q'eqchi's worked.[5] Little is known of his political initiation. "He was going to be a priest," says a family member too young to have met him, "but then he found politics." Despite this remembered worldly conversion, politics for Icó remained an enchanted vocation. An avid churchgoer, he lit votive candles to guide politicians to act justly and paid for masses to celebrate momentous events, such as national elections and the convocation of the 1945 constitutional assembly. Icó also was a *curandero*, a healer, who performed Mayan ceremonies to treat the ill. Or at least he tried. "I don't know if he had much luck curing anybody," says his great-nephew Alfredo Cucul, who is now an Evangelical Christian living in Guatemala City, with a bit of urban, protestant skepticism. With the help of his secretary, who drafted his petitions, Icó read national newspapers "religiously," a kind of secular prayer that set his life in the world.[6] Stories that equated Guatemalan plantations with Nazi concentration camps helped Icó to imagine a world catholic politics in which events in Europe were as immediate as events the next town over.[7] Many also remember him as a *quisache*—a kind of unofficial paralegal who guided Q'eqchi's through Guatemala's tortuous bureaucracy—despite being only barely literate himself.

As a folk lawyer and a folk doctor, Icó created a far-flung network of contacts that linked the Q'eqchi' countryside with national reformers and politicians. His political activism has left enduring myths: it is said that the dictator Jorge Ubico repeatedly visited Icó at his home, that Guatemala's first democratically elected president, Juan José Arévalo, invited him to stay in the national palace, and that Jacobo Arbenz paid for his funeral. Alfredo Cucul recalls being told by his mother that Icó in his youth was a "great friend of the Germans," who dominated local coffee production: "He would have lunch and drinks with *los Dieseldorff*, before they became enemies." Asked what initially kindled Icó's political ire, Cucul first speculated that perhaps it was a reaction to having Germans or Ladinos take his land, but then corrected himself to say his uncle lost his property only after he became politically active, as a result of having to raise money for his endless legal battles.[8] Aside from a brief appearance in a 1913 dispute involving forced labor, it was not until 1920, the beginning of a decade of political reform, that Icó emerged as a regional leader.

By any standard, Icó led a seditious life, refusing to bow before custom or convention or to withdraw from controversy. Against great odds, Icó overcame illiteracy, racism, violence, illness, and prison. From 1920 until his death in 1950, he led successive assaults against forced labor, discrimination, and land expropriation. Over the course of four decades, Icó drew on the ideals of liberalism, citizenship, and nationalism to undermine the exploitative foundations on which Guatemala's coffee economy was built. He earned both the hatred and the fear of local planters and government officials, who associated his infectious threat with his core being, claiming that his "absurd advice . . . maliciously inculcated" in Indians "the idea of unlimited freedom."[9] Yet this equation of the personal with the political did not prevent Icó's opponents from linking his challenge to a larger peril to their prerogatives. In 1920, two years before Guatemala would have a Communist Party and decades before such a party would have influence in the countryside, Erwin Paul Dieseldorff, one of Guatemala's largest planters just back from

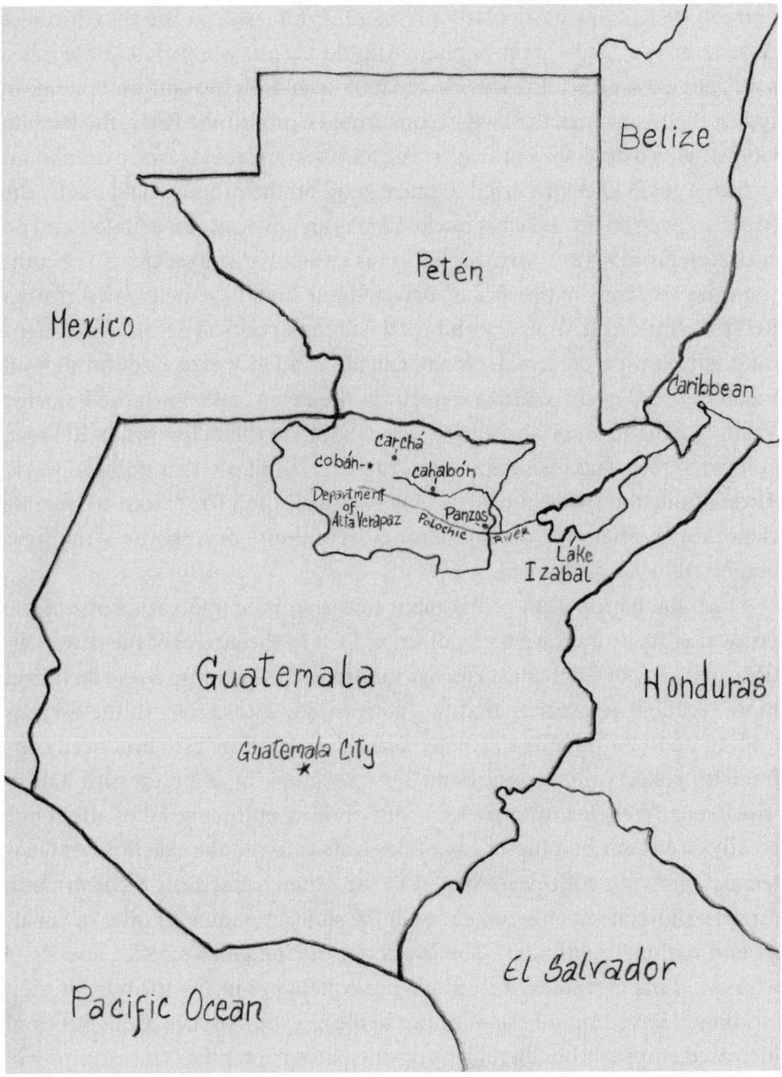

MAP 1. Guatemala (map by Mario Camacho)

a trip to revolutionary Germany, complained to government officials of Icó's "Bolshewista *[sic]* promises" to divide plantations among Indians and to drive all foreigners out of Alta Verapaz.[10] If he was not expelled from the department, Dieseldorff warned, Icó's perpetual agitation would cause great damage to the nation's coffee production.

Dieseldorff had a well-deserved reputation for foresightedness, but his opinion of Icó was particularly prescient. From 1950 to the overthrow of Arbenz in 1954, Icó's great-nephew Alfredo Cucul, whom Icó "raised as a son," carried on his uncle's work. He took over Icó's peasant union and, in 1951, joined Guatemala's newly reconstituted Communist Party, the Partido Guatemalteco de Trabajo, the PGT. For four years, Cucul played a number of critical roles as Q'eqchi's tried to make good on the promise held out by the Arbenz government. Like his uncle, he was an advocate, an agitator, and an educator. From 1952 to Arbenz's fall in 1954, Cucul organized dozens of communities to claim national and private land under Guatemala's Agrarian Reform. Nor did Icó's legacy end with Arbenz's political demise. Throughout their political careers, Icó's and Cucul's influence extended throughout much of the Q'eqchi' diaspora, north to the Petén, east down the Polochic Valley to Senahú and Cahabón, as well as south to the Achí town of Rabinal. Following 1954, successive agrarian organizers built on their political work. Throughout the 1960s and 1970s, for example, the PGT, forced to operate clandestinely after 1954, drew its strongest rural support in some of the areas organized by Icó and Cucul.

From the nationalism of the 1920s to the social democratic hope of the postwar years, from the passing of the old left to the arrival of the new, politics gave many of Guatemala's most disenfranchised a way to make their lives more bearable in a society that was increasingly intolerable. In the decades leading up to World War II, Guatemalan liberal nationalism produced contradictory effects. On the one hand, the strengthening of a repressive state in which nearly all institutions were put toward enforcing labor discipline greatly circumscribed the ability of peasants to avoid the exactions of Guatemala's growing coffee economy. On the other hand, such a constriction forced a more direct engagement with the state, including its offer of equality and national fulfillment. The hypocrisy of Guatemala's coffee liberals—who could manage to exalt freedom and equality to justify the reinstitution of colonial forced labor laws—led not to the rejection of such ideals but to an increased emphasis on liberalism's emancipating potential. The extremity of exploitation under the coffee regime, its routine experiences of subjection, vulnerability, and powerlessness, led many to rely on the rhetorical protections afforded by universal and unalienable notions of justice. Increasingly, demands on the state were no longer primarily voiced through appeals to God, king, and father. Starting in the late nineteenth century, an emergent political fluency produced generations of indigenous leaders such as Icó, who worked through national ideologies and institutions to enrich this triptych with a language of rights, citizenship, and nationalism. Just as claims to abstract liberties are most formidable when they are used to express concrete

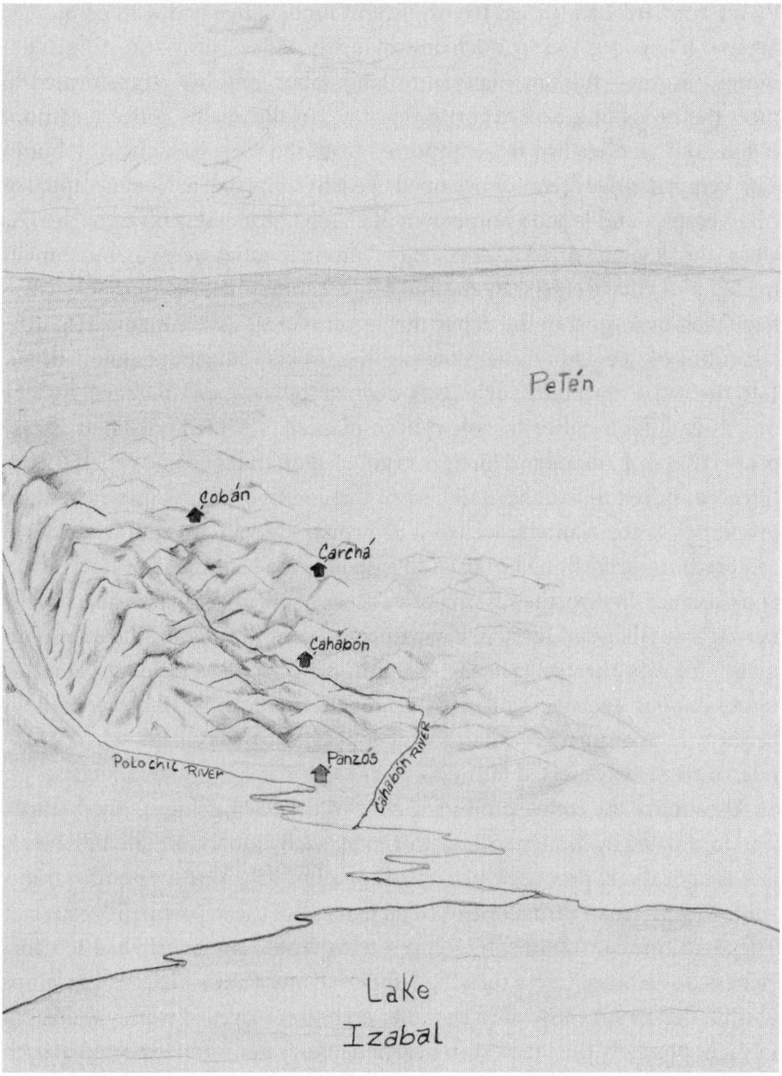

MAP 2. Polochic Valley (map by Mario Camacho)

grievances, the power of Icó's brand of insurgent individuality was that it remained rooted in and was energized by more embedded, community-based identities, relations, and ideas of reciprocity. Historians will continue to debate the degree to which liberal nationalism, either bureaucratically or ideologically, reached into the Mayan countryside, yet Icó was but one of many who called on the nation to live up to its promise.

By the time Icó had turned twenty-five in 1900, coffee had worked on Alta Verapaz like a drug, not so much destroying the old world as distorting its defining features—the raw material of land, labor, and lives transformed to meet the needs of a new export economy.[11] In the Pacific coffee piedmont indigenous workers had to be imported from the western highlands, but in Alta Verapaz coffee literally enveloped Q'eqchi's. Starting in Cobán, capital of Alta Verapaz, and in Icó's hometown of Carchá, dispossession came fast. As late as the 1860s, all of Verapaz's Q'eqchi' municipalities were run by councils made up of village elders. By the end of the century, Ladinos and foreigners had taken over most of the department's municipal governments, retaining a handful of Q'eqchi's to help oversee the town's indigenous population.[12] Into the 1860s, corn plots, or *milpas,* defined the Verapaz landscape. By 1879 over two million coffee trees had been planted.[13] Armed with new liberal property laws, Ladinos and foreigners gobbled up tracts of land ranging from fifteen hundred to five thousand acres, turning free villages into plantation property.[14] Some planters, such as Icó's primary foe, Erwin Paul Dieseldorff, acquired upward of one hundred thousand acres scattered through Cobán and Carchá.[15] In 1870, the vast majority of Q'eqchi's in Verapaz resided in dispersed free villages.[16] By 1921, close to 40 percent (57,405) of the total population of Alta Verapaz (148,425) lived on plantations as resident peons, or *mozos colonos,* exchanging their labor for the right to live and plant, either because they contracted with the owner or because their village was incorporated into a newly created farm.[17]

Also unlike the coffee-producing zone of the Pacific slopes, Alta Verapaz was dominated by foreigners, mostly Germans. By 1900, German individuals and corporations produced two-thirds of all of Alta Verapaz's coffee trade, while four German firms controlled 80 percent of the department's export.[18] They had turned Cobán, which just a few decades previously had few foreigners or Ladinos, into a thriving "imperial city."[19] New Orleans gas lamps illuminated its streets, while a chamber orchestra played at weekly waltzes in its main plaza. By the 1920s, stores carried luxury items not expected in such a remote area: "automobiles, gasoline, oils, electric light plants, in fact, almost anything one could pay for could be ordered through the German trading houses."[20] German immigrants bypassed Guatemala City and traveled from the Caribbean directly to Alta Verapaz, where they registered with Cobán's German consulate rather than with Guatemalan authorities.[21] Post–World War I German immigrants, more nationally German than their predecessors, came to dominate city government, importing a new kind of politics. Following 1933, the Ortsgruppe held weekly meetings, celebrated Nazi holidays, and held rallies and parades "with impunity."[22] Swastikas hung

FIGURE 1. San Pedro Carchá, early twentieth century (courtesy of Fototeca Guatemala, Cirma [Centro de Investigaciones Regionales de Mesoamérica]).

from municipal buildings and flew above German plantations, marks were as common a currency as Guatemalan quetzals, and the local movie house played German films—*A Trip to Beautiful Germany* and *Far from the Land of Our Ancestors*—made to warm the hearts of expatriates.[23]

Yet in important ways, the spread of coffee was less abrupt than this description suggests. New legislation allowed some, such as Icó's father, to gain title to land long in their use.[24] And with their chapels, weekly markets, scattered houses, and yearly feasts, there was often little to distinguish a plantation community from a free village. Only about 15 percent of any plantation was cultivated with coffee trees, the rest set aside for forest, pasture, water, and the plots of its resident workers, who were left free to tend their *milpas* around the seasonal needs of coffee. Plantation residence exempted Q'eqchi's from sundry taxes and military conscription, while money earned from cash advances from planters helped subsidize family and community life in a new cash economy.

But things were different. Q'eqchi's attachment to their land was now governed not by the bonds of everyday life and the needs of survival but by the vicissitudes of a global market, the caprices of a predatory state, and the ties of the law. Great investments of time and money put into obtaining titles could rapidly be lost to corrupt government agents or in public auctions. In

1890, after paying for the surveying and appraising of 580 acres, 123 Q'eqchi's lost their land to Erwin Dieseldorff, who outbid them in a public auction. Not only did they not get their property but in the process they were also transformed into Dieseldorff's peons.[25] Finally, even when Q'eqchi's successfully received title, the need for cash in an increasingly brutish market economy often led them to sell, or mortgage and then lose, their newly probated land.[26] In 1888, ninety-seven Alta Verapaz Mayans owned farms large enough to be considered *fincas,* or plantations. In 1930, the number dropped to nine. By 1949, there were none.[27]

The simultaneous growth of the state and spread of coffee capitalism caught Q'eqchi's in a pincer movement. On the one hand, an expanding government bureaucracy put all of its local expressions—department prefects, police, military, jails, telephones, telegraphs, roads, judges, and mayors—to the task of ensuring a labor force for coffee planters. Taxes, military conscription, obligations to provide free or undercompensated labor on public works, and vagrancy laws—including the 1934 decree that mandated that all men without an "adequate profession" or in legal possession of land were required to work between 100 and 150 days on a coffee finca—pushed Q'eqchi's onto the plantation. Once there, they found themselves utterly dependent on the will and disposition of the planter, in a "wild zone" of private sovereignty.[28] Plantations had their own jails, stockades, and whipping posts, and planters fought any attempt by the state to intervene in their labor relations or to use their workers on public projects.

Far from creating a juridical fiction of individualism or obscuring the "invisible threads" that bound workers to employers, Guatemalan liberalism institutionalized the collective nature of exploitation.[29] In order to cut down on paperwork, planters often ran labor contracts collectively. Consent, the autonomous self's foundational premise, could be collective: in 1898 over twenty-five hundred Q'eqchi' men gathered in front of the plantation house at Plantation Chijolóm in Carchá and listened as an interpreter read the terms of the contract, after which they issued a joint "*H'us*" (Q'eqchi' for "yes") and formalized the agreement with their thumbprints.[30] Or it could be nonexistent: in 1903 a group of Q'eqchi's complained that "it is well known that they make these contracts . . . without the *obligados* being present. We don't even know Spanish. . . . They force these books on us that are used only to throw us in jail for fraud. They write in them as they like and sign the contract for us."[31] Four-year contracts stipulated salaries and labor expectations. Workers could not leave the plantation without permission or contract with other planters; if they fled, the owner had the right to confiscate crops and apply profits from their sale to expenses incurred in their capture. Troublesome workers could be evicted; peons who had not paid off their debt by the time their contracts expired were prohibited from leaving the farm. Peasants had to carry books that recorded debts, days worked, and army service. Some planters prohibited their workers from growing commercial crops for the local market. Children inherited the debt of their parents, catching generation after generation in bondage. Land, life, and labor were literally, and legally, inextricable, as this 1922 advertisement in an Alta Verapaz newspaper testifies: "*¡Mozos! ¡Mozos! ¡Mozos!* I am selling my Plantation Sacsaminí. It has 5,000 acres and many *mozos colonos* who will travel to work on other plantations."[32]

In 1920, President Manuel Estrada Cabrera, aged, senile, and despised, lost his grip on power, exposing the coffee state he had long presided over to its first sustained challenge. A twisted heir to the worst authoritarian aspects of Latin American liberalism, Estrada Cabrera, twenty-two years in power, is remembered today as the president who turned over Guatemala's railroads, electric company, ports, and vast tracts of land to the United Fruit Company. By 1920, everybody, even those who benefited from his heavy and generous hand, knew it was time for him to go.[33] On April 8, the dictator's handpicked Congress declared him insane and elected Carlos Herrera, one of Guatemala's wealthiest sugar and coffee growers, interim president.

For the next decade, until Central America's red scare of 1932, the progressive potential of Guatemalan liberalism sprang forth. Even before Estrada Cabrera fell, Guatemala was among the first countries to join the League of Nations in January 1920, furthering an internationalism already influenced by the Mexican Revolution, World War I, and the creation of the Soviet Union.[34] Reformers of all democratic persuasions drew on global events to push for domestic reform. Guatemala City's Catholic bishop, for example, in 1919 drew parallels between the "evils" of German "tyranny" and his country's homegrown dictatorship.[35] Political clubs and unions operated with relatively little government control. Workers led an increasing number of strikes, wresting better wages and conditions from employers and a new department of labor from the government, although it was allowed to intervene only "*amigablemente*"—in a friendly manner—in labor conflicts. Political parties vied for power in relatively free elections, newspapers ran selections from John Stuart Mill on the rights of women, and *clubes femeninos* lobbied for the vote. Radicals from Mexico and El Salvador crossed into Guatemala and began organizing in the city and the country, and in the capital Communists and anarchists formed small but influential parties. A young generation of literary modernists, including future Nobel laureate Miguel

Angel Asturias, took advantage of a new freedom of the press to pronounce on social issues and develop a confident nationalism.[36] Bringing together a diverse coalition that included artisans, laborers, peasants, intellectuals, middle-class and provincial professionals, and middling planters, the Partido Unionista best represented the democratic impulse of the 1920s. No Guatemalan Zapata rode forth from the Mayan countryside carrying aloft the banner of agrarian revolution, yet the rural highlands did simmer.[37] Newspapers and government officials reported protests in a majority of rural departments among plantation workers.[38] Planters accused Unionistas of making easy and dangerous promises of agrarian reform and an end to forced labor to Indians and peasants, and the U.S. press charged the party with trying to "export" their revolution to Honduras.[39]

"We are knocking on the door of our political emancipation," wrote José Angel Icó along with 122 Q'eqchi's from Cobán's Club Unionista "La Libertad del Indio" to the national Congress on the eve of this democratic flourishing, a week before Estrada Cabrera fell. They asked for a decree recognizing the "indisputable rights of the Indian." "Throughout the republic," the petition went on,

> newspapers constantly complain of the abuses that are committed daily by the authorities against us, but nothing has been done. It is therefore necessary that we ourselves demand before the august national congress the rights that belong to us. . . . If Guatemala wants to take its place among the civilized nations of the world so as to celebrate with dignity the centenary of its independence, it needs to give the Indian his complete liberty.
>
> During its ninety-nine years of independence, the AUTHORITIES have not recognized the citizenship and liberty of the Indian. It would therefore be just, very just, to today concede the rights that belong to him so that articles 16 and 17 of the Constitution not merely be a myth: The duties of the authorities of the republic are to ensure that its inhabitants enjoy their rights, which are: liberty, equality, and security of persons, honor, and property. All power resides in the nation. Functionaries are not the masters but the repositories of authority, subject to and never superior to the law.[40]

The letter concluded with the demands that the government recognize the citizen rights of Indians; end the practice of forcing Indians to serve multiple tours of military duty; compensate compulsory public work; do away with taxes levied specifically on Indians; exempt children under the age of sixteen from municipal service; and abolish peonage contracts, "leaving in their place FREE LABOR!!" The petitioners reminded the legislators that "all eyes" were on them as they deliberated a question that could result in nothing less momentous than "liberty or slavery" for Central America's future.

By the 1920s, the potentially liberating and actually repressive elements of Guatemalan liberalism combined to transform the way indigenous representatives engaged with the government, a change marked by the above petition. The fortification of a highly militarized state, in which nearly all of its rural institutions were oriented toward the control of a workforce, limited the possibility of either evasion or violent resistance. Flight became more difficult as the state grew more capable of tracking down contract violators or debt evaders and as former areas of refuge such as the Petén or Polochic lowlands became more crowded. Riots, which under colonial and early republican rule were common means of confronting local abuses, became increasingly rare. Following a series of violent protests against coffee and settlers in 1865, 1877, and 1886, the last notable revolt against the future took place in 1905, when an indigenous preacher roamed the Verapaz woods calling on Q'eqchi's to shed their clothes, embrace poverty, and burn all coffee bushes.[41]

The repressive foreclosure on these strategies led to a more direct engagement with liberal nationalism. Turning to Ladino notaries, lawyers, and hired wordsmiths to draft their complaints, indigenous petitioners increasingly endorsed a hope that justice would be achieved not by a return to a colonial past but by the fulfillment of national and human development. As in other democratic movements of the late nineteenth and early twentieth centuries, protesters often used a distinction between slavery and freedom as a rhetorical gauge to measure this progress. "Since the French Revolution did away with lords and their privilege," forty indigenous peons in 1934 reminded the government, most likely with the help of a Ladino lawyer, "slavery has been abolished everywhere on the planet. . . . The Indian should not be exploited to the point where he is converted into a slave as in days of old. . . . We are made to work for free as it used to be done for the feudal lords."[42] In a country where forced labor was not a vestigial memory of a distant past but, for many, an active condition of the present, where the most elemental aspects of liberalism—the equality of rights and the denial of hereditary entitlements—were affirmed in the face of their absolute refusal, juxtapositions found in numerous Q'eqchi' petitions between liberty and slavery took on a vivid urgency, investing universal and abstract claims to citizenship and equality with the hope of release from everyday coercion and violence. When Tomás Pop, for instance, in 1902 demanded to be freed from his contract with Erwin Dieseldorff, he did so by drawing a distinction between "slavery" and the "human right of free labor."[43] But perhaps even more innovative than the claim that all were equal before the law was the expectation that such a claim could be fulfilled not in some hazy horizon but in the near future, that it was almost tangible enough to touch, or at least to knock on.

Likewise at play in the 1920 petition, which the Congress shelved, is a sophisticated notion of sovereignty. Its plea to centralized state power to stem the abuses of local elites is familiar enough and reflects a long-standing practice of calling on the king or the president to right local wrongs. Yet perhaps driven by the especially exploitative nature of the Guatemalan state, this appeal went a step further. The notion that the other "civilized nations of the world" were watching Guatemala foreshadows the shift toward a universal jurisdiction of rights that would not be fully developed in Western legal doctrine until the second half of the twentieth century.[44] An increased circulation of news and other printed matter that took place in early-twentieth-century Guatemala emphasized not just national progress but national progress judged against that of other countries, leading to a reconfiguration of one's place at the intersection of history and geography. Notice how the above petition justifies its demands by referencing the complaints of newspapers, presumably reformist columnists lamenting the backward state of Guatemalan society. An understanding that similar conflicts and experiences had taken place in the past or were taking place elsewhere reinforced the feeling that, as George Lukács describes the beginning of public mobilization in Europe during the late eighteenth century, "there is such a thing as history" and that it "has a direct effect upon the life of every individual."[45] And with this transmutation in the valence of daily time and space came a change in the sense of authority. "All eyes" were now on Guatemala.

In the months following the April plea, Icó, as president of the Partido Unionista's indigenous auxiliary group in Carchá, campaigned for Carlos Herrera in the August 1920 presidential elections. The sudden emergence of multiparty competition opened the way for grassroots participation in civic life as never before, and local branches of political parties worked to get out the vote. Beginning in 1879, Indians in Guatemala could participate in national elections as citizens. Literacy determined whether that vote was public or private. Yet throughout the long Estrada Cabrera dictatorship, balloting was largely ceremonial: literate Mayans and Ladinos would cast their secret vote for the only option, while illiterates—the majority Mayan—would assemble on election day and supply the requested, often collective, assent.[46] After 1920, the voting requirements did not change—illiterate citizens still had a public ballot—but now that ballot mattered. Under these new conditions, Icó, as someone who could deliver votes, posed a threat to the local status quo, and in the weeks before the election he was beaten and thrown in jail.[47]

Following Herrera's landslide victory, Icó, who now could count on the support of the Unionista department prefect, began organizing resident peons.[48] According to *finqueros* (planters), his influence reached north to the Petén and south to Rabinal. Roberto Hempstead complained of Icó's agitation as far east as his Plantation Los Alpes in Panzós.[49] They charged the Q'eqchi' leader with having a "reckless mouth," with telling peons that the new government was going to "parcel out the plantations among the Indians, that salaries were going to rise to twenty pesos a day, that foreigners would have to leave [the department], and following them, Ladinos."[50] In the majority of plantations, according to Erwin Dieseldorff, workers were not fulfilling their contracts; in Senahú "the great majority of mozos are on strike."[51] Indians of Carchá, he insisted, "are rebellious, impertinent, and lazy."[52] Because of Icó, Dieseldorff went on, "Indians all have a mistaken understanding of 'free labor,' which they believe means 'we work only as needed to support ourselves, the rest of the time we can do as we wish.'"[53] Agrarian unrest attributed to Icó in Q'eqchi' regions east of Cobán continued through 1921. In January, Hugo Droege, the owner of Plantation San Vicente, complained that owing to Icó's "intrigues" workers no longer "respect their owners."[54] Five days later, Dieseldorff again reported that his peons "do not want to work, and they have told me repeatedly that now there are no bosses."[55]

Herrera's inability to control the countryside led to his overthrow in late 1921 by a military general who, while not returning to the levels of repression that marked the Estrada Cabrera dictatorship, clamped down on agrarian protest and tamed the urban labor movement. This shift in national political power brought about a change in Icó's tactics, resulting in a more confrontational stance. Along with his brother-in-law, Santiago Cucul, he now focused on land invasions, leading forty-five other Q'eqchi's, many of them escaped peons, to plant corn on land claimed by Dieseldorff about ten kilometers north of Icó's home village. "Hypnotized by Icó's promises," Dieseldorff complained, "these mozos refuse to return [to work], nor will they pay me what they owe; they have said to my representative that I should not send a commission to arrest them, because they will shoot them with rifles."[56] For the remainder of the decade, Icó defended himself in local and national courts against an array of accusations with some success. In 1925, a judge absolved Icó of criminal charges brought by a planter who claimed he had invaded his property, passing the matter to a civil court.[57] He and his followers also won title to some of the land in dispute with Dieseldorff.[58] And in 1927, municipal authorities arrested him after he reportedly threatened another wealthy planter.[59] Upon leaving his cell after the aggrieved could not supply witnesses, Icó presented his government license to carry a gun and a knife and asked for his weapons back, suggesting that he could still count on some official favor.

By the early 1930s fortune had turned against him. The world depression had brought Guatemala's fragile democratic opening to an end, along with Icó's room for political maneuver. In 1931, a civil judge ordered that he vacate land that he had invaded, and a planter burned his house down.[60] In 1932, Jorge Ubico, at the start of his thirteen-year dictatorship, carried out a murderous crackdown on political dissent. Icó now faced criminal charges of fraud, assault, and land invasions. Admirers and detractors of Icó alike say that Ubico personally ordered the Q'eqchi' leader's arrest and made him walk the seven kilometers from Cobán to Carchá tied to the tail of a horse.[61] This humiliation was carried out, as one sympathetic local historian observed, to "mock" Icó's haughty pretense of "riding around on a horse" and to "remind him that he was an Indian." In December, a judge ruled on four pending criminal charges, sentencing Icó to five years in the national penitentiary.[62] At this point, the documentary record ends until 1944. Family members today say that he remained in prison, suffering a bad case of rheumatism in a dank cell, until he was released in 1944. One taxi driver though insists that Ubico paroled Icó early, on the condition that he attend Carchá's daily 6 A.M. mass. "I saw him knocking on the church door," he said, "crying to be let in."

Guatemala is a small country and its politics are intimate. The plantation culture that arose within the close quarters of its borders was forged from familiar, often bodily attachments. Foremen and public officials exacted compulsory labor, enforced by corporal punishment and arbitrary imprisonment, not from unknown denizens of distinct continents but from indigenous neighbors who often lived only a few miles removed from the plantation or the municipal seat. Plantation life rested as much on rape and sex as it did on forced labor. The Bostonian cousins Kensett and Walter Champney, for example, arrived in Alta Verapaz at the end of the nineteenth century, and each fathered over a dozen children with their Q'eqchi' cooks and corn grinders. "They fucked anything that moved," recalls a neighboring planter. Kensett took Catarina Choc as his common law wife-servant and made his first land purchase from her brother in 1877. The willingness of foreign male settlers to openly acknowledge, if not always legally recognize, their Q'eqchi' concubines and children created a far-flung human network of diverse allegiances, contacts, and resources, from which came many of the men and women who administered the plantation economy. Women became cooks, servants, wives, lovers, pickers, and suppliers. Some even inherited wealth and standing. Matilde Dieseldorff Cu, for example, the extramarital daughter of Erwin

Dieseldorff and Luisa Cu, grew up in her father's house, married the German Max Quirin, and, upon his death, became owner of a large plantation and a grande dame of Cobán society. Men with names such as Eduardo Maáz Spiegler and Carlos Tot Winter worked as finca administrators and bookkeepers and filled the lower ranks of an expanding bureaucracy and military. Some, such as Anastasio Chiquin Bird, after a lifetime of accumulated loyalty and, with luck, inheritance, became planters themselves.

Given the closeness of this society, it is not surprising that local explanations of national events are often expressed in terms of physical intimacy and sexual power.[63] Behind every official history lies another not so hidden story—*secretos a voces*—of faithlessness, of furtive passions, of filial grudges. Arbenz's 1952 Agrarian Reform, the most serious challenge to this system of political intimacy, elicits from Guatemalans a creative kind of historical hearsay, one that translates social histories of migration, gender, class, and race into family fables, sordidly accessible histories from below. In areas roiled by the Agrarian Reform, it is common to hear that it was the disinherited sons of planters who organized peasants to take their fathers' land. Such was the conflict that supposedly drove Emilio Caal Champney to use the reform to claim part of his unrecognized father's plantation.[64] Sex also enters the historical narrative in the guise of treacherous women or cuckolded husbands. The real reason for Arbenz's resignation, it has been said, was not the fear of a military mutiny or a U.S. invasion but because his wife, María Vilanova, and his close friend and advisor, José Manuel Fortuny, the general secretary of Guatemala's Communist Party, were having an affair.

It is among these rumors pregnant with history that we can place many of the tales told about Icó—his purported personal relationships with successive presidents, his eccentricity, his bravado. Fitting for a life married to politics. But what is to be made of stories that he was "homosexual"?

Icó had no wife or children, nor it seems was he ever in a sexual relationship with a woman. On these facts, uncommon enough in Q'eqchi' culture, his great-nephews and nieces agree. "It was somewhat rare, strange," says his nephew Alfredo Cucul, "but that's how he lived, he never had a *compañera*." Yet when asked to comment on reports that Icó was *ixqi wiinq*—a Q'eqchi' compound word meaning effeminate or, literally, a womanly man—and that in his later years he lived with a younger man whom he "kept like his wife," they respond with uneasy silence, dismissing them as hateful and jealous gossip on the part of "his enemies, the Ladinos." True enough, for although the first person to provide this unsolicited information, Eliseo Ax Burmester, identified himself as Q'eqchi', followed Icó in his youth, and described 1954 as "when we fell," subsequent confirmations were only by Ladinos, some of whom spoke eagerly of Icó's supposed preference for young boys.[65]

Like the hearsay that imparts meaning to historical events personally lived, sexual gossip and innuendo both enforce social hierarchy and account for its violation.[66] Although there is disagreement as to whether contemporary homophobia among Q'eqchi's is a new phenomenon or has long existed, nearly all those familiar with Q'eqchi' society report that they have either known or heard of men who pursued same-sex relations. And many, despite the insistence of Icó's family, say that accusations of homosexuality are not commonly used as a form of derision by Ladinos against Q'eqchi's. "Of course," says an anthropologist, himself Q'eqchi', from Cobán, "it could be an extraordinary charge leveled against an extraordinary person."

As politics turned not only more democratic but more immanent in people's lives, sex became more politicized and politics more sexualized. When people today describe Icó they none too subtly link his imagined libidinal power to his political fortune. Those who have never heard rumors that he slept with men inevitably remark on the prodigious number of offspring he sired and the number of women he kept, as if the possibility of a politics without procreation was unthinkable. Others who knew Icó yet refuse to speak about his sexual preference or why he was unmarried and childless describe a personal flair that violates the modest expectations of Q'eqchi' comportment and style: "He was a *señoron,* bald with a moustache and tall, he acted like a king." Others describe a mix-and-match native cosmopolitanism that accords with modern notions of self-presentation, a style perhaps picked up through his relations with Verapaz's foreigners. He dressed, says his great-nephew Alfredo Cucul, "like a Maya," referring to the blue wool pants, white shirts, dark jackets, and white rimmed hats worn by Carchá men decades ago, but "always very neat and trim with an umbrella hanging from his arm." Others capture Icó's subversion in his ability to combine contradictory masculine and feminine traits. "He was tall, very tall, rode a horse, spoke in a high-pitched voice, and he dominated everything," says Cucul's wife, Manuela Caal, while her husband remembers that Icó "liked to cook."

For others, Icó embodies centuries of race and class conflict. When asked what he knew of Icó, one old local Ladino politician recounted two events. First, upon learning that Indians from Chisec, to the north of Carchá, had murdered a priest, Icó headed a military expedition that burned the offending town to the ground and marched back hundreds of its residents to Carchá, where they were made to build a new church. Second, Icó led Carchá in an uprising against Cobán, which was bloodily quelled by Ladino militia. But these recollections actually closely describe events that happened before

Icó was born. The attack on Chisec occurred in 1559 and was carried out by the cacique Don Juan of Chamelco. The Carchá event, as discussed in the introduction, took place in 1865 and was led by Jorge Yat.[67] And while archival information suggests that Icó's activism in the 1920s focused on labor and land rights, a number of people, mostly Ladinos, describe Icó as heading an "uprising" against Ladinos. It would be wise to attribute most of these recollections to the Ladino inclination to interpret the simplest indigenous demands for better treatment as potential race vengeance, yet a written compilation of memories from Q'eqchi's "who lived during that time" describes a 1920 conspiracy led by Icó to burn down Cahabón, an indigenous town seventy kilometers to Carchá's east, and kill all of its inhabitants.[68] According to one account, the town and its residents were spared only by the spectral intervention of a "woman dressed in white," the Virgin Mary, who led a well-equipped military detachment that repelled Icó's would-be assassins.

Planter complaints from the 1920s often describe Icó, "the Bolshevik agitator," in the language of existential outrage, as if his very being blasphemed the social order. "Let me tell you what class of individual Icó is," started one planter before listing Icó's insults.[69] His ability to "hypnotize," as Erwin Dieseldorff repeatedly described Icó's influence, conjures supernatural powers of manipulation—powers that, it seems, could be thwarted only by divine intercession.[70] Government officials grew frustrated at Icó's habit of using different second surnames, which hampered their efforts to compile a complete legal dossier on him. Sometimes he would go by Icó Coc, other times Icó Delgado, taking "at whim" one or the other of his mother's family names. Other times he would use Icó Xol: "This results," complained Carchá's mayor, in a "detriment to justice; we can never combine all the accusations against him because we can not prove that they are all the same person."[71]

Icó's political threat resided in just this inability to pin him down. Verapaz society turned around multiple hierarchies that defined relations between planters and workers, Q'eqchi's and Ladinos, men and women, Indians and the state. In practice, however, there existed a great deal more plasticity than social conventions admitted. The spread of a juridical culture, along with the rise of liberal nationalism, transformed individuals' sense of identity, obligations and rights. Migration and labor demands, along with changes in land use, uprooted communities and families. The simultaneous fortification of the state and expansion of coffee cultivation created competing realms of sovereignty. And intermarriage and procreation among Ladinos, foreigners, and Q'eqchi's produced new generations betwixt and between exhausted ethnic categories.

Verapaz's plantation culture functioned in the precarious space between hierarchy and its transgression. A man but not married, a leader but childless, a Q'eqchi' but literate in Ladino legal and political culture, Icó lived in that space and his political activity helped push it further open. It is not hard to think that Dieseldorff had Icó in mind when he wrote to the president in 1929 to complain of legislation requiring plantations to educate the children of its resident workers. "Of what value is it to a plantation hand to be able to read and write, or to know about history and geography?" he asked, identifying the power of historical comparison, as discussed above, as a threat. "Is it not true," Dieseldorff went on, "that giving the Indian classes a higher education than their social position merits only serves to disrupt their work? We have learned from experience that the Indians who have learned to read and write are no longer useful as agricultural workers. . . . We need workers who are content with their social status, not an abundance of learned persons who look upon manual labor with arrogant disdain."[72]

The fact that Icó was not married and had no children gave him a strategic advantage in his dealings with planters and the state. The lack of a family not only allowed him some freedom for his peripatetic activism, not to mention jail time, but also prevented Icó from participating in traditional institutions of community politics. Four saint cults or *cofradías,* one located in each of the town's neighborhoods, administered the outlying rural hamlets through a network of local men charged with such duties as delivering mail, helping to compile tribute rolls, collecting sundry taxes, citing individuals to appear before the town or departmental court, and organizing public work levies.[73] Married men worked their way up this ladder, successively holding positions of increasing responsibility until attaining the rank of *principal* (elder), who then served on the town council. The coffee state grafted itself onto this dispersed system of community authority as it extended into the countryside, converting hamlet authorities into *alcaldes auxiliares* (local functionaries who executed municipal business) who, while still coming from established village families, were now "to be considered as police agents," as the 1879 decree reorganizing municipal government put it.[74] As they became more directly tied to the now Ladino-controlled municipality, their tasks increasingly pertained to the extension of state control, including the administration of forced labor. Planters had the power to appoint the alcaldes auxiliares on their plantations, who, in addition to carrying out government functions, were responsible for organizing the labor routines of the resident workers.[75]

Despite the bureaucratization of community authority, throughout the 1920s, Q'eqchi' men who served in the town government, now as subordinates to Ladinos, were still those who had attained the status of elder by rising up through the ranks of religious brotherhoods. But to do so entailed both a series of time-consuming commitments and considerable expense, as *cofrades,* as members of cofradías were called, paid for the yearly celebration to honor the patron saint. As a single, childless man, Icó was exempt from this burdensome path to community authority, which at least partially accounts for his vigorous direct engagement with the Ladino state.

Yet while Icó was spared the costs of participating in this civil-religious hierarchy, he still was able to tap into it to influence and mobilize Q'eqchi's. In 1920, one planter complained that because of Icó's "tricks," his alcaldes auxiliares had refused to force his contracted Q'eqchi's to work, resulting in a paralysis of his coffee harvest.[76] In 1931, Icó organized the alcaldes auxiliares of hamlets in the municipality of San Luis in the department of El Petén, a seven-day walk from Carchá, to collect 5 quetzals—the name of Guatemala's currency since the 1920s—from all the inhabitants in order to send Icó to the capital to petition the president to end forced labor.[77] That the alcaldes held the fund-raising in chapels underscores how Icó's power flowed through community circuits. And while Icó was never a member of a cofradía or the municipal government, many of his allies were. Eliseo Ax Burmester served in cofradías and on the town council several times, as did Santiago Cucul, Icó's brother-in-law and confidant.[78]

Icó's power came from his ability to tack between Q'eqchi' and Ladino worlds, to mobilize strikes and land invasions while at the same time enlisting the support of Ladino reformers, filing property claims, and litigating in local courts. Both in the 1920s and then again in the 1940s, provincial elites rightly viewed Icó's creation of an alternative network of rural power as a menace, one that drew from the same sources of community authority as the state but was used to fight, not enforce, the privileges of Ladino and foreign elites.

In early 1945, Carchá's mayor, Leopoldo Chavarría, ordered the brothers Mariano and Domingo Cuc to provide a week's work on the road to the Petén.[79] They refused, instead presenting the mayor with "little yellow cards" that they had been told exempted them from forced labor. An incensed Chavarría complained to the private secretary of Guatemala's new president of the "insane conduct" of José Angel Icó. Immediately after the fall of the dictatorship, Icó organized and took charge of a local Indian auxiliary section of the Frente Popular Libertador, one of the first reform parties of the October Revolution. For a ten-cent inscription fee to the party, Icó, it seems, was telling Q'eqchi's that they were exempt from unpaid public labor, which he insisted the Revolution had abolished.[80] "We used the money to hire a Cobán lawyer and print the cards," says Eliseo Ax, a founding member of the Frente, "and we would have continued handing them out to thousands, but *los contrarios* broke into Icó's house and stole them."

The 1944 October Revolution shook the foundations of Guatemalan society, but not immediately. The effects of the new government's political, labor, and land reforms were slow in coming to the distant Verapaz countryside. The Revolution's "sociological awakening," as anthropologist Richard Adams puts it, had trouble stirring a rural population living under conditions of fearsome political and economic control.[81] This control did not diminish with the fall of Ubico. The government's expropriation, at the urging of the United States, of German plantations in 1944 broke the economic and political power held by Germans in the region. Yet in Cobán and Carchá, throughout the first six years of the October Revolution, Ladinos hostile to reform benefited from the municipal autonomy granted by new legislation. They regained the authority to elect mayors, which had been taken away in 1936 with the institution of state-appointed municipal administrators, and took advantage of new freedom-of-assembly rights to revive Verapaz's Regional Planters Association, headquartered in Cobán.[82]

The ambitions of the Revolution outstripped its means. For most revolutionaries, reforming Guatemala's "feudal" labor laws was a priority. For most planters, retaining access to cheap labor was equally as urgent. The "wealth" of Cobán, as one planter put it, resided not in "the soil but the low wages of our laborers."[83] These conflicting interests flared during the debates surrounding the drafting of a new constitution, resulting in an ambivalent resolution. The 1945 constitution, following up a series of early revolutionary decrees, abrogated Ubico's horrendous 1934 vagrancy law—which stipulated that all men without an "adequate profession" or in legal possession of land were required to work between 100 and 150 days on a plantation—and the similarly horrid law that required men who could not pay a commutation fee to work two weeks a year building and maintaining Guatemala's roads.[84] The new constitution likewise placed restrictions on debt labor.[85] Vagrancy, however, remained punishable, and men were required to carry proof of employment or landownership.[86] In Carchá, the mayor, who also served as the local justice of the peace, strictly interpreted the state's continued proscription of vagrancy. Throughout 1946 the municipality arrested on average over two hundred vagrants a month.[87]

Yet the majority of peasants fortunate enough to retain land did not hold property titles and were vulnerable to charges of vagrancy. Military commissioners or police often stopped Q'eqchi' traders on market day as they left the center of Carchá to check their papers. If they did not carry proof of land or work or if they could not show that they had already served in the military, they would be subject to arrest or conscription. Since they were returning home after selling their corn, sugar, vegetables, fruits, and coffee, some could pay a bribe to continue on their way. Others, such as José Coc, complained that they were offered a choice between jail or two weeks' work on the plantations of municipal officials.[88] Alfredo Cucul remembers that the mayor made vagrants paint his house. Such ongoing harassment forced Q'eqchi's to choose between cultivating their own land and selling their labor for a pittance. Those who opted for the latter obtained from the Planters Association a work card honored by the municipality that protected them from vagrancy laws. As fifteen Q'eqchi's from San Juan Chamelco wrote to the new democratically elected president, Juan José Arévalo, in April 1947, "we are landowners and dedicated to . . . intense cultivation. Nevertheless, the large planters of Alta Verapaz force us to abandon our crops [paying us only] a work card . . . *in exchange for our free labor*" (emphasis in original).[89] That same month, Icó complained to the president that Q'eqchi's were "abandoning their land and working for planters for no other compensation than a work card."[90] Two years later, according to Icó, Q'eqchi's were still afraid "to pick their corn, for fear they will be arrested, even though they are carrying hoes."[91]

For the last six years of his life, Icó worked to make the new constitution's guarantee of equality a reality for Q'eqchi' men, focusing nearly exclusively on ending forced labor. At some point in 1946, Icó converted his Frente Popular Libertador into the local branch of the Partido de Acción Revolucionaria, or PAR, the most aggressively reformist party during the Arévalo presidency and from within whose ranks the Communist Party would soon emerge.[92] At the same time, he organized a *comunidad agraria.* Legalized by the Arévalo administration as a way to counter unrepresentative municipal governments, particularly those in heavily indigenous towns, *comunidades* functioned as something of a cross between a union and a mutual aid society and were often affiliated, as was Icó's, with the newly formed national labor federation, the Confederación de Trabajadores Guatemaltecos, or CTG.[93]

In the beginning of September 1946, Icó led a contingent of his followers to the capital. Two weeks earlier, military officers had launched a failed coup against Arévalo, and the PAR and other revolutionary parties had called a demonstration as a show of support for the revolution. The turnout was "massive," according to one newspaper, well beyond expectations.[94] Demonstrators from the countryside began arriving days before the scheduled march, filling buses, trucks, and "trains by the thousands." It took two and a half hours for the tens of thousands of demonstrators to file past Arévalo, who oversaw the procession from the balcony of the national palace. Signs and songs mocked the failed plotters, demanding that they be exiled to Franco's Spain. Other placards and chants called for agrarian reform, insisted that "Jesus Christ was a Socialist," claimed Belize belonged to Guatemala, and called on priests and the Catholic Church to support the government. Víctor Manuel Gutiérrez, head of Guatemala's labor federation and soon to be a leading member of the Communist Party, was the first to speak. He put the failed coup within a larger global context of the social struggles that had broken out following World War II, warning that Latin America's postwar political liberation was coming under attack by "reactionaries." He was right. Over the next two years, by 1948, coups and political betrayals would bring the continent's postwar social democratic opening to a truncated end, leaving Guatemala increasingly isolated. Arévalo then spoke:

> After 1944, we believed we could work in peace, to do what we could not do in 125 years of slavery. But we were wrong. The *cangrejos,* the crabs, who govern the country from the dark . . . are trying to overthrow our government elected by the popular will. We will have to do much more to achieve the economic and human liberation of the people. The socialism that guides us is the same that guides all governments that administer for the general good. It is similar to what Roosevelt did, and the bankers called him a communist.[95]

It was Icó's first and only national demonstration. A Q'eqchi' man born in the nineteenth century in a rural hamlet of a far region, he found himself at the crowded center of world-historical politics: the New Deal, FDR, Franco, World War II, the USSR, the Spanish Civil War, the meaning of Christianity and human progress. The newspaper photograph of the march, the indistinct, blurred swirl of workers and peasants, many of whom probably had never been to the capital, calls to mind Vivian Gornick's observation that the power of radical politics resides in its ability to give men and women an awareness of binding human connectedness, an individual sense of themselves within a larger social and historical whole.[96] Rather than leading to amorphous anonymity, mass mobilization here, at least judging from Icó's continued doggedness, put his political ideals and actions into bold relief.

Back in Carchá, Icó's Comunidad Agraria immediately raised the concern of local growers. In November 1946, Carchá members of the Regional Planters Association, mostly Ladinos but also a few wealthy Q'eqchi's, demanded that the municipality investigate its "intentions." José Angel Icó, the petitioners claimed, has been "preaching against the interests of planters and forcing Indian workers to pay 1 quetzal to join the Comunidad." One Q'eqchi'

AÑO XXV—GUATEMALA, C. A. LUNES 9 DE SEPTIEMBRE DE 1946.—No. 8505

PROLETARIOS EN ABRUMANTE DESFILE

Gremios y Sindicatos Marchan

Ciudad y Campo Presentes: Habló el Presidente

FERIA DEL LIBRO COMO INSTITUCION NACIONAL

La Anterior es Superada Esta Vez

Tratan de Acelerar la Paz

Posible su Firma en Nueva York

Inauguración de Casas Para Trabajadores

Estalla la Huelga en Hilados

Alumnas de Belén Irán a El Salvador

Labor Sorprendente de la Universidad de Jerusalén

FIGURE 2. Guatemala City, September 1946. Icó led a delegation from San Pedro Carchá to this demonstration in support of the October Revolution following a coup attempt (*El Imparcial*, September 9, 1946).

witness testified that "Icó told us that with the membership card, we will be free from having to work for our bosses and that if we do work, we will make between 50 cents and 1 quetzal a day. He has also been saying that we don't have to sell our corn or beans to Ladinos . . . and that the German plantations are going to be distributed among all" and that "the government was going to give each person a cow and a bull."[97] Once again Icó was arrested for extortion.

Released from jail in early 1947, Icó wrote Arévalo to complain that the mayor had refused to issue property titles, asking that the president order local authorities to grant certifications.[98] Although every member of the Comunidad had access to land, Icó went on, without titles they were subject to the vagrancy laws. In response, Verapaz's governor insisted that while he had ordered Carchá's mayor to grant certification when applicable, Q'eqchi's nonetheless have the burden "to prove that they are property owners" and that they have sufficient land to support themselves. "There exist an infinite number of Indians who are property owners," argued the governor, "but who do not have enough crops . . . to be granted the certification." He warned that considering the department's labor shortage, the exemption of all peasants

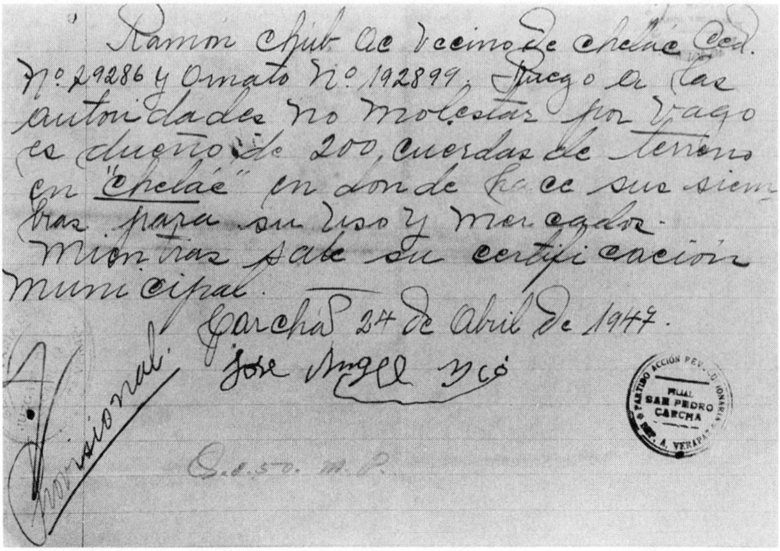
Ramon Chub Ac vecino de Chelac Ced. No. 29286 y Ornato No. 192899, Ruego a las autoridades no molestar por vago es dueño de 200, cuerdas de terreno en "Chelác" en donde hace sus siembras para su uso y mercado. Mientras sale su certificacion municipal.

Carchá 24 de Abril de 1947.

Jose Angel Icó

Provisional

PARTIDO ACCIÓN REVOLUCIONARIA FILIAL SAN PEDRO CARCHA A. VERAPAZ

FIGURE 3. Vagrancy exemption issued by José Angel Icó and affixed with PAR imprint.

from the vagrancy laws would cause great "harm to agricultural production."[99]

In the face of national apathy and local obstacles, Icó took matters into his own hands and began in early 1947 to issue his own certifications. For a small fee, he dispensed homemade credentials that read, for example, "I ask the authorities not to bother José Chub of Chelac as a vagrant. He is the owner of 50 cuerdas of land. He grows crops for his family and the market. His civil registry number is 3559. Valid until the municipal certification is extended." Signed by Icó's unsteady hand and affixed with the PAR emblem, this assumption of state power was apparently too much for Icó's Ladino allies. In July 1947, the PAR's secretary of propaganda, José Manuel Fortuny, who would soon leave the PAR to head Guatemala's new Communist Party, wrote Carchá's mayor to inform him that although the party had expelled Icó, he had so far refused to turn over its stamp.[100]

Throughout his political life, Icó pushed successive democratic movements to their limit. So disruptive were his actions, in fact, that he was expelled from the PAR by the future general secretary of the Communist Party. Icó employed a tripartite strategy of direct action, alliances with national reform movements, and engagement with the state through elections, petitions, and legal land claims to loosen the thrall of Alta Verapaz's coffee "lords." His ability to lead such a sustained and consequential challenge, one that lived on after his death, resided in his power to wed the abstractions of rights, equality, and liberty to the specifics of Q'eqchi' life, to routine struggles for survival. He was able to do so because of his unique residence in two worlds. At least until Icó reached the age of fifty, the property originally titled by his father under liberal land laws provided him the security he needed to become politically active, despite his exclusion from traditional avenues of community authority. Failure to follow Q'eqchi' paths of male power freed him to be more receptive to the possibilities offered by the rise of the liberal state. Through his work with rural civil and religious leaders, his formation of political parties and the Comunidad Agraria, and his personal appeals to national leaders, including presidents, Icó built an alternative network of rural political power that could confront local Ladino and foreign domination. And while he was not a patriarch in his personal life, he often functioned as one in his political life. It is unknown what the relationship was between Icó and the sharecroppers who worked on his farm, but his ability to gain them exemption from military service undoubtedly indebted them to him. According to family members, peasants came to him with petitions and complaints or to seek advice on legal affairs. Women approached him to intercede with government authorities, as when Dolores Mucú came to his house to ask him if he could help free her son who was imprisoned on drunk charges.[101] In exchange they left small gifts such as chickens, alcohol, and corn. This parallel system of rural authority, running outside the control of local planters and municipal officials and, at least ideally, accountable directly to the president, was in effect Icó's vision of what the state should be, and it is, as we shall see, what Arbenz's Agrarian Reform attempted to build.

Icó, while exceptional, was not unique. The social transformations brought by the coffee state provided fertile ground for similar prominent, politically consequential indigenous leaders, such as Tomás Tecú, reportedly a follower of Icó, in Rabinal, an Achí-Mayan town dominated, like Carchá, by a minority Ladino population. Tecú, like Icó, established a Comunidad Agraria, affiliated with the national labor federation, and organized Rabinal's indigenous population into the Communist Party. Like Icó, Tecú and his followers worked through existing networks of power. "In 1949, we monopolized everything," remembered one Achí participant. "We organized Indians. We created the Comunidad and the cofradía helped us. . . . We did everything like a spider, beginning in the center and then moving outward. . . . On May 1, 1949, we paraded with a thousand men under the flag with the hammer and sickle. '*¡Viva la revolución!*' we shouted. '*¡Arriba el 20 de Octubre!*' '*¡Tomás Tecú!*' The municipal authorities went crazy."[102]

In 1950, Icó, seventy-four years old, began to suffer from what was probably stomach cancer. Wasted and weak, he still made it to Cobán in May during Arbenz's only campaign visit to Alta Verapaz. The future president's speech, interpreted into Q'eqchi' as he spoke, must have felt like a fitting valediction:

> From the time when Alta Verapaz was populated by only the brave Q'eqchi' race until this moment . . . from the exploitation of the conquistadors' whip to the infamous exploitation of the plantation owners. . . . they have taken your property, your liberties, your rights. . . . Alta Verapaz workers are the most exploited in all the country. The struggle of the reactionaries, of these "friends of order" who scowl at us on the street, is to impose this regime on the whole republic. We, in contrast, want to destroy this system. It is not only agrarian reform that will resolve the problem. We need to treat Indians justly . . . with respect like human beings. We promise you better houses and a better salary. We promise you a little more justice.[103]

Planters did what they could to prevent Q'eqchi's from voting for Arbenz. Alfredo Cucul, Icó's great-nephew, remembers the vicious propaganda campaign carried out by the Regional Planters Association, which said that if Arbenz won, "women would be raised up to the same height as men and children would be taken away." During the three days of polling, buses and trucks, which were in the hands of a few Ladino families, did not run. It took days for peasants from hamlets as far as sixty or seventy kilometers from the town center to walk to voting tables, a luxury many could not afford or did not have permission from planters to do. Some remember that Q'eqchi's were cajoled, harassed, or bribed to cast their ballots for Arbenz's main conservative rival.

Dying, Icó worked for Arbenz's election. In the previous year he had campaigned hard for the PAR, and although during his life the party never managed to break the hold of local elites on the electoral machinery, more Q'eqchi's had voted than ever before. Icó, who in the 1920s rounded up groups of Q'eqchi's to give their collective public vote to Partido Unionista candidates, apparently held few illusions about the democratic nature of Guatemala's electoral process. In 1947, for example, Icó directed Juan Choc Caal back to the polls to recast his ballot after he learned that Choc did not vote for the PAR's mayoral candidate.[104] Cucul remembers his uncle operating the same way from his sickbed in 1950, ordering those whom he had influence over to cast their vote, if they could, for Arbenz: "he told them whom to vote for and they did."

November 1950 must have been a bittersweet month for Carchá's planters.

They retained control over the municipal government, the vagrancy laws were still in effect, and their longtime adversary was finally gone.[105] "They lit firecrackers when they found out Icó had died," says his nephew. When his niece went to the market to buy candles, a drunk Ladino celebrating Icó's demise attacked her, breaking her ribs. Carchá's priest refused to toll the church bells or let Icó's coffin pass through the church, saying that "Communists didn't deserve bells."[106] A month after he died, Ladinos, according to Icó's relatives, desecrated his grave so that "no one would remember him," and his tomb remains unmarked to this day. But Arbenz won the election, and the planters' troubles were just beginning.

CHAPTER TWO

An Uncorrupted Life

We are socialists because we live in the twentieth century.

Juan José Arévalo

"EVERY MORNING" says Alfredo Cucul of his education during Ubico's dictatorship, "we had to stand at attention, and the teacher would inspect our fingernails and toenails to see if they were trim and clean; then he checked for lice and if we had brushed our teeth."[1] His teacher was a nationalist and, Cucul vaguely remembers, quietly critical of Ubico. Yet he was very "disciplined, like a soldier," and for Cucul's six years of barefooted schooling, 1935 to 1941, martial exercise took equal place with other rote studies, such as penmanship, grammar, geometry, history, music, and natural sciences. Cucul still bears the emblems of Ubico's highly regimented public education, not only in his posture and handwriting—at seventy-eight both still measured and straight—but in an unyielding moral rectitude. Cucul, now an Evangelical Christian living in Guatemala City, is disgusted with the world of men. About unions, human rights, peasants, and international affairs, he talks with a harsh aloofness. The edge in his voice undercuts the indifference of his words as he tries to reconcile the fact that things did not turn out as they were promised. Politics, he says now, is a corrupted, degenerate realm of human endeavor. But it was not always so.

Like the personal life of his great-uncle, José Angel Icó, some things are still not easily discussed in Guatemala. During our first interview, Cucul openly talked about his membership in the Partido Guatemalteco de Trabajo (PGT). He explained how he joined and what his activities were, yet avoided speaking about what it meant to him to be a member. This reluctance deepened in subsequent meetings, and Cucul increasingly deflected specific questions concerning the party. Yet this reserve did not signal an unwillingness to discuss his uncle's politics or his own role as a peasant organizer. On these matters he talked at great length. When Cucul learned that Guatemala's national archives held papers describing his or Icó's political activities, he insisted I take him and show him. When he came across a document relating the workings of a peasant union that did not mention his name, Cucul said, "That was us. We taught them how to do the paperwork to make the land claim." Reading some of the property certificates his uncle gave to Q'eqchi's to elude the vagrancy law, Cucul pointed out that the handwriting was his. Cucul would not talk about his own experience with the PGT, yet he denied anti-Communism's legitimizing premises. Asked if Arbenz was a Communist, he responded, "Maybe he was, but look what he did for Guatemala, the labor code, the Agrarian Reform, the Institute of Social Security, the Atlantic highway. I have my pension because of him."[2] When I asked him what an "anti-communist" is, he unfailingly responded: "An enemy of peasants." He refused to forsake Arbenz.

For four years, beginning in 1950, Cucul carried on his uncle's work. He defended Q'eqchi's in court, organized unions, worked to end compulsory unpaid labor, planned a literacy drive, and campaigned for revolutionary candidates. Through the Agrarian Reform legislation, he helped fulfill Icó's effort to build an alternative network of rural power that could undermine the control planters held over peasants. While his uncle attended rallies, Cucul spoke at them. All this ended with the overthrow of Arbenz in June 1954, when Cucul was beaten, jailed, and exiled from Carchá. "To this day," he says, "they treat me like I have a disease."

As he and his wife, Manuela Caal, talk about that time, their sense of betrayal is palpable. Manuela is less comfortable speaking Spanish than her husband, but her outrage helps fend off his attempts to cut her off. "They received land, money to plant, even animals, but they tried to kill him," she says, pointing at Alfredo. "We earned nothing, not one cent," Alfredo says, "but now they are in it for their personal interest. That is why I don't believe in politics." "He fought hard, for nothing, nothing," Manuela continues; "when Arbenz fell, they stole our beans, corn, cow, even our chickens." Cucul interprets that betrayal through Christian fidelity: "After 1954, I saw many men who said that they were with the Revolution deny Arbenz. That is why I left politics and found God. Only God is faithful." He draws repeated parallels between the integrity of politics during the October Revolution and the purity of evangelical grace. Everything in between, including subsequent guerrilla and peasant movements, is corrupt. In fact, Cucul believes that the problems of Guatemala after 1954—intractable poverty, violence, and delinquency—are God's punishment for turning against Arbenz.

Cucul's description of his teacher's daily inspection illustrates the extending reach of the Guatemalan government. During Ubico's thirteen-year rule, the state, to an ever-greater degree, came to stake out its sovereignty over the personal and social lives of its citizens, reaching even into the corporal territory of skin and scalp. Most historians describe Ubico's reign as a flawless dictatorship.[3] His rule rested on a far-flung network of spies, regular use of torture, arbitrary imprisonment, and public executions. Ubico expanded the army and government bureaucracy, militarized public education, and rigorously enforced a number of laws designed to secure cheap, often unpaid labor for plantations and public works. The 1944 October Revolution is often presented as a reaction to this repressive system, yet in a way it was actually the dictator's perverse brand of liberalism that spawned the revolt. Ubico's long rule put two popular conceptions of the state into sharp opposition. On the one hand, many rural peasants, the majority indigenous, saw the state as predatory, as existing to collect ever more sundry taxes and fees and to enforce bonds of labor oppression. On the other hand, owing to the influence of ideals of justice and equality, which, thanks to the Mexican and Russian Revolutions, had reached new heights in the 1920s, many peasant leaders, union activists, and middle-class reformers acted as if the state were potentially liberating, as if it were the only viable means to rein in planter impunity.

The notion that it was the government's purpose to bring order and justice to daily life ran deep in Guatemalan society, fusing colonial conceptions of a common good with a nascent liberal nationalism. Ubico did not so much silence expectations of state intervention as personalize them, assuming the role of benevolent father—*tata presidente*—who would arrive yearly in indigenous communities to attend to assorted complaints, often acting against local elites. Today in Guatemala individual memories swing wildly between hatred and fondness for Ubico. Cucul, for example, recalls with horror how as a boy blood splattered in his eye as he watched an execution ordered by Ubico that took place in Carchá's cemetery. Yet he also talks approvingly of Ubico's law-and-order approach and suggests that Guatemala needs a new vagrancy law. This surprising endorsement of a practice he and his uncle helped abolish springs not just from Cucul's revulsion at today's dismal state of affairs. Cucul is a product of Ubico's state, and his conception of justice is animated perhaps less by the ascendant rights consciousness of his youth than by a sense of order drilled into him during six years of martial education. In addition to a notion of progressive national history and Spanish literacy, Ubico's schools gave Cucul the discipline and solidarity needed to stand up to the racism and abuses of Carchá's Ladinos.

Ubico presided over a society that produced a generation of politicians, many of whom were educated in his schools and trained in his army, that expected the government to dispense justice. Activists from this generation existed not only in Guatemala City, where they would lead the first rushes of the October Revolution, but also in the country's more remote regions, such as Carchá, where it would take men such as Cucul more time to make some of the promises of the Revolution a reality. It was not just that Ubico's heavy-handed brutality failed to exterminate expectations of state-delivered justice; his insertion of the government into all aspects of social life inevitably bred such hopes. In this sense, the October Revolution, especially when one considers the caution of its early reforms, represented less a break with Ubico's state than a fulfillment of its promise to intervene against the private power of local planters.[4]

Consider Guatemala's 1947 Labor Code. Although it provided its fullest protections only to large-scale enterprises, the code marked a watershed in Guatemala's republican history. It granted (but also restricted) the right to unionize and strike, protected against unfair firings, mandated a forty-eight-hour workweek, regulated the labor of children and women, and set basic health and safety guidelines for the workplace.[5] Most important, for the first time the state offered an avenue of redress for labor grievances that did not depend on executive paternalism or local government officials.[6] As Edgar Champney, grandson of the Verapaz planter Kensett Champney (who died in 1939), put it, "If my grandfather rose from his grave today and I showed him the labor code, he would drop dead again of fright."[7]

An avalanche of questions and complaints poured into the new labor ministry attempting to define the rights of workers and the limits of state intervention in labor relations.[8] The Robert H. Hay Company, which was conducting oil exploration in the Petén jungle, wanted to know if it had to supply food to its migrant workers.[9] Municipal councils asked if plantation alcaldes auxiliares should be paid by the township or by planters.[10] The union at the Compañía Agrícola de Guatemala needed clarification on a number of points related to overtime: "What is the pay rate for Sunday work?" "If a worker refuses to work Sunday, can he be fired?" "What is the legal difference between sick days and absences?"[11] A planter inquired as to whether he could deduct doctor fees from the half salary paid to sick workers.[12] "If it rains and work is halted, do we have to pay a full day?" asked another.[13] "Can municipal secretaries organize a union?" "If so, can they do so with other municipal workers?"[14] "Does an eight-hour day include lunch?"[15] Many questions concerned the rights of resident peons over their subsistence production: Planters asked if mozos who left to work on another farm forfeited the right to harvest their corn ("no!" someone from the ministry exclaimed in the margin of one such letter).[16] Other finqueros wanted to know how many days they had to give resident workers to plant, weed, and harvest their crops.[17]

Most scholarship on Guatemala's labor movement during the October

Revolution focuses on the large agricultural, industrial, and professional unions—United Fruit Company workers, railway men, and civil servants. Yet workers from the smallest, economically inconsequential outfits also used the code to their advantage.[18] Petén lumberjacks and *chicleros,* nurses in children's hospitals, taxi and bus drivers, salt workers, employees at small artisan workshops, even steamboat operators on Lake Izabal and Lake Atitlán all formed unions.[19] The marginal work of many of these associations contrasted with the ambition of their slogans: "For Economic Liberation and Social Justice in Guatemala," proclaimed the letterhead of the candy makers union.[20] In 1944, hardly any unions existed. By 1954, three hundred thousand members filled the ranks of nearly two thousand rural and urban unions. At over 60 percent of the total 1950 voting population, organized labor suddenly held decisive political power.[21]

In the four months following the adoption of the code, the labor ministry intervened in 281 conflicts.[22] Many of these were small disputes. In Santa Cruz el Quiché, far from Guatemala's agro-industrial zones, the eleven-year-old servant Justa Pú quit her two-cents-a-day job after being mistreated by her employer, Josefa Tamúp. Tamúp owed Justa a month's pay, and her father wrote the ministry asking for help in collecting the balance.[23] In 1948, employees of the dry goods store Tienda La Chichicasteca—also located in the provinces—complained that their employer had not provided them with vacations, enrolled them in Guatemala's social security program, or equipped the store with a first aid kit.[24] And in 1951, the widow Raymunda Rivas convinced the ministry to force her deceased husband's employer to pay for his funeral.[25] Such small unions and minor conflicts did not have a great impact on the economy or development. The labor ministry dismissed most of the disputes as beyond its legal or practical reach. Yet they do indicate just how deep and far expectations of state-mediated justice ran, extending to some of the country's most vulnerable citizens.

Guatemala's labor code was fundamentally moderate—even the U.S. Embassy conceded it was fair and properly reformist.[26] By affording its most important benefits and protections to industrial laborers or permanent employees on large plantations, it precluded, to the dismay of Guatemala's more radical democrats, possible alliances between workers and peasants. A stretched-thin labor ministry likewise diluted the code's effect. Understaffed and short of funds, the ministry focused its vigilance on Guatemala City and the plantations of the southern and Atlantic coasts.[27] Alta Verapaz, with its roadless plantations that often took days on horses or canoes to reach, was practically ignored. The hostility and power of planters, who still for the most part controlled municipal governments, reinforced this isolation. As Arbenz noted in his 1950 campaign speech, Alta Verapaz was the most extreme case of planter power. But it was extreme in degree, not in kind. Despite eight years of reform legislation, planters throughout Guatemala managed to retain a good deal of sway over rural workers.[28] Not until June 17, 1952, with congressional approval of Decreto 900, the Agrarian Reform, would this authority be fundamentally challenged.

Until recently, scholars attempting to answer why the United States intervened in Guatemala in 1954 have focused on the threat the Agrarian Reform posed to U.S. economic interests, particularly to the United Fruit Company. Lately, however, historians have stressed the growing influence of the PGT—the Communist Party—over Guatemalan society and over Jacobo Arbenz, the quiet, serious army colonel picked by the revolutionary coalition to succeed Arévalo. While United Fruit complained incessantly first about the labor code and then about the Agrarian Reform, the company played only a peripheral role in Eisenhower's decision to act against Arbenz. According to this perspective, the United States was neither contemptuous of the kind of third-world nationalism represented by Arbenz, nor fearful of a more democratic distribution of political power, nor mobilized in the defense of private economic interests.[29] Rather, Cold War anti-communism and an accurate evaluation of the PGT's strength drove U.S. agents. Yet interpretations that highlight the political culture of the Cold War in order to counter less sanguine accounts of U.S. motivation often miss a key point: there would not have been a significant expansion of democracy in Guatemala were it not for the PGT.[30]

Guatemala's first Communist Party, formed in 1922, was destroyed by Ubico ten years later. In 1949, young, middle-class teachers and students led by José Manuel Fortuny, most of whom had previously been active in the PAR, met clandestinely (Arévalo had cracked down on an earlier attempt to organize a Communist party) to form what became known as the Partido Guatemalteco de Trabajo.[31] According to anti-communist writers and U.S. officials, Arbenz and the young men who formed the PGT were the best the October Revolution had to offer.[32] The CIA thought the president "brilliant" and "cultured." One PGT opponent admitted that the Communist leader of the national labor federation, Víctor Manuel Gutiérrez, was honest, soft-spoken, humble, and revered by Guatemalan workers.[33] The deputy chief of the U.S. Embassy remembered that non-Communist politicians "were a group of bums of first order; lazy, ambitious, they wanted money, were palace hangers-on. Those who could work, had a sense of direction, ideas, knew where they wanted to go, were Fortuny and his PGT friends; they were very honest, very committed. This was the tragedy: the only people who were committed to hard work were those who were, by definition, our worst enemies."[34] Descriptions of Arbenz and other PGT leaders relate a respectful democratic manner in their political relations with their supporters. They were men who rejected, by choice or by instinct, the caudillo paternalism that characterized the performance of many Guatemalan politicians. Such a style was evident in Arbenz's speeches, where he insisted on treating his marginalized audience as human beings capable of making their own decisions. In 1950, for instance, at the Alta Verapaz campaign rally attended by Icó, Arbenz told Q'eqchi' listeners that he had been advised not to bother to speak to them since they would vote as they were told, without knowing whether they were voting for "the candidate of the Revolution or the candidate of the reaction." He ended his remarks by saying that he had "faith that you will go to your villages and tell them that there are men who come not only to ask for your votes but who come because they care about your problems—whether you vote for me or not."[35] Such sentiments were not only needed in a country that had suffered decades of graft, dictatorship, and poverty but practically insurgent in a polity that expected little more than manipulation and opportunism from its rulers.

Although the party grew rapidly—from less than one hundred members in 1950 to five thousand in 1954—and made impressive showings whenever it fielded candidates in local or national elections, it gained most of its strength from its fortuitous alliance with Arbenz, who legalized the party and its commitment to reform.[36] The PGT never placed more than four deputies in the national Congress, yet it had a great influence in drafting and passing the October Revolution's most democratic legislation, especially the Agrarian Reform.[37] While the party did not come to control the labor federations or occupy high offices in the government, it was often its members, such as Alfredo Cucul, who worked the hardest to realize the reforms of the Revolution. Alfonso Bauer Pais, who served as minister of labor, recounts that practically the only incorruptible labor inspectors were PGT members who, owing to their "willingness to work directly with the rural population, played a great role in carrying the Revolution forward."[38]

For all its importance, the PGT was merely one part of a larger democratic universe. Every viable political party called itself social democratic, had some design for an agrarian reform, and competed for organized labor's suddenly vital support. Every newspaper liberally used terms such as "proletariat," "feudal landlords," and "reactionaries," had sections devoted to the peasantry and the working class, and supported, at least nominally, the modernizing goals of the October Revolution. Many provincial activists, in Alta Verapaz and elsewhere, kept their PGT membership secret while working in a union or the PAR. This was necessary because of the deep anti-communism that had existed in the countryside since 1917, as we saw with the accusations leveled at Icó. Yet the ease with which individuals moved between the PGT and other reform parties after 1954 suggests that this "double militancy," as Bauer Pais describes it, was less a strategic artifice and more a testament to the organic role that the PGT played within Guatemala's reform movement.[39] According to Bauer Pais, "the PGT under Arbenz, and even after, was the maximum expression of our revolutionary élan that grew out of the world wars and the unionist movement of the 1920s. I was never a member, but I had good relations with its leaders."

The idealism that drove the founders of the PGT was fortified by a compelling vision of political and economic modernism, and this is what attracted Arbenz, as a presidential candidate, to the PGT. Fortuny recounts that prior to his electoral campaign, Arbenz began to invite the young Communists to his home, where he would question them on their platform and ideas. Fortuny explained to Arbenz that Latin America was "semicolonial" and that the principle task was to "do away with all the backward relations of production or legacies of feudalism or colonialism."[40] Guatemala needed a "profound change in its agrarian structure," one that would distribute uncultivated land to peasants and "increase their consumptive capacity." Whatever the limitations of economic strategies of import substitution, what is historically important is that the PGT's vision of development was cohesive and coherent in comparison with those of other Guatemalan political parties. "The other parties were always twisting themselves up with phraseologies," says Fortuny; "they would go on and on about liberty, justice, and democracy, but it was all in the abstract." In the end, "all of this opaque rhetoric said nothing" to the practical Arbenz, who soon asked Fortuny to write his campaign speeches.[41] It was the practicality of Marxism, its claim to put social enfranchisement within reach, and not its distant theoretical utopianism, that accounts for its appeal among many of Guatemala's political elite.

The PGT's Agrarian Reform, made law in June 1952, sought to advance national capitalism through the extension of democracy in the countryside. Through the creation of an administrative structure designed to weaken the ironclad grip planters had over rural life, the reform hoped to empower peasants to demand higher salaries for their plantation work.[42] Better wages, it was believed, would not only turn rural laborers into consumers of national manufactures but force planters, historically addicted to cheap, often free labor and land, to invest in new technologies and rationalize production in order to make a profit.

The centerpiece of the PGT's vision of democratic modernization was the agrarian committees, Comités Agrarios Locales, or CALs.[43] By bypassing institutions controlled by planter interests, such as municipal governments, the Congress, and the courts, CALs turned rural relations of domination and deference upside down. They received the initial land claims by peasants and unions, reviewed the documentation, conducted a survey, and passed their recommendation on to the department-level Comités Agrarios Departamentales, or CADs, which ruled on the expropriation. For their part, planters had the right to appeal decisions first to the Agrarian Reform's national oversight board and then to the president, defined in the legislation as the "final arbiter of all disputes." The composition of the CALs likewise shifted the balance of power in the countryside. CALs had five members, of which peasant unions appointed three and the municipality and departmental governor named the remaining two. Many times, the president of the union and the president of the CAL were the same person, and little practically separated the two institutions. In other words, the leader of the peasant union petitioning for land was often the government representative charged with initially ruling on the petition.[44] In Carchá, for example, barely a month after the adoption of the Agrarian Reform, the Comunidad Agraria named Cucul and two other members to the CAL, which outraged the mayor.[45] Not only did he complain to the governor that Cucul should not serve as president of both the union and the CAL, he asked that the two institutions conduct their business in separate locations. "In my opinion," he wrote, "the CAL should work in a different office from that occupied by the Comunidad Agraria, which is a biased party."[46] That the office in question was Icó's old house underscores the continuity between the Agrarian Reform and Cucul's uncle's lifelong efforts to circumvent planter control through the creation of a parallel structure.

The PGT's Agrarian Reform aligned cross-ethnic and cross-class interests. In nearly all areas where Decreto 900 had a deep impact, residents talk of organizing teams comprising Q'eqchi's and Ladinos.[47] Local Ladinos promoted reform for a variety of reasons, motivated by a mix of idealism, nationalism, opportunism, and resentment of the power wielded by large finqueros. Some were the educated children or grandchildren of medium-sized planters and earned their living as either provincial merchants, professionals, or civil servants. In every important town of Verapaz, there existed a nucleus of activists, often affiliated with the PGT and grouped around one or two families. In Purulhá, the municipal clerk Porfirio López, along with his son Vinicio, a first-generation university graduate, joined the PGT, traveling down the southern bank of the Polochic River on horseback helping to form unions and CALs on plantations as far east as Panzós. In the hamlet of La Tinta, in Panzós, Marcela Lemus, a schoolteacher and the owner of

FIGURE 4. Alfredo Cucul addresses an assembly in Guatemala City to demand land reform, May 1952. Víctor Manuel Gutiérrez sits behind him (courtesy of Alfredo Cucul).

a dry goods store and *comedor,* an informal restaurant, along with her lover Herculano Hernández, were members of the PGT and used their establishment, known as *el comedor de los comunistas,* as a meeting place.[48] Up the Polochic River, in Tecurú, Marcela's cousins, Mario and Napoleón Lemus, also children of middling planters, were PGT activists. After the fall of Arbenz, Mario became third-in-command of Guatemala's first guerrilla organization.[49] Within months of the passage of the Agrarian Reform, Ladino and indigenous activists had established 185 unions in the Q'eqchi' and Poqomchi' towns of Chahal, Lanquín, San Juan Chamelco, Santa Cruz, Senahú, San Cristóbal, San Pedro Carchá, Tactic, Tamahú, Tucurú, Cahabón, and Panzós.[50]

The Agrarian Reform endowed rising local leaders with considerable political power, a threat identified by the reform's opponents. In his post-1954 condemnation of the October Revolution, for example, Guatemala's archbishop, Mariano Rossell y Arellano, cited the emergence of exactly the kind of political outspokenness voiced by Icó and Cucul as one of democracy's more notable sins. Organizers would select a peasant "gifted with facility with words and a certain ability to get along with local people, overwhelming him with money, travel, public posts, and indoctrinating him thoroughly in their cause. They brought him to the Capital . . . taught him to speak in public."[51] And looking at the May 1952 photograph of Cucul addressing fifteen thousand demonstrators in Guatemala City, with the PGT's Víctor Manuel Gutiérrez, who invited Cucul to speak at the rally, sitting attentively behind him, one can imagine that the cleric had some such scene in mind (see fig. 4).[52] Sharing the stage with prominent politicians, including José Manuel Fortuny, the man who five years earlier had expelled his uncle from the PAR, Cucul congratulated the crowd on its spirit and called on Congress to quickly pass the Agrarian Reform.[53] Yet Cucul's political engagement with a wider world remained rooted in community, which is what gave the Revolution its menace.[54] He spoke in Q'eqchi', and his words were broadcast throughout the country, including Carchá, where Manuela remembers gathering with members of the Comunidad Agraria in Icó's old house to listen to her husband.[55]

In 1952, at the age of twenty-six, Alfredo Cucul, now head of his uncle's Comunidad Agraria and president of the CAL, found himself one of the most important men in San Pedro Carchá.[56] It was during his frequent trips to the capital on union business that Cucul made friends with Gutiérrez and other

FIGURE 5. Village leaders of Carchá's Comunidad Agraria posed for this photograph the day after Congress passed the Agrarian Reform legislation. According to Alfredo Cucul, third from the right in the second row, the celebrants spent the previous night in a local cave performing Q'eqchi' rites of gratitude. Later in the day they joined with other *comunidades agrarias* in Alta Verapaz to continue the ceremony in Cobán's general cemetery (courtesy of Alfredo Cucul).

leaders of the PGT, drawn to them because, as he recalls, they possessed a kind of astringent integrity that contrasted with the more unctuous mannerisms characteristic of many revolutionary caudillos. It was on account of these "friendships," remembered tenderly in the way Cucul drops his customary severe tone for a softer, more reflective voice—the state would disappear Gutiérrez in 1966—that Cucul joined the party.

By August 1953, Cucul, along with PGT member Miguel Guzmán, had organized eighteen peasant unions and numerous CALs in plantations and villages throughout Carchá.[57] By 1954, he had helped with the expropriation of over twenty thousand acres from ten plantations and facilitated the distribution of livestock from nationalized German plantations.[58] Yet it was not just the Agrarian Reform that provided rural workers with some independence from their bosses. The Instituto Guatemalteco de Seguridad Social (IGSS)—modeled on the U.S. social security payroll tax but also including health care and accident insurance—provided an escape from the private paternalism on which so many peasants relied in times of crises.[59] Under IGSS auspices, Cucul and the departmental PAR's general secretary, Hugo de la Vega, formed a local credit union as a way of offering an alternative to the foremen's practice of "holding" the workers' earnings in the plantation's safe and skimming off "interest" for themselves. When a bull gored a resident worker to death, Cucul and de la Vega publicly presented his widow insurance money while at the same time explaining to assembled workers the goals of the Revolution. "I tried out my Q'eqchi' but nobody understood me, Alfredo had to interpret," remembers de la Vega. The interlocking relationship between newly established bureaucratic social service programs and supposedly nongovernmental labor organizing proved essential since activists often relied on state salaries and equipment in order to conduct their work. Availing themselves of IGSS jeeps, phones, and office supplies, Cucul and de la Vega helped organize unions in the mines of northern Carchá, in San Cristóbal's shoe factory, and among Carchá's tanners.[60]

The importance of the PGT in advancing the reforms of the October Revolution is underscored by the appointment of Víctor Lucas, a party member, as head of Carchá's Guardia Civil, Guatemala's national police force. Until late 1953, the Partido Revolutionario de Guatemala (PRG) ran Carchá's municipality. Nationally, the PRG supported Arbenz, but throughout the countryside its local leadership had grown increasingly hostile to his reforms. San Pedro Carchá, more than Cobán even, was, according to de la Vega, an "anticommunist redoubt," and reformers were constantly harassed and threatened.[61] Lucas's 1952 arrival helped level the field for agrarian organizing and fair voting.[62] In 1953, for example, the PAR won all but one of Alta Verapaz's municipal elections, including Carchá's.[63] Furthermore, according to Cucul, it was Lucas who finally brought a definitive end to the municipality's enforcement of vagrancy laws. "He made a difference," remembers de la Vega.

By the time Arbenz fell, the government had expropriated nearly one and a half million acres to the benefit of roughly one hundred thousand families.[64] Yet the reform lasted only two years, and the amount of property transferred on paper does not neatly match peasant memories. Crops planted on land expropriated during the reform's final months were for the most part never harvested, as planters, after Arbenz's fall, quickly reclaimed their property. Cucul at first insisted that only one private plantation in Carchá was expropriated, but changed his mind when he read the documentation describing other cases. "The thing is," says Cucul, "we were only just beginning. It was over before we got most of that land."

Despite the Agrarian Reform, planter power persisted by means of an ongoing application in many areas of vagrancy laws, control over subsistence production, and an alliance with local priests against the secularizing thrust of the Revolution. In 1954, Leonardo Castillo Flores, head of the national peasant federation, complained of the "pamphlets, flyers, radio programs, and newspapers" planters had at their disposal to spread lies about the Agrarian Reform: they told peasants that they would forfeit their union membership if they received land, that they would no longer receive food rations or material to repair their houses if they joined a union, and that the government was going to take away their wives and children.[65] Castillo Flores also noted attempts to divide the rural population, such as offers of better salaries for loyal workers and rumors that land granted by the reform would be invaded by free peasants. Routine physical and verbal violence likewise diluted the effectiveness of local political democracy, wearing activists down with a constant, low-intensity harassment. Following Arbenz's election and Icó's death in 1950, for example, assaults and taunts against Cucul and other peasant leaders grew worse. Manuela Caal, who had her ribs broken by a drunk celebrating Icó's death, remembers Ladinos throwing rocks through her windows. She hated going out because of the insults she would suffer. Alfredo complained that Ladinos ridiculed his attempt to organize adult literacy workshops, saying that the "only way Indians could learn Spanish is if you split their skulls with an ax and pour it in."[66] And despite the establishment of networks of authority outside the control of planters, local courts and municipalities still held considerable power. Cucul remembers how judges in

Carchá and Cobán would react to complaints from Q'eqchi' workers of physical abuse, employing the colloquial *vos* verb tense and the lordly *don* to underscore the subordination under which Q'eqchi's lived: "'*¿Qué querés? ¿Qué querés?* Tell me, tell me. Who hit you?'" says Cucul, spitting out the words. "Then the *don* would come and they would say to him, 'This mozo claims you hit him,' and the *don* would laugh, 'Ha, it was he who threatened me with a machete.' '*Vos,* you are the guilty one,' they would say and throw the Indian in jail for a week." For many rural workers, to support the Revolution meant in effect to side with the state against planters. This entailed a great risk, for the benefits of plantation loyalty were often more tangible than revolutionary promises. Planters cultivated allegiance by protecting their workers from the worst abuses of the state, paying taxes and fees, obtaining for them exemptions from military service and public work obligations, and defending them in court.[67] A sober assessment of power meant to take serious account of the common planter threat, repeated in differing versions but to the same effect, "If you quit the PAR, you will have a house and land. If not, the street will be yours."[68]

Planter power was also perpetuated by a politicized form of racism, which, as we saw in the case of Icó, had long been aimed at indigenous leaders. In fact, during the October Revolution, the term *líder* itself became a pejorative accusation, used as a self-evident synonym for the impertinence attributed to indigenous activists, almost as damning as the charge of bolshevism.

The 1953 shotgun murder of the Q'eqchi' Santiago Saquil by his neighbor, the Ladino peasant Emilio Alvarado, in a small hamlet of Carchá is a case in point.[69] The father of six children, Alvarado had lived his entire life next to the Saquil family, making his living, as did Saquil, as a tenant farmer. The two families were twined through marriage—Alvarado's Q'eqchi' common law wife of thirty years was Saquil's cousin, and his Ladino brother married the Q'eqchi' sister of Saquil's wife. The Alvarado brothers spoke Q'eqchi' with their family and did not teach their children Spanish. Cucul, who helped Santiago's family work through the legal system, insists that although Santiago was the president of his hamlet's CAL and, since the time of Icó, a member of the peasant union, the conflict between Alvarado and Saquil was not over land or economics. Alvarado hated Saquil, says Cucul, because Saquil was a "leader" who did not know his place. Santiago was killed, as his wife testified, for being politically active, for "being a member of the *campesinado.*" In fact, Cucul points out, Alvarado could have benefited from the Agrarian Reform but opposed it because he was a Ladino and thought he was "*más que uno*"—better than us.

The incarceration of Alvarado for Saquil's murder became a cause célèbre in Verapaz, helping to unite various strains of anti-communist sentiment. Carchá's Catholic priests celebrated masses for his release and used the opportunity to preach against the Comunidad and the Agrarian Reform. Arturo Nuila, a planter, lawyer, and one of Cobán's most powerful men, agreed to defend Alvarado pro bono. Although Nuila traveled in circles far from Alvarado's peasant world, a shared opposition to insolent Q'eqchi's brought the two together. The trial represented an opportunity to blend publicly racist stereotypes with anti-communist fears, a deadly mix that would become increasingly toxic in the decades after 1954. Nuila marched a parade of character witnesses before the court. Rural Q'eqchi's, notable Ladinos, and Carchá clergy testified that Saquil was "bellicose and aggressive," "corpulent and strong," "lived in a state of drunkenness," was "out of control, bad tempered, and rash" and "a hostile man." Shortly after Arbenz's overthrow, Nuila entered a motion to drop charges against Alvarado. Saquil's family, he said, "was badly advised by Alfredo Cucul, the *líder instigador.*" His client was of "irreproachable conduct who saw the need to commit a painful act because of the unjustifiable actions of a Communist leader animated by the circumstances that prevailed in the country during that time." Cobán's anti-communist newspapers *El Sulfato* and *El Impacto* campaigned for Alvarado's freedom, which he received in February 1955.[70] All he did, commented *El Impacto,* was "kill a Communist leader."

Cucul insists that the Agrarian Reform had overwhelming support among Q'eqchi's. When asked who was against it, he answers: Ladinos. When asked if any Q'eqchi's opposed the reform, he confesses that a few did but they were wealthy and lived in Carchá's center. When questioned about the rural Q'eqchi's who testified on Alvarado's behalf, or about why supposed support quickly turned after the fall of Arbenz, Cucul admits that there were some who did not agree with the Revolution: "They didn't know what they were doing, they went with both sides. Some were very *pegados,* attached, to their bosses. They were like dogs who barked when ordered. They did what they were told." Since its inception, the October Revolution had generated natural opponents, not only among those who profited from the old order but also among those who found safety and meaning in its hierarchy and authority. As the Revolution progressed, a diffuse defense of the disciplined security of the plantation and hostility to challengers to social hierarchy cut across class and ethnic lines, bringing together men as different as Nuila and Alvarado. Race and class divisions proved so potentially powerful that they could also divide supporters of the October Revolution. The organizer of Cobán's 1953 May Day celebration, for instance, reported that the "sparse" numbers of white-collar government workers who attended refused to "march with their more humble [peasant] *compañeros*," acting instead like "disgraceful aristocrats."[71]

In an attempt to weaken the considerable power planters continued to hold over the rural population, the Agrarian Reform advanced a considerable amount of unregulated power to local agrarian activists. These activists often drew on their authority as community leaders, politicians, or patriarchs to mobilize threatening numbers of followers in support of specific goals, such as land, better working conditions, higher wages, and political autonomy. This mobilization tore up and remade social relations and expectations throughout Guatemala. But it is on its Spanish-literate leaders, such as Cucul, that it had its greatest ideological impact, sharpening their understanding of rights and political power backed up by state intervention. Yet despite the spread of parties, unions, and CALs, this mobilization was launched through many of the same hierarchical relations of deference and obligation that structured rural society—hierarchies that were themselves not fundamentally challenged.[72] Notwithstanding the democratic style employed by a handful of Communist and other revolutionary leaders, populist authoritarianism still served as the most powerful organizing device. Icó, it is to be recalled, treated his followers much as any local caudillo would, rounding up Q'eqchi's to vote for revolutionary candidates and repeatedly referring to his followers as "my Indians."[73]

The political leadership of Francisco "Pancho" Curley reveals the force and faults of the mobilization that took place under the Agrarian Reform. Curley, the descendant of an Irish immigrant planter grandfather and Guatemalan grandmother, was born in 1917 in Cahabón, one of the original colonial Q'eqchi' settlements east of Carchá.[74] Educated to the sixth grade in a Guatemala City Catholic school, he became Alta Verapaz's most infamous Arbencista, a notoriously abrasive and controversial person. Alfonso Bauer Paiz remembers Curley as "extremely theatrical, and aggressive and abusive" toward political opponents. Cucul only shakes his head and smiles when Curley's name is mentioned, and one gets the feeling that it is with Curley that Cucul compares himself when he says he did not earn one cent from his political activities. The only thing he will say is that Curley always "wore his hat tilted on his head, covering part of his face." Revenge reportedly drove Curley's political passion, exemplifying how social conflict is often blamed on personal motives. Kensett Champney dispossessed Curley's widowed mother of a ten-thousand-acre plantation after her husband died in

1931 indebted to Champney. "Something just snapped in him," says Kensett's grandson, Edgar. "It wasn't even just a matter of getting back the land, it was like a sickness. He became obsessed with destroying first my grandfather and then my father."

Under the aegis of the Agrarian Reform, Curley joined with Federico García of the neighboring town of Senahú to build an extensive structure of power and patronage. Along with allied relatives and indigenous leaders, they held multiple offices in the new institutions created by the October Revolution, dramatically shifting power relations in the countryside. Curley was in charge of organizing in Alta Verapaz's branch of the national labor federation, served as the peasant federation's delegate to the Department Agrarian Commission, held various positions in the unions he helped form, headed Cahabón's PAR and CAL, and was elected mayor in 1953.[75] Federico García was the general secretary of Alta Verapaz's national labor federation and its delegate to the Department Agrarian Committee. García's cousins, along with their Q'eqchi' associates, most notably Marcelino Xol, Vicente Acté, José Hor, German Che, Marcos Che, Pedro Caal, José Caal, Manuel Tex, Vicente Chub, and Pablo Maquin, filled the leadership positions in both unions and CALS. It was a formidable network of power reinforced by ties with national politicians. It was, for instance, Curley and García who interpreted Arbenz's 1950 campaign speech into Q'eqchi'. While required for the extension of democracy in the countryside, this network was itself decidedly not democratic.

Throughout his activity during the October Revolution, Curley faced repeated charges of fraud, patronage, and coercion. In late 1953, for example, Pedro Quib, from a small village in Cahabón, accused Curley of placing his Q'eqchi' supporters in positions of power, demanding money from every household that received cattle, and threatening those who complained with expulsion from their recently acquired land grants.[76] Quib testified that when he voiced his objections to Curley, Curley struck him. Other *campesinos* (peasants) reported that every year Curley "sends us to work on his plantation," which he told them belonged to Arbenz, "paying them absolutely not one cent."[77] At the same time as Curley faced criminal charges of corruption and abuse, he and García fought attempts by national revolutionary leaders to force them out of their many positions of authority. The general secretary of Alta Verapaz's PAR complained that the intrigues of Curley and his followers were "deforming the ideology of the PAR." They are "false leaders," he wrote, "who use the Agrarian Reform as political bribery to tie peasants to a new type of exploitation."[78] In turn, Curley and García red-baited their detractors, organizing anti-communist demonstrations to disrupt attempts to remove them from their office.[79]

When opponents today speak of the application of the Agrarian Reform, they inevitably focus on the kind of transgressions and corruptions attributed to Curley as proof that the reform had run amok.[80] Historians, on the other hand, have gone to great lengths to prove the opposite—that, except in occasional cases, the reform's application was orderly and legal.[81] Yet the fact is that in many cases abuses such as those associated with Curley were a constituent element of the reform's strength. As mentioned earlier, in order to dilute planter authority, the reforms of the October Revolution, particularly the Agrarian Reform, greatly empowered local leaders. At best, these leaders mobilized followers through patriarchal compulsion, drawing on their influence over women, family members, and other dependents to create a zone of sovereignty not subject to the punishments and blandishments of planters. At worst, as seems to have been the case with Curley, they employed a more bullying force.

In some sense, the coercion employed to enact the Agrarian Reform approximated the power the reform contested. This was both the reform's strength and weakness. If Alta Verapaz was, as Arbenz noted in his 1950 campaign speech, the most exploited department in the republic, Cahabón was the most subjugated municipality in Alta Verapaz. As in Carchá, the municipality vigorously applied vagrancy laws that forced peasants to work on plantations in order to avoid jail or fines. The territory of nearly half the municipality, over a hundred thousand acres, was owned by one man—Benjamin Champney. Prior to Arbenz's election, the rise of the PAR, and the enactment of the Agrarian Reform, Champney controlled the town council, local courts, and the police of both the municipality of Cahabón, where the majority of his plantation lay, and the municipality of Senahú, where the plantation's main house and productive land were located. He paid no salary to his resident peons, offering them in exchange for their labor only access to land. According to his son, he "strode around like he was the marquis de Cahabón." Curley's concentration of power among allies, his flagrant bestowal of rewards on favorites, his intimidation of peasants perhaps more beholden to Champney than to Arbenz, his passion fired by revenge, and his larger-than-life audaciousness—according to one witness, upon receiving news that the government had approved the expropriation of Champney's land, the peasant union carried Curley through the streets of Cahabón "like a saint, burning incense and banging a drum"—created an effective counterweight to the plantation's power over the lives and livelihoods of Cahabón's rural workers.[82] Spurred by Curley's constant harassment, which drove Benjamin to flee Guatemala for New Orleans, the state expropriated nearly half of Sepacuité's more than a hundred thousand acres. "They had the whole valley organized," says one longtime PGT activist of Curley and García. "They controlled an impressive number of peasants," remembers Hugo de la Vega.[83]

Guatemala's 1999 truth commission report notes that many of the reforms of the October Revolution did not have time to mature. Despite attempts to transform Guatemala's "archaic judicial system," courts were ill prepared for the conflicts generated by the "rapid incorporation of new rights" activated by the labor code and the Agrarian Reform.[84] The reforms both let loose pent hatreds—whether in the form of acts of vengeance by the sons of dispossessed widows, brawls between family members, or efforts by indigenous communities to regain land lost decades previously—and created new tensions that threatened to widen every fissure of Guatemalan society into gaping rifts. For individuals long politically marginalized and economically disenfranchised, the power granted by the Revolution could be intoxicating. In 1952, when Eliseo Ax Burmester, a founding member of Icó's Comunidad and political party, lost his job as a custodian of a local school because a Ladino accused him of stealing, Ax ordered him to leave town and threatened him with his life. "I have plenty of Indians under my command to hurt you," Ax reportedly said, apparently referring to Carchá's Comunidad Agraria.[85]

The number of court cases exploded. Judges, even assuming their impartiality, could not mediate the swirl of accusations or evaluate opposing testimonies. Since in the electric air of the October Revolution even the most mundane conflict became charged with political importance, neither could they satisfy—again, setting aside the probability of corruption, racism, and reaction—the competing expectations placed on their decisions. Many cases, such as those against Alvarado and Curley, sputtered on for a time after the overthrow of Arbenz, eventually to be quietly dismissed. Emilio Alvarado's release was clearly a political act, yet even the charges against Curley were dropped for lack of evidence. Curley was arrested for being a Communist, but like the majority of the thousands of others taken into custody after the fall of Arbenz, he was eventually freed. Savage violence, including assassinations and massacres, took place in the weeks following Arbenz's resignation.[86] Yet once order was restored, once planters felt the threat to their power was safely contained, they attempted to return to the world of deference and largesse unhinged by the October Revolution.

If the strength of the October Revolution resided in its vanquishing the notion that injustice was fated, then the power of the counterrevolution resided in destiny's resurgence, for people, as Barrington Moore observes, "are evidently inclined to grant legitimacy to anything that is or seems inevitable no matter how painful it may be."[87] According to many accounts of those who lived through Arbenz's 1954 overthrow, the theatricality of the CIA's psychological war created the illusion not only of an opposition but of a dramatic unfolding of events, of inescapable confrontation, which effectively turned potential actors into passive spectators. Not wanting to antagonize the military, revolutionary leaders reinforced this watch-and-wait attitude, demobilizing potential defenders and reassuring them that the loyal army was repelling the mercenaries.[88] Alfredo Cucul remembers being bewildered by Arbenz's resignation speech, for he had been told throughout the preceding week that the U.S.-trained mercenaries were in retreat. Where worker committees did offer resistance, such as in Puerto Barrios, they were betrayed by the army. From Cobán, Walter Overdick remembers heading toward Guatemala City with hundreds of other students and peasants before being intercepted by the military and taken to a military base where, they were told, they were to form a militia to defend the government. Overdick soon realized that they were in fact prisoners.[89] For its part, the PGT leadership found itself "overtaken by events," as one of its founders, Alfredo Guerra Borges, puts it.[90] The party provided Arbenz with unsure counsel and talked of mounting an armed underground resistance, but after four years in power, they "did not even have a mimeograph machine hidden, not one piece of clandestine equipment, not to mention money, food, guns, or any of the other basics of underground life."[91]

Confusion reinforced the counterrevolutionaries, who quickly moved to fill the vacuum of state power. In Alta Verapaz, local politicians hostile to the direction of the Revolution transformed affiliates of political parties into provisional anti-Communist defense committees and took charge of municipal and departmental offices.[92] The new government set up the National Defense Committee against Communism, giving it both judicial and executive authority to investigate, arrest, and try suspected subversives. The Preventive and Penal Law against Communism empowered the committee to create a register "of all persons who in whatever form participated in Communist activities" and by November 1954, with the help of the CIA, had compiled a list of over seventy-two thousand names.[93] Communism was defined so loosely that one U.S. Embassy official boasted that "with this law we can now pick up practically anybody we want and hold them for as long as we want."[94]

In the months following Arbenz's resignation, the police, military, and ad hoc vigilante groups, at the command of either anti-communist committees or private planters, murdered between three thousand and five thousand

FIGURE 6. Court records document a number of violent deaths in the Verapaz countryside in the weeks following the overthrow of Arbenz. This forensic sketch depicts the death of Francisco Cucul, a peasant leader from Gualibaj, Cahabón, whose death was ruled a suicide (AGCA J-AV, index 107 60G).

Arbencistas.[95] In the town of Escuintla, where the PGT had won the mayoralty in 1953, its leaders were arrested, tortured, and executed.[96] At the United Fruit Company's Plantation Jocotán on the southern coast, upward of one thousand plantation organizers were murdered after being taken into custody. In the plaza of the banana town of Morales, United Fruit's head foreman, Rosendo Pérez, fired his machine gun into the face of Alaric Benett, an Afro-Guatemalan union leader and PAR congressman. He then executed over two dozen other captured unionists.[97] These large-scale killings aside, most violence took place quietly, against troublesome yet less prominent activists who lived in remote areas not covered by national or international press. At the request of the CIA, the *New York Times* did not send reporters into the countryside following Arbenz's overthrow.[98] Thousands of urban activists—including Arbenz and most of the PGT leadership—sought asylum in foreign embassies, while some rural Arbencistas fled to Belize, Mexico, Honduras, or more remote areas of Guatemala. Well before the new government officially

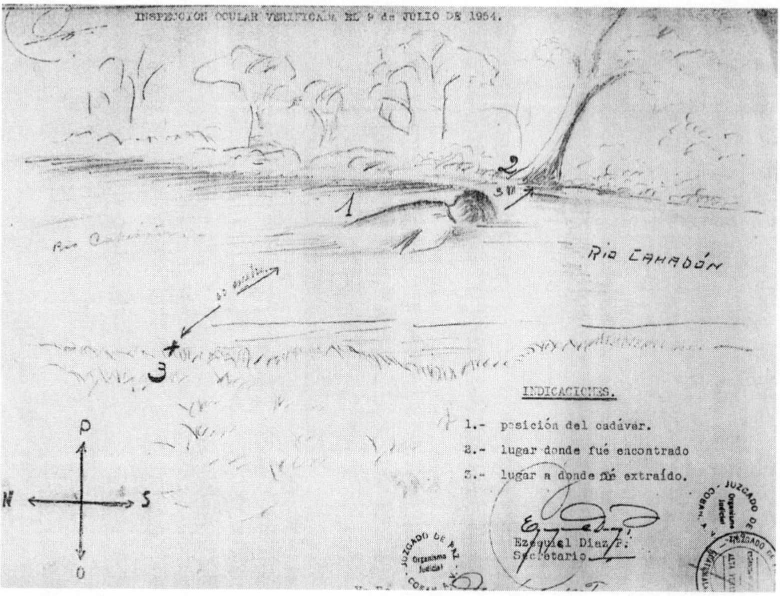

FIGURE 7. Ezequiel Chen was a union activist at Alta Verapaz's electric plant. His corpse was found floating in the Cahabón River in August 1954 (AGCA J-AV, index 107 60H).

overturned the Agrarian Reform, planters reclaimed land and livestock while many peasants who allied themselves with the new order seized the moment to settle old scores and pilfer their neighbor's property.[99]

Despite the violence, most of the roughly twelve thousand captured were not executed.[100] Provisional authorities sent local Arbencistas to the capital and either released secondary leaders after a few months or brought them up on charges under new anti-communist legislation. Provincial trials served not so much to jail or punish suspected enemies of the new state—nearly all those legally processed were eventually released—as to elicit contrition and condemnation of the past regime and disengage peasant activists from their leaders. In Carchá, for example, anti-communists arrested twelve members of the peasant union of the San Vicente plantation, including the son of Santiago Saquil, in July 1954.[101] Their interrogation consisted of asking them if they could prove that they were not Communists or members of the PGT or that they did not "hold Marxist ideas during the past regime." In being forced to prove a negative, the accused were compelled not only to deny any relation to the PGT, which they in fact did not directly have, but to renounce the *substance,* that is, the specific material benefits accrued, and *spirit,* the right to citizenship based on political participation, of the October Revolution. Pedro Mucú said he had never joined a party but that "Alfredo Cucul obliged me to receive a parcel of land." When asked what party they belonged to, all responded that they did not know its name but were forced to affiliate by Alfredo Cucul. Marcelino Che Bo said that Cucul and Miguel Guzmán arrived at his house to "press his fingerprint in a book, saying that if I didn't I would be thrown out of my house." Others called on prominent Ladinos to testify to their "good habits," "faith in God," and qualities of a "good worker"—in effect reestablishing patronage relations severed by the October Revolution.[102]

After Arbenz's resignation on June 27, 1954, Cucul decided to hide at a friend's home a day's walk from the center of Carchá. During the previous months, a sense that the Revolution's days were numbered emboldened his opponents, and taunts against him and his wife steadily increased.[103] While Cucul was away, soldiers ransacked his house, looking for weapons, burning documents, and threatening family members. The next day, a crowd of Q'eqchi's and Ladinos armed with sticks and machetes trampled his corn plot and made off with his livestock. Fearing continued harassment against his family, Cucul turned himself in to the police in Cobán—rumors of beatings and murders led him not to trust Carchá's authorities. By the time he surrendered, Alta Verapaz's anti-Communist forces had arrested about three hundred men, placing Ladinos and Q'eqchi's in separate holding areas. Cucul's captors gave him a steady if somewhat desultory rain of kicks, punches, and insults and after about two weeks sent him and about thirty others to the central police station in downtown Guatemala City. His wife, Manuela, remembers the six months Cucul remained locked up as the hardest and hungriest of her life. She and her nephew traveled to Guatemala City, getting by on handouts from political contacts and the relatives of other prisoners after losing all their savings, including their property, to pay a woman who falsely promised to use purported connections to get Alfredo out of jail. After six months of little more than waiting, the brother of a recently released prisoner told them to ask the secretary to the new *ministro de gobernación* for Alfredo's release. "But be sure to speak in Q'eqchi, because he is from Alta Verapaz," he said. They did as instructed and Alfredo was discharged. Following his release, Alfredo and Manuela went to the secretary to thank him and ask him what they could do to repay the kindness. "Nothing," said the secretary, "just send me a chicken when you get back to Carchá." Manuela and Alfredo decided not to return to a world in which favors—be they jail pardons or chickens—served as the currency for what they now viewed as an immoral economy of restored subservience. They stayed in Guatemala City, where, with help from acquaintances, they started a new life for themselves and educated their children.

No matter what part of the past Cucul recounts, it is to the betrayal by his imprisoned *compañeros,* along with the attack on his house and crops, that his thoughts invariably turn in the end. When Cucul describes these events, his attribution of total support for Arbenz ("only the Ladinos were against him") melts into emptiness ("I was alone"). Yet it is a declension drained of the specifics of history, for he refuses to talk about his life after 1954 except in the absolute terms of religion. Cucul gives the impression that he gave up politics and converted to Evangelical Protestantism immediately after Arbenz's overthrow, but according to his son, who says that Alfredo talked about the Vietnam War and taught him Marxism into the 1970s, this apparently was not the case. Often those who lived through the "trauma of 1954," as the truth commission describes the overthrow of Arbenz, repeatedly, compulsively, affirm that the October Revolution could have succeeded had it not been for U.S. intervention. History may have been violently interrupted in June 1954, but, for many, history remained an impassioned possibility. Not so for Cucul, who while he talks proudly of the Agrarian Reform and fondly of many of its protagonists, especially Gutiérrez, Castillo Flores, and Arbenz, believes that it was a fundamentally futile endeavor. While family members suggest that it actually took Cucul decades to reach this impasse, that he now dates it to 1954 speaks to the psychic power of that year in the minds of a postwar generation who experienced little distinction between personal and national progress. For Cucul, the trauma not only cut short the possibility of politics as an avenue of upward human mobility but also ended any prospect that that mobility, which he pursued through other means after 1954, could be anchored in his community. Alfredo and Manuela never returned to live in Carchá, and their conversion to Evangelicalism, whatever spiritual nourishment it offered, is an element of their emotional exile, revealed in Cucul's stinging criticism of superstitious Q'eqchi's who blindly obeyed the anti-communism of the Catholic Church.

Manuela and Alfredo remember 1954 as an end to history and politics. But others, on both sides of the revolutionary divide, experienced that year as a radicalization of both. For many who worked for social change, memories of the October Revolution strengthened their resolve, for it confirmed to them that reform was indeed possible. The desire to redeem the democratic promise of 1944 drove their politics, and many of their children's politics, for the next four decades. For those who feared change, 1954 was at first a welcomed relief. But a return to an idealized past of security and deference would prove no less utopian than the revolutionary hopes they fought against. There was no going back, and those "friends of order," as Arbenz called them in 1950, would steadily come to rely on new ideologies, new technologies, and an ever greater dependence on the United States to counter challenges to their authority. In short, the expectations of 1944 kept running into the reality of 1954, resulting in the political polarization that defined much of the Latin American Cold War.

CHAPTER THREE

Unfinished Lives

Come, I will make the Continent indissoluble.
Walt Whitman

"I'M NOT SURE I can explain it," says John Longan of Guatemalan violence during the 1960s; "it is inbred in them, and they hate pretty deeply."[1] Longan, who had previously worked as a law officer in Oklahoma and Texas, arrived in Guatemala in 1957 as part of the first wave of advisors sent by the United States to foreign countries, a police corps to train local security forces "to destroy the effectiveness of the Communist apparatus in free world countries."[2] He stayed for two years and then moved through other Cold War trouble spots—Brazil, Venezuela, Thailand, and the Dominican Republic. In December 1965, Longan returned to Guatemala on a temporary assignment to set up a rapid-response security unit. Within three months this squad, working under the name Operación Limpieza (Operation Cleanup), had conducted over eighty raids and multiple extrajudicial assassinations, including an action that during four days in March captured, tortured, and executed more than thirty prominent left opposition leaders. The military dumped their bodies into the sea while the government denied any knowledge of their whereabouts.[3]

Among those murdered in March 1966 were Víctor Manuel Gutiérrez and Leonardo Castillo Flores, the respective leaders of Guatemala's labor and peasant federations during Arbenz's tenure. Coming on the eve of the election of a civilian president who pledged to reinitiate the reforms of Arévalo and Arbenz, just as the left was fracturing between the old and the new, these disappearances destroyed the possibility of a negotiated end to Guatemala's escalating civil war. The most forceful advocates of dialogue on the left, such as Gutiérrez, were eliminated, while a newly fortified military saw no need to settle. In effect, the March 1966 murders offered in one act a repeat performance of Guatemala's democratic decade: reformers and revolutionaries hoping to recreate the alliances that had led to the 1944 political opening now faced a new set of internationalized repressive capabilities, put in place in 1954, that ensured that those coalitions could never again be replicated.

Just as the overthrow of Ubico signaled one of the first and most enduring democratic experiments in postwar Latin America, and the 1954 demise of that experiment marked the first U.S. Cold War intervention in the hemisphere, 1966's Operation Cleanup marked a decisive step in the radicalization of the continent. It bolstered an intelligence system that in the course of Guatemala's civil war metastasized throughout the body politic, able and resolved to conduct perhaps the cruelest campaign of state repression in twentieth-century Latin America.[4] It presaged the installation of counterinsurgent terror states throughout much of the continent, most notably in Brazil in 1968; Chile and Uruguay in 1973; Argentina in 1976; and El Salvador in the late 1970s. While Latin American dictators such as Trujillo, Batista, and Somoza had long practiced extrajudicial kidnappings, torture, and executions, counterinsurgent military regimes through the work of technically armed and ideologically fired intelligence agencies perfected the signature act of Cold War violence: the literal disappearance of political opponents.[5] *Disappearances* created a climate of uncertainty and confusion in which the state was able to "deny its crimes because there was no concrete evidence, no bodies, no arrests, no formal charges, no trials, and no imprisonments."[6] The *disappeared* left behind families and friends who spent their energies dealing with government, police, and military bureaucracies only to be told that their missing probably went to Cuba, joined the guerrillas, or ran away with a lover. Relatives of those kidnapped in March 1966 filed over five hundred writs of habeas corpus answered with nothing but state silence.

The government murdered 200,000 people in Guatemala, 30,000 in Argentina, 50,000 in El Salvador and at least 3,000 in Chile. Security forces throughout the continent tortured tens, possibly hundreds of thousands more. To a large degree, it was the expertise supplied by the United States, including the training provided by men like Longan, that made such industrial terror possible. Following the costly Korean War, U.S. foreign policy moved away from frontal assaults on Communism toward more indirect methods of containing subversion, primarily the strengthening of the internal security capabilities of its allies.[7] In its sphere of influence in the third world, the United States helped to establish or fortify central intelligence agencies. Through financing and training, its agents encouraged local officials to forgo self-interested, criminal behavior and adopt more professional attitudes. U.S. advisors such as Longan coordinated the activities of the police and the military, set up command centers and units that could quickly analyze and archive information gathered from diverse sources, and trained domestic security forces to execute operations against suspected subversives. The United States supplied intelligence agencies with phones, radios, cars, guns, ammunition, surveillance equipment, explosives, cameras, typewriters, carbon paper, filing cabinets, and training. In Argentina, U.S. agents worked with the Secretaria de Inteligencia del Estado; in Chile, the Dirección Nacional de Inteligencia; in Brazil, the Sistema Nacional de Informações; in Uruguay, the Dirección Nacional de Información e Inteligencia; in El Salvador, the Agencia Nacional de Servicios Especiales.[8] Throughout the 1980s, the CIA supported Operation Condor—an intelligence consortium established by Pinochet that coordinated the activities of many of the continent's security agencies and orchestrated an international campaign of terror and murder. Yet for all its lethal potency, the U.S.-exported counterinsurgency campaign could not have succeeded without willing allies and versatile ideologies within Latin America.

Latin America's counterrevolution could work only by offering an ideological and institutional alternative to the challenge it sought to reverse. The strength of Guatemalan democracy between 1944 and 1954 was that through politics it offered a vision of participatory democracy, a vision in which individual activists were able to engage the state while remaining connected to their local communities. To counter such attractions, clerics and anti-communist militants during the campaign to oust Arbenz offered their own conception of participant citizenship. The modernizing, exclusionary liberalism of coffee planters had spent itself, and it was up to Catholic radicals and anti-communist militants to revitalize the ideology of the ruling society. Drawing from Spanish fascism, counterrevolutionaries promoted a potent Catholic folk nationalism based on social harmony, deference, and duty. Yet the emotive power of family, God, and nation proved insufficient absent repressive persuasion. Despite Arbenz's quick defeat, successive governments could not establish legitimacy. The left proved too resilient and the rich too venal. As opposition, including an armed guerrilla insurgency, spread in the 1960s, the military and right-wing political parties came to rely on urban death squads, such as that which carried out the March 1966 disappearances, to terrorize political opponents. In the countryside, as an antidote to the unions and parties established during the Agrarian Reform, counterrevolutionaries organized peasants into vigilante and surveillance groups, tapping into a deep-seated agrarian tradition of armed defense of the state.[9] By the mid-1960s, in the opinion of the United States, the "counterinsurgency" was "running wild." Its death squads and rural paramilitary organizations were carrying out a merciless "white terror."[10] Throughout the course of Guatemala's four-decade-long civil war, the United States tried to distance itself from such revanchist violence, condemning it as beyond the bounds of its efforts to "modernize" the country's national security capabilities. Yet little distinguished the official counterinsurgency from extrajudicial death squads. U.S. support for the former directly empowered the latter. In fact, as officials would occasionally admit, the wrath of these private avengers was just as fundamental to U.S. goals as were the zeal and enthusiasm of PGT activists to the democratic achievements of the October Revolution.[11]

The 1954 overthrow of Jacobo Arbenz would not have occurred had it not been for the United States.[12] There were far fewer coups and plots against Arbenz than there had been against Arévalo, and as a military officer Arbenz commanded greater loyalty from his officers than had his predecessor. While the increasing authority of the PGT in Guatemalan politics made some officers anxious, the party's influence did not threaten the autonomy of Guatemala's armed forces, whose members enjoyed unprecedented privilege under Arbenz. Unrest in the countryside was manageable, even declining according to some estimates, and many anti-communists felt that the PGT's ascendance would stall when Arbenz's term ended in 1956. There was opposition—over a hundred thousand Guatemalans voted for Arbenz's 1950 opponent—but by the CIA's calculations it was "passive" and divided.[13] Members of the landed oligarchy were too discredited, demoralized, and hesitant to risk their considerable remaining comforts in a quixotic campaign against a popular and apparently secure president. Industrial, commercial, and agricultural associations and many newspaper editorialists, especially after the adoption of the Agrarian Reform, waged an unrelenting campaign against Arbenz, often calling for open rebellion.[14] But these groups had no "positive program," according to the State Department. They did little but rail.[15]

Even before Arbenz's inauguration, would-be liberators began a steady march to the U.S. Embassy seeking patronage.[16] While State Department officials politely turned them away, the CIA, which had commenced operations in Guatemala in 1947, started to cultivate potential assets. With the Cold War under way, Washington began to view with increased suspicion the nationalism that energized Latin America's post–World War II democratic openings and quietly encouraged its containment. Arévalo's moderate support of United Fruit Company labor unions and opposition to Central American and Caribbean dictators made U.S. officials nervous, but his continued proscription of Communism calmed some of their fears.[17] In July 1952, a year into Arbenz's tenure and a month after the passage of the Agrarian Reform, the State Department gave the CIA orders to overthrow Arbenz, yet quickly called off the operation after Nicaragua's Anastasio Somoza began talking openly of invasion plans. A year later, in March 1953, an antigovernment uprising financed by the United Fruit Company failed to elicit public support. Its quick suppression by the military led to the demoralization of the plot's leaders and either the exile or the imprisonment of many of the CIA's best contacts.[18]

So when the new Eisenhower administration decided in August 1953 to restart the campaign against Arbenz, it realized that a simple military revolt or invasion would not work. Arbenz and the Agrarian Reform were deeply popular, the military quiet, and the opposition divided and still. PBSUCCESS, as the CIA dubbed the campaign, became the Agency's most ambitious covert operation and would serve as a model for future actions. It lasted nearly a year, as opposed to the six weeks it took the Agency to overthrow Iranian prime minister Mohammad Mossadeq in 1953.[19] From Langley to Madison Avenue, the United States mobilized every facet of its power to end the October Revolution. It used the Organization of American States to isolate Guatemala diplomatically, worked with U.S. businesses to create an economic crisis there, and funded and equipped an exile invasion force based in Honduras. The U.S. navy searched all ships entering Guatemalan ports for arms. The "blatant illegality" of such action was not lost on the Guatemalan government, which fruitlessly appealed to international law in defense of its sovereignty.[20] The State Department assigned hard-line anti-communist ambassadors to Guatemala, Nicaragua, and Honduras and threatened to withhold much-needed trade concessions and credit from other Latin American countries unless they acceded to U.S. plans for Guatemala. The CIA used techniques borrowed from social psychology, Hollywood, and the advertising industry to erode loyalty and generate resistance. Radio shows incited government officials and soldiers to treason and attempted to convince Guatemalans that a widespread underground resistance movement existed. Claiming to be transmitted from "deep in the jungle" by rebel forces, the broadcasts were in fact taped in Miami and beamed into Guatemala from Nicaragua.[21] Operatives mined pop sociologies such as Robert Maurer's 1940 *The Big Con* and Paul Linebarger's 1948 *Psychological Warfare* for disinformation tactics.[22] The Agency planted stories in the Guatemalan and U.S. press and engineered death threats and sabotage to create dissension and confusion within the Arbenz government.

Yet while the counterrevolution would not have taken place were it not for the United States, neither would it have achieved its durability and strength had it not connected with oppositional currents within Guatemala. As we saw in the last chapter, planters trying to generate popular support against the Agrarian Reform, community authorities threatened by the secularization and pluralization of local politics, revolutionaries fighting over resources and members, and local Ladinos, rich and poor, attempting to contain suddenly empowered indigenous "leaders" such as Saquil and Cucul found ideological reinforcement in the rise of Cold War anti-communism. Yet this opposition generated no obvious leaders.[23] Planters were too isolated and scared to act except locally, while the officer corps remained loyal as long as its interests were not threatened by Arbenz's "communist friends."[24] It was up to the Catholic Church and anti-communist nationalist students to throw themselves into the fight with a zeal equal to that generated by the expectation of democracy and justice.

Catholicism was not the faith of the coffee state, and this was the Church's best advantage in its fight against the October Revolution. Many of the nineteenth- and early-twentieth-century planters turned presidents and governors were nominal Catholics, but their freemasonry, positivism, and vilification of colonial institutions led them after 1871 to legally separate the Church from the state, limit its right to own property, encourage Protestantism, and greatly restrict the ability of the priests to engage in politics. By the eve of the 1944 Revolution, there resided in Guatemala only 126 Catholic priests for over three million Guatemalans—forty of whom ministered to the capital's 170,000 inhabitants.[25]

At first, Guatemala's archbishop, Mariano Rossell y Arellano, viewed the 1944 overthrow of Ubico as an opportunity to restore the authority of the Church. Yet the cleric grew increasingly belligerent as it became clear that Arévalo would not reverse previous anticlerical legislation. When the Congress declared in 1945 that welfare should be considered a "right" and not a "humiliating charity," the archbishop began a decade-long assault on the October Revolution that culminated in an April 1954 call to insurrection.[26] In a steady issue of pastoral letters and sermons, Rossell y Arellano equated Arévalo with previous liberal dictators and laid out a conception of human misery based not on class conflict but on the secular erosion of colonial institutions and protections, which for centuries, he insisted, had provided meaning, dignity, and welfare to Guatemalans. The prelate blamed the brutality of World War II on the Enlightenment and viewed Allied victory not, as many others at the time believed, as a chance to consolidate democracy but rather as heralding the victory of godless "materialism."[27] The French Revolution let loose a "rising tide of evil" and introduced "liberty without conscience" and an "oppressive capitalism" without "God and without heart."[28]

The Catholic Church could rightly point to a long history not only of government harassment but of insurgent defense of peasants against liberal land and labor expropriation, and Rossell y Arellano tried to depict the October Revolution as an extension of this predation: "The hatred of Liberalism for the Church was not based on opposition to its theological doctrines so much as on the role of the Church as protector of the Indian and a dyke against the greed of those who wished to exploit the peasant."[29]

At the beginning of the October Revolution, Rossell y Arellano's anti-Communism was vague, directed at distant international threats.[30] His harangues against "godless totalitarianism" often missed their mark. In an attempt to steer a middle course in the polarizing atmosphere of the Cold War, Arévalo also criticized Soviet materialism and promoted a "spiritual socialism" aimed at returning to "men" an "integrity denied to them by conservatism and liberalism."[31] Even the most militant revolutionaries were not Jacobin anticlerics of the sort found in neighboring Mexico. There was no attempt in Guatemala to replace the language and ritual of Catholicism with a new state cult of the secular, no effort to scour religious belief from the soil. On the contrary, what so irritated the archbishop was that the October Revolution rather than rejecting Christianity sought to redefine its meaning. Rossell y Arellano complained that revolutionaries "made gifts to the village . . . they would present an image of the Blessed Virgin and call her 'Our Lady of Carmen of the PAR.' . . . Slates of candidates for Deputy were engraved on the backs of medals of the Sacred Heart. . . . They offered the villages to repair their churches."[32] And after the first serious coup attempt against Arévalo in 1946, supporters poured into the national plaza with placards insisting that "Jesus Christ was a socialist." To counter such efforts to recruit Jesus into the ranks of democrats, Rossell y Arellano increasingly articulated a position that allowed no middle ground. To Arévalo's socialism of the soul, the archbishop countered that all forms of socialism were anathema to Catholicism and served only to foment class warfare and sow "hatred in the heart of the proletariat." Socialism was merely Communism's "ridiculous, shameful puppet."[33]

The threat of modern politics forced the Church to update its message. Rossell y Arellano was sympathetic to fascism, yet he distrusted its appeal to mass political action. He was willing to use contemporary political tools such as balloting and education, however, to the degree needed to prevent being overrun by modernity. While he appealed to a past in which the Church was properly the bearer of morality and the mediator of conflict, he grounded his tactics in the present. The archbishop preached against the divisive effects of democratic pluralism, arguing that "liberty left to the caprice of each individual, far from uniting our people in their advance toward progress, only disorganizes them into opposing bands."[34] Yet he declared it a sin not to vote against anticlerical candidates. His newspaper criticized Ubico's policy of public education, writing that "books are too fragile a staircase for our Indians to climb to civilization."[35] But the archbishop established a number of indigenous schools. And while he loathed popular politics, he promoted Catholic Worker Leagues and established a catechist program in the countryside to counter the spread of unions and political parties.[36]

Rossell y Arellano's criticism of Arévalo was strident, but his attacks on Arbenz went further. The fight was no longer between the city of God and the city of man but between the city of God and "the city of the devil incarnate."[37] He joined planters in attacking the "completely Communistic" Agrarian Reform, which would lead to an "agrarian dictatorship."[38] The archbishop tapped into the growing anxiety that the reform would subvert proper relations between Ladinos and Indians and men and women. He condemned revolutionaries for teaching peasants such as Cucul how "to speak in public."[39] While politics mostly empowered men, occasionally women would take advantage of new channels of participation. "When a woman of one village or another displayed gifts of proselytism or leadership," wrote Rossell y Arellano, "she was given a high and well-paid position in official bureaucracy. [Revolutionaries are] the professional corrupters of the feminine soul among the women of the worker and peasant classes."[40]

Rossell y Arellano drew from fascism to promote a spiritual vision of social unity, an antidote to the fragmentation and divisiveness brought about by secular democratic pluralism. Prior to the October Revolution, the Spanish Civil War provided the possibility of a rapprochement between the Church and the state. Ubico, despite his liberal pedigree, mimicked Mussolini's style, quickly recognized Franco's rebellion, and offered refuge to Spanish exiles fleeing republicanism, many of them priests. The Falange was strong among Guatemala's one thousand Spanish émigrés, and it injected into the Catholic Church a restorative mystical nationalism. "We do not want a cold Catholicism," proclaimed its weekly, "we want holiness, ardent, great and joyous holiness, . . . intransigent and fanatical."[41] Fascist rituals, such as a 1938 high cathedral mass celebrated for the victims of Spanish Republicans and attended by government officials, gave the Church a way to reconsecrate its relationship with a state that had long ago stripped itself of the ceremonial trappings of Catholicism.[42] A contrived appreciation of the folk allowed Rossell y Arellano to promote a Catholic nationalism that bypassed the state to align the Church with the nation's soul. "The disorganized tribes that inhabited our America," the archbishop wrote, "would have disappeared had not the Spanish conquest arrived so providentially to unite them and give them their triple gifts of religion, blood, and language."[43] In place of democracy's exaltation of secular justice and individual rights, he offered Christian unity, deference, and duty: "In the shade of Christ's cross was forged the temperate character of our ancestors, to whom we owe what is noble and generous in our high classes and patient and abnegated in the popular classes."[44]

The archbishop's promotion of folk Catholicism helped him to enlist in his crusade rural cofradías, the saint cults through which much of local political life took place.[45] In 1953, Rossell y Arellano organized a tour of the Black Christ of Esquipulas, considered "the heart and soul of Guatemalan Catholicism" and the country's patron saint since 1916.[46] Alfredo Cucul's memory of the arrival of the itinerant clerisy in Carchá matches the archbishop's description: thousands greeted the icon as it passed through each of Carchá's four cofradías before entering the Church, and "peasants poured into the streets en masse to detain the holy image, to prostrate themselves before it and to kiss its blessed feet."[47] The pilgrimage did more "against Communism," claimed the archbishop in 1955, "than if a hundred missionaries and millions of books and hundreds of Catholic radio programs had led the anticommunist campaign."[48]

Throughout the countryside, Catholic anti-communism also passed from the pulpit to the populace through the Church's network of priests and catechists. In an effort to cultivate good relations with the Vatican, Arbenz continued Ubico's policy of allowing more foreign priests to work in Guatemala.[49] Many of them arrived from countries where they suffered republican or socialist anticlericalism, such as China, Spain, Mexico, Hungary, and Czechoslovakia, and adopted an anti-Communism bred from persecution and even torture. A number of Guatemala's Spanish and Italian priests were fascist sympathizers.[50] In Carchá, Ubico had allowed the Salesians to establish a ministry, and its three priests, led by Father José Dini, who had preached against Cucul and refused to let Icó's body enter the church, were strongly anti-communist.[51] Other clergy came from the United States, and their anti-communism was less passionate and theorized, more instinctual. From 1951 to 1954, Father Sebastian Buccellato was one of two U.S. Franciscan priests stationed in Asunción Mita, in the eastern department of Jutiapa. He remembers his opposition to Arbenz as being driven less by politics and more by fear of atheism: "We were Americans, we didn't like Mussolini, we wanted free speech and democracy."[52] Asunción, he recalls, was a "Communist stronghold," and in order to avoid the ban on clerical politics, he and another U.S. priests trained a group of thirty-five lay catechists. "We weren't allowed to preach against Communism, but natives could, so we instructed them on the evils of Communism and then they went out and taught others in villages. We taught them Catholic doctrine and that Communism denies God and says the government is more important than the Church. We told them that the Communists were trying to make a paganistic society. We told them to resist."

The moral authority the Catholic Church held over the Guatemalan population was considerable, yet its political influence was limited. The Church remained overextended. Father Sebastian remembers that he was one of only four priests in all of Jutiapa. The archbishop launched a catechist program aimed to broaden the Church's reach, but it arrived in many communities late in the Revolution.[53] Likewise, despite the unprecedented freedom of speech that characterized the Arévalo and Arbenz administrations, priests did have to tread carefully, for preaching against the government was a crime, as Father Sebastian learned when he was expelled in early 1954. The Church's "lack of a constructive social program," the U.S. Embassy noted, limited its influence, while the CIA believed that the tangible benefits of the Agrarian Reform undercut the Church's anti-communism.[54] Peasants may have prostrated themselves at the feet of the Black Christ, but a hundred thousand families received land and livestock. So in April 1954 when Rossell y Arellano exhorted Guatemalans to "rise as one man to fight the enemy of God and their country," it was up to others to deliver the message.[55]

Conceding that the fight in the countryside was lost, CIA agents worked primarily with the Comité de Estudiantes Universitarios Anticomunistas (CEUA), a group of about fifty young university students mostly from the capital but also from the provinces.[56] Led by Mario Sandoval Alarcón, Lionel Sisniega Otero, Mario López Villatoro, and Eduardo Taracena de la Cerda, these professional students, often the sons of middle planters, affected an energetic internationalism.[57] They formed émigré groups in Mexico, El Salvador, and Honduras and organized an international letter-writing campaign to demand the release of Sandoval following his imprisonment; established front solidarity organizations, such as the Comité México; and promoted the "salvation" of Guatemala as merely the "first step" in freeing Latin America from Communism.[58] They created a tight organizational structure and demanded party discipline. As insurgents, they sought, as did the archbishop with whom they closely worked, to destroy any possibility for compromise: "Atheistic Communism and Christianity were two philosophies in conflict." The choice was absolute: "slavery of man within a totalitarian system" or "democracy."[59] Armed with U.S. training and equipment, they mounted an escalating campaign of terrorism that included sabotage, bombing, and propaganda which they hoped would inspire "people to take up arms, to punish those responsible, and to eradicate Communism totally and definitively" and fill them with a "great patriotic fever and a great spirit of struggle."[60]

The CEUA was formed in September 1951, but its roots go back to the debates that gripped Guatemala City's political class surrounding the adoption of a new constitution in 1945. While issues such as women's suffrage, vagrancy laws, welfare, and Church-state relations produced multiple proposals and opinions, two broad factions emerged: those who wanted to advance social liberalism and those who sought to contain it. The latter at first was composed mostly of economic elites, the Catholic hierarchy, *cachurecos* (slang for ultra-Catholics, often applied to oligarch members of the defunct Conservative Party), and obdurate elements of the military. Revolutionary contretemps deepened this schism, charging every act with political meaning, transforming every event into a provocation, and winning new adherents to either side. When a railroad workers' strike coincided with a Church-sponsored Eucharistic Congress, the Church charged that the work stoppage was intentionally staged to prevent the rural faithful from entering the city.[61] When the remains of Rossell y Arellano's predecessor were repatriated in 1948, the archbishop used the occasion to condemn the government's recent closure of a Falange radio station. Shortly after his sermon, rumors spread that the government was to exile the prelate, provoking a large Catholic protest that dispersed only after Colonel Francisco Arana gave his assurances that no such action was planned.[62]

Colonel Arana was the man around whom opposition to the October Revolution coalesced. When he was accidentally killed by government forces while being arrested for his involvement in a plot to topple Arévalo in 1949, his death provoked a military uprising put down by Arbenz, loyal police, and civilian volunteers.[63] Yet the counterrevolution had its first martyr —to this day the right in Guatemala considers his killing as marking the beginning of the civil war—and Arévalo's bungled attempt to blame Arana's death on "reactionaries" served only to confirm to the colonel's supporters that Arbenz premeditatedly murdered his opponent in order to secure his position as Arévalo's successor. Arévalo declared five days of national mourning, yet his effort to claim Arana's death for the Revolution was betrayed the following year, 1950, when he decreed a holiday to celebrate the defeat of the rebels. In response, anti-communist university students organized a counterprotest, which set off a week of street fighting between pro- and antigovernment factions.[64] Arévalo encouraged his supporters from the balcony of the national palace. Businesses struck. Flying squads organized by unions looted the homes of suspected counterrevolutionaries. An average of two people died a day in a week of protests that ended only after Arévalo promised to dismiss the head of the national police and the minister of the interior. Theodore Draper, who covered the disturbances for a U.S. periodical, described the anti-Arévalo protesters as gangs of jeunesse dorée, noting that it "was easy to distinguish between the two sides in this conflict—the poorly dressed and the better dressed. . . . It was like the old class struggle in reverse. The workers were riding high with government protection, and the middle class was on strike."[65]

The year 1951 saw the entrance of the city's popular classes into oppositional politics. Led by Eduardo Taracena, the CEUA organized market women into anti-communist committees to demand the restitution of nuns who had just lost their jobs in the national orphanage to social workers.[66] Anger at the secularization of state welfare institutions combined with an anti-Communism energized by the increasing visibility of the still illegal PGT. Protesters destroyed a PGT office and chased party members through the streets. It was a "truly impressive crowd," admits Fortuny, who spent the night in the Colombian Embassy.[67] The next day, Arbenz on advice from the PGT restored the sisters in order to calm tensions. Nevertheless, the police violently dispersed the crowd gathered in front of the palace, wounding many and killing twelve.

Well before the United States definitively decided to oust Arbenz, two camps were coming into focus, and every action taken by one was used by the other to cast its rival as a "universal aggressor in a zero-sum political struggle that brooks no compromise."[68] Despite their shared nationalism, each side draped their fight in the banner of internationalism. Left unions and the national Congress held a minute of silence to mark Stalin's death. Anti-Arbenz students established ties with anti-communist groups in Bolivia, Argentina, Brazil, and Asia. And when organizers of the left-wing International Congress for Peace held a mass, Rossell y Arellano unexpectedly seized the pulpit to pray for peace, but for "the Peace of Christ" and not the "farce of the peace congress."[69]

The CEUA distinguished itself from the dozen or so other anti-communist groups that formed in the wake of the 1951 protests by the ardor of its members, and the CIA, desperate to find activists to work with among the divided and opportunistic opposition, used them as the foot soldiers of Operation PBSUCCESS.[70] At the beginning of the campaign, the students imagined a period of mass political education that, again evoking language associated with the left, would "form the consciousness" of all Guatemalans.[71] Through newspapers, comic books, and leaflets, they proposed to teach in simple terms the meaning of counterrevolutionary keywords, such as *God, Country, Law, Justice, Truth,* and *Work:* "*Truth* as the emblem of sincerity and the realization of high ideals and as the antithesis of lies; *Work* as a noble attribute of human beings, a fertile expression of the spiritual creator of man [and] not as the exploitation of man by man, as it is preached by Communism." They advocated an anti-communism that not only did not deny social injustice but sought to rectify it. "Our campaign should have as its goals," wrote the CEUA in 1953, "the humanization of the capitalist economic system, the alleviation of the misery in which the great majority live, the elevation of the standard of living of workers," and an "agrarian reform designed to create new property owners."[72]

CIA field officers, in particular the chief of the mission in Guatemala, George Tranger, had other ideas. They insisted on a strategy designed more to inspire fear than virtue. Propaganda designed to "attack the theoretical foundations of the enemy" was misplaced. The point, Tranger wrote in March 1954, was "to (1) intensify anti-Communist, anti-government sentiment and create a disposition to act; and (2) create dissension, confusion, and FEAR in the enemy camp." Psychological efforts should be directed at the "heart, the stomach and the liver (fear)."[73] "We are not running a popularity contest but an uprising," rejoined one agent to student concerns that the campaign was too negative.

The Agency had its way. Its plan to sow "distrust, division, suspicion, and doubt" overrode student efforts to raise political consciousness.[74] Students posted fake funeral notices to Arbenz, Fortuny, and other government and PGT leaders and pasted stickers reading "A Communist Lives Here" on the doors of Arbenz supporters.[75] They mailed "black letters" from a fake "Organization of the Militant Godless" to arouse Catholic fears and spread rumors that the government was about to seize bank accounts, collectivize all plantations, and ban Holy Week. They circulated the archbishop's writings, including his April 1954 call to insurrection, and sent notes to military officers informing them that their friends were spying on them for the PGT and to Víctor Manuel Gutiérrez saying that Fortuny was plotting against him, "and vice versa." It was a yearlong escalating campaign of sabotage, political agitations, rumors, and propaganda designed to destabilize and demoralize government supporters, create dissension in the military, force Arbenz to crack down on dissent, and energize and unify the opposition. By June 15, 1954, when the colonel handpicked by the United States, Carlos Castillo Armas, invaded from Honduras, the CIA had succeeded in all its goals except the creation of a unified internal resistance movement. There was no need. The United States skillfully manipulated the tension between public denial of its involvement and private displays of antipathy. While the invasion was clumsy and could easily have been defeated by Guatemalan troops, officers nonetheless abandoned Arbenz because they feared the power of the United States, which they knew had organized, trained, and paid for the invasion.

A COUNTERINSURGENCY RUNNING WILD

"We confront two enemies," proclaimed CEUA leader Mario Sandoval Alarcón in 1957; "the first is regressive recalcitrant reaction that governs with whip in hand. The second is the destructive force of human values whose system of government consists in demagoguery, hunger, and crime."[76] Sandoval made his comments before the nominating convention of the party that came to be called the Movimiento de Liberación Nacional (MLN), which ruled Guatemala from 1954 to 1957. Formed from the various anti-communist groups that opposed Arbenz and led by the young ideologues, such as Sandoval Alarcón, who spearheaded the resistance, the MLN tried to situate itself in opposition to both communism and the dictatorships that had dominated Guatemala prior to 1944.[77] Borrowing contradictorily from liberal democracy, Spanish fascism, and anti-communist Catholicism, the MLN at first promoted a forward-looking vision of development and nationalism.[78] Sandoval Alarcón, for example, announced to loud applause in his 1957 speech that anti-communism stands for "the liquidation of social injustice," while the party's 1958 platform declared that the "dispossessed represents the majority and weakest part of society. . . . A true democracy benefits the majority of its inhabitants, a fact that is recognized and accepted by the free nations of the world and affirmed in the Universal Declaration of Human Rights."[79] Yet the MLN soon found it was not so easy to let go of the whip.

After the departure of Arbenz, the U.S. Embassy installed the anti-communist standard-bearer Colonel Carlos Castillo Armas as president.[80] But once in power, the counterrevolutionary coalition came apart. Castillo Armas, despite his nominal support for "free trade unionism" and other democratic reforms, was too beholden to a powerful economic coalition—members of the landed oligarchy now diversified into cotton, sugar, finance, and industry and U.S. economic interests that included both old East Coast capital and new "sunbelt" real estate, cattle, lumber, and oil concerns—to seriously implement them.[81] Despite the rhetoric of liberal democracy used in the fight against Arbenz, national elites were not willing to follow a reformist program that could produce either government legitimacy or national stability, even if they had not been constrained by the dictates of foreign capital. While the government pacified the labor force and largely restored the agrarian tenure system to how it had stood prior to Arbenz, it shunted aside the

MLN's strident brand of anti-communism.[82] Within the military, tensions soon emerged between officers who saw the army as an institution with its own interests and those who gravitated toward the MLN and wanted to use the army as an instrument of the landed class. An important sector of the Catholic Church and its affiliated unions and political parties came to repudiate Rossell y Arellano's ultraconservatism and follow a road that would increasingly lead to revolutionary militancy, forsaking, as Sandoval Alarcón put it, the late archbishop's "beautiful vision." For its part, Washington distanced itself from the increasingly feverish anti-communist movement and supposedly embraced the goals of modernization, but refused to back any serious economic or political restructuring that would undercut the power of Guatemala's most recalcitrant elements, which the United States ultimately came to see as a needed backstop against Communism. Likewise, a resurgent armed and pacifist left had deep support in the countryside and could more legitimately claim to be the defenders of social justice and freedom than could the MLN.

Following the 1957 assassination of Castillo Armas by his bodyguard, the anti-Communist students who had led the fight against Arbenz increasingly found themselves estranged from state power. The MLN continued to engage in politics, using its ties to the military, countryside, and elite to influence successive governments. Between 1966 and 1974 Sandoval Alarcón served as president of the Congress and vice-president. Yet after the 1958 election of Miguel Ydígoras Fuentes, who represented the less inflamed wing of the counterrevolutionary coalition, to the presidency, the MLN returned to its insurgent roots. At the same time, it abandoned its effort to fashion itself as an agent of progressive liberal democracy, instead transforming into a brute defender of the agrarian oligarchy.

The MLN turned to the countryside. Just months after the Cuban Revolution and well before any group on the left had made such a move, MLN member Raúl Estuardo Lorenzana, who would later found Guatemala's first death squad, organized in February 1959 a short-lived guerrilla *foco* called Acción Nacionalista to overthrow the government.[83] While this effort failed, the MLN effectively built a social base that linked planters, provincial military officers, and paramilitary organizations led by military commissioners. Prior to 1954, there existed about one commissioner for each of Guatemala's three hundred municipalities, mostly enforcing military conscription and exercising loose surveillance. By 1966 the number had grown to nine thousand.[84] Fortified by new legal powers, commissioners aligned military and planter interests. They doubled as spies and plantation security, worked closely with regional army officers, and organized peasants into vigilante groups, most prominently in the eastern part of the country where by the early 1960s insurgents had begun to operate and where the memory of the Agrarian Reform remained strong.[85] This network served as the counterrevolution's answer to the CALS, unions, and political parties of the 1944–54 period.[86] The U.S. Embassy estimated that in eastern Guatemala between three and five thousand commissioners worked with "local army field commanders as intelligence sources and paramilitary auxiliaries in counter-insurgency operations. Many of the Comisionados are members or supporters of the MLN and manifest a virulently indiscriminate anti-communism."[87] In some places, the MLN's rural vigilante structure became the state. In one coastal town a rural worker remembered that the commissioners "had all the people tied up. We had to carry MLN membership cards in order to avoid problems. It was worth more than our citizenship papers."[88]

Starting in the mid-1960s, death squads and paramilitary groups unleashed horrific repression against suspected guerrilla supporters, serving as the frontline in the military's campaign against the small but growing insurgency. In the city, in collaboration with police and military units, the MLN operated under the name Mano Blanca (White Hand) to represent its five-man cell structure. Staffed by army officers, funded by planters, and supplied information by military intelligence, Mano initiated a campaign of, as the State Department put it, "kidnappings, torture, and summary executions."[89] With information acquired from military intelligence, Mano published death lists, giving targets short opportunity to leave the country. Mutilated bodies appeared on city streets and country roads.

In addition to attacking the proscribed left, the MLN also decimated the anti-communist Partido Revolucionario (PR), the most important reform party allowed to operate after 1954 and the MLN's chief rival in the countryside. The U.S. Embassy reported that the Mano Blanca and military commissioners had "teamed up in certain regions and are conducting operations (liquidations, etc.) against leaders and members of the PR."[90] In many rural areas, the PR built on the now clandestine yet still extant base created by the Agrarian Reform. In response, planters stepped up their cultivation of peasant support. In San Vicente Pacaya, for example, Manuel de Jesús Arana reclaimed land taken from him under the Agrarian Reform yet granted small lots to thirty-three families, who would go on to join the MLN.[91] Throughout the 1960s, tensions escalated between these MLN peasants and Arbencistas turned PR activists. Arana was the uncle of Colonel Carlos Arana, the infamous MLN commander of the Zacapa military base who became president in 1971. Immediately following Carlos Arana's inauguration in January, a detachment of troops aided by local MLN commissioners occupied San Vicente for over a month, raping women, capturing and torturing dozens of peasants, and executing at least seventeen PR members, many of whom had been involved with the town's CAL or peasant union during the time of Arbenz. The violence destroyed the Partido Revolucionario in San Vicente and ended all legal efforts to attain land.

In the wake of 1954, revolutionary and counterrevolutionary forces and ideas fed off each other, leading to a downward spiral of crisis and terror. Yet much more than the left, it was the advance guard of the right that propelled this cycle, its militant absolutism unbound by a society and polity that allowed no reform. By the mid-1960s, the MLN had shed its progressive posture and turned into a vengeful protector of planters, its earlier language of justice and modernization degenerating into the virulent idiom of "armed struggle without quarter, a true national crusade." It had become, as Sandoval Alarcón famously proclaimed, "the party of organized violence," a "vanguard of terror."[92]

The PGT's resort to violence was less sure, more tortured. In 1952, barely three years old with its influence and power greatly outpacing its age and experience, the party held its second congress calling for a broad national alliance with democratic parties to end feudalism in the countryside, establish political independence, and promote economic modernization.[93] While its leaders believed that world socialism was inevitable, they had minimal contact with the Soviet Union or other Eastern Bloc countries.[94] And although U.S. hostility and elite efforts to block reform increased its anti-imperialist and class conflict rhetoric, neither of these two sentiments figured into the PGT's vision of development or democracy (except perhaps in its attacks on the landed class). They were naïve, yet party leaders embraced a terminal but still potent popular-front vision in which the United States was part of the democratic, modern world, and socialism, when it came, would be a natural evolution of that world. Two years later, that vision lay in ruins, and Arbenz and his Communist advisors as well as many non-Communist activists such as Castillo Flores and Joaquín Noval were either dead, exiled, trapped in foreign embassies, or imprisoned.

The events of 1954 sparked analysis among supporters of the October Revolution as to what had gone wrong. In its 1955 "*autocrítica*," the party, after a review of errors committed during Arbenz's presidency, adopted a more militant, anti-imperialist, and antibourgeois stance. Although the document did not mention armed struggle, implicit in its analysis was the opinion that change could not be brought about through elections.[95] At the same time exiled Marxist and non-Marxist intellectuals began to publish similar criticisms, rebuking Arbenz and the party for failing to see the imperialist threat, for trusting the army and the bourgeoisie, and, especially, for not creating armed people's militias.[96] Alfonso Bauer Paiz, for example, began to sketch out an analysis of "monopoly imperialism," pointing out how the confluence of interests between the U.S. State Department, local economic elites, and foreign monopolies, most notably the United Fruit Company, would never allow reforms such as those advanced by the October Revolution to mature.

Yet even with this bitterness, some Communists held onto their original inspiration for a democratic socialism, one that could humanely combine internationalism and patriotism, cosmopolitanism and localism, solidarity and individuality.[97] From exile in Mexico, Huberto Alvarado Arellano, one of the founders of the party, composed, as he acclimatized himself to the "empire of intimidation," a treatise on Walt Whitman as the embodiment of this vision. "Universal culture," he wrote, "is forged from national cultures. In order to be universal, one has to be from somewhere . . . Walt Whitman celebrated democratic and progressive ideas . . . he exalted the individual but he wrote for millions. . . . during this shadowy and shining moment, when there are new roads to destruction and death yet there is also a bright horizon . . . it is imperative that we go back to lessons provided by the great North American poet and remember his prediction that the 'sweetest songs remain yet to be sung.'"[98] The state kidnapped and executed Alvarado in 1974.

By 1958, the PGT had regrouped and begun to grow from its exiled rump. Important activists and intellectuals who were not members prior to 1954, such as Leonardo Castillo Flores and Joaquín Noval, an anthropologist and former head of Guatemala's National Indigenista Institute, joined its ranks. Following the 1957 death of Castillo Armas, activists crossed into Guatemala and reestablished contacts in San Marcos, Escuintla, Quetzaltenango, Guatemala City, and the eastern departments of Zacapa and Izabal. By 1960, there were roughly six hundred members working in Guatemala.[99]

Despite its more militant official stance and despite the triumph of the Cuban Revolution in January 1959, the party's position on armed struggle was by no means settled. In 1960, the PGT adopted a resolution that endorsed "all forms of struggle consonant with the concrete situation," and many took this to mean support for a Cuban-style insurgency.[100] Yet it was difficult to translate this new resolve into action. Interestingly, those who joined after 1954, such as Castillo Flores and Noval, were more belligerent than many of the party's founders and leaders.[101] Even for those committed to armed struggle, there remained a large gap between theory and practice. Many of the founders of the party, such Huberto Alvarado, Mario Silva Jonama, and

Alfredo Guerra Borges were heirs to Guatemala's first generation of literary modernists. They were urbane, cultured, and literate, more oriented toward Paris than Moscow, Beijing, or even Havana. As Guerra Borges puts it, it was unclear how "a vice-minister of education who taught Rousseau and grew emotional listening to Mozart (Silva Jonama) or a writer interested in Breton and Vallejo (Alvarado) could turn himself into a military commander."[102] Cuba was an inspiration and a goad. PGT leaders had to put up with Che's repeated boasts that Cuba "will not be Guatemala."[103] But so was Spain, and some leaders such as Guerra Borges found inspiration in the Spanish Communist Party's attempt to find a "democratic solution" in its fight against Franco.[104] The party continued to talk of allying with "progressive" members of the military and worked to have a democrat voted mayor of Guatemala City.[105] In 1959, the PGT adopted a policy of "national reconciliation," calling on its supporters to vote for Ydígoras in order to defeat the MLN, and speculated that his victory would once again allow "democratic forces to advance."[106] As sociologist Carlos Figueroa writes, the central tension that defined the 1954 afterlife of the party was to be found not in debates between Soviet Leninism and Cuban Guevarism but in the "oscillation" between an "awareness for the need of armed revolution" and a "sensitivity to the possibilities of democratic openings."[107]

The PGT continued to be overtaken by history, as Guerra Borges described its 1954 defeat. The challenges to the counterrevolution were mounted from outside the PGT. On November 13, 1960, nearly a third of the Guatemalan military revolted in protest at government corruption and Ydígoras's having allowed the United States to train anti-Castro Cubans in national territory in preparation for the Bay of Pigs invasion. Although the revolt was suppressed within a week with the help of CIA B-26 bombers piloted by the anti-Castro Cubans, some of its leaders refused to surrender, instead continuing to stage guerrilla raids while at the same time establishing contacts with Cuba.[108] Throughout the late 1950s, students from the national university, which had previously been the seedbed of anti-communist dissidents, organized successively more aggressive demonstrations, which often were met by fatal repression, producing, as did the protests against Arévalo and Arbenz in 1950 and 1951, new revolutionary martyrs. And while many students joined the PGT's youth organization, the Juventud Patriótica de Trabajo (JPT), their support for the Cuban Revolution put them at odds with the PGT leadership.[109] In the countryside, peasants from highly politicized areas fought attempts to restore the status quo ante, often forcing the PGT to take a more confrontational stance than it had planned. Efraín Reyes Maaz, a Q'eqchi' party member who fled to Mexico in 1954 but returned in 1957, remembers his experience trying to educate United Fruit plantation workers in Santa Lucia Escuintla. "We held study groups where we would read *La Verdad* (*The Truth*, a PGT underground newspaper). They said to me, we're tired of *The Truth*, we want arms." And in March 1962 protests led by high school students in Guatemala City exploded into two months of riots and pitched battles with the national police. *Las Jornadas*, as the disturbances became known, drew on all sectors of society (even the MLN!), left dozens dead, and continued the radicalization of domestic politics. "1968 came six years early for us," remembers one participant.

The PGT was by no means disconnected from these events. Its influence spread through the university, and it slowly rebuilt support in the countryside. It had some contacts with the military rebels and had provided important if not always coherent leadership in the 1962 protests. The party also by 1960 had taken control of the officially anti-communist labor federation, the Federación Autónima Sindical de Guatemala (FASGUA). Nevertheless, its ambivalent stance toward armed revolution put the party at odds with many of its more militant, Cuba-fired members, while its constant attempt to respond to this or that political opening, or this or that potential collaborator, led it to forsake what it had done best during the October Revolution. As Deborah Levenson observes in relation to the urban labor movement, PGT leaders hailed "one politician or another as a harbinger of new times [and] constantly scrutinized formal politics for allies. They did not look with the same intensity and passion at what urban wage earners were thinking or doing to see how their power could be mobilized. Fragile at the point of production, where the Communists represented a reduced number of their precoup base of craft workers in small shops, they did not offset this vulnerability by building a constituency" among the rapidly growing industrial working class.[110]

In late 1962, after a disastrous attempt earlier that year at starting a guerrilla movement, a failure that further discredited the PGT in the eyes of the USSR and Cuba, party representatives met in Havana with members of its youth section, the JPT, and remaining rebels from the November 1960 army revolt to create the Fuerzas Armadas Rebeldes (FAR).[111] Operating as the armed wing of the PGT, the FAR's first combatants were young party and JPT activists who had gone to Cuba on education scholarships but once there opted, without obtaining permission from party leaders, to receive guerrilla training.[112] In theory, the PGT would be in charge of political work and armed actions in the city, while the FAR would establish itself in the eastern departments of Izabal and Zacapa.[113] In practice FAR leaders felt used. They dismissed the party's political maneuvers as misguided and antiquated and grew annoyed at the PGT's failure to provide equipment.[114] César Macías recalls a meeting where the PGT promised to supply material support: "We thought that finally the strong arm of the USSR would come to our aid. We thought they were going to send us MIGS."[115] The USSR had no intention of getting involved, while the PGT only reluctantly carried out its military responsibilities.[116] Guerra Borges recalls being told by the party's general secretary, Bernardo Alvarado Monzón, that if they did not go out and engage in acts of sabotage, then "those from the FAR and the JPT would accuse us of being cowards."[117]

Despite its nominal support for armed revolution, the PGT leadership still looked for electoral openings. Led by Víctor Manuel Gutiérrez, the PGT in early 1966 decided to support Julio César Méndez Montenegro as head of the Partido Revolucionario in the March presidential election. As mentioned earlier, the PR, along with the Christian Democrats, was the only effective reform party allowed to operate in the 1960s. Yet by 1966, in order to exist in Guatemala's repressive political atmosphere, the party had purged from its leadership its most progressive members and had grown corrupt and compromised.[118] Despite this conservative turn, Méndez Montenegro, predicted to win against the military's Partido Institucional Democrático (PID) in a landslide, promised to reactivate the reforms of Arévalo and Arbenz and install the "third government of the October Revolution."[119] As Gutiérrez put it in a January opinion piece published in *La Hora,* "the principal task" was to "end the military dictatorship and establish a democratic and patriotic regime that is respectful of human life."[120] Most of the PGT leaders were much less optimistic than Gutiérrez in his public statement, yet they were constrained by their own ambivalence toward guerrilla warfare and conscious of the PR's support. There was little choice but to support Méndez Montenegro, who had "stirred hope in a people tired of the repression."[121] The FAR likewise decided to support the PR. Despite its commitment to armed revolution and distrust of Méndez Montenegro, it too had no alternative. Emilio Román López, an Achí from Rabinal who led FAR forces in Baja Verapaz, admitted that his civilian support committees were made up of PR members, an assessment shared by other rebel commanders, including Leonardo Castillo Flores, who by that time was in charge of guerrilla operations in San Marcos.[122]

The debate over whether or not to support Méndez Montenegro reflected a growing rift within the Latin American left, as young militants increasingly viewed the electoral tactics of Communist parties as "obstacles" to revolutionary victory.[123] In Guatemala, this conflict exploded in a plenary meeting held by the PGT and the FAR in the town of Amatitlán just outside of

Guatemala City in late February 1966.[124] The FAR and its younger supporters in the PGT demanded a firmer commitment to armed revolution from the party's leadership.[125] Fernando Hernández, former general secretary of the PGT's youth league, launched a personal, virulent attack on Gutiérrez for his lack of revolutionary will and his support for the PR.[126] Gutiérrez was too demoralized to respond, but others came to his defense. After two days of heady Marxist theorizing, revolutionary posturing, and charges and countercharges of left adventurism and right conservatism, the standoff of two heavily armed factions nearly exploded.[127] The PGT's agreement to replace some of its older leaders on its political commission, including Gutiérrez, with JPT and FAR members defused tension and deferred for the time being larger strategic questions.

That a hundred PGT and FAR activists were able to meet in a "simple and vulnerable" house about thirty minutes outside of Guatemala City for three days without being detected speaks to the ongoing deficiency of Guatemalan intelligence—a deficiency that even as the conference proceeded was in the process of being remedied.[128]

OPERATION CLEANUP

The November 1960 military revolt mentioned above purged from the ranks of the army potential reformers who had survived the 1954 counterrevolution, leaving in their place an officer corps that was corrupt, opportunistic, and ever more brutal.[129] The 1962 riots and protests weakened Ydígoras, confirming the growing consensus shared by domestic elites and U.S. officials that he had to go. Both events increased the toxic effects of anticommunism, which in the wake of the Cuban Revolution had risen to yet more poisonous levels. Every revolt, protest, or opposition movement, no matter how pacific or explicitly anti-communist, was now thought by both Guatemalan and U.S. officials to be either "instigated" or "inspired" by Cuba.[130] And even when U.S. officials admitted that opposition was homegrown, they still feared that such movements would serve as a cat's-paw for the PGT, paving the way for its return to legality and influence. While CIA director Allen Dulles admitted that Cuba had had nothing to do with the 1960 army uprising, he still knew that "Castro-itis" was spreading throughout Central America.[131]

Eisenhower ordered the State Department to "beef up" Guatemala's intelligence system after 1960, yet U.S. officials continually complained of Ydígoras's refusal to fully cooperate in such efforts.[132] Ydígoras fell further out of favor with the United States by his heavy-handed response to the 1962 protests, which not only did little to end the disturbances but left scores dead and wounded. Embassy officials used the event to argue that a modernized professional police force could better counter subversion.[133] Juan José Arévalo's expected return from exile to participate in the scheduled 1963 presidential elections added to U.S. disquiet, for while the ex-president remained a stated anti-communist, his anti-imperialist pronouncements had been growing more strident. "Many people believe Arevalo is most likely to be elected Guatemala's next president," reported the embassy secretary, but "for what it's worth, the Country Team, and the American community in Guatemala, and more than that, many, many Guatemalans, believe he is the least desirable [candidate], to put it mildly."[134] By October 1962, the United States had resolved to "discourage by all available means Juan Jose Arevalo from returning to Guatemala or running for President" and to "exert every effort to preclude and prevent his attaining that office."[135]

In March 1963, a military coup deposed Ydígoras and installed Colonel Enrique Peralta Azurdia as president.[136] In the past, army officers had served as presidents, yet the Peralta regime from 1963 to 1966 brought a new stage in the militarization of Guatemala's political and economic life. From this point forward the army would rule, either directly or indirectly, as an institution, taking over government bureaucracies, organizing large-scale modernization projects, founding banks and other financial enterprises, and building a counterinsurgent state.[137] The coup pleased the State Department, which noted that by "eliminating the threat of a return to power of Arévalo through the scheduled 1963 elections, the immediate primary objective of our Internal Defense Plan was effectively implemented."[138] Central to that plan, and to efforts to fortify third-world domestic security forces, was the strengthening of domestic intelligence capabilities.[139] The coup allowed the United States to intensify its military and police aid. It sent instructors and equipment to help the Guatemalan army's effort to uproot the FAR, provided officers and soldiers with training at military bases in the United States and the Canal Zone, and financed military "civic action" programs designed to win the "hearts and minds" of the rural population. Advisors helped establish a Central America–wide defense council to coordinate counterinsurgent activities throughout the region, supplied the equipment, technology, and funds to create a regional communications system, and trained police in the latest tactics of crowd and riot control.[140]

Throughout this buildup, the embassy distanced itself from the more indiscriminate violence of MLN death squads and paramilitary groups. Embassy officials occasionally admitted that such repression operated either in coordination with or under the direct command of the military and that lists of victims, both communist and not, were compiled from the intelligence system they had helped put in place.[141] State Department analysts tried to maintain a rhetorical division between the vengeful violence that was decimating acceptable reformers and the more precise, counterinsurgency procedures directed against the PGT and the FAR.[142] Yet the very process of professionalization rendered such a distinction increasingly irrelevant. The private terror executed by the MLN, once it had destroyed the social base of the FAR, was brought directly under military control. But more than this, it was impossible to eliminate the PGT and the FAR without also draining the larger democratic sea of which they were a part.

In response to a request from U.S. Ambassador Gordon Mein, John Longan arrived in Guatemala from his post in Venezuela at the end of November 1965 to train Guatemalan authorities in "techniques and methods for combating terrorists, kidnapping and extortion tactics."[143] Throughout the mid-1960s, the expansion of FAR operations in the countryside matched a rise in urban revolutionary violence. Young PGT and FAR members blew up electric towers, occasionally attacked military installations, and were the first Latin American guerrillas to rob banks and kidnap members of wealthy families in order to finance their operations.[144] Despite their initial pleasure with the Peralta government, by the beginning of 1965 U.S. officials still felt it came up short in its central objective of creating an intelligence system "worthy of the name" that could gather, analyze, and archive information and act in a precise, rapid manner.[145] The embassy also complained of rampant incompetence and corruption that implicated the police in many of the robberies and kidnappings that were publicly blamed on the left.

Upon his arrival, Longan identified a need for "fundamental elementary work in organization, coordination, and basic police activity." On December 5, he held the first in a series of workshops with the heads of the judicial and national police, military officers including Colonel Rafael Arriaga Bosque, and two other U.S. public safety advisors.[146] Longan laid out plans for combined "overt" and "covert" operations collectively called "Operación Limpieza" (Operation Cleanup). In the overt phase of the operation, the "Army, the Judicial Police, and the National Police" would carry out sweeps in "suspect areas in hope that some criminal or subversive elements could be caught in net and lead to further openings."[147] Longan instructed the officers in a maneuver dubbed the "frozen area plan," which entailed cordoning off a four-block radius, establishing an outer perimeter, and searching the secured area for subversives and information. On the covert side, Longan recommended the creation of a small "action unit to mastermind campaign against terrorists which would have access to all information from law enforcement agencies."[148] A team of "trusted investigators" would work from a "special room to be called 'The Box,'" a twenty-four-hour nerve center equipped with telecommunications and electronic surveillance equipment staffed by military colonels and captains and located at Matamoros, the military's general headquarters in downtown Guatemala City.[149] Responsibility for the full operation, including command of "The Box," was given to Arriaga Bosque, the commanding officer of Matamoros. The overt and covert sides of the proposed operation complemented each other. Intelligence picked up from wide sweeps using the frozen area plan was to be sent to "The Box" to be analyzed and deployed in more focused clandestine raids, which in turn would provide information for larger dragnets.[150]

By January 1966, the embassy was pleased with the results. Arriaga appears to be "doing relatively good job," said one report, noting that "National and Judicial Police forces now repeat now actually cooperative with each other and with army (military police) both in collection, analysis of intelligence and in actual operations. . . . Security forces under Arriaga are conducting large-scale joint 'sweeps' of suspect urban areas."[151] By the end of February, eighty raids and a number of executions had taken place. Then in March 1966, on the eve of Méndez Montenegro's election, Operación Limpieza scored its most impressive success. On March 2, the military and police picked up three guerrilla leaders. On the third, the police captured Leonardo Castillo Flores and three other PGT-FAR members on the south coast. The next day, the fourth, special security officers from Guatemala City arrived to interrogate the prisoners, which according to a CIA document apparently yielded information on Guatemala City safe houses.[152] The following day, the police and military detained a number of PGT leaders, including Víctor Manuel Gutiérrez, who was in Guatemala to attend the party's contentious plenary meeting mentioned above. By March 5, security forces had captured scores of members of the PGT, FAR, and MR-13 (a Trotskyist group split from the FAR) in coordinated operations throughout the country, including the capital, the southern coast, Zacapa, San Agustín Acasaguatlán, and El Progreso.[153] The oft-stated U.S. goal of effective use of intelligence and coordinated operations between police and military and between the countryside and the city was now a reality.

Judicial police took Gutiérrez to their downtown headquarters, where they submitted him to a torture dubbed *la capucha*. They covered his head with a cowl and shocked him with electric currents, which according to one witness quickly proved too much for Gutiérrez, who suffered from a frail heart. Security forces transferred most of the rest of those captured in Guatemala

City to the Matamoros military base, where The Box was located. They were interrogated, tortured, executed, and their bodies placed in sacks and dropped into the Pacific.[154] Years later, Longan recalled that some of their remains washed back onto the shore.[155] The exact number is not known, but, along with Castillo Flores and Gutiérrez, the police and military murdered at least thirty people over the course of four days. In July, a defector from the national police told the newspaper *El Gráfico* that execution orders came from Arriaga Bosque, the man in charge of the new U.S. "action unit."[156] U.S. Embassy officials admitted that the killings were carried out under the auspices of Operación Limpieza. The embassy's March progress report, which enumerated its paragraphs, stated in paragraph 4 that the Guatemalan government scored "a considerable success when they captured a number of leading Communists, including Victor Manuel Gutierrez [and] Leonardo Castillo Flores." Paragraph 23 then matter-of-factly noted that the police "have conducted 80 raids during the past month using the 'frozen area plan.' The raids have been productive in apprehensions (see paragraph 4)."[157]

Coming literally on the eve of the election of Julio César Méndez Montenegro, who promised during his campaign to initiate negotiations with the guerrillas, the executions seem to have been carried out to prevent a peaceful resolution to the growing armed conflict. The CIA and the State Department also worried that the left's endorsement of Méndez could provoke a military backlash or pave the way for a return to legality of the PGT.[158] For its part, following the elections, the Guatemalan military forced the president-elect to sign a "secret pact." The army agreed to let civilians elected in the recent vote be inaugurated. In exchange, the new president promised not to negotiate with "subversives" and granted the army complete autonomy, along with all the "help needed to eliminate" the guerrillas.[159]

Operación Limpieza was a decisive step forward in the strengthening of an intelligence apparatus that would go on to mutate and expand throughout the course of Guatemala's armed conflict, the cornerstone of a state repression that by war's end was responsible for over two hundred thousand deaths and countless tortures.[160] It invested awesome power in Arriaga Bosque, whom the new civilian president would soon appoint defense minister and whom the U.S. Embassy in September 1966 complimented as one of Guatemala's "most effective and enlightened leaders."[161] In October, a few months after the March executions, he carried out with the help of the MLN Guatemala's first scorched earth campaign, killing eight thousand to defeat a few hundred guerrillas.[162] Soon after this successful campaign, Arriaga Bosque consolidated military authority over Mano Blanca and other right-wing groups.[163] As the war dragged on, individual and collective disappearances

4. Extreme left activity during the month was relatively limited since the Communists had announced earlier they would do nothing to disrupt elections (they had, of course, anticipated that the PID would win by imposition and that this would provoke a popular uprising which would be made to order for terrorists and agitators). Additionally, the GOG forces apparently did score a considerable success when they captured a number of leading Communists, including Victor Manuel Gutierrez, Leonardo Castillo Flores and Francisco Amado. While the press reported the capture and the execution of the prisoners, the GOG remained steadfastly silent about the whole matter.

23. The police in Guatemala City have conducted 80 raids during the past month using the "frozen area plan". The raids have been productive in apprehensions (see paragraph 4). They have also produced great quantities of Communist documents, printing material,

USAID/GUATEMALA TOAID A-579 ~~CONFIDENTIAL~~ w/UNCLASS. ATTACH. 7

guns and ammunition. They feel that these raids have reduced the initiative of guerrillas and terrorists.

FIGURE 8. "A Considerable Success" (from Department of State, "Public Safety Monthly Report, March 1966"). GOG refers to the government of Guatemala.

became the signature trait of Guatemalan terror, including the 1972 extrajudicial executions of nearly the entire PGT politburo and the 1980 capture of forty-three labor unionists in two separate operations.[164] Like the March 1966 killings, subsequent terror radicalized democrats and furthered the polarization of domestic politics, which the CIA often acknowledged.[165] Two years after the killings, Longan himself admitted that it "seems evident" that Guatemalan security forces "will be continued to be used, as in the past, not so much as protectors of the nation against communist enslavement, but as the oligarchy's oppressors of legitimate social change."[166]

The distinction of Operación Limpieza is measured by the fact that just three years earlier, in 1963, the police had captured Gutiérrez but released him to the legal system in response to a court order.[167] This time, despite pleas from Guatemala's new archbishop and over five hundred applications of habeas corpus, the state remained silent.[168] The fight now was to the death.

"Guatemala is a violent society," wrote the U.S. State Department in a 1986 retrospective survey of two decades of state terror:

The conscious acceptance and use of violence as an instrument of politics contributes to the extraordinary levels of murder, kidnapping and disappearances.

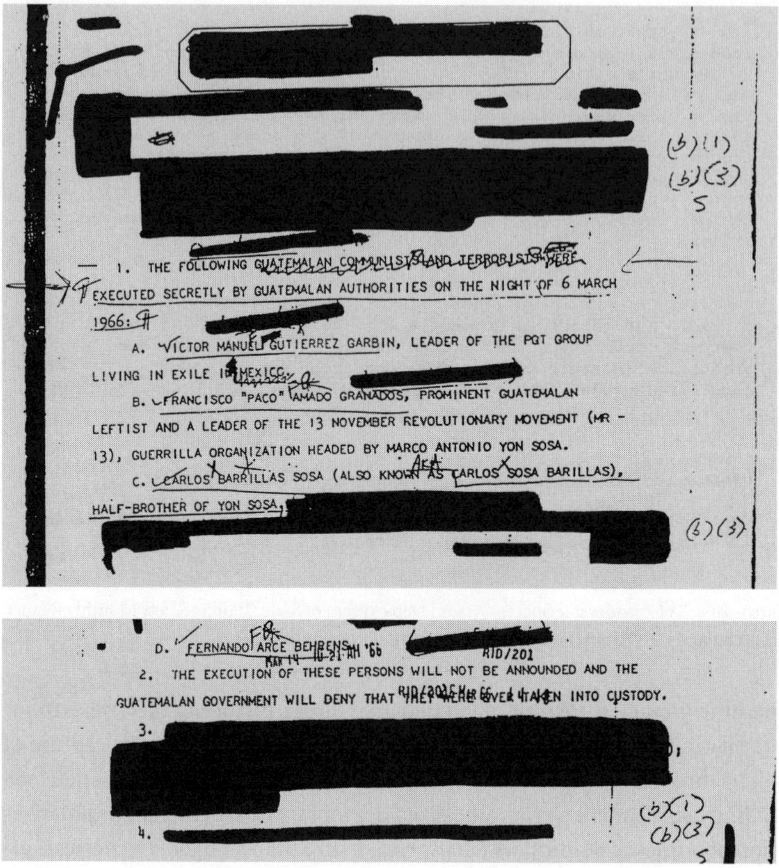
[redacted]

(b)(1)
(b)(3)
S

1. THE FOLLOWING GUATEMALAN COMMUNISTS AND TERRORISTS WERE EXECUTED SECRETLY BY GUATEMALAN AUTHORITIES ON THE NIGHT OF 6 MARCH 1966:

A. VICTOR MANUEL GUTIERREZ GARBIN, LEADER OF THE PGT GROUP LIVING IN EXILE IN MEXICO. [redacted]

B. FRANCISCO "PACO" AMADO GRANADOS, PROMINENT GUATEMALAN LEFTIST AND A LEADER OF THE 13 NOVEMBER REVOLUTIONARY MOVEMENT (MR-13), GUERRILLA ORGANIZATION HEADED BY MARCO ANTONIO YON SOSA.

C. CARLOS BARRILLAS SOSA (ALSO KNOWN AS CARLOS SOSA BARILLAS), HALF-BROTHER OF YON SOSA, [redacted] (b)(3)

D. FERNANDO ARCE BEHRENS [redacted]

2. THE EXECUTION OF THESE PERSONS WILL NOT BE ANNOUNCED AND THE GUATEMALAN GOVERNMENT WILL DENY THAT THEY WERE EVER TAKEN INTO CUSTODY.

3. [redacted]

4. [redacted]

(b)(1)
(b)(3)
S

FIGURE 9. March 1966 CIA document reporting the execution of Víctor Manuel Gutiérrez.

First used systematically by the security forces against the Communist Party and members of the moderate left beginning in 1966, the practices of kidnappings became institutionalized over time. . . .

Guatemala's high violence levels cannot be accounted for by economic or political variables. Equally poor nations in Africa, Asia, and Latin America have lower violence levels. The explanation for Guatemala's high level of violence probably is rooted in cultural and sociological factors unique to Guatemala. Guatemala is distinguished from other Central American nations by the duality of its culture where a wealthy ladino minority lives side by side with an impoverished Indian majority largely marginalized from national political and economic life. . . . The use of violence to settle disputes of almost any nature is accepted in Guatemala's indigenous culture.

The plantation system which historically generated Guatemala's exports and wealth has relied on Indian labor to function. . . .

> Fear of revolution stems from the Arbenz period when the first political efforts to involve peasants and Indians in national life began in earnest. . . . Following Arbenz' ouster in 1954, saving the country from communism and personal self interest thus blended to form a psychology conducive to supporting physical repression of workers and peasants in the name of anti-communism.[169]

In this document and in many like it, the imaginative projection of violent propensities upon Guatemalans abetted official amnesia about U.S. collusion in repression—an amnesia that, to borrow from the document itself, became institutionalized over time. Denial became deniability. While acknowledging the importance of the years 1954 (the overthrow of Arbenz) and 1966 (Operación Limpieza), the analysis conveniently omits any actions taken by the United States at these two junctures. With the United States expunged from the narrative, a fairly perceptive critique of how anti-communism had been used to protect the economic and political privileges of an entrenched elite turned into a dubious armchair anthropology of "cultural and sociological factors unique to Guatemala"—an anthropology that holds Indians accountable for counterinsurgent disappearances. Brutality here is a part of the past in which Guatemala is trapped. Guatemala's failure to modernize, to move beyond its native particularity toward a tolerant U.S.-style pluralism, thus explains, or rather explains away, a descent into political terror that the United States was instrumental in initiating.

Víctor Manuel Gutiérrez and Leonardo Castillo Flores both took different roads to the PGT, and their unfinished lives testify to the force of Guatemalan revolution. Born in the Ladino department of Santa Rosa, Gutiérrez was a twenty-two-year-old technical school teacher in Guatemala City at the time of the October Revolution. Like Alfredo Cucul, he used Ubico's public schools to achieve both social and political mobility, helping to found the national teachers' union, joining the PAR, running successfully for Congress in 1945, and becoming general secretary of the labor federation in 1951. He was nicknamed "the Franciscan" for his ascetic demeanor, and even his detractors described him as "honest, humble, and soft-spoken" and a "revered leader."[170] His self-taught Marxism helped him understand Guatemala's October Revolution within a larger post–World War II global history, an analysis he shared in countless public speeches, such as the one attended by José Angel Icó in 1946.[171] He started out too far left for the PGT, at first organizing a Marxist party to be led by workers rather than middle-class intellectuals. By the time of Gutiérrez's murder, history, to use once again the image evoked by his friend and comrade, had overtaken him, the reality of a counterinsurgent security state destroying the political world that allowed the October

FIGURE 10. Víctor Manuel Gutiérrez.

Revolution to come about. He was scorned by younger revolutionaries who—however mistaken in hindsight their revolutionary romanticism may have been—saw more clearly the impossibility of peaceful reform. For its part, the PGT posthumously judged Gutiérrez's political position as "conservative and traditionalist."[172]

Leonardo Castillo Flores, six years older than Gutiérrez but like him a schoolteacher, union organizer, and PAR congressman, found little use for Marxism. Castillo Flores helped found and lead Guatemala's first national peasant federation during the October Revolution, over the protest of the PGT which felt that a separate peasant organization would divide the labor movement. Although Arbenz's patronage and planter opposition to the Agrarian Reform drew him closer to the position of the Communists, he did not join the party until 1957. Like other newcomers, he proved more militant than many of the party's Arbencista leaders, especially his counterpart

Gutiérrez, and along with his son Leonardo Castillo Johnson he organized a guerrilla front in the coffee zone of San Marcos. The fate of Castillo Flores's son tragically illustrates the brutalization of politics that took place following Operación Limpieza. Two years after his father's disappearance, Castillo Johnson learned of the murder of his lover, Rogelia Cruz. An architecture student, JPT member, and former Miss Guatemala, Cruz was not the first woman to be killed by security forces, but her publicly displayed mutilated and raped corpse announced that the military had crossed yet another line. In response, Castillo Johnson let loose a day of mournful rage, exacting, as the U.S. Embassy put it, "revenge on a spectacular scale."[173] Before being shot to death in downtown Guatemala City, he assassinated two U.S. military advisors and an MLN member and launched a grenade attack on the military base where most of those murdered in March 1966 had been detained.[174]

Rather than a return to the past, the Guatemalan counterrevolution ushered in a new, deeply polarized world. On one side of the Cold War divide stood the coalition that drove Arbenz from power. Rent by competing interests and visions, unable to establish a stable governing coalition or political

FIGURE 11. Leonardo Castillo Flores, in the center dressed in khaki.

legitimacy, haunted by the legacy of Arévalo and Arbenz, and frightened by a resurgent, militant national and continental left, counterrevolutionaries embraced terror with such zeal that at times even the United States blanched. On the other side were the diverse heirs of the October Revolution. It was an irony lost on U.S. security advisors that Communists—"the original targets of the 'white terror'," according to the State Department—could not claim this inheritance because they did not resort to violence as eagerly as did their opponents.[175] That task would be left to others. After the 1967 defeat of the FAR, its survivors regrouped to found new guerrilla organizations unaligned with the PGT. Throughout the 1970s and 1980s, the PGT divided and divided again, continuing to offer only unenthusiastic recognition to an insurgency that had long since passed it by. Nevertheless, the party's legitimacy continued to resonate among some intellectuals, unions, rural workers, and, as we shall see, Q'eqchi' communities in Alta Verapaz.

CHAPTER FOUR

Clandestine Lives

> Clandestinity is the form of illegal organization adopted by revolutionary movements when reactionary classes employ violence to prohibit open political struggle. This form of organization has its laws, rules, and particular methods of work, as well as special forms of relations between our organization and the masses in which it operates.
>
> *PGT, Basic Rules of Clandestinity and Means of Security, ca. 1983*

WHEREAS ALFREDO CUCUL found conversion the only way to hold to his convictions, Efraín Reyes Maaz discovered revelation in exile. Born to a peasant family in the Q'eqchi' town of Lanquín in 1917, Reyes worked for the United Fruit Company as a dockworker throughout the October Revolution. "I should have been a Ubiquista," Reyes says, meaning a peasant supporter of the dictator, but credits his union work, particularly his contacts with Cuban longshoremen who once sent provisions to aid a strike, with pointing him to the PGT. But he joined *"a lo ciego,"* blindly, not knowing what it meant to be a Marxist or a party member. After participating in the defense of Puerto Barrios against Castillo Armas's invaders in 1954, which he can describe with bewildering detail, Reyes and a dozen other PGT members fled first to Belize and then, with the help of a Mexican Communist Party women's support committee, to Campeche and finally to Mexico City. He was given a place to live and a small stipend, and then the "doubts began." Reyes asked the PGT's legal advisor to United Fruit's dockworker union, Virgilio Guerra, "*Mire compañero*, what happened?"[1]

Guerra gave Reyes a copy of the PGT's 1955 *"autocrítica."* "I read it, and reread it, and read it again, and suddenly I understood," says Reyes: Arbenz fell because of a "foreign intervention" allied with "Creole anti-communists" and the Catholic Church. But that initial answer pushed him to read more, not only the *Communist Manifesto* and Lenin's *Imperialism* but the Bible as well. Reyes identified with the eschatological vision of the Book of Revelation, written as it was by another persecuted exile similarly trying to find meaning in history. Yet he filled the prophecy with social content, consciously repeating Marx's adaptation of Hegel's historicism. Reyes read in the darkness of his own flight Revelation's prediction of the coming of a seven-horned lamb—Christ—who would destroy the Roman Empire and install a just ultramundane kingdom. Conflating a number of the book's images, he interpreted the "seven horns as the seven empires," the last of which is the United States, which "has tried to dominate the world with a dogmatic idealist philosophy." From his studies and experiences, he developed a scorn for idealist obscurantism that he has carried with him throughout his life. He uses the distinction between materialism and idealism to distance himself from, as he puts it, "ignorant peasants" easily manipulated by the army, the Church, and planters, and he prides himself on a certain scientific skepticism, a capacity to observe and learn. "I'm a bit like Santo Tomás," he says referring to the doubting apostle, "the first materialist. I believe only what I see."

Marxism in both theory and practice opened up the world to Reyes. "Every revolutionary," he says, "carries around an entire world in his head." He returned to Guatemala in 1957 and began to rebuild the party among displaced United Fruit plantation workers in Santa Lucía Cotzumalguapa on the Pacific coast. Exhausted after three years, he went to Cuba in 1961 to recover and receive some training in guerrilla warfare. He returned at the end of 1962, and after he had helped to set up a FAR guerrilla front in the Sierra de las Minas, the PGT placed him in charge of reestablishing contacts with its Arbencista base in Alta Verapaz. Except for a brief stint in Quetzaltenango in the late 1960s, the Polochic Valley would be Reyes's principal theater of operation for the remainder of his political career. Alternately using the names Carranza, Tono, and Marcelino, he traveled with his mule through the valley's communities and plantations as an itinerate merchant. One Ladino relative of a plantation administrator in Tucurú joined the PGT because of Reyes. "After a day of selling his products," he recalls, "Reyes would return at night and preach about how we were going to make a better world, a new Cuba." "Wherever people were organized," remembers a Q'eqchi' PGT member from Panzós, "they knew Tono." In the 1970s, the PGT through the labor federation, the Federación Autónoma Sindical de Guatemala (FASGUA), would hold weekend workshops around Cobán, and Reyes would bring in small groups of Q'eqchi's and act as the interpreter. An economics professor from the national university who led many of the sessions remembers "talking for two, three minutes and that Carranza would go on for ten." It was Reyes's ability to understand and translate Marxism into a Q'eqchi' cultural vernacular that made him an indispensable organizer. "We used to ask the *ancianos*," remembers Reyes, "what did the Spaniards bring when they came? God, the mirror, and the cross in the sky. All idealist symbols. But what did you worship before they came? Water, earth, the sun, and corn, all material factors in the relations of production."

A life lived underground has given Reyes a rigidity no less severe than Cucul's. His eighty-five-year-old mind is hardened, and the world Marxism

FIGURE 12. Efraín Reyes Maaz.

gave him is ossified. Vivian Gornick has written that the tragedy of Marxism is that in satisfying a passion to live a life with "moral meaning," it inevitably becomes dogma. What was "compellingly humanizing" becomes "compellingly dehumanizing," for the "law of passion is that it is all."[2] And there is something of this in Reyes, for now that all around him has crumbled, now that the war is lost, the USSR is gone, and Cuba is disenchanted, to lose his Marxism would be to lose his core being as he himself identifies it. Yet more than some flaw intrinsic to Marxism, it was this "ideological armour" that protected him throughout decades of clandestine life.[3] He survived capture and torture three times and bore the murder of countless allies: "Galileo said the world was round," Reyes responds to my question as to the costs of dedicating a life to a failed revolution, "but the powerful wanted everybody to believe the world was flat, so they persecuted him. But today we know that the world is round, not flat." Rather than dissolving his identity in a larger ideological solution, as Marxism is often accused of doing, the Communist Party helped Reyes emerge from an exploitative, deeply deadening system, to develop a sharpened sense of himself as a critical being, able to observe, act in, and change the world. "If I hadn't studied Marx I wouldn't be *chicha ni limonada*," he says. "I'd be nothing. But reading nourished me and here I am. I could die today and nobody could take that from me."

The work Reyes carried out in the Polochic Valley testifies to the enduring power of the PGT's original vision. Even as the countryside militarized, repression grew, and the war escalated, the party continued to work with local Q'eqchi' leaders and other reformers to end forced labor and redistribute land. Under Reyes's organizing, the PGT achieved one of its most impressive post-1954 victories in Cahabón, where throughout the 1960s unpaid labor was still a common practice and more than half of the municipality was owned by the Champney family. "Now there are no planters," smiles Vicente Toc, noting that his father, who for most of his life was a resident peon on Champney's plantation, has a plot of land where his extended family grows corn, coffee, and achiote for the regional market. Since the war's end in 1996, a majority of Cahaboneros have repeatedly cast their ballots for the left in local and national elections, and today a portrait of Che hangs in the mayor's office.[4] While this transformation came about at immense human cost and by no means solely through PGT acumen, the party's at times successful persistence in helping communities work through the courts and governmental land and labor ministries demonstrates that its post-1954 strategy was not entirely misplaced. In effect, the PGT helped accomplish in some parts of Cahabón what it had hoped to do for all of Guatemala with its Agrarian Reform: transform a private fiefdom into a community of small property owners who vote for the left.

In 1939, Benjamin Champney Choc inherited the plantation Sepacuité from his father, Kensett Champney Brooks.[5] The Boston-born son of a Hudson Valley landscape painter, Kensett arrived in the Polochic Valley at the end of the nineteenth century. With access to North American capital and aided by generous land laws, he began to build Sepacuité, purchasing the original plot of land from the brother of his common-law Q'eqchi' wife. Throughout the early twentieth century, the plantation grew through a series of claims, purchases, and foreclosures. "It was like a chessboard," says his grandson Edgar Champney, "with black and white squares that bit by bit turned all black: Sepacuité."[6]

After a failed attempt to produce rum with imported Jamaican indentured labor, Kensett, now joined by his cousin Walter Champney, began to plant coffee.[7] The cousins apparently offered good terms to Q'eqchi's from the highlands around Carchá who were then leaving to escape labor and tax demands. Migrants established small villages on Champney property, subject only to the relatively light work requirements of an embryonic plantation. Yet as coffee production increased, so too did labor needs.

By the 1930s Sepacuité, rising from fifteen hundred to five thousand feet, had become one of the most prosperous coffee plantations in Guatemala, occupying close to the entire eastern half of Cahabón and spilling into neighboring municipalities. The plantation produced mostly coffee but also cacao, fruit, maguey, and some cardamom on seven thousand acres in its southern reaches, below the Cahabón River. North of this commercial production, nearly half of the population of the municipality of Cahabón lived in seventeen plantation communities, trading one to two weeks of labor a month for housing and plots to grow their subsistence crops. Roughly one hundred thousand acres of plantation property surrounded these settlements, sown with corn and beans and cut through by wide patches of dense forestland whose stony and steep inclines protected water sources and provided a habitat for game animals.

More than extracting the labor needed to grow coffee, the Champneys and other Anglo and German planters who settled in the Polochic Valley, such as the Hempsteads, Sappers, Birds, and Owens, used their resident workers to create the comforts of a colonial society in a jungle frontier.[8] Corps of Q'eqchi' women worked as domestic servants in estate houses, serving as wives, wet nurses, and mistresses. Kensett and Walter each fathered over a dozen children with their wife-cooks (no one in the family today can say exactly how many). Q'eqchi' men worked as porters, hauling the supplies and equipment of amateur anthropologists, biologists, and topologists as they trudged through the jungle in search of new discoveries. They carried on their backs not only goods but children and at times adults up from the port town of Panzós. One older planter from the region recalls that before the Champneys built a patio to sun dry the coffee crop, Q'eqchi' men took turns standing in a large cast iron pot stirring beans heated by a wood fire below.

"It was pure feudalism," says Benjamin Champney's son Edgar; "my father strode around like he was the marquis of Cahabón." After acquiring the plantation in 1939, Benjamin expelled his many relatives from the property and tried to modernize production. He used his bequest to import quality livestock from New Orleans and Texas and to buy coffee futures from his neighbors at depressed prices, making a fortune when World War II drove them high again. He had also initiated small-scale mining on his property of nickel, copper, and zinc. All this activity continued to be based on forced free labor, as his son admits. "Until 1944, the salaries were low, about five cents a day," he says, "but workers were paid either with plantation scrip or with salt, sugar, and other things."

Perhaps even longer than elsewhere, the reforms of the October Revolution, which included the abolition of pay in scrip or in goods, took time to come to Sepacuité. It was only after Francisco Curley and Federico García were able to create a credible counterweight to Champney's network of alcaldes auxiliares, foremen, and municipal police, as discussed in chapter 2, that residents were able to refuse to work unless properly compensated. Now Cahabón's remoteness, which had previously served to fortify Champney's authority, turned against him as he was increasingly subject to the intimidations of Curley and García and their mobilized followers.[9] Champney left Sepacuité in 1952, apparently in fear for his life, to wait out Arbenz in Cuba and New Orleans, leaving the plantation's administration in the hands of his head foreman. In 1954, the state expropriated nearly half of Sepacuité, about fifty thousand acres. The Agrarian Reform did not disturb the plantation's physical landscape since it left productive land untouched. Yet by nationalizing the plantation's roads, villages, and part of its forests and distributing among the resident workers corn land, pastures, and houses, the reform transformed its social geography. With residential security, free mobility, and land, freed workers would now be in a better position to sell their labor to Champney for a better wage.[10] Yet this expropriation merely ratified what had already occurred on the ground. Following Arbenz's 1950 election, resident workers in the seventeen communities in the northern part of the plantation organized by Curley and García had begun to withhold their labor in lieu of pay and to claim the land they lived on and planted as their own.[11]

The government legally returned most of Champney's land to him in 1956, yet this restoration was likewise a formality. Following Arbenz's overthrow, Sepacuité's foremen immediately moved to restore the status quo ante, enforcing labor requirements in place prior to Arbenz. Champney did not live long enough to enjoy the restitution of his land. As he was flying on a commercial flight from Guatemala City to Panzós in 1956, his plane crashed, killing him, his wife, and, coincidentally, his longtime adversary Federico García. Since Edgar left no will, his out-of-wedlock but acknowledged son Edgar Champney and two unrecognized siblings, Jaime and Erika, disputed his legacy. Sepacuité alone was valued at over two million dollars.[12] After six years of legal wrangling that transferred much of the worth of his father's legacy to lawyers, Edgar in 1962, "in order to put an end to litigations, differences, and demands," gave Erika and Jaime the eastern half of Sepacuité, nearly sixty-four thousand acres, with Erika quickly losing her share to her lawyers and Jaime.[13]

In 1962, Edgar and Jaime divided a plantation in bad straits. The October Revolution, the Agrarian Reform, Benjamin's exile and death, and the siblings' legal conflicts hurt coffee production, which had fallen from an annual high of twenty-eight thousand quintals to six thousand.[14] Most of Benjamin Champney's prized livestock had been pilfered. Soil exhaustion had led to a decrease in the corn yield, and Sepacuité could not produce enough to feed its workers, a central bond in the tenant-planter compact. In the year before his death, Benjamin had to import fifty thousand dollars' worth of corn to feed his workers, provided in lieu of payment. Legal costs drained capital, credit was hard to come by, inheritance taxes of over $130,000 forced the Champneys to mortgage part of their holdings, and the military state began to levy duties on unused land, especially on those plantations not owned by members of the traditional oligarchy.

Even more vexing, neither Edgar nor Jaime could hope to command rural workers the way their father and grandfather had. The counterrevolution destroyed Arbencista parties and unions and killed or otherwise neutralized activists, but agrarian politics continued through other means. The revised 1956 labor code banned rural unions, yet it allowed peasant leagues to function.[15] The MLN, the PR, and later the Christian Democrats vied for support by working with local leaders on various community development and improvement projects, including the solicitation of land through post-1954 agrarian legislation.[16] In 1961 Guatemala joined the Alliance for Progress and established the Instituto Nacional de Transformación Agraria (INTA), a corrupt, military-controlled bureaucratic leviathan that nonetheless promoted colonization and established mechanisms for communities to solicit collective title to unused national and private land.[17]

Efraín Reyes Maaz arrived in Sepacuité in 1963 to find that the PR, through the renewed work of Francisco Curley, had established itself on the ruins of the plantation's Arbencista network and had begun to register complaints with the ministry of labor, organize work stoppages, and petition INTA for land.[18] Once again Curley was agitating against the Champneys, who, undercapitalized, were once again paying with goods or promissory notes in lieu of the twenty-five cents a day minimum wage. "They gave us four cigarettes, soap, and a can of sweets once instead of a week's salary," says Manuel Caal. And as did their father and grandfather, Edgar and Jaime counted on the municipality now run by a party allied with the military to enforce revitalized vagrancy laws, which remained in effect throughout the 1970s.[19] Work conditions were terrible. Manuel Coc recalls his father having to give two seven-day shifts a month, which did not include the one-day walk from Sactá, where they lived, to the coffee fields. Tomás Coc remembers working alongside his father, "sleeping between mud and cow shit, under a roof with no walls with their fires, tortillas, and chili."

Since 1954, the PGT had adopted a more traditional Leninist structure, allowing only a handful of selected individuals to join. There was no attempt at mass consciousness-raising of the kind carried out by the new guerrilla movements of the 1970s. Yet frontline organizers such as Reyes worked with community improvement associations, land committees, and peasant leagues to attend to various conflicts and to identify local leaders who could eventually be recruited as members. The pursuit of "immediate reforms," as the party's 1970 program put it, was theoretically part of a forward march toward heightened revolutionary awareness. But in reality the PGT had deferred the revolution indefinitely.[20] Although throughout the 1970s various factions would split from the party because of its reformism, its more traditional rump, through Reyes, remained in control of organizing in the Polochic Valley. In Cahabón, where he spent most of his time, Reyes carried out the "slow boring of hard boards."[21] Patient but persistent, he took a job as a finca worker, set up a household with the daughter of an Arbencista contact, and established relations with a number of PR activists, most importantly Marcelino Xol.

Born in 1901 in the neighboring town of Senahú to free peasants, Marcelino Xol moved to Cahabón as a young man and established himself as an itinerate merchant.[22] At some point in the 1930s, perhaps as a result of the Depression, he became a resident worker for Champney, cultivating a corn plot on Sepacuité in exchange for work. As was often the custom of Q'eqchi's who could afford to do so, he maintained ties to the town center of Cahabón, holding positions of responsibility in its principal cofradía, Santa María, and its municipal government. Immediately after Arévalo's 1944 election, Xol, according to legal charges filed by Benjamin Champney in 1947, led a number of land invasions, organizing male resident workers of his extended family to clear land and plant corn.[23] Expelled from Sepacuité in 1947, Xol aligned himself with Francisco Curley, who not only provided Xol with political tutelage but gave him some land. After 1954, when persecution abated, he and Curley once again joined forces, this time under the banner of the Partido Revolucionario, and it is this team that all identify with organizing the work stoppages and salary demands of the early 1960s.

Clandestine politics demanded a more covert, natural style, symbolized by the transition from Curley and the PR to Reyes and the PGT as the principal agents in Cahabón. Curley's ostentatious manner increasingly clashed with Guatemala's repressive climate, and his high-handed and dishonest politics could not deliver the material benefits it had during Arbenz's tenure. Reflecting the rightward drift of the PR, he became increasingly conservative and his corruption more barefaced. As Curley lost influence among resident workers, Reyes moved in, working closely with a number of leaders, particularly Xol. In the mid-1960s, around 1966, Xol was kidnapped, beaten, and left for dead, probably by a group organized by Jaime Champney's chief administrator, Norman Prado. He survived the assault, after which he joined the PGT.

If José Angel Icó represented the deviation from traditional community leadership, the point in local politics where the secular and the sacred diverged, then Xol perhaps embodies their reunion. Where memory today paints Icó—Xol's "teacher" according to one account—in terms of transgression and outrage, Xol, a Spanish-illiterate husband and father of seven children, prompts only admiration. He is unanimously described as "humble" and a "natural leader." Where Icó's sexual and financial motives are repeatedly questioned, Xol is described as honest, without "political interests." Reyes claims that Edgar Champney offered Xol a large bribe to desist from his political work, which, according to Reyes, he of course refused. His authority came from speaking "campesino truths," remembers one PR activist, and only those closely connected with him or the PGT acknowledge his eventual membership. Most insist that Xol "didn't belong to any political party." Where Icó's political strength came from his ability to transcend the local, Xol's authority was firmly embedded within the community, as a patriarch whose influence grew as he aged and as a religious leader who held political meetings in cofradía chapels. One plantation administrator remembers that Xol would bootleg corn liquor used in Mayan rituals and lead ceremonies "burning incense and candles, sacrificing a turkey. They believed it gave force to their petitions."[24] While Icó was larger than life, Xol was so common as to be almost invisible, even in death: Edgar Champney's son recalls with some wonder that when military commissioners finally arrested him in 1972, they found him hiding in "a very small box, no bigger than a trunk."

Confronted with obstinate protest and aware that the paternalism of his father and grandfather would no longer hold together labor relations, Edgar Champney, twenty-two years old in 1962, adapted himself to new times. At a cost of $10,000 to be paid over a period of ten years, he sold lots of between five and six thousand acres to the same communities who had briefly received land under Arbenz.[25] Through these sales, Champney hoped to settle a number of problems. By transferring ownership of the land from the plantation to the communities, he would no longer be responsible for the survival of his workers, a burden that became increasingly onerous as Sepacuité's tired soil produced less and less corn. The sales would also exempt him from post-1962 agrarian legislation that subjected undeveloped property to both higher taxes and the possibility of expropriation. "It was a sale in place of a donation," says Edgar Champney; "I didn't want to give it to the government." Furthermore, the need to raise money to make the yearly payments would ensure a willing labor force, as the terms of the transaction required residents to work for Champney until the mortgage was fully paid. Finally, Champney calculated that the property transfer would win support among an increasingly alienated peasantry: "With this move, I disarmed Curley and Xol, I took away their slogans," he says with a grin.

The sales violently divided the affected communities between those willing to raise the money and buy the land and those, organized by Curley, Reyes, and Xol, who refused, instead demanding of INTA that the land be granted to them to make up for back pay and historical grievances. Manuel Caal was one of the first leaders of the group in Sactá opposed to the purchase and remembers it as a "trick, nothing more, by that Champney, who wanted to keep us tied to him." Caal recalls his father saying that the land was given to them by Arbenz, and "besides, we were natives to the land and were forced to work like slaves." Other families recall less militant motives. They simply had no money to participate. The first transactions were to take place in the villages north of the Cahabón River, in Sactá, Gualibaj, Sepoc, and Sequixpec. In 1966, families in three of the four communities had raised the 1,000 quetzals needed for the first installment, yet when their representatives traveled to Cobán to make the payment they were arrested. Marcelino Xol had reported to the police that they had extorted money from frightened peasants.[26] All four communities were divided down the middle, with a slight majority being in favor of making the deal with Champney. Tensions came to a head in 1973 when the families who opted to pay violently expelled those who refused, burning down their houses and destroying their crops.[27]

The torching of the property of dissenting families followed a common pattern of community violence, for fire was often used to settle local disputes.[28] Occasionally it was a weapon in class conflict, such as when three workers set Plantation Joaquín's sugar mill ablaze in 1934 after its German owner tried to evict them for being "contrary" to the plantation's "internal order" or when planters burned down the homes of *agraristas* after the fall of Arbenz. Yet more often than not arson was practiced by resentful neighbors or disciplining husbands.[29] "Questions of jealousy" apparently moved Aurelia Caal to set fire to Carmen Xol's house in Carchá in 1933.[30] Between 1926 and 1942, 221 suspicious conflagrations were reported in Alta Verapaz, the majority in thatched peasant homes.[31]

The land conflicts that exploded after the 1962 establishment of INTA increased the incidence of acts of popular justice, and planters harnessed them to their own profit. In 1963, Erika Forst of Panzós sent teams of mozos under the command of a local military commissioner to pull up the corn of workers attempting to claim land through INTA.[32] In the village of Pinares in 1979, anti-communist peasants burned down the homes of PGT activists. Throughout the Polochic Valley, as communities responded in different ways to the challenge of securing access to land, divisions became endemic. Conflict often revolved around charges of corruption. Peasant leaders attempting to raise money for various legal fees and land transactions were often accused, as they were in Cahabón, of blackmail by their opponents. In 1963 in Panzós the police arrested Emilio Caal Tení and Nery Gutiérrez after a number of peasants charged them with extortion. After a lengthy and disputatious investigation, Cobán's public prosecutor, Arturo Cruz, a proven anti-communist, dropped the charges because he believed they were orchestrated by "interested persons" who wanted to stop the accused from collecting funds to petition INTA for land titles.[33] While peasants aimed most violence laterally at neighbors, increasingly throughout the 1960s they directed their anger upward at local planters or government agents. In 1963 a group of resident workers stoned their village's alcalde auxiliar for trying to conscript labor for a public works project. That same year Mariano Caal cut off the hand of an alcalde auxiliar on plantation Pachilhaj with an ax.[34] In 1966, authorities arrested Juan Coc for trying to kill his finca administrator.[35]

As the countryside grew more violent, planters began to depend to an ever greater extent on military commissioners, martial administrators, and the army, which by the 1960s had identified the Polochic Valley as a strategically important corridor in its expanding counterinsurgent strategies.[36] A process of selection took place in which those who were either undercapitalized or lacking military contacts sold their land to more potentially violent planters. This hardening of the local landed class itself had a class dimension, as often it was aspiring elites who took advantage of rural turmoil to improve their social standing. These nouveau planters, such as Jaime Champney, Ernesto Fratz, and Flavio Monzón, were reputed to be more ruthless than established coffee growers. At times, new planters would do away with the troublesome resident workers of their predecessors by transforming a coffee estate into a cattle farm. Ernesto Fratz, Cahabón's mayor in 1965, for example, expelled two hundred families from a recently acquired property, using a military detachment to load them onto trucks and drop them off in a neighboring municipality.[37]

Rural residents who participated in the organizing against Champney tend to speak of the twenty years after 1954 as of a piece: two decades of low-grade harassment, displacement, flight, and occasional murder. In most accounts of the war, ambient violence gives way by the early 1970s to more precise repression carried out against specific leaders. Many participants accuse the Champneys and other planters of bribing the military with either money or land to deal with troublesome workers. Edgar Champney denies the accusations. "Maybe some did, but it wasn't common," he says. "There was no need because the alliances were natural, the army was on the side of the powerful. So money, no, but a bottle of whiskey, a woman, yes." Edgar (the recognized, educated heir) and Jaime (the semi-illiterate pretender who according to one relative had never traveled beyond the borders of Sepacuité) had different administrative styles. Jaime was more brutal and directly involved in carrying out violence against defiant resident workers.[38] His heavy-handedness was aggravated by the fact that in the 1962 division of Sepacuité, Edgar gave him the most underpopulated section of plantation, thus making labor procurement difficult. Edgar, for his part, tried to temper his labor relations with more *tino*, more subtlety and grace. Yet circumstances overwhelmed him, for he, along with Jaime, came to rely on Norman Prado, Cahabón's infamously violent military commissioner. By his own admission Edgar Champney first hired Prado as a teacher in a plantation school in the early 1960s to spy on peasants in Gualibaj, one of the insolent villages north of the Cahabón River. Later in the decade Prado assumed the triple role of administrator on Jaime's estate, Cahabón's military commissioner, and army informant.

Invested in Prado was the compounded power of private and public repression. As plantation administrator and military commissioner he was in charge of a corps of underlings—foremen, alcaldes auxiliares, and assistant commissioners, most of whom were Q'eqchi'—that allowed him to enforce labor discipline throughout Sepacuité. Tomás Cac remembers once being too wasted from dysentery to work and having one of Prado's alcaldes auxiliares cut his hammock strings. As Cahabón's chief commissioner Prado was also an intelligence agent, serving as an important connection between the army and planters. Until the 1970s, the military did not have much of a presence in Cahabón, instead focusing its attentions on the area south of the Sierra de las Minas where the FAR mostly operated. It was under Prado's direction, according to eyewitnesses, that troops arrived on January 15, 1975, to break up a meeting in Seasir between FASGUA representatives and the community to discuss petitioning INTA.[39] On at least three separate occasions, Jaime Champney and Prado chased away FASGUA delegates at gunpoint.[40] Survivors of the violence also hold Prado and Jaime Champney responsible for the 1980 murder and decapitation of Emilio Rax Pop, an old Arbencista turned PGT leader. They placed his headless body on public display, ordering

Champney's workers to file past it.[41] Prado developed a reputation as a *matón* (cold-blooded killer), and many say he orchestrated the capture, torture, and murder of Marcelino Xol in 1972. Some say Prado personally cut Xol's tongue out, extracting his teeth with a pair of pliers.[42]

Prior to the early 1980s, when all that Cahabón's PGT activists had built was swept away, party strategy seemed to be gaining ground. The 1973 migration of two hundred or so families from the four northern communities, following their expulsion from their homes as discussed above, to villages located south of the Cahabón River—Seasir, Setzacpec, Chíax, Balamte, Salac, and Chiacach—created a unique situation in Sepacuité.[43] Before the arrival of these families, a confluence of events had already made these six communities especially combative. After 1954, Benjamin Champney forced their residents once again to work on Sepacuité, yet technically the government did not legally restore the corn land that surrounded the communities to the planter. While Edgar and Jaime treated their inhabitants as if they were peons, Edgar could not include them in his pacification strategy to sell land to workers. In the 1960s, these communities had been the most aggressive in demanding an end to free labor and retroactive compensation for time worked, a militancy that became sharpened by Jaime's coercive attempts to secure workers. They were "pure guerrillas" says Edgar's son, who claims that in 1968 they "ambushed Prado and tried to kill him."

The coming of the two hundred dispossessed families in 1973 further condensed their militancy. Many of the fathers and sons of those expelled from the north were either members of or sympathizers with the PGT, and activists used their recent experience of divisionism, violence, and failed struggle to create a more disciplined and unified clandestine structure. The villages south of the Cahabón River joined the PGT wholesale, with Reyes the main link to the regional and national party structure. A high-ranking party leader who came to the area in 1981 recalled that he "arrived to find that the party had thirty thousand members. Who knew?" While a deliberate exaggeration, the remark does capture how the PGT's wide network of subterranean support remained invisible even to the party's urban leadership. This support existed not just among the "guerrilla bastions," as Edgar Champney describes Seasir, Setzacpec, Chíax, Balamte, Salac, and Chiacach, but throughout the Polochic Valley from El Estor to Chahal. Part of the reason for the invisible nature of Q'eqchi' support stemmed from the distinction the party made between members and sympathizers.[44] Adopting a closed structure after 1954, the PGT allowed only an elect few to join. In the 1970s, it counted on roughly four hundred members throughout the valley, organized like other besieged

Communist parties throughout the world in small cells of four to six people. But in the zone south of the Cahabón River, the cell structure was nonexistent. While technically there were only a few score of official members, the *simpatizantes* of each free community were organized en masse in base committees of women, youth, and elders. "Compartmentalization," recalls a national-level PGT member, designed to ensure secrecy, gave way to "wholly organized villages."

Reyes's rebuilding of the PGT in Alta Verapaz is all the more impressive when one considers the failure of guerrilla groups to make inroads into the area. From the 1960s onward, those groups proved unable to gain a foothold in the Polochic Valley, and their leaders complained of the "taciturnity" of Q'eqchi's, often contrasting them to the more militant Achí and Ixil.[45] The PGT on the other hand was able to draw from second-generation commitment, working with the sons and daughters of activists from the October Revolution. Tomás Cac, who led the successful land struggle in the 1970s, was the son of an Arbencista turned PGT member in the late 1960s. Repression steeled political dedication, as many of the children of murdered parents, such as the daughter of Emilio Rax Pop, killed by Jaime Champney in 1980, became more active in oppositional politics.[46]

While probably overdrawn by the precision of hindsight, the following comparison made in different versions by many involved in Polochic politics between the Q'eqchi' Mario Botzoc from San Juan Chamelco and Marcelino Xol's daughter, Herlinda Xol, highlights the distinction between the successfully cautious politics of the PGT and the confrontational stance of younger revolutionaries associated with FAR rebels: In the early 1960s, Botzoc, Herlinda, and a handful of other Q'eqchi's traveled to Cuba for basic education and some military training.[47] Upon returning to Guatemala, Herlinda took the pseudonym América and joined her father to quietly rebuild the party in the Polochic Valley, continuing with the PGT until her murder in the early 1980s. Before leaving Cuba, some remember, she taped revolutionary messages in Q'eqchi' to be broadcast into Guatemala from Havana.[48] Botzoc, in contrast, came back to join the FAR, "believing," according to one account, that "he would have the support of his race, that he was going to make the revolution." But he had little success. Supposedly betrayed by Chamelco Q'eqchi's and surrounded by the military, Botzoc reportedly blew himself up with a hand grenade in March 1967.

Energized by the arrival of militant families in 1973, the six Sepacuité communities scored a number of successes in their struggle for back pay and land. Starting in 1970, the PGT, through the labor federation FASGUA, stepped up its direct legal and financial assistance to Cahabón communities.

The federation not only provided free legal services and financial aid but helped set up meetings in the capital between community leaders, government ministers, and the Champney brothers. For Tomás Cac, the ability to meet outside of Cahabón was crucial. "Jaime and Edgar always insisted we meet near the plantation house, but whenever FASGUA would show up, they would be harassed." Cac remembers Jaime Champney and Norman Prado once threatening FASGUA advisors at gunpoint, refusing to let them into the plantation. "They treated us like stupid animals. But in the city, with FASGUA and the government, they had to show more respect." In early 1975, the ministry of labor ruled that the Champneys not only had to discontinue paying their workers in kind or in promissory notes but had to compensate back pay. And later that year, INTA provisionally approved a number of land claims, including those of the six villages south of the Cahabón River, and began plans to survey boundaries.

The PGT's success in eastern Alta Verapaz—at a time when in other areas the party was yielding to new guerrilla groups or social movements—can partly be explained by the fact that the Catholic Church in eastern Alta Verapaz did not provide a venue through which communities could channel political demands. There existed few radical priests, such as those found among the Spanish clergy in Quiché, the Belgians on the southern coast, or U.S. Maryknolls in Quetzaltenango and Huehuetenango.[49] In Carchá, the Salesians continued to be conservative and orthodox and openly sided with the state against the left.[50] In Cahabón, nuns, priests, and Catholic lay activists who did try to engage in political work were much more restricted by local planter power than their counterparts in other areas, and the Christian Democrats did not emerge as they did elsewhere as the successor to the reform aspirations of the PR. In 1978, for example, security forces kidnapped, raped, tortured, and left naked on the border of El Salvador a Spanish nun working in Cahabón, reportedly in retaliation for her work on behalf of the Christian Democrats.[51] The Benedictines in the late 1960s did start a catechist program, and some of the young Q'eqchi's who later joined the PGT did become radicalized through its work, but most of the clergy remained either conservative, apolitical, or silenced. Vicente Toc, one of the PGT leaders of the land struggle in the community of Pinares, was in charge of hundreds of Cahabón's catechists, but he eventually broke with the local priest because "all he wanted to do was pray."[52] Planter power was so fierce east of Cobán that you did not "raise your voice or your head," remembers one catechist.[53] The clandestine structure of the PGT, absent any alternative, proved to be the only viable venue for political work in many areas of the Polochic Valley, particularly in Cahabón.

More than offering just a concealed organizational structure, PGT Marxism resonated with the lived experience of many Q'eqchi's in the lower Polochic Valley. Unlike the newer guerrilla groups, which relentlessly criticized the party not only for not incorporating "race" into its analysis and strategy but for the petit bourgeois urban condescension of many of its leaders, the PGT never much evolved beyond its class-based understanding of revolutionary consciousness and action.[54] Since its inception the PGT had condemned discrimination, yet in the transformation to clandestine life it resisted adopting a model of "internal colonialism," that is, one that viewed Guatemalan society in specifically racial terms. To the degree that the party did address the "Indian Question," it was through the writings of Joaquín Noval, the ex-head of the Guatemalan Indigenista Institute, who rotated his time between teaching anthropology at the national university and heading the PGT's military commission. In a series of writings, Noval defended himself against the attacks of younger New Left intellectuals such as Carlos Guzmán Böckler, Julio Quan, and Jean-Loup Herbert, deriding their romantic and thin understanding of an indigenous culture that supposedly would automatically lead to revolutionary solidarity.[55] Whatever the deficits of his at times instrumentalist analysis of ethnicity, Noval in retrospect granted indigenous culture and society significant complexity, and his ethnographies and theoretical writings have survived much more intact than have those of his detractors.[56]

By not overtheorizing ethnicity, by not assigning it a surfeit of either revolutionary virtue or counterrevolutionary vice, the PGT in effect allowed for the emergence of a syncretic Q'eqchi' interpretation of Marx, a kind of Mayan Marxism that filled the ideological vacuum created by the overthrow of Arbenz. Post-1954 repression destroyed the nascent language of agrarian radicalism through which indigenous peasants had made demands on the state, an apprenticeship reinforced by the material rewards of the Agrarian Reform. In other areas of Guatemala, liberation theology and Christian Democratic politics would fill this void, but in Alta Verapaz, planter and Ladino power greatly limited their effectiveness. PGT intellectuals argued that colonialism had effectively used distinctive cultural "traits," such as language, dress, and local political and religious institutions, to segregate "the great indigenous masses" into easily controllable "small particular groups," yet in eastern Alta Verapaz PGT organizers made no attempt to destroy these "divisive elements."[57] They instead attempted to recast them as universal and critical signifiers. Between 1977 and 1979, for example, an economist working with the PGT front organization, the Escuela de Orientación Sindical, traveled to Cobán every weekend to hold workshops for about twenty Q'eqchi's at a time.[58] "It was a great lesson in pedagogy," he says, "one that tried to explain concepts such as alienated labor in relation to communal work and collective life of their ancestors. I had to take their daily experience and move it to another level, trying to clarify social relations of production based on their own lives, working under foremen and landlords. My goal was to give them theory to understand the concrete way they experienced exploitation."

It was through Reyes—who took ten minutes to say what Ladino instructors said in two—that most of this conversion took place. He not only often served as the interpreter at study groups and as the primary liaison between the local party structure and the national leadership but also ran political meetings. Such autonomy kept Ladino condescension to a minimum and allowed Reyes to preach his unique brand of Marxism. For instance, the youthful, literate intellectualism of the PGT in the 1950s had by the mid-1970s grown sclerotic, its Marxism as taught by party allies at the national university rigidified by Soviet dogma—especially its interpretation of dialectical materialism in which economic base was separated from ideological superstructure. Yet it was this conceptual division between the material and the ideal that most fired Reyes's imagination, and he repeatedly refers to it in his accounts of his activism and his attempts to define himself. He often invokes Lenin's elaboration of the "unity of opposites" concept to answer questions, at times quoting the Russian revolutionary from memory to explain historical motion: "Development is a struggle of opposites, the ideal and the material." Reyes offers as an answer to why he left the PAR to join the PGT in 1950: "When a man is born, he has baby hair, but as he ages, he grows a beard. A leaf is green because of its chloroform, but then it turns. Quantitative and qualitative change."[59]

As Marxism converted into hollow theoretics for PGT intellectuals and political leaders, for Reyes it remained a powerfully dynamic explanatory tool in his organizing work, one he used to convert the experience of nearly a decade of promissory notes into mordant aphorisms. "Idealism," he offers as a definition, "says we will be rewarded in the afterlife. Materialism says we want our pay now." Reyes explains how he would prod Q'eqchi's to stand up to Sepacuité's administrators and at the same time teach them about their surplus labor value. When a worker named Miguel voiced concern that he would be accused of being lazy for refusing to work without pay, Reyes told him to tell the administrator, "If we are not worth anything to you, then plant the money you should pay us under the coffee bush and see what happens, see if it brings you a profit." It is this capacity to elucidate, to clarify, to replace obscurant faith with critical thought that gave Marxism its value to a number of informants. For Tomás Cac, to become more involved in the PGT and to become educated were one and the same, and both were driven by *necesidad,* by not so much a need for survival, although that was present too, as a desire to understand: "No sense getting killed if you don't know why. They took many who were involved with the church, with other organizations, who didn't know anything. *Mejor que sepa, me metí,* it is better to know, so I joined. The struggle of Marxism was a struggle of necessity. If we didn't, we would have continued being tricked and exploited by the landlords."

For Reyes, the ability to assess and explain was a supreme value, one that trumped even gender prejudices. Elena Chuc, a PGT organizer in the 1970s, was according to Reyes a "*cuadra más inteligente en charla,* she knew how to explain why there is poverty, why we are slaves, why we are subjugated, why the boss does not pay, all of these questions she was good at explaining." And for Reyes the antithesis of this quality is religion, be it Christian or Mayan. He described Vicente Toc, a longtime member of the PGT and currently general secretary of the left's political party in the department of Izabal, as "ideologically influenced by capital" because Toc participates in Mayan ceremonies and was educated by the Church. "It takes time to shake free of it," says Reyes.

But Reyes was in most ways an outlier in how Q'eqchi's interacted with the ideological tenets and political structure of the PGT. National PGT leaders tended to be atheists, and doubt worked its way into the minds of regional Q'eqchi' activists. As Tomás Cac put it, "Yes, the leaders who know more say that Marxism teaches that there is no God. Well, there was one, but he was persecuted for speaking the truth. His words survived, and this is what we have, but he doesn't exist any more. But in the communities, we couldn't talk about that." As part of its general indifference to the subject, the national PGT leadership neither opposed Catholicism nor took a position in regard to Mayan religious practices in Alta Verapaz. "Each had its own practices, *costumbre,*" says Inocente Cac of Mayan and Communist rituals and beliefs, "but the PGT always respected and never repressed Mayan traditions, you could be part of a cofradía and PGT member." Until the violence of the early 1980s made it no longer possible, PGT committees throughout the 1960s and 1970s worked with Mayan folk priests who practiced a fusion of Catholic and Q'eqchi' rituals, some of whom were party members. One elderly member recalls that in the 1970s, "the elders, *los viejos,* would do their ceremony, a *mayejak,* and between a hundred and two hundred people showed up. We would ask for a change, for a better pueblo, a better Guatemala. We would petition the mountain, the sun, the sky. We would go pray in caves, with drums, *harpas, chirimías.*" Such local rites put traditionalists at odds with Catholic Action "modernizers" who sought to instill a more orthodox Catholicism. In other areas of Guatemala, new insurgent organizations tended to ally with these catechists, which often put the left at odds with traditionalists.[60] In the Polochic Valley, however, the relatively slight influence of liberation theology allowed the PGT to more directly engage Q'eqchi' spiritual beliefs and practices, accounting for the party's successful blending of the sacred and the secular.

Reyes's repeated evocation of Mayan materialism is more than just a gratuitous comparison, for other less theorized informants suggest a deep resonance between Marxism and Q'eqchi' spirituality.[61] In Alta Verapaz, as in other majority indigenous areas of Guatemala, local religious beliefs melded with Catholic doctrine to produce to different degrees an integrated and eclectic set of practices and convictions centering on the cofradía complex. Yet unlike other Guatemalan Mayan groups, Q'eqchi's do not worship animal spirits or alter egos. Instead they conjure a sacred landscape of mountain spirits known as *tzuultaq'as,* or "tellurian gods" as anthropologist Richard Wilson describes them, that bind together and influence all animate and inanimate objects.[62] Celestial gods exist in Q'eqchi' folk religion, including the Catholic images of Christ and the saints, but they are distant, less immediately powerful than are *tzuultaq'as.* These earth gods provide Q'eqchi's with a hierarchical and interlocking set of geographic and moral coordinates. Each community is thought to be owned by a specific *tzuultaq'a,* while thirteen more potent mountain spirits surround the Q'eqchi' linguistic area. For traditionalists, these mountain spirits regulate the sexual and agricultural reproduction of the entirety of Q'eqchi' life and are easy to offend. They demand adherence to a set of ritualistic practices, including respect for taboos and offerings before planting, harvesting, traveling, hunting, sex, and childbirth. They also insist on a life lived in harmony with neighbors, the fulfillment of expected obligations to spouse, family and community, the granting of respect and deference to male heads of households and community elders, and the containment of individual ambitions and the excessive accumulation of wealth in an increasingly commodified and commercial world.

Within this moral polity—it cannot be called an economy for implicit was the notion that the world could be changed by extra-economic interventions—the PGT's vision of social justice, its hierarchical party structure and demands for discipline and unity, as well as some of Marxism's philosophical conceptions, took root. Most powerful was the party's legitimate claim to be the heirs of the Agrarian Reform and the party's ongoing promotion of an ethical society centered in the just distribution and use of land, for Q'eqchi' society and culture continued to be largely linked to subsistence corn production despite the disruptions of coffee capitalism. Traditionalists hold that humans do not own the land but only have access to it as a "renewable usufruct," a belief that party activists used to frame their demand that disputed land be granted them free of charge.[63] In 1979, an INTA surveyor, for example, complained of a "group of rebellious peasants who refused to be surveyed because they say that INTA does not have the right to give the land, because *siendo de Dios, a ellos les pertenece*"—being of God, it belongs to them.[64] If the PGT had gained power, its promotion of development and productive capitalism might have conflicted with anti-entrepreneurship elements of Q'eqchi' life. Yet that tension never had a chance to materialize. Rather, the two worldviews shared a certain appreciation of the "use value" of goods. Vicente Toc reports that elders used only subsistence and local crops such as cacao, corn, and turkeys as well as homemade candles in their offerings, as *tzuultaq'as* did not appreciate commercial products such as coffee or cardamom, for once goods are sold they lose their holiness, or *xtioxila'*.[65]

Offerings and sacrifices were no organizing artifice, for many Q'eqchi' PGT activists shared this sacred vision of the world and structured their organizing work accordingly. They did not seek guidance directly from *tzuultaq'as*, but until the escalation of violence made such time-consuming routes to decision making less viable, they took advice from community elders who shared through dreams a more proximate relation with mountain spirits. These dream counsels helped local leaders decide not only on larger courses of actions but on the more routine aspects of clandestine life—where to rendezvous, where to hold political meetings, what route to travel. Before performing any such tasks, they would make small offerings and say little prayers "to ensure, well, that the road was safe." And while Reyes explains his organizing strategies in Q'eqchi' communities within classic consciousness-raising terms, others remember joining the PGT through more traditional, hierarchical mechanisms of community decision making. Pedro Maquin remembers that in the late 1960s, the "elders" of the PGT came to speak to the "elders" of his village, who made a collective decision to accept their help.

As does Marxism, Q'eqchi' animism emphasizes the interconnectedness of everyday life, binding the world through the inseparability of the animate and the inanimate, the secular and the sacred, the material and the ideal. In trying to recall what Marxism meant to him, the son of Adelina Caal, who helped organize the Panzós protest discussed in the next chapter and is now an Evangelical Christian, says that the "party taught us what we already knew, that the world was one." *Tzuultaq'as* literally means "mountain-valleys," and this duality is the essence of their power. They are both man and woman, Q'eqchi' and European, "the land as well as the spirit inhabiting it."[66] This echo of Reyes's dialectical "unity of opposites"—a belief that everything contains within itself its own contradiction—resonates in less theorized form among many of the surviving PGT Q'eqchi' activists. In explaining the distinction between idealism and materialism, Tomás Cac says that idealism "is something that is born within you but that you haven't tried. It could turn out good or bad." For Cac, political consciousness develops through action, or, in other words, praxis. "It means not simply to wait, to not do anything to make the ideal happen," he says, "but to become organized since nothing comes on its own, from heaven."

The successful efforts of PGT communities to obtain a favorable ruling from INTA in 1975 took place during a brief national political opening allowed by president Kjell Laugerud, who presided over Guatemala from 1974 to 1978. In an attempt to build legitimacy and garner support for the military's modernizing project, Laugerud lessened repression, at least in comparison with what had come before and what lay ahead. Yet the opening was short-lived, and the cycle of reform and violence that constituted Guatemala's postwar history continued to spin forward toward its resolution.

By the mid-1970s, the PGT had long since lost most of its influence over Guatemala's growing oppositional movement, yet through FASGUA the party continued to work on behalf of a number of communities throughout the country, including Cahabón, Panzós, San Martín Jilotepeque, San Marcos, Santiago Atitlán, and Santo Domingo Suchitepéquez.[67] As in Cahabón, the party's legal maneuvers were at times successful. In Santo Domingo, for example, five hundred peasants involved in a land struggle working with FASGUA were financially compensated by the legal owner and promised work and land elsewhere.[68] For the first time in the "history of the campesino movement," enthused one newspaper, "dialogue carried out with a spirit of understanding and humanism, leaving aside foreign influences, helped resolve a conflict" and set a "precedent of how to resolve problems without violence."[69]

It was an optimism unwarranted in hindsight. By the late 1970s, the PGT's strategy, notwithstanding such occasional important victories, was fraying. In Cahabón, the party had won land concessions not only in the six villages south of the Cahabón River but in Pinares, Seguamó, and Salamtun as well, yet activists found it difficult to follow up initial successes.[70] Originally, INTA granted the communities of Chíax, Balamte, Chiacach, Salac, Seasir, and Setzacpec 3,300 acres each, but a state hydroelectric project, which flooded the Cahabón River, cut the concession to 2,200 acres.[71] INTA bureaucracy dragged on. Land had to be surveyed and families needed to have all their paperwork in order, which cost time and money.[72] Planters obstructed the process at every point. Jaime Champney disputed INTA's measurements and tried to scare peasants who participated in the land grant with loss of work.[73] As the promised property was slow to materialize, tensions within the communities flared, aggravated once again by a dispute over whether or not to pay INTA for the land, as INTA insisted, or to demand it as a grant. At first the communities united behind the insistence of local PGT leaders that the concessions be free, but they divided as time wore on, violence rose, and planters schemed.[74]

Cahabón's land struggles were just a few of the hundreds that roiled Guatemala by the mid-1970s.[75] INTA became overwhelmed with requests from communities either for titles or for help in settling problems, many of which INTA itself had aggravated through its corruption, lethargy, or ineptitude.[76] As in the Polochic Valley, violence escalated throughout rural Guatemala. In 1978 in Santa María de Jesús, peasants complained that land they had purchased thirty years earlier was being claimed by a local planter who worked with the military to have their leaders arrested and threatened with death. In 1977 in Mazatenango, the tortured corpses of three peasant activists who recently had led a land invasion appeared under a bridge.[77] In Concepción Chiquistepeque, a planter reportedly placed a bounty on the heads of local peasant organizers. The press reported increasing incidences of evictions, such as the one in 1978 in La Gomera, Escuintla, where a planter used pesticides and other poisons to drive three hundred contentious peasants off disputed land.[78]

Most troublesome for the government was that in some areas, well before the 1980 militant southern coast plantation workers' strike, peasants were increasingly striking back. In Santa María de Jesús, leaders told a reporter that they would "fight until death" to remain on their land. In 1977 in Huehuetenango, members of Finca El Herrador's peasant league murdered the son of the plantation owner.[79] By 1977, a wave of land invasions had led to the militarization of many municipalities, with invading families growing increasingly belligerent. In San Antonio Suchitepéquez, five hundred campesinos sang Guatemala's national anthem as they faced down twenty armed men trying to prevent the takeover of the plantation Los Tiestos.[80] In Santo Domingo Suchitepéquez, nine hundred families frustrated by eight years of bureaucracy swore to defend land they invaded with "machete in hand."[81]

To acknowledge rural militancy is not to suggest that peasants are innately revolutionary but merely to admit that they share a common human sentiment, the ability to hate. There has been much debate on the political consciousness of Guatemala's indigenous peasants but surprisingly little written on the sheer rage that ran through rural activists by the late 1970s, many of whom not only were embittered by failed reform but mourned the murder of family and friends and wore the scars of torture. Anthropologists today talk about fear as if it were hardwired into the Mayan psyche, but in the late 1970s it was fury that drove many rural indigenous activists. By the end of the 1970s, the party's strategy of working to settle conflicts with private planters through state agencies had reached its limit, but the truth is that the PGT was barely in control of events even in eastern Alta Verapaz. National PGT leaders grew anxious at the acts of open militancy that were taking place in the Polochic Valley around Panzós. In other areas where the party pursued the same reformist strategy, such as the southern coast and Chimaltenango, its influence waned not just because insurgents or radical priests usurped its authority but because peasants became confrontational through their ongoing exposure and vulnerability to an intransigent, brutal state. In Cahabón, peasant activists still distinguished between the government, which they continued to call on for help, and planters and their military and civilian allies, whom they feared and fought. In early 1978, for example, Tomás Cac led a delegation to the capital to complain to the minister of defense about planter and army violence. But peasants also increasingly demanded guns, which the PGT's national leadership refused to supply. Even Efraín Reyes Maaz, who tends to dismiss inchoate peasant anger as insufficiently conceptualized, grew irritated with party leaders who agreed to provide some armed self-defense training but no arms. "What good does it do if you take the guns back to the city with you?" one of the instructors remembers Reyes complaining. It was not until late 1981 with its membership dispersed and its local structure largely broken that the party established an armed front in Cahabón. Yet by then, according to Reyes, ever attentive to the correct interpretation of historical conjunctures, "it was too late."

In Cahabón, genocide finished what the PGT started. The military's 1981–83 scorched earth campaign—which razed hundreds of Mayan communities, committed over six hundred massacres, murdered over a hundred thousand indigenous peasants, tortured thousands more, and drove, in some areas, 80 percent of the population from its homes—was specifically designed to destroy rural support for the powerful insurgent group known as the Ejército Guerrillero de los Pobres (Guerrilla Army of the Poor [EGP]) that operated mostly in the country's western highlands. In eastern Alta Verapaz, however, PGT communities during those years experienced a similar yet slightly modified pattern of counterinsurgent terror.

As part of its effort to undercut guerrilla support and devolve responsibility for antisubversive policing to communities themselves, the military ordered all able-bodied men to serve in civil patrols.[82] Militias, or PACs by their Spanish acronym, were central to the counterinsurgent campaign, for as one study put it, they transformed a war between rebels and the army into a civil war among indigenous peasants.[83] In most areas, the army initiated PACs in late 1981 and 1982, that is, after regular troops committed massacres. Yet in Cahabón what were in effect if not in name civil patrols had existed since the late 1970s, when planters and the military organized peasants hostile to the PGT, mostly in the villages north of the Cahabón River, into anti-Communist brigades. By 1978, for example, Francisco Curley, who had disavowed his radical youth but not his militant tactics, had claimed land in Setzacpec for himself and had organized groups of peasants from the villages of Chitcoj and Chimenchen to harass the PGT communities.[84] Likewise, Jaime Champney and Norman Prado had armed groups of Q'eqchi's from the villages north of the Cahabón River. While in other areas the army initiated large-scale repression, in Cahabón between 1980 and 1983 it was these ad hoc groups led by military commissioners and planters that began an escalating campaign of torture, murder, and rape, primarily singling out PGT members of land committees.[85] Politically divided communities, such as Pinares, Tzalantun, and Chivite, turned on themselves. In Pinares in January 1979, for example, tensions between peasants organized by the PGT and demanding that INTA make good on its 1975 land concession and another group aligned with planters erupted into open physical conflict.[86] Soldiers occupied the town, while anti-PGT leaders took advantage of their presence to torch the houses of their opponents, leading to a temporary exodus into the mountains of three hundred families. For their part, the six more unified communities south of the Cahabón River—Seasir, Setzacpec, Chíax, Balamte, Salac, and Chiacach—found themselves isolated, ringed by villages increasingly allied with the military or planters.[87] "The truth is," says Inocente Cac, "we were surrounded."

In June 1982 after completing its first sweeps through Chimaltenango and Quiché, the military arrived in Alta Verapaz.[88] Following their pacification of the EGP communities in western Alta Verapaz, troops moved east to Cahabón, committing massacres in Seasir, Setzacpec, Chíax, Balamte, Salac, and Chiacach. In July, soldiers decapitated seven party members in Setzacpec. A month later in Seguamó, the military and civil patrollers carried out Cahabón's worst slaughter, murdering 106 people, mostly women, children, and elderly refugees from PGT communities whose husbands had fled, believing their wives and children would be spared.[89] Pinares, identified in party documents by the pseudonym Esperanza (Hope), suffered seven massacres at the hands of civilian patrols and the military between December 1981 and December 1982.[90]

As a response to the diagnosis that rural subversion spread in the absence of government, military strategists designed an operation that was merely the first stage in a longer stabilization project that entailed "integrating" indigenous communities into the state. Yet before such steps could be taken, all opposition had to be destroyed. This meant not just physically eliminating the guerrillas and their real and potential supporters but colonizing the spaces, symbols, and social relations analysts believed to be outside of state control. Terror was made spectacle: soldiers, commissioners, and civilian patrollers raped women in front of husbands and children. In September 1982, in Sechaj, Cahabón, civil patrollers captured, beat, and tortured PGT activist Francisco Xi, then turned him over to soldiers. Before executing him, soldiers amputated his tongue and testicles and put them on public display, rendering—none too subtly—impotent his voice and virility.[91] In Cahabón, security forces publicly tortured and killed groups of men in village chapels, disposing of their bodies in sacred caves.[92] They turned churches into torture chambers and singled out traditionalists for murder.[93] "They say that the soldiers scorched earth," said Manuel Caal, who fled his home in Salac, "but it was heaven that they burned."

In those villages that remained united, the military forced intracommunal violence. It was a common tactic to make members of a community commit violence against their neighbors.[94] In 1982 in Salac, for example, soldiers and military commissioners captured eighteen members of the community and took them to a military camp where they separated the victims into two groups, the strong and healthy and the weak and infirm, forcing the former to beat the latter.[95] In the same village the previous year, one survivor says that the military made residents execute by machete seventeen refugee families who had recently fled repression in their home community of Senahú. Often the army encouraged their civilian allies to avail themselves of their victims' property and surviving wives and daughters.[96] One military commissioner was forced to murder his PGT parents, severing the kind of generational political ties discussed earlier.[97] Such terror not only broke local solidarity but, following the primary objective of the pacification campaign, bound the perpetrators in an impious blood ritual to a larger impersonal state collective as represented by the military.

In response to the increasingly unbearable situation, Q'eqchi' activists demanded that the PGT help them organize armed resistance. In late 1981, the national leadership finally relented and sent an organizer to set up a front.[98]

The idea was to open a liberated corridor running north of the Santa Cruz mountain range from Seguamó in southeastern Cahabón to Belize. A desperate effort, the front had no hope for success. Although the unit had quickly grown to over a hundred men, the arms the party sent were useless, and the EGP columns to the west and south with whom they hoped to ally were in the process of being decimated. Military repression directed at PGT communities forced a massive exodus into the northern mountains, cutting off an important source of the guerrillas' material support. The party disbanded the front at the end of 1982, its members either joining their communities in the mountains or traveling to insurgent territory in El Salvador to regroup. Fight or flight, however, was not the only choice. In Seasir, identified in party documents by its apposite pseudonym, La Tumba (The Tomb), seven PGT activists committed suicide by poisoning themselves in September 1982.[99]

The PGT's land reform, which began in 1950 when residents refused to work for Champney, was completed by the counterinsurgency. The war drove many planters, including Edgar Champney, to sell off their remaining land and leave. Jaime Champney died of kidney cancer in 1982, and his mortgaged property passed to the state.[100] In 1983, the military, for its part, began to implement the second phase of its pacification campaign, resettling refugees in reeducation centers, model villages, and other more controllable populations. Unlike the EGP, which urged its fleeing supporters to resist such efforts and to organize themselves into mobile "communities of people in resistance," the PGT, short on resources, counseled its members to accept the government's 1983 amnesty offer. As refugees came down from the mountains, the military resettled them on the land granted by INTA in 1975 but never titled.[101] The families began to make payments in 1984. They received their deeds in 1998.[102]

Despite the horrific violence visited on PGT families, an oppositional political culture in Cahabón survives. The municipality elected an ex-insurgent mayor in 1998. The old PGT-organized villages, including the six "guerrilla bastions" south of the Cahabón River, have proven somewhat better able than others to work with state and nongovernmental organizations to bring water, light, and medical services to their communities, although high levels of poverty persist. The ongoing vitality of the left in Cahabón stemmed from the PGT's ability to tap into a local history of struggle that, owing to extreme planter control, found no outlet other than the party's clandestine politics. In no other region of Guatemala did the history, vision, and goals of the PGT mesh so seamlessly with local knowledge as they did in Cahabón. While Cahabón was an ancient town, one of the original colonial Q'eqchi' settlements, the villages where the PGT was strong were not old. They shared no primordial foundation myth or venerable institutions stretching back through the ages. Nor did they suffer the trauma of primitive capital accumulation, the "blood and fire" that often accompanies the alienation of land and labor needed to begin commodity production.[103] Rather, these communities were created at the end of the nineteenth century by migrant Q'eqchi's, pushed by a highland intensification of plantation labor demands and pulled by the promise of land in exchange for toil that was relatively light, at least at first. Yet they did share a common linguistic and ethnic identity that gave them a means to make transcendental claims on the land, claims that were reinforced by a relative absence of economic stratification. A shared political culture of combativeness, which many date to the 1950 election of Arbenz, along with the collective experience of extreme exploitation and violence, fortified these claims. Blood and fire came not with the creation but with the maintenance of coffee capitalism.

In order to succeed, the Guatemalan counterrevolution had to adopt elements of the challenge it sought to contain. One aspect of that challenge was the expectation of state-administered justice. As we have seen, planter control over the bodies of workers was an elemental part of plantation life. Along with the ability to exact labor came the power to incarcerate, whip, and rape with near complete impunity. The extension of the liberal state was a fundamental precondition of this private power, limiting the possibility of flight and other forms of evasion. Yet at the same time, this extension forced a more direct engagement by marginalized groups with the state. Beginning at least in the time of José Angel Icó and even earlier, rural activists called on the government to temper planter authority. For ten years between 1944 and 1954 it did, or at least its promise to do so seemed credible. The alchemy of postwar counterinsurgent repression transfigured this promise into terror. After 1954, the state continued to intervene against planter sovereignty. That intervention, however, increasingly took the form of a nationalization of the relations of violence. Rape, mutilation, torture, and murder were no longer everyday acts of planter control but increasingly became both the representation and the essence of public state power. In this sense, government repression was both a backlash against the ongoing legacy of the October Revolution and the revolution's perverse realization, the hope of a postwar social democratic state mutated into the nightmare of a counterinsurgent terror state.

But not everybody experienced the nightmare. In response to the revolution's rural organizing, the military, the state, and private counterrevolutionaries built their own institutional bases of peasant support. In the last chapter, we saw how the MLN through military commissioners, planters, and paramilitary groups created a network of rural power, tapping into community divisions and hostility toward political liberalization. In the 1980s, the civil patrols continued this tradition. Although PACs have received a good deal of attention from human rights advocates and anthropologists, few scholars have connected them to Guatemala's long history of popular participation in local militias, allowing for something of a popular Jacobin citizenship asserted through armed defense of the state.[104] As did the organizing associated with the left, the civil patrols provided an effective venue for local interests and factions to speak in the name of the community, to impose stability, and to make claims on the government. In many towns, for example, at the same time as the patrols allowed the army to consolidate its rural authority, they also empowered indigenous leaders to loosen local Ladino control of politics and the economy.

Finally, many of the reforms the left long struggled for were achieved not through victory but by defeat. In Guatemala, the postwar "transition to democracy" was, along with genocide, a fundamental element of a larger counterinsurgent plan.[105] The military promoted a guided return to constitutional rule in order to stabilize national politics and obscure its own ongoing power. In the countryside, after the massacres, the army permitted and at times even advanced a restricted program of reform. In Cahabón as throughout Guatemala, Mayan communities are no longer dominated by cliques of Ladino merchants, planters, politicians, and labor contractors. Land reform initiated by the PGT was finished by the military as part of its resettlement program. This is not to devalue the experience of the left in the Polochic Valley. On the contrary, the force of the reaction can be understood only by the strength of the threat.

Over the course of four decades, the nature of that threat changed as the government's capability for repression increased. In other areas of the country, decades of violence and intransigence on the part of the state and the oligarchy led new guerrilla movements to reject PGT reformism and to pursue more militant, armed tactics. Nevertheless, in the Polochic Valley the party continued in the face of escalating terror to caution moderation and to keep on organizing communities to work through government agencies. In the town of Panzós, however, down the valley from Cahabón, popular outrage overflowed PGT restraint. While the 1978 Panzós massacre is today understood as a prelude to genocide, at the time many saw the killing as a breaking point in state-society relations, where a long-standing peasant tradition of protest, negotiation, and concession gave way to direct confrontation.

CHAPTER FIVE

An Unsettled Life

> In the plaza of Panzós, a hundred flowers have been planted, and in the struggle of campesinos, there are now another hundred hearts.
>
> *"Las cien flores"*

ADELINA CAAL, also known as Mamá Maquin, has haunted this book, and not just because her life tracks its narrative. Born in San Pedro Carchá in 1915, she migrated with her husband to the village of Setzacpec on Champney's Sepacuité, where they exchanged their labor for a place to live and farm. They received property under the Agrarian Reform, but after Arbenz's fall they opted not to suffer Champney's restoration. With other former resident workers they moved further down the Polochic Valley to Panzós, settling on a strip of national land called Soledad along the banks of the river. Through Efraín Reyes Maaz, Adelina and her husband, Luis, joined the PGT in the mid-1960s and began to organize support for FAR rebels. She and her son Manuel, who became a party member in the early 1970s, were the principal leaders of the land movement that ended with the military's 1978 massacre of scores of Q'eqchi's in Panzós's town square, of which she was the first victim. In quietly accompanying this story's progress, Mamá Maquin fittingly represents two conditions difficult to discuss. The first has to do with her gender, the second with her outrage.

By all accounts, Maquin's leadership, reported as belligerent by allies and foes alike, formed part of a larger regional phenomenon in which women starting in the early 1970s became increasingly involved in local PGT-led struggles. The party preached gender equality. Its 1969 program, which did not have a specific section on indigenous rights, contained a detailed elaboration of the rights of women, including full parity before the law, equal salaries, and special protections for working and single mothers.[1] Yet on the ground its hierarchical structure drew on and reinforced local patriarchal ideologies and relations, allowing at first only modest room for women's involvement. Throughout the late 1960s and early 1970s, female members for the most part were expected to do little more than to organize other women into support committees. An exaltation of unity and discipline served to politicize routine tasks such as cooking, child rearing, and agricultural work already expected of women. In other words, women helped maintain the sea in which PGT men swam. Q'eqchi' society's limited acceptance of polygamy, for example, allowed Reyes access to a number of households maintained by women throughout the Polochic Valley.[2]

Yet clandestine organizing in an increasingly repressive climate undermined these relations. As selective terror killed men and as increased surveillance made it hard for survivors to organize, women came to play an increasingly important role in local clandestine politics. Gender ideologies and practices facilitated this deeper involvement. Women's actions tended to be more covert, as planters, military commissioners, and the like were less likely to recognize them as agitators than they were men. Adelina Ax, a PGT organizer in the 1970s, explained how a certain invisibility facilitated her organizing. "As an indigenous woman, I lived a clandestine life," she said to explain how she often was exempt from searches. Women also did much of their extracommunal organizing during market days when there was increased travel between communities. While this political work entailed specific tasks like passing messages and party directives back and forth, it also included gossip about shared indignities and promised redress. The mobilization of large numbers of women through auxiliary support committees came to overwhelm the party's clandestine cell structure. In Panzós, Maquin was technically the head of Soledad's women's committee but became de facto leader of an increasingly exposed land movement. Usually the most involved women filled voids left by murdered fathers or husbands, but in Maquin's case her husband, Luis, also a party member but apparently much less keen for the fight, was still alive.

Participation in oppositional movements gave marginalized groups, including women, not just a means to attain material benefits but help in achieving a heightened sense of self within a larger world. By 1982, for instance, in the middle of the dislocation caused by the military's scorched earth campaign, the PGT sent a Ladino activist to Cahabón to hold a meeting with seven Q'eqchi' women to talk about the current "political conjuncture."[3] Listed only by their pseudonyms—Ofelia, Amalia, Angela, and the like—the women took advantage of the meeting to complain and to assert their own sense of worth. "Angela" protested that a "woman's head shouldn't be used solely to carry water. Our heads need to be used to help fortify the party." After affirming that she was "ready to give her life to the party," Ofelia, who had recently withstood her father's demands that she marry, complained that women can do more than "throw a handful of beans into water."[4] The women asked to learn Spanish, to be trained to administer medicines, and to be taught how to sew. That they demanded to learn skills associated with female activity underscores how politics both flowed through gender expectations and undermined the ground on which those expectations rested. The PGT continued to underestimate their value. For all their importance in the field, Q'eqchi' women never held regional or community leadership positions. Yet the party did help them to slyly critique their depreciation. "Of course," Ofelia said, in reference to their complaints of exclusion, "it is not your fault, *compañeros*, it is the fault of imperialism and capitalism."

Women's involvement in community affairs was not a new thing. Without romanticizing highland indigenous life, or suggesting that there existed parity in the authority men and women exercised over each other, most ethnographies have noted the looseness that governed gender relations in Q'eqchi' societies. Women could for example choose and divorce their partners with relative freedom.[5] They participated in nearly every aspect of the local political economy, picking coffee, sponsoring religious ceremonies, and sharing in the deliberation by which leaders were chosen, even though they themselves were excluded from the higher echelons of community authority.

Yet as government bureaucracy expanded, much of women's activity was either ignored in official record keeping or contained to the domestic sphere. This "modernization of patriarchy," as one historian has described the process of national state formation, created an actual and ideological distinction between the public and the private: actual in the sense that despite their continuing political and economic activities women were legally disempowered and marginalized; ideological in the sense that men's endeavors came to define the normative political and economic realm.[6] Consider the following example: In 1934, the government abolished debt labor and prohibited cash advances to workers, instead putting in place a vagrancy law designed to force those with no property titles or wage employment into plantation work. Erwin Dieseldorff wrote to the minister of government asking for clarification.[7] He wanted to know if women were subject to the new rules; if not, could planters continue to lend them money to secure their labor? Women, he said, were "indispensable" and better "pickers than men"; deprived of their labor, Alta Verapaz would "lose half its harvest." Despite this emphatic plea from one of Guatemala's most productive planters, the minister answered that "under no conditions" were women to be advanced money or to be subject to the vagrancy law. "Women have their own function in the home," he said, "where they fulfill an irreplaceable role supporting the family, and in consequence, society." This projection of a state-defined separation of proper male and female roles not only rhetorically denied the centrality of women's economic activity but, by prohibiting cash advances that allowed women to sponsor religious feasts, limited their access to money and curtailed their influence in community rituals. In a similar manner, the secular civil regulations that came to define municipal administration displaced local administrative practices, and with them women's influence.

Court records, while incomplete, indicate that Q'eqchi' women's engagement with an expanding government was ambiguous and double-edged.[8] Men used the extension of the legal system under Ubico to discipline women, who were frequently brought up on charges of adultery, abortion, or infanticide by husbands, parents, employers, or plantation administrators.[9] In 1963, for example, María Choc Coc, a thirty-year-old daughter of a resident plantation worker in Lanquín who had somehow managed to hide her pregnancy from her parents, went to her father for help after her baby died stillborn. When he cast her out of his house, Choc turned to the plantation's administrator, who promptly had her arrested for infanticide. On a plantation far from the department's administrative center, the law served to reinforce the woman's dependence on family and plantation authority, a dependence underscored by the fact that the accused did not have citizenship papers because "neither her parents nor her ex-husband, who abandoned her a long time ago, bothered to document her."[10]

Yet women who either found avenues of patriarchal redress closed or sought to widen those approaches often turned to the state for protection, initiating legal action against thieves, trespassers, rapists, child abusers, and other transgressors.[11] In 1934, when her husband suddenly died without a will, Dominga Xol from San Juan Chamelco successfully petitioned the court to evict a group of fifty-one Q'eqchi' men who had invaded her property and planted corn.[12] Angela Xoy, forty-four and single, accused two Ladino thieves of stealing her livestock.[13] Candelaria Maquin filed charges against her ex-husband for burning her *huiple* and *corte* (traditional indigenous skirt and blouse) when she refused to have sex with him.[14] Other times women used the courts less for retribution than for vindication. In San Pedro Carchá, María de Jesús Yat went to the police to press charges against her neighbor, who supposedly bit off a piece of her ear. When the police ignored Yat, she obtained a lawyer and demanded that the local court not only arrest her attacker but order the police to explain why they did not act "even though they saw she had only half an ear."[15]

Despite the many instances in which poor Q'eqchi' women and men used the court system, the liberal state, for all of its powerful promise, was woefully inadequate in providing either safety or redress for the majority of Guatemalans. Not only was the legal system corrupt, racist, and strongly tilted toward maintaining class and patriarchal privileges, but it simply did not exist in most rural areas, while a lack of evidence left the majority of conflicts that did find their way to court unresolved. Acquittal of the accused often weakened whatever satisfaction women may have found in receiving a public hearing of their grievances. The court found Candelaria Maquin's ex-husband innocent of burning her clothes. A judge absolved Carlos Paau of beating his wife to death, even though his mother-in-law witnessed the murder.[16] And when women did receive a favorable verdict, at times countervailing social pressures could diminish the effects of liberal jurisprudence. After the court convicted and sentenced her common-law husband for the rape of her thirteen-year-old daughter, María Cristiana Max Pop pardoned him because, according to the case transcript, "it suited her interests."[17]

Born in 1915, coming of age under Ubico, receiving land under Arbenz, and then losing it in 1954, Maquin led an unsettled life that paralleled the expansion of the state with all its benefits and disadvantages. For Maquin, the aborted promise of state-administered justice is perhaps best symbolized in a rather routine bureaucratic task. The two times she applied for her citizenship identity papers *(cédula)* were in Cahabón in January 1954, when she and her husband needed to register in order to participate in the Agrarian Reform, and in Panzós in August 1977, when she needed to reapply in order to facilitate their INTA claim.[18] The first time ended with exile, the second with death.

The second associated difficulty in relating Maquin's life is describing her outrage. Available records suggest that the political passion exhibited by Maquin and other women in the 1970s was not so much a new thing as it was the exposed core of a society split open by repression and rage. In Guatemala as elsewhere during moments of crisis, the institutionalized segregation of the public from the private broke down and women carried out what was often an aggressive defense of their communities.[19] In Panzós, the disruptions of migrant life furthered community secularization. Religious brotherhoods and traditionalists had less influence in settlement communities than they did in Cahabón and Carchá. Yet where the separation of the secular from the sacred in established villages had the effect of disempowering women and rendering their politics invisible, the extremity of daily life in Panzós—the inflammation of political passions, the militarization of local relations, the incompetence and corruption of government agents—worked to make the actions of women like Maquin more public and the women themselves militant and ultimately vulnerable.

It is testimony to the fictive power of the domestication of women that in the memorializing of such crises their politics are denied. On one level, women actively help perpetuate this denial, as repeatedly throughout colonial and

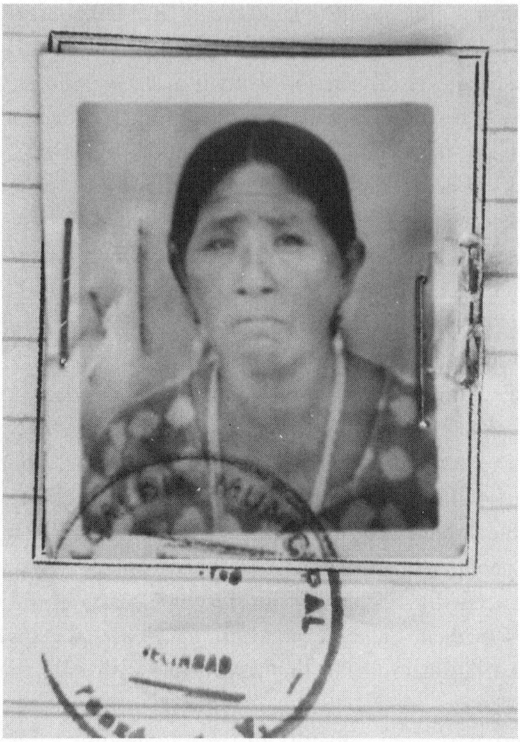

FIGURE 13. Adelina Caal, or Mamá Maquin, in the Panzós civil registry.

republican rule it was a common strategy of the wives of jailed protesters to assume the role of blameless innocents and to beg patrician pardon for the husbands.[20] Yet the suppressed remembrance of women's activism is also related to the containment of that activism. In the Polochic Valley today, with the legalization of the left following the war's 1996 end, there has been something of a patriarchal restoration, with women's participation exceedingly rare in the successor political party to the underground opposition. For men, ongoing partisan engagement serves as a memory bridge helping them to recount with more precision the politics of the past. While memories are shaped by the tragic quietus of the struggle, as well as by the psychological and political needs of the present, continuing activism leavens the stories men tell of the past, providing a textured diversity, accented with narrative details, the very inconsistency of which provides traction for historical inquiries.[21] In contrast, even taking into consideration the probability that women talk less freely to outside inquirers than do men, a fact that is itself directly related to the gendered segregation of the public realm, surviving women seem to have a less direct connection to their more activist pasts. Because they are excluded from current politics, their recollections tend to dilute their own sense of agency, and political commitment fades from their stories. While Inocente Cac continues to participate in left politics, his wife, Manuela Rax, whose father was killed by Jaime Champney, does not. She recounts her past with detachment, with few specifics, despite the fact that many stress her importance in Cahabón's land movement.

The ferocity of repression further removed political engagement from history for both men and women. The horrors of the razing of hundreds of Mayan communities by a national army, along with the failure of the revolutionary project and the inability of the guerrillas to protect their supporters, likewise led many to deny indigenous peasant involvement in the mobilization leading to the 1981–83 genocide.[22] The legal difference between combatants and civilians was meaningless, as state terror made no distinction. Only by claiming "innocence," which in Guatemala meant renouncing all political commitments and emotions, could one hope for salvation. We have seen this once already, when in 1954 Carchá beneficiaries of the Agrarian Reform betrayed not only Alfredo Cucul but their own politics. The need to counter the deeply entrenched penchant on the part of Ladinos to see all indigenous mobilization as innately violent and provocative reinforced this retreat from politics. Throughout the twentieth century, the national press obsessively resurrected colonial fears of machete-wielding rural Indians descending on a town to exact race vengeance.[23]

As an indigenous peasant woman, Mamá Maquin, for over a decade a member of the Communist Party, has become a symbol of this political purity, her name now claimed by a national Mayan women's human rights organization. In most presentations of the Panzós massacre itself, pacific Q'eqchi's humbly assemble to request redress for historic injustices only to be met with an aggressive military response. A fuller rendering of the event is necessary not simply to restore political agency, however that may be defined, but to try to show what was at stake in the conflict and what was destroyed by the repression. The rural civil war in Guatemala was fought to establish land rights, end forced labor, and assure the ability simply to survive. But perhaps the most bitter struggle was over the role of the state in society, definitions of citizenship, and the limits of political participation. In Panzós this fight reached a fever pitch, and it was led by an illiterate Q'eqchi' peasant woman who could not speak Spanish.

The marshy Polochic delta around the area that would become Panzós had served for centuries as a place of refuge and profit, of fleeting booms and dragged-out busts. In the early 1600s, Spaniards settled the short-lived colony of Nueva Sevilla. Two centuries later, the British established the equally ill-fated New Liverpool.[24] As a connection between the Polochic River and Lake Izabal, which opened to the Atlantic market, the area around Panzós during the colony attracted traders, bootleggers, and smugglers who openly flouted royal prohibitions against navigating the Polochic.[25] With little royal or republican authority until the 1860s, the region provided sanctuary for escapees from the Atlantic coast prisons of San Felipe and San Tomás.[26] Starting in the 1860s, Q'eqchi' migrants from the Verapaz highlands settled in the region, hoping to avoid the increasing labor and tax demands of a centralizing state and an expanding coffee economy.

Yet this lowland refuge did not last long, for fast on Q'eqchi' heels came perhaps the most impressively rapacious land rush in Guatemala's history. Most of the lower Polochic Valley, including the area north of Lake Izabal, not only was untitled but had nebulous political status, passing back and forth since independence between the bordering departments of Alta Verapaz and Izabal. Starting in the late 1880s, however, the state began to hand out deeds. By 1915 Ladinos and foreigners had claimed close to 300,000 acres, mostly in 1,550- to 3,100-acre lots.[27] Surveyors moved so quickly through the valley that they measured land in triangles rather than quadrangles so as to save time.[28] As early as 1892, the department's governor complained that wealthy outsiders had gobbled up the best lands, including Panzós's common pastures and woodlands.[29] Nearly overnight, newly established free Q'eqchi' migrant communities became incorporated wholesale into plantation villages.[30] The prefect groused of speculators who promised to cultivate sarsaparilla, rubber, cacao, and mahogany but ran only cattle, which wracked havoc on corn production.[31] Small groups of local Ladinos quickly took over the new municipal governments of Senahú and Panzós.[32] Concentration of land had grown so severe that the official went so far as to call for large estates to be broken up and given to those in need, since, he said, it is well know that "land distributed among a hundred produces more than if it is concentrated in one."[33]

With the rise of Verapaz's coffee economy, the region's importance grew as nearly all of Verapaz's exports passed through the "fluvial port of Panzós," mostly coffee but also pepper and later cardamom.[34] Steamships and barges from the Caribbean plowed through Lake Izabal to its dock. Starting in 1910 a rail line built and run by the German Verapaz Railroad Company climbed the valley twenty-six miles before giving way to a mule road connecting to Cobán.[35] In 1922, United Fruit began production under the name Polochic

FIGURE 14. Panzós, ca. 1860.

Banana Company on the 165,000-acre plantation Las Tinajas. Until Panama disease wiped out its operations in the late 1930s, two thousand workers, including Efraín Reyes Maaz, lived in company houses and shopped in the company's commissary. An odd assortment of international travelers and settlers, along with a contingent of railroad and steamship workers from New Orleans or the Caribbean, gave the town a honky-tonk feel.[36] Crime was high. Small freight boat operators slept anchored in the middle of the river protected from common thieves but vulnerable to mosquitoes. And murder was almost as common as malaria.[37]

The first land rush produced a concentration of property and monopolization of trade and transport in the hands of a few foreign corporations, including the German-owned Verapaz Railroad Company and United Fruit.[38] A second wave of entrepreneurial migrants arrived in the 1930s and 1940s, led by middle-class Ladinos with planter pretensions and German nationals such as Máximo Wohlers and Hugo Droege, who had had their property expropriated during World War II and were looking for a new start. Droege, who had lost his Carchá plantation in 1944, started his "second stage of life" in Panzós as a finca administrator before using his credit connections to buy a new estate.[39]

Flavio Monzón García headed the family most often accused of organizing the 1978 massacre, and it is he who best represents the pathological trajectory of this new class. Born in the highlands in 1910, Monzón moved to Panzós at the age of sixteen, where he worked on the railroad before becoming the town's postmaster in Ubico's expanded mail service.[40] He became a landowner in 1940, when the municipality granted him a modest stake.[41] In 1944 Monzón supported Arévalo and went on to be elected mayor. Perhaps more than elsewhere, provincial middle-class support in Panzós for the October Revolution was driven by a desire to break the stranglehold that large landowners had over local politics and economics.[42] In this case, Monzón represented landowners who had for decades not only complained of the railroad, steamship, and plantation monopolies but chafed at the dictator Ubico's control of local municipal politics.[43] The world depression of the 1930s and the onset of Panama disease, which had forced United Fruit to suspend operations, had already loosened foreign domination of the regional economy.[44] The October Revolution gave local elites a way to finish the job. In 1952, Monzón and his brothers helped organize a number of CALs and peasant unions, successfully working with plantation workers to demand the expropriation of enormous tracts of land held by outside corporations and large local planters.[45] With the 1954 overthrow of Arbenz, however, Monzón turned. Appointed the town's MLN mayor, he helped lead the crusade against his former revolutionary colleagues, calling for, in his words, the "total eradication of Communism from the country's soil."[46]

The fall of Arbenz relieved local planters and ranchers of the burden of reform, allowing them to use their recently restored autonomy to their own ends. After 1954, Monzón served five times as mayor, reinstituting vagrancy laws and public works requirements for those peasant families living and planting on national land.[47] The revival of forced labor resulted in the plummeting of daily wages from sixty cents a day during the "time of Arbenz" to fifteen cents during the "time of Monzón." While in other areas, the overthrow of Arbenz led to the restitution of expropriated land to its original owners, in Panzós much of the property claimed by the Agrarian Reform was nationalized or left in nebulous legal status. This led to a free-for-all. Peasants moved onto uncultivated land and created settlements, while planters used post-1954 land legislation to claim large lots as private property.[48] Shoddy record keeping, inaccurate surveys, disappearing natural boundary markers, and overlapping government concessions aggravated conflicts between competing claims, with the resulting confusion benefiting those who could afford legal services and government bribes.[49] After 1954, United Fruit's Las Tinajas, for example, experienced thirty-two divisions and countless subdivisions, with the rump going to Flavio Monzón.[50] Older Q'eqchi's remember Monzón tricking settlers from one community on Las Tinajas in the early 1960s into affixing their thumbprints onto a document that was supposed to solve their land problem: "Monzón gathered the population together," says Mateo Pop, "and got the *ancianos* [elders] to sign a paper asking for their land. He returned later and said that INTA had made a mistake, that the land appeared in his name and we were kicked off."[51] Walter Overdick, the mayor at the time of the massacre, describes many of the land conflicts that afflicted Panzós as a battle for the valley's flatlands. Every year, he says, "planters pushed peasants further up into the slopes of the Sierra de las Minas."

This land grab left peasants with little room to maneuver. For at least a century starting around the time of the 1865 Carchá protest described in the introduction, the Polochic Valley served as a valve for the pressures of highland coffee production. A permeable and ill-defined frontier allowed Q'eqchi's some leverage in dealing with an expanding state and economy. For example, in the late nineteenth century, peasants who lived in the Cahabón River valley, which separated Alta Verapaz from Izabal, hopscotched from one side of the river to the other, claiming to live in Izabal when agents from Alta Verapaz showed up and vice versa.[52] By the 1960s, this frontier had all but closed. Q'eqchi' families increasingly sought refuge from the labor demands of local planters on the banks of the numerous rivers that crisscrossed the municipality, taking advantage of legislation that set aside as national property a hundred meters on either side of a waterway.[53] But even this recourse came under assault. In 1963, Eusebio Chún Pop, "a poor campesino," wrote Cobán's *El Norte* to complain that since 1954 he and his neighbors had been intimidated by planters to stop cultivating the banks of the Polochic River, which they had been doing since 1944. The sons of Hugo Droege, he complained, even beat him with rifle butts and carried off his corn.[54]

While both peasants and planters turned to the government for help, the state, increasingly reducible to the military, had its own interest in the area. During the last decades of colonial rule, successive governments encouraged migration to the region, offering various tax, seed, and land incentives to settlers.[55] In order to stem contraband and quell the "rumors of indigenous uprisings," the state in 1868 established an artillery battery in Panzós.[56] The rise of coffee and the improvement of rail, road, and river transportation brought the area more directly, if still uneasily, under state control. In the 1930s, Ubico established a permanent military detachment and expanded the national police. By the 1960s, the twinned concerns of commerce and security fused into counterinsurgent developmentalism. The army increased its presence in the valley, which they had identified as an important corridor connecting the eastern lowlands to Verapaz and beyond, to Quiché and the Ixcán.[57] After a few successful incursions by FAR rebels into Panzós in the early 1960s, the military began a program of road building and civic action in the area, using troops to dispense medicine and build schools.[58] At the same time, the government promoted a developmental policy designed to address the causes of subversion and integrate isolated populations and regions into "the march of the nation toward a better future."[59] INTA was part of this journey, as was a slew of other institutions—the Secretaria de Bienestar Social, the Servicio de Fomento Económico Indígena, the Programa de Desarrollo de la Comunidad—aimed to promote colonization, advance credit, provide technological advice and services, improve literacy, and teach Spanish.[60]

Standing at the epicenter of these contending planter, peasant, and military histories was the Panzós community of Soledad, where the Maquins and other families settled after 1954. Located about five kilometers outside the center of Panzós and comprising close to six thousand acres, Soledad is bordered by the Cahabón River to the east, the Polochic River to the south, and a smaller tributary to the west. At the time the Maquins arrived, the land was owned by the nationalized Verapaz Railroad Company, and most of Soledad's new settlers, including Luis Maquin, took jobs with either the railroad or its steamship operations in exchange for the right to live and plant.[61] When the railroad ended operations in 1965, forty families led by Luis Maquin and counseled by FASGUA began to solicit titles, making their first official claim to INTA in 1970.[62] This petition seems to have been a defensive move, for when the train stopped running, outsiders to Soledad began to stake out lots.[63] The forty families in 1973 asked for title for forty-four hundred acres of land, yet by the time INTA approved the concession in June 1975 the size had dropped to a little under three hundred acres, while the number of petitioning families had grown to sixty-six.[64] Despite these hitches, PGT guidance, as in Cahabón at this time, seemed to be successful. Along with the 1975 Soledad concession, that same year INTA provided provisional collective title to 188 families in adjacent Cahaboncito, another FASGUA-advised community.[65]

Success was short-lived. By 1976, Soledad had divided into contending camps. On one side were the Maquins, affiliated with the PGT and representing about twenty-five families. On the other side stood nine families led by Mario Bac Maas and Joaquín González, the head of Panzós's military commissioners and administrator of a nearby plantation. Along with two Ladinos who did not live in Soledad, Raúl Aníbal Ayala and Carlos Aldana Tejada, González and Bac organized a land committee, the Comité de Tierras de la Comunidad de Soledad.[66] Those who opposed the Maquins today say that the main point of conflict was their insistence that INTA grant the land to Soledad for free, a position that did correspond with the PGT's earlier stance in Cahabón. Yet INTA records indicate that Luis Maquin and three of his sons who headed households made the initial 1975 payment of 96 quetzals (equivalent to 96 dollars), the first of what were to be ten yearly installments.[67] The problem was not that they did not want to pay but that many could not. That first year, two other of the Maquins' sons who were on the original list of petitioners were unable to make the down payment. "Despite the effort made it was impossible to raise the money," they wrote, promising to do so when they brought in their October harvest.[68] The following year, more families could not scrape together the 96 quetzals. Yet since the payment to INTA was collective, and the property was granted collectively, González and his allies paid the yearly difference and pushed those families who could not pay, which by 1977 had grown to twenty and included most of the Maquins, to the worst and most sterile land.[69] These PGT-affiliated families demanded that INTA halt their dispossession, lower the yearly payment, and conduct a new survey.[70]

Panzós unlike Cahabón offered peasants who tried to contest such abuses other options besides the PGT. The Partido Revolucionario, Christian Democrats, and even the social democratic Frente Unido de la Revolución, which operated relatively unrestrainedly during the brief political opening of the mid-1970s, organized cooperatives and helped peasants solicit land from INTA. Likewise a Christian Democratic labor federation, the Confederación Nacional de Trabajadores, began to make inroads in the area. Starting in the late 1960s, the PGT, because of the more open nature of the region, developed in Panzós a more traditional clandestine structure than it did in Cahabón. In the early 1960s, FAR rebels counted on Arbencistas throughout the Polochic Valley for material support. After the defeat of the FAR in 1968, Efraín Reyes Maaz helped rebuild this network, which included both peasants and provincial Ladinos who, unlike Monzón and other MLN planters, remained committed to democratic reform.[71]

As it did on the national level, in Panzós the party sought reform through alliances with local political elites. In 1976 it organized its members and sympathizers to vote for the successful Partido Revolutionario–Frente Unido de la Revolución fusion mayoral candidate, Walter Overdick. Overdick, who beat an MLN planter, had democratic sympathies. He volunteered to defend Arbenz in 1954 and along with his brother joined the FAR in the early 1960s. After he was wounded and his brother killed in battle, Walter traveled to Cuba to recover. He returned to Guatemala to take over his father's plantation in Panzós and, believing the armed struggle fruitless, joined the PR. Yet as mayor he could do little but raise unrealizable expectations while serving as a lightning rod for the anger of peasants, who arrived regularly at his office to demand that the "mayor solve their problems." Planter power enjoyed near absolute impunity. A promising but never complying state only helped fuel the crisis. "Every time there is a problem," Overdick complained, "INTA sends surveyors. They stay for two or three days, offer to give the peasants land, but then never return."[72] And his position as a Ladino landlord who employed Q'eqchi' day laborers and resident workers inevitably created antagonism, suspicion, and distance between himself and the PGT's social base.

For many informants, there existed untranslatable differences between how reform-minded Ladinos and Q'eqchi's understood politics and democracy, with Ladinos favoring secular developmentalism and wealth distribution and Q'eqchi's acting on a religiously informed understanding of justice and action. Miguel Lobo, a Ladino shopkeeper who for decades provided first the FAR and then the PGT with provisions, complains today that the protesters lacked "revolutionary consciousness" and that they "confused politics with religion." Worlds of social and cultural distance separated the Maquins from Ladinos such as Lobo, who employed the Maquin sons as day laborers on his small farm. Lobo supported land reform but says that escalating and bewildering Q'eqchi' demands prohibited INTA from doing its job. The Maquins, he says, wanted "to install an Indian king, they said that the land belongs only to God and therefore it should be granted to them free of charge. They dipped their machetes and sticks in chicken blood to give them more power." The air of confrontation that hung over Panzós in the months leading to the massacre undoubtedly sharpened the distinction in the minds of reforming Ladinos between the supposedly messianic and superstitious impulses behind Q'eqchi' mobilization and the worldly, state-centered politics of the PGT. The town's chief of police reportedly lived in fright of Q'eqchi' hexing powers and refused to act on behalf of the planters.[73] While no Q'eqchi' survivor of the massacre explicitly corroborates the supposedly millenarian goals of the protesters—generally described today by Ladinos as a demand for a Mayan king or president or a desire to "cleanse" the town of foreigners—some do admit that there existed a cultural divide. "They didn't like our *costumbre*," one Q'eqchi' woman remembers; "they said it was witchcraft."[74] Others report a similar consecration of the ideas and practices of the PGT that took place in Cahabón. Yet because the land struggle in that municipality was more focused, directed against a core of large planters, and had very little support from local Ladino reformers, the fault lines between secular and sacred politics remained subterranean. In Panzós, the more diffuse nature of the fight, aimed not at a couple of families but at a broad front of ascendant planters, along with the PGT's more sustained attempt to work with local reformers, brought that tension to a head.

FIGURE 15. Military occupation of Panzós (courtesy of Fototeca Guatemala, Cirma [Centro de Investigaciones Regionales de Mesoamérica]).

By 1977, over twenty-three land skirmishes throughout Panzós threatened to turn the town into a war zone.[75] The response time between repression, protest, and reaction accelerated. By November 1977, soldiers stationed in the Panzós garrison were making regular incursions into communities considered troublesome. On a number of occasions, they entered Soledad to harass families who could not make their payments yet refused to vacate their share of the concession. On April 7, 1978, a group of peasants from the community of Cahaboncito nearly beat a municipal agent to death whom they accused of trying to rape a minor.[76] In retaliation, troops arrived in Cahaboncito, kidnapping and torturing those identified as responsible for the beating. When relatives of the arrested traveled to the municipality to demand their release, soldiers fired over their heads.[77] By all accounts, both planters and peasants grew more confrontational. One Ladino witness recalls overhearing a meeting brokered by Overdick between opposing parties in the hope of easing tensions: "I fed your grandfather, I fed your father, and I fed you," stated one planter, to which an unmoved peasant leader supposedly retorted, "No, you exploited my grandfather, you exploited my father, and now you are exploiting me."[78]

On May 3, 1978, less than a month before the massacre, a group of peasants met with Overdick to complain that Flavio Monzón had claimed land that they had been working on the bank of the Polochic. They demanded that

INTA grant them legal ownership and threatened to begin planting with or without titles.[79] As residents of Monzón's plantation San Luis, they were fighting less for land as such than for relief from uncompensated plantation work. Two days later, Monzón along with Raúl Aníbal Ayala and Joaquín González traveled to Cobán to meet with Alta Verapaz's military governor to complain of land invasions and to request the establishment of a permanent detachment of troops to be stationed in Panzós's plaza to protect against growing "concentrations of peasants."[80] That Ayala and González, two of the Ladino protagonists in the Soledad conflict, attended the meeting confirms that that dispute was at the center of tensions in Panzós. The governor granted the request, and on Saturday, May 27, a detachment of about thirty soldiers, armed with Israeli-made Galil assault rifles, bivouacked in Panzós's main plaza.[81] The arrival of the troops set loose pent-up anger, and fights took place throughout the municipality. Soldiers and members of the Monzón family confronted some four hundred peasants on the banks of the Polochic. Monzón reportedly raised a red flag and threatened that its color was that of the "blood that would run" if the peasants persisted in their efforts to plant and title the land. Military commissioners waylaid and beat a group of PGT peasants returning from a meeting in Cahabón.[82] Planters took advantage of the presence of the military to run their cattle over campesino corn, and today indignation is indexed to the height of the stalks—that they were a meter tall is a shared detail in memories of that day. Some say that on that first day the detachment committed a number of rapes in the center of the town, and others claim they detained and tortured a group of peasants.[83] The large number as well as the heinous nature of the crimes attributed to the troops on that Saturday suggests that memory here may be compressing a more dispersed history of violence into a compact overture to the massacre that would occur three days later.

Clearly the PGT influenced events in Panzós. Yet as in Cahabón the party succeeded in cultivating support almost despite itself because it built on social patterns, expectations, and relations that structured and gave meaning to local society. This is especially true for gender relations as the PGT's hierarchical organization melded at first almost seamlessly with the popular patriarchy that marked Q'eqchi' communities. As two of the original settlers of Soledad, Adelina Caal and Luis Maquin, in their sixties, enjoyed significant prestige. The informality of migrant and settler life augmented their standing, opening up channels of community ascension outside of the traditional civil and religious chain of authority that structured more established towns. While cofradías were founded in settler communities, they played less of an entrenched role in conferring authority. Rather it was the struggle for land that became the primary venue of local leadership. In that struggle, the Maquins took leading roles. Luis led the first petition to INTA, and Adelina organized women to support the struggle. As we have seen, the PGT heavily invested in reform politics, in avenues of influence usually dominated by men. Luis Maquin organized the first solicitation to INTA for Soledad titles. His sons led the delegations to complain to the mayor. And his grandson Sebastián traveled to Guatemala City to meet with FASGUA. Yet the party's strategy of working with local male leaders to pursue electoral openings, legal petitions, and political alliances reached a point of diminishing returns and came under violent, sustained assault. This breakdown in turn allowed Q'eqchi' women's activism to become more important and visible. For both sides of the conflict, Adelina Caal, known locally as Mamá Maquin because she was the head of a large family, became the principal protagonist not only in the Soledad land struggle but in a number of conflicts taking place throughout Panzós. The commander of Cobán's military base directly blamed the massacre on her, while Juan Cus remembers that the Maquins "always carried the voice for our communities."[84] "They lived together in a group," says Emilio Ical, a member of one of the Soledad families that opposed the Maquins. "There were twelve of them, twelve *pisados*, bastards. They always worked together to fuck with those who weren't in agreement with them."[85]

To say that PGT influence flowed somewhat easily through Q'eqchi' institutions and values does not mean that community divisions did not exist. Despite its valuation of harmony, the complex set of Q'eqchi' beliefs and practices did not create a balanced, reciprocal polity. Domestic and neighborly violence according to court records was a constituent element of daily life. Planters systematically took advantage of peasant conflict to secure their continued authority. Yet Panzós and other cases suggest that intracommunal schisms are a precondition as much for resistance as for domination. Just as Cahabón's PGT families used their 1973 experience of divisionism, violence, and expulsion to create a more disciplined, unified clandestine structure, Panzós activists fought, sometimes violently through ejections of their own, to maintain party/community discipline. In Soledad on the Saturday the soldiers arrived in the center of town, the Maquins reportedly led a rampage against the families allied with Monzón and González, the military commissioner, setting their corn on fire and driving them out of their homes.[86] One of the dispossessed insists that the Maquin brothers hacked Pedro Cuc to death with a machete, and indeed there is such an entry in the Panzós civil death registry for that day.[87] Refracted through the prism of popular Q'eqchi' notions of justice and unity, such clashes helped activist families define themselves and their fight. They did so both negatively by providing an internal opponent that could help sharpen resolve and positively by creating through struggle a vision of a deserving community. "We won because we had more *xtioxila'* [holiness]," according to Inocente Cac when contrasting PGT communities in Cahabón with those villages that compromised with Champney. In Panzós, the arrival of the troops and their reported crimes were the breaking points of community anger, or at least that part of the community represented by the Maquins. The violent, possibly deadly expulsion of their opponents galvanized not only the outraged but the wavering. Not every family prior to that Saturday took equally militant stances in the land conflict. Roughly twenty-five families could not pay INTA and were dispossessed by about nine families led by Joaquín González. The day's events forced the remaining ten or so families to participate more fully in the coming protest, a participation sanctified the following Sunday evening by a *mayejak*, a ritual ceremony.[88]

After the ejection of the families from Soledad, Adelina Caal's grandson Sebastián Maquin returned from a meeting with FASGUA in Guatemala City with a letter addressed to the mayor announcing the pending arrival of a delegation to discuss peasant complaints.[89] Since the municipality was closed on Sunday, Soledad's remaining families decided to march to the municipal building and collectively present the letter to Overdick on Monday, the twenty-ninth of May.[90]

Survivors of the massacre understandably stressed the pacific goals and manners of the protesters. "We only went peacefully to see the mayor," said one participant to a *Newsweek* reporter; "if we had gone to attack, we would not have taken our women and children."[91] Sebastián Maquin, who led a group of survivors to the capital to provide the first eyewitness accounts to the press, said that they decided to go to the plaza in a group "because we were scared."[92] They saw the troops, about one hundred fifty of them according to Maquin, but did not pay them attention, instead approaching Overdick to hand him the letter. It was then that fifteen soldiers came forward and fired.[93] One witness reported that just before the shots, another soldier yelled, "If it is land you want, land you will have, but in the cemetery."[94] "Maybe they all fired, maybe only a few, I don't know," said Sebastián Maquin, "We only went to ask a favor of the mayor to explain to us what was happening with these lands."[95]

The military and the government immediately accused the protesters, the

Ejército Guerrillero de los Pobres, Fidel Castro, and the Catholic Church, everybody but the PGT.[96] By 1978, the party had become much less of a threat than other movements, as is confirmed by the fact that the state took little interest in publicly blaming it for events leading up to the killing. The army insisted it acted in self-defense, exhibiting a dozen old rifles that the Q'eqchi's supposedly carried and making available to reporters a number of wounded soldiers.[97] Private Pedro González suffered a machete wound to the head and testified that the demonstrators arrived armed with rocks, sticks, and machetes and were yelling that they were going to "do away with the army."[98] Maquin opponents supported the official version. Luis Bac attributed the initial provocation to Adelina Caal. "A woman" leading the protesters, he said, "swung a machete at a soldier, cutting him. The soldiers reacted and began to fire, that is how Mamá Maquin fell, dead."[99] Walter Overdick, who today says the military committed the massacre with premeditation, at the time confirmed the bellicose nature of the crowd, noting that the Q'eqchi's demanded "that positions of authority be held by Indians, and they even demanded that the president of the republic be an Indian."[100]

Yet other, less compromised accounts narrate a political thickness usually expunged from the record of attenuated extremes of absolute aggressiveness or total passivity. Carlos Roberto Pazos, who was in Panzós doing his medical internship, testified that on the morning of the massacre six to seven hundred Q'eqchi's marched to the plaza "inflamed" and "furious," shouting "vivas and slogans, raising their sticks and machetes and demanded a just repartition of land."[101] Representatives came from at least ten of Panzós's far-flung villages, some a few hours' walk from the center of town.[102] Juan Cus, whose father was killed in the massacre, gave the following testimony immediately after the event:

> What really happened is that a few days prior [to the massacre] in the hamlet Soledad two groups of campesinos fought. The brothers Maquin led one group. One of them calmed the conflict down and proposed that we advise *compañeros* from other communities . . . that we should arrive together to demand the land that had been taken from us. My father had returned from San Juan Chamelco Monday morning when a number of campesinos passed our house to bring us to the mayor's office where we would present a note that would resolve the problem. . . . When we arrived in the plaza on the side of the market we saw that other *compañeros* also advised by the Maquins were entering from other directions, but the mayor's office was blocked by soldiers who would not let us pass. [Adelina Caal] pushed a soldier to get through, but he would not let her in. One of the sons jumped in front to protect her, and in reaction the soldier fired, shot, and killed the mother. This enraged us, and when they said that they would not let us in, it is true, we took out our machetes, but by then it was too

late because the soldiers were firing more and more. In the firefight many campesinos that were with their wives and children fell, a great many of them. We ran, and when we arrived at our house only our father was missing.[103]

The process by which accounts of peasant politics become pacified is visible in Cus's testimony. Given just a few days after the killing, it admits emotion and commitment, but almost apologetically, tempered by a carefully crafted sequence of reactive causality: When Caal was shot, it "enraged us." After the soldiers refused to let them pass, they, "it is true," took out their machetes. Cus's own sense of conscious involvement and that of his murdered father are virtually washed away by a wave that sweeps them to the plaza.

The FASGUA letter to Overdick announcing the arrival of a delegation has become the centerpiece of survivors' memories. In a largely illiterate society, the written word comes to represent the state, taking on fetishistic power. It sanctions, mobilizes, and, after mobilizations meet with tragedy, rationalizes. As in past instances of protest and reaction, survivors assume a certain naiveté to both justify and distance themselves from their actions. Today, Cristina Choc, who was present that Saturday, says that the Soledad families decided to present the letter as a collective to Overdick so he could read the missive out loud since they did not understand Spanish. Yet considering that Sebastián Maquin met directly with FASGUA representatives, it is doubtful that the leaders did not know the letter's content. Rather than being mystified by the written word, it seems as if Soledad's leadership turned its power to their own ends, to turn out their followers. Juan Cus, in the testimony cited above, said that he was told that the letter would redress their demands, while Carmelina Pop told a reporter that she was told to go to Panzós where they were going to "read a piece of paper."[104]

Accounts from the time reported that the protesters carried their machetes, but that was "common" for peasants, and if "we had gone to attack, we would not have taken our women and children."[105] Yet other sympathetic witnesses recalled that women were not "taken" to the plaza but actually led the column of demonstrators. The mood according to a few survivors was one of anger and agitation but also somewhat "*alegre*" (happy).[106] While the military's insistence that Q'eqchi's carried rifles was a complete fabrication, many did carry sharpened sticks—an already established practice that earned some of the more confrontational communities the epithet "*paleros*."[107] A number of those who either participated or uneasily stood on the sidelines reported that on the way to the plaza, well before any provocation by the soldiers, men banged their machetes together to produce a "fine, high-pitched ringing," a practice that greatly unnerved their opponents.[108] Another witness testified that the protesters "raised their machetes and clubs, making them buzz incessantly."[109] One witness said that women carried "chili, salt, and limestone they were going to throw in the soldiers' eyes."[110] The marchers chanted a number of slogans suggesting that land was not the only issue on their minds. Overdick still insists that they called for indigenous municipal authorities and an "Indian president." Other participants today remember that they demanded that the army withdraw and stop its violence. "The Maquins arrived in the plaza thinking that they were going to *hacer justicia* [do justice]," says Emilio Ical, who blames the protesters for the massacre; "they thought that they were going to kick out the army." The march itself, like many episodes of indigenous protest before it, notwithstanding whatever goals it hoped to achieve, symbolically, briefly, overturned the marginality, subservience, and repression that were the daily life of most Q'eqchi' campesinos. Spurred by an intensification of repression and emboldened by their liberation of Soledad on Saturday, not only did the marchers take over the plaza but their ringing machetes decolonized sound, penetrating the shut doors and windows of Ladinos.

"Solid, frenzied gunfire," as Marlise Simons in the *Washington Post* reported, probably lasted less than a minute, but survivors remembered a more sustained assault.[111] Some insisted that the military threw hand grenades into the crowd, while others claimed planters joined in the shooting, singling out children and women.[112] Protesters fled terrified, many into the Polochic River where some drowned, others back to their communities or into the mountains where many died. According to Miguel Lobo, a military helicopter fired on a boat of protesters fleeing down the Polochic, killing twenty-five. During the days following the massacre, a large number of Q'eqchi's came into Lobo's dry goods store to purchase black plastic sheets to use as shrouds for those who had escaped the plaza but died later of wounds. Panzós's civil registry lists three times as many deaths that June of snake bites and respiratory infections than had occurred the previous June,[113] indicating that many died taking refuge in the surrounding mountains. Later on in the afternoon of the massacre, the military placed thirty-four corpses—twenty-five men and nine women between the ages of six and seventy-nine, the majority between nineteen and twenty-nine—in the back of a truck and brought them to just outside Panzós's general cemetery, where they were placed in a common grave.[114] Unlike the mass burials that would occur three years later, the interment was not a clandestine affair. Mourners placed a makeshift wooden cross over the site, replaced a few months later with a crucifix made of train rails. When

FIGURE 16. Hauling away the dead.

forensic anthropologists exhumed the grave in 1997, they found the remains lying neatly, placed with some respect. The afternoon of the killing, Walter Overdick recorded twenty-four deaths, marked only with XXX.[115] Over the entry of the twenty-fourth someone later added the name Adelina Caal.

Despite this attempt to render a more complicated description of events leading to the Panzós massacre, accusations of premeditation and conspiracy should not be readily dismissed. It is commonly believed that Monzón bribed the military to move into the plaza. Efraín Reyes Maaz still insists that the planter paid the army 25,000 quetzals to do away with peasant activists.[116] One report cites witnesses claiming that Monzón organized a meeting on the day before the massacre between planters and the military and that he ordered a large grave to be excavated in preparation for the killing to come. Others place the planter at the center of Monday morning's events in a military jeep directing operations. Sebastián Maquin told reporters that Monzón bragged that he had direct orders from the president to "do away with all the *indios* who are fucking with the land."[117] Walter Overdick today agrees that there was a conspiracy to act.[118] Planters did request the help of the military to confront peasants, he says, but doubts that money changed hands. Like Edgar Champney, Overdick suggests that it was a convergence of interests and affinities that brought the soldiers to Panzós that Saturday. The military's chief of staff, Arturo de la Cruz, who arrived by helicopter thirty minutes after the killings, was an MLN member from Alta Verapaz and had "spent his youth with the Monzóns" and other valley planters. In the plaza that morning there occurred a "confrontation of two brute forces, but the army did not shoot first and the peasants were not armed." According to the mayor, after a brief scuffle the initial tension calmed down. But then Flavio Monzón's son, a municipal councilman allied with the planters, and Joaquín González fired their guns. The noise caused the crowd to surge forward into the edgy and scared soldiers. Miguel Lobo today insists that soldiers aimed at specific leaders, intentionally firing directly into Adelina Caal's face. This targeting, if it in fact did occur, perhaps explains why young men were the majority killed, even though by many accounts women led the march. That the troops were not from the local garrison and that de la Cruz arrived at the scene in short order are all, for Overdick, further evidence that the massacre was intended.[119]

Ultimately, however, the importance of the Panzós massacre resides not in the intention of individual actors, however vile, battered, or belligerent they may have been. The killings marked a watershed in Guatemala's war, an overdetermined moment of cause and effect. Perhaps no other event had such far-reaching political and symbolic consequences, consequences that rang

FIGURE 17. Burial site.

FIGURE 18. Exhumation of remains, 1997 (photo by Marlon García).

through all levels of society—the left, unions, indigenous movements, the insurgency, the Church, the military, and the state.

Unlike the massacres that were soon to come, Panzós was not denied. Despite the best efforts of the military to cordon off the area, stories in the national and international press quickly circulated. Six survivors, including Sebastián Maquin, fled Panzós by canoe down the Polochic and across Lake Izabal. They arrived at FASGUA's office in Guatemala City just as a number of young PGT members were planning a protest march to commemorate the murder of Mario López Larrave, a labor lawyer murdered on June 8 the previous year. The presence of the six Q'eqchi's in the capital visiting the offices of unions, political parties, the Church, and major newspapers brought together the diverse urban left, which organized a quick demonstration three days after the massacre.[120] A week later eighty thousand protesters overwhelmed the memorial march for López Larrave, turning it into a more immediate protest for justice in Panzós.[121] The demonstrations following the Panzós massacre were an important step toward open rebellion. For the first time since 1954, protesters publicly accused the state of assassination and genocide. Marchers carried placards accusing the government, Flavio Monzón, and the army of being "assassins of the peasantry" and demanded that they "return the land you robbed from the Indians."[122] According to one newspaper report, peasants from thirty-nine municipalities were present, including one hundred Q'eqchi's from Panzós.[123] Unions, religious and professional groups, and university associations—almost every existing social organization—published paid ads denouncing the crime.[124] The Catholic Church—itself torn by competing left and right factions—issued its most damning condemnation of the government until that point, demanding an "integral, just, and equitable agrarian policy." Led by Oliverio Castañeda de León, the university's student association conducted its own investigation and insisted on an exhumation of the graves.[125] Criticism against the government was unrelenting.

In the national Congress, the massacre sparked three months of debate and calls for reform, even agrarian reform.[126] Representatives revisited at length Guatemala's long history of land expropriation. The delegate from the department of Quiché linked that history to more immediate concerns of rising political violence against his indigenous constituents.[127] Others quoted John Kennedy's warning that those "who make peaceful revolution impossible will make violent revolution inevitable."[128] Many deputies called for a restructuring of land-titling procedures, INTA, and other government land and credit agencies. Yet the majority of MLN and conservative Christian Democrats blocked any substantive legislation. "Agrarian problems," one congressman recognized, "are as old as human history, as we see in many European countries, the French jacquerie in 1330, the Neuster peasant rebellion in

FIGURE 19. Protest in Guatemala City, June 8, 1978: I.

FIGURE 20. Protest in Guatemala City, June 8, 1978: II.

Germany, as well as in the great rebellions prior to the Mexican Revolution." While he went on to admit that land was the root of these uprisings, he maintained that Guatemala did not have an "institutional framework that would permit an agrarian reform."[129]

As late as 1978, the October Revolution continued to weigh on the minds of Guatemala's political class. MLN congressional deputies yearly called for a moment of silence to honor the 1949 death of Francisco Arana, who was killed while being arrested for his role in a plot to overthrow Arévalo.[130] On the other side of the aisle, Alberto Fuentes Mohr, a social democrat elected in 1977, served as the Revolution's standard-bearer, framing all relevant debate as a choice between despotism and democracy. To the chagrin of his MLN colleagues and the planters they represented, he supported the Sandinistas and condemned Nicaragua's Anastasio Somoza as an "archeological remnant of prewar dictators."[131] Following the Panzós massacre, Fuentes Mohr unsuccessfully attempted to push through forceful reform and strongly criticized colleagues who held out the colonization of the Petén jungle as a panacea for the country's agrarian conflicts.[132] He also insisted on more precise language, on not diluting responsibility in passive vagaries. When the Congress passed a fuzzily worded resolution clearly meant to evade taking a responsible stance, Fuentes Mohr chided his colleagues, saying that "unless I have completely forgotten the grammar I learned in school . . . we are approving a phrase in a resolution that says absolutely nothing."[133]

Less than a year later Fuentes Mohr paid for his precision. Security forces executed him on January 25, 1979. His death was part of a broader campaign of repression against all potential political opposition. Between 1978 and 1981, death squads killed scores of social and Christian democrats, murdered an average of one trade unionist a day, and singled out for elimination university professors and students. This violence was not just directed at present enemies but at past memories, particularly those associated with the 1944 October Revolution. After giving a speech in the main plaza marking the thirty-fourth anniversary of the Revolution, Oliverio Castañeda, the president of the university student association that was investigating the Panzós massacre and working with survivors, was machine-gunned to death in full view of hundreds of spectators and scores of national police.[134]

For the PGT, the Panzós massacre was the effective end. Twelve days after the killings, a more militant faction within the party retaliated and killed nineteen military police in Guatemala City.[135] After a week's debate, the party's central committee repudiated the action and denied responsibility, insisting that justice for Panzós did not mean "indiscriminate revanchist actions."[136] The party split.[137] The more conservative wing retained authority in Alta Verapaz, yet by 1979 its influence on a national level was nil. In Panzós and elsewhere, the PGT's decimated structure was replaced by armed insurgents, most notably the Ejército Guerrillero de los Pobres (EGP), which now included in its ranks Adelina Caal's son and grandson.

For their part, trade unionists active at the time viewed the Panzós massacre not as one more rural massacre but as the culmination of a campaign of violence directed against the efforts of Guatemala's fast-growing Confederación Nacional de Trabajadores (CNT). The CNT started out as a moderate, anti-Communist Christian democrat labor confederation but had grown increasingly combative and had begun to expand into the plantation economy and provincial cities. Between 1974 and 1978 the government of General Kjell Laugerud lessened repression in the city. Yet in the countryside, military violence continued not only in EGP areas but wherever unions or peasant organizations had made inroads. In the Verapaces, the CNT had organized Chixoy dam workers, reestablished unions destroyed in 1954 in Carchá's mines and in Cobán's shoe factory, and was gaining support in rice plantations and a Canadian-owned nickel-mining complex in the Polochic delta. According to a CNT activist, the killing at Panzós was part of a larger repressive drive that *prior* to the massacre had already eliminated the leadership of most of these provincial unions.[138]

Even among the most militant, there existed a good deal of overlap between reform and revolution, with the boundary between the two soft. In her study of the ethos of urban trade unionism, Deborah Levenson argues that despite common affinities, there remained a gap between antireformist, radical workers and the cadres affiliated with the armed insurgency who joined their unions. It may have been "hard to find a procapitalist worker in Guatemala," and many unionists may have welcomed a revolution arriving from the countryside to rescue them from hellish violence, but that did not necessarily mean they thought they were "building a revolution."[139] Yet the Panzós massacre hardened for many the border between reform and revolution. Gabriel Méndez, a labor organizer, remembers that among the leaders of FASGUA the killing accelerated a debate already under way as to the meaning of revolution: "We always projected into the countryside the idea of a revolution, but of a long-term revolution, of a parliamentary revolution. Many continued to believe in democracy, in elections. The massacre was practically a declaration of war, after which the state started its social cleansing. Some used the killings to say, 'see, we told you.' The massacre created a split within FASGUA." Méndez went on to convey the difficult step between debating the meaning of revolution and actually entering into one: "We were asked to join the revolution, but we had legal cases pending, we had open activities. You can't just give them up. I was among those who argued against revolution, that it was not the adequate moment." When asked when he changed his mind, he answers, "When they came to kill me."

For many indigenous activists taking part in the assorted strands of opposition politics, Panzós came to represent a change in the relationship between indigenous communities and the government. By the late 1970s the chronic failure of reform combined with intensifying repression to reach a level of crisis never before experienced. For many leaders, the massacre, itself largely adhering to older patterns of protest and rule, marked this turn, and they seized on it to transform it into something more. Two days after the massacre, on the eve of the first protest, about a thousand indigenous members of the Comité de Unidad Campesina (CUC) filled a religious convent in downtown Guatemala City to attend a mass in honor of the victims. Operating mostly in the western highlands and along the southern coast, the CUC was Guatemala's first national peasant federation organized and led by Mayans. While state terror would soon force the organization to merge with the EGP, in 1978 it was still relatively independent, one important part of a growing social movement that for the first time identified Indians as the subject of oppositional politics.[140] An old indigenous catechist from San Martín Jilotepeque, who had been a member of the PGT and FASGUA, gave the memorial sermon, accusing the government of trying to destroy the decade-long, growing peasant movement. That night a member composed a song, "Las cien flores," enshrining the Panzós massacre in CUC folklore. In the coming years, CUC and EGP activists used events in Panzós as part of their organizing work through the western highlands.[141]

The next day, the CUC issued a press release denouncing the killing, making known its frustration with reform, with the "numerous petitions that are answered only with ridicule by functionaries and repression against leaders."[142] It was later that month that the CUC, through an anonymous spokesman attending a conference at the national university, presented its most eloquent statement:

> We will try to give you a picture . . . of what it is like to be an Indian in this context of repression, exploitation, and discrimination. The Panzós massacre is not an isolated incident. It is one link in a larger chain . . . a continuation of the repression, the dispossession, the exploitation, the annihilation of the Indian, an inhuman situation that began with the Spanish invasion. . . . It is enough to mention the massacres that occurred in the colonial epoch, the slow massacres that took place when they forced Indians and poor Ladinos to work in the coffee fields. It is enough to mention the massacres that have been committed by the right since the fall of Arbenz, the thirty thousand or more dead during the last twenty-five years. . . . Our history has been this, and even more, because there are more that have been forgotten, buried, existing only in the heart.[143]

Using the ordinariness of the massacre to claim its universal resonance, the CUC began to articulate here a vision of national history that would become commonplace for the left in the years following the Panzós massacre but was at the time unique. It was an interpretation that saw colonialism and racism not as how PGT Ladinos saw them—as residues held over from Spanish rule that continued to deform social relations in the countryside—but as the central contradictions of national history, the fundamental conditions of an unbroken chain of exploitation and repression. By emphasizing its routine nature, the CUC used the Panzós massacre rhetorically to link isolated conflicts into a larger national struggle, to "reveal the roots of a system of exploitation . . . that we have been living for four hundred years," and "to do away with that system." By 1980, the CUC had incorporated its support base, in many cases entire communities, into the EGP-directed insurgency.

For the military government, the Panzós massacre signaled the intersection of the two different, yet related, forms of repression discussed in the last chapter: one decentralized, indiscriminate, and often carried out on behalf of economic elites, and the other rationalized, military-directed, and conducted in the name of national stability.

General Kjell Laugerud, who served as president between 1974 and 1978, took advantage of the pacification conducted by his predecessors to pursue a program of modernization that included a hodgepodge of U.S.- and AID-funded cooperatives, road and dam building, an expansion of government development agencies, promotion of mining and oil drilling, and colonization of the northern lowlands. He made peace with the MLN by giving its leadership key government posts, while at the same time trying to undercut its support in the military and rein in the death squads. Laugerud even permitted the formation of a number of social democratic parties and urban and rural unions. This political opening caught the government in a bind. On the one hand, it allowed rural organizing and promoted, through INTA, land reform aimed at "transforming" Guatemala's unproductive agrarian economy. On the other hand, the corruption, intransigence, and avarice of army officials and the ruling class led to increasing violence against the growing oppositional movement. The 1978 massacre not only was an expression of this contradiction between reform and reaction in Panzós but became its symbol on a national level as well.

Criticized by the foreign press, censured by Jimmy Carter's State Department because of increasing human rights violations, faced with a strengthening popular movement and widespread land invasions, and under attack by the MLN for allowing the situation to get out of hand, Laugerud, with one month left in his term, dealt with the fallout from the massacre with a number of contradictory moves.[144] He lashed out at the left, unions, and the Catholic Church, while threatening to jail Flavio Monzón.[145] Within less than a week of the killing, INTA announced it would speed up issuing titles to national land claimed by peasants in the Polochic Valley.[146] At the same time, the president suspended all future land claims, quipping that Guatemala would have to be "three stories high" in order to satisfy them.[147] Inaugurated a month after the massacre, Laugerud's successor, General Romero Lucas García, facing an unprecedented popular movement and a spreading insurgency, let loose the death squads.

Yet at the same time Lucas was ratcheting up the repression, there emerged within the military a cohort of officers who increasingly identified the kind of chaos that led to the Panzós massacre as an obstacle to national security and stability. Since the 1962 coup, the Guatemalan military had evolved from the protectors of the landed class into a vested institution with its own economic and political interests. Both as individuals and as stakeholders in a larger military corporation, officers moved into real estate, industry, and finance, fattening themselves at the trough of development and colonization projects—many of them in and around Panzós—over which they themselves presided. While a number of officials remained MLN stalwarts and sympathetic to the plight of planters, the military as an institution increasingly saw its interests as not always in harmony with those of the landed oligarchy.

This shift was heralded by the events in Panzós. On July 5, Colonel Valerio Cienfuegos, the commander in charge of operations in Panzós, called a meeting of forty-two planters including all those implicated in the massacre to scold them that "the army can't act in favor of one group to the detriment of another." He went on to say that he had knowledge that planters were threatening "their workers with bringing in peasants from other areas." When one of the reproached tried to blame outsiders who "poison" the "little Indians" with "bad ideas," Cienfuegos, who himself made similar statements to the press, cut him off. "The peasants say they are being paid 50 cents a day and you say you pay them 1 quetzals," the colonel rejoined, "but after a detailed investigation we have learned that the peasants are telling the truth."[148] In the years to come, generalized, indiscriminate killing would bring the state almost to the point of collapse, yet already by 1978 young officials disillusioned with the corruption and inefficiency of their superiors had begun to sketch out a more efficient counterinsurgency strategy, one less beholden to the interests of local planters.[149] To be sure, military officers continued to view national security as synonymous with a defense of social hierarchy. At the regional level planters and officers, such as de la Cruz and Monzón, still shared many of the same interests and aspirations. Yet increasingly an ascendant sector of strategists believed security could be achieved only through a centralization of power in the hands of the military, which at times put the army at odds with planter interests.

As it did on a national level, the massacre brought talk, just talk, of reform to Panzós. Local planters, encouraged by Colonel Cienfuegos, organized a "Welfare Committee" charged with "helping the poor, humble peasants."[150] In August, the army brokered a truce in which peasant representatives agreed to halt invasions and planters promised to respect peasant property.[151] The peace did not last long. The Welfare Committee was composed mostly of local planters and headed by Fidel Ponce, who by September was himself accused, as he had been prior to the massacre, of usurping campesino land.[152] And by January 1979, the CNT had issued a number of complaints against landowners who continued to use groups of peasants to displace other peasants.[153]

Troops occupied Panzós for a month, conducting land and air sweeps through the area with a "fine-tooth comb."[154] Cienfuegos said the patrols were necessary in order to deter "Indians who again want to provoke soldiers."[155] Dozens of peasants refused to return to their homes, sealing their doors with mud and taking refuge in the mountains or neighboring towns. Soledad stayed deserted for months until the peasant families opposed to the Maquins, along with newcomers uninvolved in past troubles, moved in.[156] A number of PGT families sought refuge in Cahabón. Eventually, most returned after the military withdrew from the plaza, and a tense semblance of normal life was reestablished.

In the following years, Panzós experienced a pattern of violence different from that of many other mobilized communities. The 1978 killing and the ensuing repression decimated campesino opposition well before the military initiated its 1981 scorched earth campaign, making the widespread massacres that took place elsewhere unnecessary.[157] Planters took advantage of the crisis to drive out bothersome peasants and to reassert control over their workforce. Organized communities such as Cahaboncito, Telemán, Concepción, Río Zarco, and Trece Aguas suffered disappearances and executions.[158] In 1978 Abelino Cuz Mo from Cahaboncito, who along with his family had taken to sleeping in the mountains in order to avoid the military, disappeared after going to bathe in the Polochic.[159] In 1979 Francisco Jalal, a labor activist on the plantation Miramar, killed himself because of constant planter and military persecution.[160] On that same plantation in 1980, military collaborators executed two other activists after they complained of not being paid for their work.[161] In 1981 the army set up a garrison on Monzón's plantation Las Tinajas, where it tortured and disappeared suspected guerrillas and peasant activists until the early 1990s.[162] Between 1978 and 1983, 231 violent deaths were recorded in the Panzós civil registry, many of them by strangulation, gunshot, drowning, and decapitation.[163] Corpses revealed trauma, such as cut jugular veins, broken ribs, contusions, bullet wounds, and burns.[164] Activism continued. The village of Cahaboncito, for example, which used to be organized by the PGT, became an important base of support for the EGP. Yet it was a defensive, clandestine politics, fighting for survival more than transformation. The anger and open mobilization that had gripped Panzós prior to the massacre gave way, for those who dared to continue, to a kind of covert mourning, a continuation of state repression by other means. "My husband died in the plaza," says a survivor, "and then my baby died because I passed my sadness and fear to him through my milk."[165]

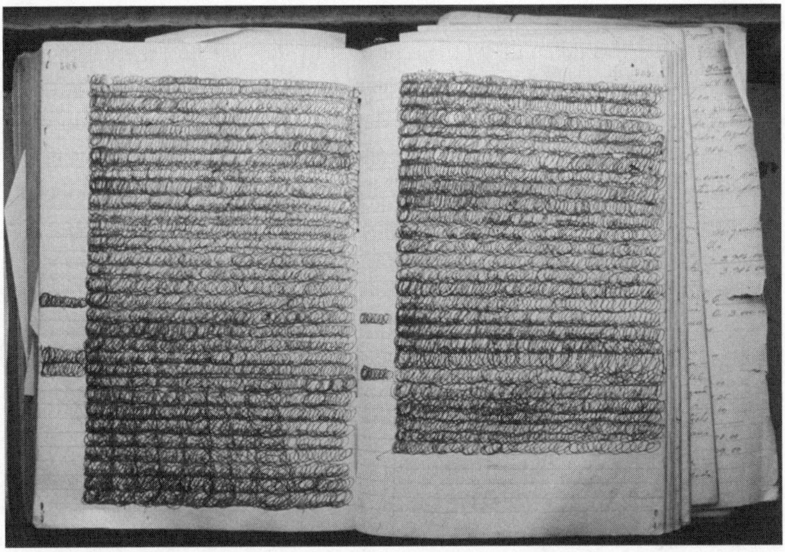

FIGURE 21. Minutes of Panzós municipal council meeting the day after the massacre (photo by Marlon García).

The Panzós massacre galvanized the national left, providing a focal point of unification. The killings further radicalized politics and destroyed the lingering ability on the part of not just the PGT but a range of other parties, organizations, and individuals to work through state institutions. It not only brought together the city and the country but rhetorically merged isolated land conflicts into a single movement with a common enemy. But more than this, the massacre made more explicit the tendency to understand relations of rule and resistance in racial terms. The left-Ladino account of national fulfillment, of which the October Revolution was the measure and the promise, gave way to a more culturally inflected narrative, one that found little to redeem in five centuries of repression and terror. As for the state and the military, the massacre also highlighted an evolving transformation in Guatemala's long history of political repression, marking a breakdown in the counterinsurgent ruling consensus and the immediate emergence of a more chaotic savagery. Death squad executions and disappearances, which had been partially quieted during the quasi-reform government of Laugerud, returned with a literal vengeance. Yet this brief interregnum was not a return to some brutal past but the threshold of an even more violent future. Following the destruction of unions, political parties, and religious and peasant communities, the army in 1981 unleashed in the countryside a more precise but no less bloody genocide.

Adelina Caal—Mamá Maquin—lived the history of the old left, yet it was her death that was taken up by the new, first by the CUC and then in 1990 by an EGP-affiliated refugee women's organization in the camps in southern Mexico that housed Guatemalans fleeing from the military 1981–83 scorched earth campaign. After the genocidal defeat of the revolutionary movement, Caal would be transformed into a virtuous symbol of political innocence, yet immediately following the massacre it was her combativeness, the fact that she fought back, that appealed to CUC activists. The CUC highlighted the ordinariness of the Panzós massacre—"one link in a larger chain"—not to emphasize the fated nature of exploitation but to imagine a new national narrative that would break the cycle of violence. Panzós may have been more of the same, but it would be distinct in that it would be the last of its kind. The CUC was right, but not in the way that it had hoped. Not only did the army decimate the social base and military structure of the guerrillas in its 1981–83 genocide, it transformed the terms of the national debate. While the war would persist for another fourteen years, after 1983 the rhetoric of the left changed. The struggle was no longer a progressive, historically inevitable fight for a more socially just nation—a fulfillment of the expectation offered by the 1944–54 democratic spring. It became a rearguard fight for survival, an attempt to establish the rule of law and respect for basic human rights.

The expansion of the liberal state during the first half of the twentieth century entailed a contradictory strengthening of both private power and public sovereignty. On the one hand, the government devoted nearly all of its expressions to forcing peasants onto coffee plantations. At the same time, rural people increasingly turned to the state to limit planter impunity. This process, however, affected men and women differently.

The development of bureaucratic national societies both defined and confined female activity to specified spheres, greatly circumscribing the ability of women to claim the status of citizen. If men were universal, women were particular. If men were political, women were the bearers of culture. If men were individuals, women were communal. Feminist theorists have approached the construction of such difference in two ways. Liberals tend to treat the disparities, contradictions, and paradoxes of actually existing democracy "as embarrassing, but essentially corrigible, misconceptions" that can be remedied through a progressive extension of equality.[166] Postmodern thinkers, however, contest the very notions of citizenship, equality, and the rights-bearing subject, arguing that the construction of such categories is the root cause of domination.[167] By requiring the "very difference that the idea of the prototypical human individual was meant to deny," the discursive logic that creates supposedly liberating concepts such as equality, citizenship, and political activism at the same time produces their opposite: inequality, exclusion, and disempowerment.[168] Diana Taylor, for one example, draws from this tradition to conclude that the Argentine Mothers of the Plaza, by mobilizing around their identities as mothers and grandmothers to demand the appearance of their relatives disappeared by the military, played into and reinforced a "national fantasy predicated on sexual difference that explains male potency and dominance and the female's lack thereof." Their "very subjectivity was a product of their position in the drama."[169] The violence directed at Q'eqchi' women who violated expected gender roles, as well as the thoroughness with which female revolutionary activity was either suppressed or transformed into an acceptable narrative of chastity, goes far to support a similar conclusion. Yet such approaches tend to be static, offering an all-or-nothing view of politics that too readily dismisses as inconsequential variations in forms of domination. For individuals living under extreme conditions of exploitation, physical violence, forced labor, state-sponsored racism, and sexual repression and exclusion, variations matter. Such readings also often downplay the importance of politics as a realm of human activity, ignoring how within this realm conflicting and competing interpretations of ideals of equality, rights, and justice by those most denied such ideals contribute to their evolution and always faltering, easily reversible fulfillment.

Like others whose lives have been recounted in this history, Adelina Caal was on the frontline of many of the fights that made up the Latin American Cold War. At their most elemental level these conflicts often involved little more than access to land in order to live. Yet like the massacre in which Caal died, such mundane struggles were—to return to the CUC's understanding of the importance of the Panzós killing—"this, and even more." They were fundamentally constitutive of transformations in the experience of citizenship and political participation, the actuality of equality before the law, and the shape and function of the state in society. While it is impossible to know how, exactly, Caal interpreted notions of parity and reciprocity between Q'eqchi's and Ladinos and between men and women, her actions not only contributed to their redefinition but changed history.

CONCLUSION

Children of Abel: The Cold War as Revolution and Counterrevolution

ON ACCEPTING the Nobel Prize for literature in December 1982, Gabriel García Márquez felt he needed to remind his Swedish hosts that in Latin America reality often outran his own celebrated imagination. Since the early 1970s, he said, the continent had "not had a moment's rest":

> There have been five wars and seventeen military coups; there emerged a diabolic dictator who is carrying out in God's name the first Latin American genocide of our time. In the meantime, twenty million Latin American children died before the age of one—more than have been born in Europe since 1970. Those missing because of repression number nearly one hundred and twenty thousand, which is as if no one could account for all the inhabitants of Uppsala. Numerous women arrested while pregnant have given birth in Argentine prisons, yet nobody knows the whereabouts and identity of their children. . . . Because they tried to change this state of things, nearly two hundred thousand women and men have died throughout the continent, and over one hundred thousand have lost their lives in three small and stubborn countries of Central America: Nicaragua, El Salvador and Guatemala. If this had happened in the United States, the corresponding figure would be that of one million six hundred thousand violent deaths in four years. One million people have fled Chile, a country with a tradition of hospitality—that is, ten per cent of its population. Uruguay, a tiny nation of two and a half million inhabitants which considered itself the continent's most civilized country, has lost to exile one out of every five citizens. Since 1979, the civil war in El Salvador has produced almost one refugee every twenty minutes.

In describing this "unbridled reality," he continued, "our crucial problem has been a lack of conventional means to render our lives believable."[1] In fact, the power of García Márquez's writing has been his ability to condense unwieldy, inassimilable truths into manageable historical parables. *One Hundred Years of Solitude*, especially, captures Latin America's sprawling history—from the genesis of conquest and settlement to the rise of nationalism, from the obstinate persistence of social violence to the equally stubborn endurance of religious and secular beliefs in human dignity and the possibility of redemption. The birth and destruction of the fictional town of Macondo, along with the fortunes of the Buendía clan, are an allegory for economic imperialism. The coming of a North American banana company violently thrusts the town into modernity, a modernity signaled not only by the railroad, electric lights, and moving pictures but by ever greater control exercised by the state and the company over the lives of Macondo's inhabitants. Overnight the town is transformed into the plantation's dependent appendage, its inhabitants having lost sovereignty over their lives, even over their memories. The amnesiac quality of Cold War terror—which was aimed not only at repressing political opposition but at obliterating political alternatives as well—is captured in the novel's climax. The beginning of the end of Macondo comes when the national military, in the service of the North American plantation, slaughters three thousand strikers in the town's plaza. The profane fury of modern imperialism is transformed into otherworldly wrath when an interminable whirlwind conjured up by Mr. Brown, the banana company's envoy, washes away not only Macondo but any memory of the massacre. As the storm that would destroy his town gains force, Aureliano, the last Buendía, reads the gypsy prophecy written a century earlier in backward time forecasting the end of his life, his family, and his community. As he skims ahead to read of himself reading of himself, Aureliano realizes that he will soon die and that his history, and the history of Macondo, will be forever "exiled from the memory of men."[2]

Critics have recently taken García Márquez to task for his apocalyptic conclusion, which grants near omnipotent power to foreign economic interests to shape Latin American history. One historian has pointed out that the novel's depiction of the massacre, which was based on a 1928 killing of Colombian workers striking against the United Fruit Company, greatly exaggerates the numbers killed in the real event.[3] Another has stressed that although the story ends with the destruction of Macondo, "in reality the United Fruit Company did not obliterate" Colombia's Magdalena banana zone, the region on which Macondo is based.[4] But the light of these criticisms dims before the fact that *One Hundred Years of Solitude* was published in 1968, that is, before the litany of terror García Márquez recounted in Sweden took place. If it is true that the Magdalena region was neither figuratively nor literally destroyed in an apocalyptic rain, many other Latin American communities, in fact, soon would be. In some way, the gypsy's prophecy, and the novel itself, can be read as a kind of anticipatory truth commission, a revelation of terror to come.

A decade after the publication of *One Hundred Years of Solitude,* the Guatemalan military's massacre in Panzós seems hauntingly familiar.[5] As in Macondo, trains, roads, and a U.S.-owned banana plantation, which even had its own North American administrator named Mr. Shaw, helped bring an uneven capitalist modernity to Panzós. And like García Márquez's fictional town, which was founded by an act of incestuous, *machista* violence that resulted in the birth of a child with a pig's tail, Panzós even has its own bestial origin myth. According to a local chronicler, "Indians still say" that Jorge Yat, who, it is to be recalled, led a Q'eqchi' migration down the Polochic River valley to the lowlands around Panzós after an 1865 highland protest turned deadly, "had a tail, like the devil."[6] News of the killing was not silenced. Panzós was not destroyed. Yet beginning less than four years later hundreds of communities soon were in a quiet genocide, ignored by the national and international media and dishonestly denied by Reagan's State Department.

It would be comforting to believe that the prescience of *One Hundred Years of Solitude* derives from the mantic talents of its author. But García Márquez is no Old Testament prophet. The kind of political repression described in the novel has been a common fact of Latin American life, and its reoccurrence is all too mundanely simple to describe and predict. This testimony from a witness to the days following the Panzós killing is as eloquent as it is obvious: "Every day when I went to work, I dreamed that they were the same bodies that floated down the river. Even though I knew it wasn't possible, it was too awful to believe that each day the river brought new dead."[7] The past keeps intruding on the present, not, however, in the form of repressed memory—even though we would like to convince ourselves that political violence is a thing of the past—but in reality, in the form of new victims.

Along with other post–World War II dissenting writers and intellectuals, García Márquez rendered sensible the senselessness of Latin American political terror. Part of this senselessness derives from the dissonance between the democratic and humanist ideals that run so strong in Latin American history and the felt reality of recurrent political repression. The authority of many Latin American novelists and intellectuals rests in their ability to present an alternative, progressive nationalist history that can explain the latter while affirming the former. Since violence is always present in the founding and preservation of political societies, the trick of nationalism, as Hannah Arendt put it, is to turn that violence into "cogent metaphors or universally applicable tales."[8] Usually, the "violence of foundation"—be it conquest, war of liberation, or revolution—is highlighted, while the "violence of conservation," which maintains that new order, is concealed.[9] García Márquez and other popular writers turned this formulation on its head. They sought to construct competing myth-epic national or continental histories that reveal the continuous, enforcing violence of the state in order to both discredit that state and create the possibility of a new, more genuinely popular, revolutionary identity: "From the ancient cordilleras executioners protruded like bones," wrote Pablo Neruda after he was driven from Chile into exile in 1948, "like American spines on the hirsute back of a genealogy of catastrophes: they were encysted in the misery of our communities."[10]

But this myth rendering of Latin American violence cuts two ways. While it unveils the criminal acts of governments that seem to exist merely to serve the interests of a blessed minority, it also has the danger of portraying Latin Americans as children of Cain, unable to erase their father's mark and unable to escape a land where brutality is bred in the primal bone. (Despite its reputation, Latin America has historically been considerably more peaceful than other comparable regions, including Europe.)[11] Too many observers, including many scholars from across the disciplines, have taken the kind of repetition that allows for García Márquez's foresightedness as fate.

Sociologist Edelberto Torres-Rivas, for example, states that during the 1970s and 1980s Latin America "passed through one of those authoritarian cycles, to which the region appears to be fated, in its oscillating path between democracy and dictatorship. . . . Dictatorships have been a recurrent element in the region, and up until now there is no evidence to suggest that . . . we shall not see them again in the future."[12] As it was in the beginning, so it shall be again.[13] In Guatemala, observers describe victims of the 1981–83 genocide not so much as descendants of Cain but as children of Abel, incapable of escaping the weight of centuries upon centuries of violence. The "most recent brutal period of violence against the Mayas in Guatemala is neither an aberration nor a blip in the historical record," recently wrote one anthropologist: "The dirty war in Guatemala is a piece of a whole that extends from the arrival of the Spanish conquistador Pedro de Alvarado in the early 1500s to the present period."[14] By not historicizing Cold War repression, these scholars naturalize it, evoking an image as close as can be imagined to Walter Benjamin's famous aphorism of a "state of emergency" that is not the "exception but the rule."[15]

THE LATIN AMERICAN COLD WAR AS REVOLUTION AND COUNTERREVOLUTION

The idea of revolution is usually used to describe a circumscribed moment of condensed crisis, unfolding in various definable phases provoked by a sudden, often violent assault on an established, relatively sovereign state and society representing incumbent "elites, status, class relations, institutions, values, symbols and myths."[16] This assault is led by insurgents with mass support and a more or less coherent opposing worldview based on innovation and not restoration. The degree that such a clash breaks and recasts political and social relations and values is the degree that it is a political and social revolution. Yet recently in the wake of Nazism and Stalinism some historians and political thinkers have pushed the concept further to entail not just an exchange of power holders and a rearrangement of class relations but a drive toward utopia.[17] Motivated by a messianic schizophrenia that divides the world between the pure and the impure, revolutionaries of both left and right varieties mobilize the masses in order to create a "new man" or to bleach the blackened soil of the nation clean. One scholar has even gone so far as to argue that genocide is if not synonymous with then at least constitutive of revolution.[18] Yet the history recounted in this book, as well as similar episodes of crisis in twentieth-century Latin America, provide a more grounded view of how ideological hardening and polarization unfold chronologically, a view that refuses to posit radicalism as the cause of radicalization. Instead it forces an appreciation of the catalytic power of political reaction to breed accelerating rhythms of frustration, fear, and extremism.

Historian Arno Mayer, in his comparative history of terror in the French and Russian Revolutions, argues that the militancy that compels political violence takes place on two overlapping and interdependent fields of political and social power.[19] The first is national, where the attack on the established rule—in terms of both political authority and worldview—leaves multiple zones of unstable, fractured sovereignty. This national field is largely mirrored in the rural/urban divide. The fact that the countryside often is actually a formidable bastion of the institutions and mores of the ruling classes is multiplied by the cosmopolitan condescension of urban militants. While resistance to revolution is real and obstacles to reform formidable, insurgents often take the natural resistance engendered by the creation of new forms of legitimacy and centralization to be more coherent than it often is, leading to an ever-intensifying friend-enemy disassociation. Revolutionary contretemps widen schisms, investing every act with political meaning, transforming every event into a provocation, and gaining new adherents to either side.

The second field is the inter-state system. While taking place within the conceptual borders of the nation-state, revolutions are by their very nature international. The universal, ecumenical, and world-historical claims of revolutionaries spill beyond national frontiers and as such pose a threat to the international order's ruling states and classes, a threat often inflamed by fleeing émigrés warning of apocalypse. The contagion is spread by proselytizers of the revolution itself, who are often driven by both idealism and a practical desire to diversify the ideological and political challenge to the inter-state system so as to deflect that system's wrath.[20] These two fields of national and international power feed off each other. Foreign intervention and siege serve as powerful radicalizing agents for not only domestic but international politics as well, quickening the pace of domestic social transformation and the intensity of political militancy, both domestic and foreign.

At the risk of attenuating the above description beyond recognition, I want to say that the Latin American Cold War as a whole represented a protracted revolution, dispersed through time and space yet entailing a coherent and legible logic of insurgency, violence, and transformation. Not only did each of Latin America's twentieth-century revolutions take place in domestic and international arenas simultaneously, each contributed to an accrual of experience and perception that challenged in increasingly focused terms the authority of the United Sates as an ascendant world power. Starting in Mexico and continuing to Nicaragua, successive revolutions functioned as radicalizing transit points where itinerant activists sought sanctuary, applied theory, gained knowledge, and carried the message elsewhere, throughout not just the Americas but the world. They served as workshops to the international left, providing apprenticeships to untold numbers of activists as well as to some of its most notable luminaries, such as India's M. N. Roy and France's Régis Debray. Sequential foreign interventions led by the United States combined with domestic reaction fed this amplification of experience, leading to ever-widening circles of radicalization and militancy. The threat that each revolution posed varied according to its specific economic and geopolitical moment, yet in broad terms the challenge evolved from an effort to fulfill the ideals of democracy and capitalist modernization that many in Latin America saw the United States as representing to an understanding of the United States as not only an impediment to but an active enemy of those ideals. While the Latin American Cold War comprised multiple fronts, each of its four decades produced a representative conflict. In the 1950s, the U.S. overthrow of Arbenz brought the continent's post–World War II democratic opening to a definitive close. In the 1960s, that overthrow reverberated in Cuba, as the CIA sought to duplicate its 1954 success and the revolutionary government maneuvered to avoid Arbenz's mistakes.[21] In the 1970s, Washington's assault on Allende increased after it realized that he would not turn Chile into a Cuban style Soviet satellite.[22] In the bipolar stasis of détente between the United States and the Soviet Union, which gave the United States breathing room as it set about to rebuild a foreign policy wrecked by Vietnam, the threat that *la via chilena* posed was that it provided an example of a popularly elected Marxist government that insisted it was possible to combine democratic pluralism and real socialism. For the United States, this was an unacceptable alternative in an international struggle it increasingly viewed as primarily revolving no longer around an East-West axis but a North-South one.[23] And in the 1980s, following the 1979 Sandinista Revolution, the Reagan administration decided to take what it described as a final stand against world bolshevism in Central America.

THE COLD WAR AS REVOLUTION

Starting with the great Mexican Revolution of 1910, nearly every Latin American nation contributed to a continental cycle of insurgent politics that paralleled during its most intense stage the trajectory of the Cold War, ending with the electoral defeat of the Sandinistas in Nicaragua in 1990. Each country's contribution to this history was distinct: definable revolutions took place in Guatemala in 1944, Bolivia in 1952, Cuba in 1959, Chile in 1970, and Nicaragua in 1979; guerrilla movements occurred in Argentina, Uruguay, and to a lesser extent Venezuela; and full-blown civil wars erupted in Colombia, Peru, El Salvador, and Guatemala. A degree of mimesis fueled this history, as revolutionaries analyzed their own experience, particularly in terms of the national and international obstacles to their goals, in light of the fate of previous revolutions. Yet the lessons drawn from the past did not provide rigid roadmaps but rather evolved to incorporate new values and tactics—guerrilla warfare, peasant mobilization, radical Catholicism, New Left consciousness-raising, anti-Stalinism—and to fit specific national histories. "Cuba will not be Guatemala," Che was fond of repeating to provide historical justification for restricting the political rights of opponents, but Allende and the Sandinistas struggled to prevent Chile and Nicaragua from becoming Cuba. While sympathetic to the Cuban Revolution, they refused in the teeth of overwhelming intimidation by the United States to forsake political pluralism and to fully radicalize the revolutions they presided over. This cycle also refracted world politics. Latin American revolutionaries drew inspiration from and measured themselves against not just the Russian Revolution but the Spanish Civil War, the antifascist popular front, the Chinese Revolution, decolonization movements, Algeria, and Vietnam. "Are we in February 1917 or October 1917?" was the question according to historian Peter Winn at one socialist meeting in Chile in July 1973 on the eve of the coup against Allende.[24]

In some cases, ideology magnified left brutality, as when the Shining Path in the 1980s interpreted Peru's long history of political corruption and compromise through the lens of Maoist purity to execute a vengeful, clarifying violence.[25] Yet on the whole, ideology in Latin America moderated the left's reaction to political frustration and state terror. The Popular Unity coalition, writes Winn, consciously debated its response to escalating counterrevolutionary violence in the light of historical antecedents provided by a larger international radical history.[26] Influenced by Chile's deep democratic tradition, the leadership deliberately refused to launch a *levée en masse,* pursue Soviet terror, or embark on Guevarist armed struggle, instead modeling itself on the antifascist popular front struggle of World War II. Nicaragua's Sandinistas for the most part rejected repressive revolutionary justice, instead attempting to articulate a new radical Christian ethos of forgiveness based on the prominent role that liberation theology played in their movement. And as we have seen in the case of Guatemala, the PGT after the overthrow of Arbenz fashioned its actions more on the Spanish Communist Party's peaceful resistance to Franco than on Cuba. Apart from the Shining Path, the two most violent manifestations of the left are decidedly nonideological. Colombia's Fuerzas Armadas Revolucionarias is bereft of ideas and instead wages a low-intensity war over resources. And while ruthless against perceived opponents, the Cuban Revolution through the course of nearly five decades has not resorted to cyclical purges and terror spectacles to justify its endurance. Unlike other mobilized regimes, the Revolution has not devoured its own. Considering the repression it suffered throughout the twentieth century, the Latin American left on the whole responded with extraordinary restraint, almost in inverse proportion to the torment inflicted on it by the state, domestic elites, and the United States.

Revolutions are distinguished by their most contingent conjunctures, moments of perceived historical openness the resolution of which is often used to account for the outcome of specific revolutionary histories. In Latin America, the immediate post–World War II period, as sketched out in the introduction, could be considered one such instance, representing a highpoint of mobilization and interclass oppositional alliances and kicking off nearly a half century of turbulence.[27] The years 1944 to 1946 witnessed widespread social democratic reform throughout the continent. Between 1946 and 1948 there was a successful elite counterthrust (which Guatemala barely escaped). The relative importance of these conjunctures differs greatly according to country, yet many could trace the most visible origins of their ensuing crises to this period. Notwithstanding important differences in social structure, the content and manifestation of popular politics, and the ferocity of elite reaction, Argentina, Chile, Brazil, Uruguay, and El Salvador fit best the pattern I have described for Guatemala. Each country suffered prolonged periods of counterinsurgent dictatorship aimed to crush an increasingly radicalized mass movement. Colombia and Peru experienced the Cold War in more chaotic terms, yet each witnessed at the end of World War II a truncated democratic opening that influenced the successive political history of each country.[28] Costa Rica and Venezuela bucked the continental trend and solidified, at least for a time, relatively stable welfare states, yet both countries could trace the immediate roots of their democracies to the postwar period. Mexico, Nicaragua, Cuba, and Bolivia achieved social revolutions with different chronologies yet nonetheless similar sharp arcs of mobilization and reaction.[29] Mexico managed to establish a legitimate revolutionary nationalism and consolidate an absorbent clientalist state because its revolution took place prior to the Cold War, with its more radical reforms being carried out during the Depression when U.S. attentions were turned inward.[30] But even Mexico experienced the swings of postwar democratic expansion and containment, including a wave of strikes led by the Marxist Vicente Lombardo Toledano, a rapid reaction on the part of the state in the form of a curtailment of the labor movement and a clampdown on independent, potentially mass political parties, and increased and enhanced government repression.

Throughout Latin America, mid-century oscillations between democratic promise and reaction not only radicalized actors but polarized the political field, accelerating confrontation. In Guatemala, as we have seen both with the 1966 murder of Leonardo Castillo Flores and the 1978 Panzós massacre, frustrated reform militarized not just individuals but successive generations. In Rabinal, for another example, a town in Baja Verapaz that in 1982 suffered over twenty massacres, the experience of mobilization during the October Revolution led a number of young Achí-Mayans first to join the FAR in the early 1960s and then to form part of the rebel group that would become the Ejército Guerrillero de los Pobres.[31] On the western side of the highlands, in the K'iche'-Mayan town of Cantel, David Ordóñez Colop, as head of the local peasant union, successfully obtained under the aegis of the 1952 Agrarian Reform the return to the municipality of over a thousand acres seized in 1884 by a Ladino town. An Arevalista in 1944 and an Arbencista in 1950, in 1967 he successfully led the town in stopping the army from building a base on a site considered sacred, foreshadowing the Mayan cultural rights activism that would occur much later. In 1982 as an old man he was one of the leaders of a successful fight to reject the military's attempt to establish a civil patrol.[32] Security forces captured and tortured Ordóñez in 1981 and executed him in 1984. Ordóñez never joined the guerrillas, but his sons did: "I am a *revolucionario histórico,*" he would say to his impatient sons, while they regret that he "never understood the armed struggle, the struggle of the masses."[33]

Yet more than just composing variations on a theme of mobilization and reaction, the post–World War II period represented a generalized insurgent threat to Latin America's ruling classes. Latin American labor historians writing in the 1960s and 1970s tended to judge this period as a failure, highlighting the taming of mass movements through their "incorporation" into populist or social welfare projects.[34] Viewing rank-and-file aspirations through the lens of dependency theory, these scholars downplayed the importance that claims to citizenship and national inclusion had for peasants and workers. In many studies, the state was the enemy, and appeals for citizenship rights were portrayed as all but unintelligible to the great mass of the disenfranchised and the marginalized.[35] A post–New Left generation of scholars, however, while not necessarily denying the pessimistic conclusions of their predecessors, has instead insisted on the resonance that liberalism, nationalism, and democracy had in the lives of working-class and peasant families.[36] Worlds of political and experiential differences separated, say, Argentine Peronism from Colombian left-liberalism, or Bolivia's indigenous peasant movement from Chile's socialist labor unions. Yet recent scholars all share strikingly similar opinions.[37] Daniel James writes that Peronism represented not just higher wages but a "political vision which entailed an expanded notion of the meaning of citizenship" and "a denial of the elite's social and cultural pretensions."[38] John Green argues for a reassessment of the strength of the postwar Colombian left and for the inclusion within that left of Jorge Eliécer Gaitán's liberal populism, which posed a clear danger to "Colombia's oligarchic democracy."[39] Brooke Larson notes that after Bolivia's Chaco War in 1935, a regional indigenous peasant movement demanding education began to connect with a national left, linking calls for land restitution to a broader "project of popular citizenship and democracy, labor rights and economic justice."[40]

Most Latin American countries on the eve of World War II were deeply undemocratic, and not just in terms of suffrage rights. While the spread of capitalism and the extension of bureaucratic states are often identified as requisites for political liberalization, in Latin America this was not the case. A majority of the region's nations beginning in the late nineteenth century did come to be ruled by modernizing, often professedly liberal elites, yet the states and societies they presided over were in practice anything but liberal. In many countries, republican governments resurrected a range of colonial coercive mechanisms, from debt peonage and vagrancy laws to government-organized labor drafts, in order to secure workers for agricultural commodity production.[41] Forced labor, in one form or another, continued to prevail throughout much of the countryside well into the twentieth century. Intensified forms of racism, in some ways more poisonous than colonial blood strictures, both justified these practices and provided the foundations for exclusionary nationalisms. The rise of bureaucratic governments, far from freeing women from restrictive patriarchies, deployed new civil codes and ideologies of citizenship that both legally affirmed and perpetuated the "social superiority of elite males."[42] With the exceptions of Mexico and Argentina, the landed class, along with Catholic hierarchs and the military, dominated national and regional politics. Their values suffused national cultures, cultures of order, deference, patriarchal allegiance, and praetorian virtue.

A new rural and urban proletariat, along with an increasingly dispossessed or otherwise threatened peasantry, entered the public arena with a vengeance, providing the reformist, radical, and populist political parties that tested this order with direct, participatory support.[43] While experienced differently according to gender, class, ethnicity, and region, these new political actors shared a powerfully ambiguous, dialectical relationship to their modern world. Many retained if not firsthand experience then at least second- or third-generation memories of what it meant to exist in a community that was not as commodified or bureaucratized as the one they lived in, of local, spiritual, and community-based ethics, of social relations not necessarily routed through the state or through the market. This relatively late commodification and bureaucratization, at least in relation to Europe and the United States, also meant that many participants in Latin America's mid-century mobilization personally suffered the traumatic violence, the "blood and fire," needed to break up community land and force peasants into a labor market, as Jeffrey Gould has demonstrated in Nicaragua and El Salvador and I have tried to show for Guatemala. Yet at the same time, an ever greater number turned to the government, including its rhetoric of democratic equality and justice, for help in meliorating the often brutal effects of capitalism, even though paradoxically the coercive labor and loss of access to subsistence production were in fact made possible only by government intervention. The idea of the state as both an oppression and an emancipation had deep roots in society, the first notion drawn from the experience of steadily increasing tax and labor demands, land loss, conscription, and subjugation, and the second from diverse currents of Catholic humanism, liberal nationalism, local norms of justice, socialism, and conservative defense of collective privileges.

Visions and programs of modernity and national fulfillment, a central preoccupation of Latin American elites, became socialized, democratized, and diversified. While at the time, the theoretical distinctions in Peru between, for example, the Marxist José Carlos Mariátegui and the populist Víctor Raúl Haya de la Torre undoubtedly mattered a great deal, today it is their similarities, especially their insistence that development would come about through an extension of democratic empowerment to the most excluded and their promotion of a national and continental identity that reconciled elements they identified as modern and premodern, that are historically most important. Their grappling with the disjunctures of the modern world, with the expectation of equality and the realities of difference, allowed the politics of philosopher-organizers as dissimilar as Haya and Mariátegui to gain traction, to connect with popular classes, and to promote a vision of development and democracy based on enfranchisement and direct action. The extremity and unstable dynamism of Latin America's capitalist development—simultaneously experienced as both crisis and expansion—led Latin America to produce throughout the twentieth century some of the world's greatest modernist productions, including José Martí's political writings, Rubén Darío's *Azul,* Octavio Paz's *Labyrinth of Solitude,* the work of the Mexican muralists, and Gabriel García Márquez's *One Hundred Years of Solitude.*[44] The very uncertainty as to the best direction to take that invested these novels, meditations, paintings, and poems with their restive spirit also gave life to the concept of revolution, as intellectuals and politicians came together over the need to overthrow the old rural oligarchies yet divided over the nature of the society that would result. Democratic-capitalist? Anti-imperialist? Socialist? Rather than leading to political dissipation, such debates, passionately fought throughout much of the twentieth century, worked to make the revolutionary idea tangible and, in many cases, real.

Perhaps most importantly, the political movements that defined the midcentury represented a unique conjuncture in the relational development of the self to society. Mass politics helped constitute among many of the most marginal a sharpened sense of political agency, integrity, and consequence. Such an assertion flies in the face of much contemporary political thought. At least since the atrocities of Nazism and Stalinism, but even earlier, political theorists have mostly defined the relationship of the individual to mass society and mobilization in negative terms. The dislocations of modernity brought about a profound sense of "homelessness on an unprecedented scale, rootlessness to an unprecedented depth," that left human beings lost, at best to the crowd, at worst to the Party.[45] In the postwar years, this critique became the foundational premise that joined together as twins Communism and fascism, opposing both as enemies to the individual that is liberalism's centerpiece. For early Cold War warriors, many themselves former Communists, the worst thing about Communism was not the loss of life but the loss of self, the subjugation of individual thought to an all-enveloping and unquestioned system of belief and behavior.[46] Totalitarianism came to be defined as the unmediated relationship between a mass of humans and the state, and much ensuing political theorizing has been aimed at deflecting people's attention away from the government as a site of personal fulfillment and toward civil institutions and faiths that could provide both spiritual nourishment and protection from the predations of a perpetually expanding bureaucracy.

Yet the history of democracy in Latin America in the twentieth century offers a less pessimistic account of the relationship of the individual to mass movements. It was through political action most often associated with the left, including the Marxist left, that many of Latin America's most disenfranchised, from rural communities, plantations, and factory floors, found a way to negotiate and psychically stem, at least partially, the disruptions caused by capitalism. Rather than eliminating the boundaries between self and society, collective action distilled for many a more potent understanding of themselves as politically consequential individuals. Such insurgent individuality, I argue, was fundamentally necessary to the advancement of democracy, to the end of forced labor, and to the weakening of other forms of exploitation and domination.[47] But this sense of agency was defined neither by radical autonomy nor by isolated freedom: rather, collective action laid bare the social foundations of the self.

Most historians of Latin America date the spread of individuation to the late eighteenth century, focusing on the political, economic, and cultural transformations brought about by the modernizing Spanish Bourbon court.[48] The extension of commodity exchange and wage labor allowed the possibility of survival outside of the productive and reproductive relations of family and community. The evolution of bureaucratic states fragmented human behavior into separate spheres and defined the category of individual autonomy. A growing emphasis within Catholic doctrine on pious self-discipline, as Pamela Voekel has argued for Mexico, helped "generate the individual at the heart of the Bourbon assault on corporate privileges."[49] Yet while the rise of capitalism and secular states made possible an identity defined apart from family, community, and religion, it was at the same time fortifying throughout Latin America hierarchical and collective forms of exploitation and domination.[50] Starting in the late nineteenth century, the acceleration of export commodity production reactivated and intensified colonial practices of coercive, non-market-based labor recruitment. In Nicaragua, coffee brought about the solidification of seigniorial relations in the countryside. In Guatemala, as we have seen, liberal contract law, applied en masse, far from obscuring the social relations of exploitation, confirmed them, as did collective, miserably compensated corvées, vagrancy laws, and debt peonage targeted primarily at indigenous peasants. Much more than an automatic reflex of capitalism or modern state formation, the insurgent individuality that threatened this system was deeply rooted in the institutions and experiences of mass radical politics.

All the lives depicted in this book existed in tension between an extending political horizon and local struggles, cultures, conflicts, and identities. Starting in the mid-nineteenth century, at different speeds depending on region, the rapid spread of a plantation economy roiled villages and peoples, leading in some areas to migration and the formation of new communities, and in other places to a reconfiguration of the ways individuals related to each other and to the state. Politics both further opened up prospects and helped individuals situate themselves within this broadening vista. It did so through institutions, by creating the parties, unions, and legislation, such as the Agrarian Reform, that allowed activists like José Angel Icó, Alfredo Cucul, Efraín Reyes Maaz, and Adelina Caal to link their local aspirations to larger national movements. And it did so through ideas. Marxism, as a theory of how to understand and act in the world, gave inhabitants in what was one of the most subjugated regions not only in Guatemala but arguably in Latin America a means to insist on their consequence. It was Marxism that helped Reyes Maaz develop his capacities as a critical thinker, to bridge the ruptures caused by plantation work, imperialist intervention, exile, and clandestine life. Marxist politics and ideas aided Q'eqchi' women in breaking through the diffuse anonymity in which their lives were often enveloped, not only by society in general but also specifically by their Ladino organizers, so that female PGT members could insist that their "heads" could be used more effectively, that they were willing to give their lives to the struggle, and that they could do more than throw a "handful of beans into water." This extraordinary assertion of political agency comes into even sharper relief considering not only that their names were unknown (necessarily so considering the repression) and that their urban Ladino organizer was not sure if they were members of the party proper or its youth group, but that such self-determination was voiced at the fulcrum of the most vicious and destructive counterinsurgent terror in the Americas. That the women blamed their depreciation not on Ladino racism and sexism but on "imperialism and capitalism" underscores how left politics provided those triply subordinated by gender, ethnicity, and class a framework to define their experiences within an enlarging world. In fact, it seems that the very clandestine fragmentation demanded of many of the subjects of this book in order to survive an increasingly repressive state—Icó's permutations of his surname to escape the compilation of a legal record, Reyes's multiple noms de guerre, or the ornate Spanish pseudonyms of the Q'eqchi' female party members—was inversely indexed to self-definition. But perhaps the most extraordinary, and inexplicable, instance suggesting the connection between personal resolve, a key element of individuality by any standard, and politics is that Icó apparently willed himself to live long enough to see Arbenz elected, dying the day after victory was confirmed.[51]

Guatemala was not unique. Most of Latin America's testimonial literature, for example, likewise conveys how politics helped define people's self-understanding.[52] In Argentina, María Roldán, the first female shop steward in the city of Berriso's Swift meatpacking plant and a lifelong Peronista labor activist, recounts how when she was a child, well before Peron, politics literally captured her roving imagination and provided her a forge in which she could cast her life: "I was a young girl who liked to roam. I was very predisposed to curiosity as a kid, to know what was going on here and there, where there was a political meeting, for example, there I would be, listening. I remember May first meetings commemorating all the blood spilt in Chicago, the taking of the Bastille when men, women, and children fought for their freedom, which is the most important thing in life; without liberty why should we live? . . . for me to stay shut up with a needle, sewing and hemming and things like that, was a waste of time, I thought that you had to go beyond that and do other things."[53] In Brazil, Chico Mendes, an early member of the Workers Party and martyred environmentalist, describes how in 1962 an old Communist who participated in the revolutionary politics of the 1920s gave him a political education and taught him how to read by poring over months-old newspapers.[54]

Yet while politics allowed many to "do other things," their expanding identity remained rooted to, and drew its formidable strength and definition from, social solidarity. As PGT founder Huberto Alvarado put it in his treatise on Walt Whitman, "to be universal, one has to be from somewhere." As we saw throughout this work, increasing appeals to abstract individual rights were always defined in relation to more encumbered social and cultural identities. The mutually reinforcing relationship between individual leaders and their communities also materialized by means of the social relations and hierarchies through which oppositional politics took place. While Icó's freedom from family allowed him to deal effectively with new and expanding government institutions, it was his ongoing capacity to mobilize his followers through community structures and expectations of reciprocity that reinforced those dealings with social power. An ability to live in two worlds—as a nascent liberal subject and as a local patriarch (although unmarried and fatherless!)—fueled Icó's political energy. Likewise, Reyes was able to survive because he had access to a number of households maintained by women that provided him with both cover and nourishment. These networks, hierarchies, and values did not compose an autonomous or more culturally authentic arena of subaltern politics.[55] Instead, they overlapped with and were shaped by the larger society in which they were located. The Ladino activist Francisco Curley, for example, marshaled indigenous peasants on behalf of the Agrarian Reform through patronage relations that not only mirrored the system that he contested but were often no less abusive. And Adelina Caal and other PGT Q'eqchi' women carried out their organizing within a gendered division of activity that was if not created then at least institutionalized by a modernizing state.

Latin America's old left, defined in the most generous terms possible to include multiple, at times rivalrous, mass movements and their associate political parties, bridged the fault lines of modernity, linking nation and world, community and state, and self and society. It comprised remarkably diverse alliances, bringing together at different moments intellectuals, elite politicians, workers, and peasants, producing a richly synthetic political culture that allowed its component parts to press their diverse interests and visions of a just society. It is only by acknowledging the power that post–World War II democratic politics had in providing an alternative to the disruptive antinomies generated by capitalism and state formation that we can appreciate the intensity of the state terror that spread throughout Latin America starting in the late 1960s.

THE COLD WAR AS COUNTERREVOLUTION

The Latin American counterrevolution, at least at first, had a less punctuated and more graduated progress than did its more historically conscious counterpart, revolution. To be sure, more than a few national and international agents of containment understood themselves within a larger world-historical continuum. Repression against the left was measured against comparable acts of violence in Europe. Argentina's ruling class equated 1919's Semana Trágica (tragic week), when nationalist brigades killed seven hundred striking socialists, anarchists, and trade unionists, to the almost simultaneous suppression of the German Spartacus uprising. In this wave of repression, and in many similar ones especially throughout the southern cone countries, anti-Semitism functioned as the language of right-wing internationalism.[56] In El Salvador, the 1932 slaughter of over ten thousand mostly indigenous peasants affiliated with the Communist Party resonated with the destruction of the Paris Commune sixty years earlier. The slander "Bolshevik" became continental currency to describe all forms of political activity; Erwin Paul Dieseldorff, returning from revolutionary Germany in 1920, used the word to describe Icó. The evolving Cold War offered a new repertoire of reference. "There is a graveyard smell to Chile, the fumes of a democracy in decomposition," reported the U.S. ambassador to Chile upon Allende's 1970 victory; "they stank in my nostrils in Czechoslovakia in 1948 and they are no less sickening today."[57] There were intellectual traditions and political models to draw on, such as Franco's Spain and Salazar's Portugal, yet conservatism's supposed rejection of abstraction and exaltation of particularity did not at first lend itself easily to universal emulation.[58] Conservative thought during the early Latin American Cold War remained in the realm of affective feelings, and elites tried to ensure their privileges by defending an underconceived celebration of family, religion, property, and a minimal state, positioning themselves not in opposition to modern life but as a needed bulwark against its excesses.

While more reactive than innovative, the Latin American counterrevolution was nonetheless dynamic, pulling together a diverse cross-class coalition.[59] Economic, political, and cultural elites, except in some cases such as Nicaragua in the late 1970s, tended to cohere rather than fracture in the face of insurgent threats. They adapted themselves to emerging bureaucratic structures, interest politics, and state institutions, infusing them with the personal loyalties characteristic of Latin America's Catholic, patrician landed society. In Chile and Argentina, sectors of the oligarchy that had previously despised mass action began in the 1930s to patronize fascist and populist movements, despite the fact that they themselves had been previously targeted by such movements as degenerate and deserving of destruction.[60] More decisively, the ruling classes proved able to draw new groups to protect their interests. Military officers throughout the continent, even when, as in the case of Guatemala, they at times contested their subordination to civilian economic elites, interpreted national security as homologous to defending the established social order.[61]

For the most part, the fight against the new world was directed not by those at society's commanding heights but by middle-class ideologues who first revitalized and then radicalized conservative thought and practice. Their affective investment in, yet sufficient distance from, the beleaguered order allowed them to breathe new life into its conventions, traditions, and values. The counterrevolution drew support from large segments of agrarian and urban popular classes, powered by subterranean currents of status anxiety, race hatred, and fear of social liberalization, which for men could mean a loss of prerogative and for women a loss of protection.[62] Anti-communism as a spreading global ideology served as a circuit that routed these isolated, local currents into an international movement with universal pretensions. As the insurgent threat continued, conservatism moved from an instinctual defense of hierarchical privilege into a more contrived ideology confected from component parts of radical Catholicism, martial nationalism, and patriarchal allegiance. In Guatemala anti-communist Catholic students fashioned themselves as the vanguard of a global movement, working with an archbishop who declared himself in opposition not just to social security but to the Enlightenment as well. With the help of the CIA, these students affected an insurgent internationalism exuberant in tone and content, communicating with other anti-communist movements not only throughout Latin America but in Asia as well, and promoted the "salvation" of Guatemala as merely the "first step" in liberating Latin America from Communism. It was this impassioned middle sector that functioned as a broker between the upper echelons, both domestic and foreign, of reaction and the street thugs and paramilitary forces responsible for some of the worst acts of counterrevolutionary terror.[63]

Counterinsurgency—the technical art of counterrevolution—enjoyed a defined learning curve, and as the Cold War advanced it assumed a greater weight in the counterrevolutionary equation. As described in chapter 3, the overthrow of Arbenz was the most comprehensive covert operation at the time, employing nearly every facet of U.S. power—political, economic, cultural, diplomatic, military, psychological—and would come to serve as a model for future actions. At times in Latin America success proved a poor advisor, blinding strategists to the specific conditions of the present. When the United States tried to replicate its Guatemalan achievement against Castro in the Bay of Pigs invasion, it failed spectacularly, helping to radicalize not just the Cuban Revolution but the Latin American Cold War as a whole. Yet for the most part, the accumulation of counterinsurgent knowledge was effectively adapted to the developing revolutionary threat. Latin American militaries applied tactics perfected by the United States in Vietnam, the French in Algeria, and England in Northern Ireland.[64] Following the success of the Cuban rural insurgency, militaries quickly learned not only to terrorize the population to dry up guerrilla support but to incorporate it into new ideological and political structures of authority. Destabilization, psychological operations, internal policing, and low-intensity warfare filled an arsenal to be flexibly deployed as the situation dictated. In particular, the devolution, as Martha Huggins describes the process, of executive repressive power to quasi-autonomous death squads staffed by army and police officers supplied with information by rationalized military intelligence agencies and often trained by the United States was a common element in the creation of many of Latin America's counterinsurgent terror states.[65]

The burden of defense of the status quo is considerably lighter than that of innovation. Insurgents, in contrast, have to establish sovereignty over a social terrain that they themselves shattered, using violence not only to neutralize opposition but to incorporate popular demands for justice and revenge into new state structures. In Latin America, Cuban revolutionaries staged public executions not only to channel grassroots vengeance into a new system of legitimate authority but to contrast the transparency of revolutionary justice with the covert repression of the Batista regime.[66] Counterrevolutionary terror in Latin America, on the other hand, has for the most part tended to do its work more covertly and with considerably less vocal justification. Pinochet, in contrast to Che, carried out his post-coup military executions in private.[67] The Contra War was perhaps the most fully coherent counterrevolution, bringing together a diverse foreign and domestic coalition to lay siege to and contain the Sandinistas. In Nicaragua's interior, the U.S.-funded, trained, and equipped Contra rebels destroyed cooperatives, schools, health clinics, and other government projects and murdered civilians to demonstrate to a wavering rural population that the Sandinistas could not establish effective sovereignty—that is, protect against counterrevolutionary violence.[68] Again, white terror found its effectiveness in stealth and unpredictability, while revolutionaries had the liability of having to establish public and comprehensive rule and security.

Latin America's counterrevolution responded in diverse degrees to threats, at times with excess carnage, such as in Central America and Argentina, and at other times with more surgical restraint, such as in Uruguay. Yet counterrevolutionary terror was much more driven by emotive wrath and the desire for retribution than revolutionary violence was, accounting for its barbarism in such places as El Salvador in 1932 and Guatemala in 1981–83. In Chile in 1973, for example, the U.S. State department noted that a "puritanical, crusading spirit," a "determination to cleanse and rejuvenate Chile," led the military junta to execute not just leftists but "petty criminals."[69] In some countries, as the threat of mass mobilization proved inextinguishable by ordinary means, state repression became more spectacular and verbal in its self-justification. In Argentina, for instance, the junta issued a steady barrage of commentary to annotate its atrocities.[70]

Counterrevolutionary terror was inextricably tied to empire. Present at its birth in 1954 and nurturing through its adolescence in the 1960s, the United States was a distant yet still involved patron during the Guatemalan genocide. Jimmy Carter would cut off direct military aid in 1977 owing to human rights abuses, yet the United States continued to provide training, funds, and material through other avenues.[71] After Ronald Reagan's 1981 inauguration, the State Department vigorously lobbied Congress to restore direct support. As it did in El Salvador following the 1981 El Mozote massacre, the U.S. Embassy and the State Department refused to consider mounting evidence gathered by their own agents that, as the officer in charge of inter-American affairs put it in a November 1982 memo to the U.S. secretary of state, "the military continues to engage in massacres of civilians in the countryside."[72] A month later, in December 1982, during the apex of the bloodletting, Reagan met in Honduras with Ríos Montt, the military general who as president presided over the most severe phase of the genocide, and declared to the press that the general was getting a "bad deal" from his critics and that he was "totally committed to democracy."[73]

In Europe and Japan the United States could ally with center-left politicians to carry out preventative modernization—land distribution, social welfare provisions, land and tax reforms, and industrialization. Yet in much of Latin America, as elsewhere, no such alliance was possible, and the United States inevitably sided with reactionary civilian and military forces as a bulwark against communism. That Washington was not solely responsible for the coups and atrocities carried out by their agents, and at times had no involvement at all, matters less than the fact that it did little to discourage them. Again, compare the U.S. response to the trials and executions immediately following the Cuban Revolution, which became a focal point of worsening relations between Washington and Havana, and its silence toward Pinochet's military tribunals, despite having detailed and up-to-date reports of the killings.[74]

The fearsome power of Latin America's counterrevolution resided in the synthesis of the rationalized, precise counterinsurgent tactics and more furious sentiments and aesthetics. Professional intelligence agencies trained, funded, and equipped by the United States, such as Argentina's Secretaria de Inteligencia del Estado, Chile's Dirección Nacional de Inteligencia, El Salvador's Agencia Nacional de Servicios Especiales, and Brazil's Sistema Nacional de Informações, worked closely, often indistinguishably, with death squads that had adopted Nazi terror tactics of disappearances, torture, and murder.[75] In Guatemala, the 1981–82 genocide was surgically precise. Military analysts marked communities and regions according to colors. White spared those thought to have no rebel influence. Pink identified areas in which the insurgency had limited presence; suspected guerrillas and their supporters were to be killed but the communities left standing. Red gave no quarter; all were to be executed and villages razed. "One of the first things we did," says Héctor Gramajo, one of the young colonels who designed the operation, "was draw up a document for the campaign with annexes and appendices. It was a complete job with planning down to the last detail."[76] Yet the actual operations were savage beyond belief, carried out with a racist frenzy targeted not just at Indians but at all things considered indigenous.[77] A similar tension between rationality and rage ran through nearly all aspects of Latin America's terror states. The Argentine junta, for example, worked with University of Chicago economists to install free-market economic policies and contracted the services of the Madison Avenue public relations firm Burson Marsteller in order to "bring Argentina into the twentieth century." At the same time, however, it also waged a viciously anti-Semitic terror campaign and declared its three principal enemies to be "Karl Marx, because he tried to destroy the Christian concept of society; Sigmund Freud, because he tried to destroy the Christian concept of the family; and Albert Einstein, because he tried to destroy the Christian concept of time and space."[78] Rationalization and revanchism fused. It was the only force that could destroy—by suppressing the egalitarian potential of Latin American democracy while elevating its individualistic, market-oriented elements—the ideological and political challenge set loose in the years following World War II.

Yet it would be wrong to simply equate the rational side of this equation with the United States. Radical critics of U.S. foreign policy contributed to the belief that the Cold War was a rivalry for dominance between the twin heirs of the Enlightenment—liberal democracy and communism. The New Left's damning analysis, for instance, of "Cold War liberalism"—whose rational, procedural sterility it held responsible for the destruction of Vietnam—advanced the notion that the United States was waging a liberal crusade. Robert Jay Lifton, for example, described a "grotesque technicizing" that measured progress in the war by body counts.[79] Gabriel Kolko condemned a "liberal myopia" that interpreted the chronic devastation wrought by U.S. foreign policy only in terms of isolated "errors" and that served as a "defense against reality as well as a means for its perpetuation."[80] Robert McNamara, who took over as secretary of defense after serving as the president of Ford Motor Company, came to embody the "impersonal, mechanistic aspects of the Vietnam War" through his use of "cost effectiveness" to justify waging "mechanized, dehumanizing slaughter" from the skies.[81] Likewise Noam Chomsky borrowed from Randolph Bourne to blame the desolation of Vietnam on the "young liberals" who made "themselves efficient instruments of the war technique, accepting with little question the ends as announced from above."[82]

In Latin America, these criticisms certainly hold. Throughout the Cold War in the decades following the Korean War, the United States poured money, technology, and advisors into the region in an effort to reform national security forces and intelligence capabilities so that they could better respond to subversive threats. The stated goal was to move away from "thuggish," self-interested behavior toward a "rational," "modern," and "professional" army and police. In Guatemala, for example, embassy analysts mostly ignored or downplayed evidence that the intelligence system they had helped put in place was conducting an unrelenting campaign of terror against all political activists, communist or otherwise. As the bodies mounted, they simply reiterated like a mantra their desire to modernize Guatemala's economy and polity, to identify and work with members of a "democratic left" whom their own apprentices were then slaughtering.[83] John Longan, the U.S. advisor who trained the unit that in 1966 carried out Operación Limpieza, describes himself as a "technician" whose "job was to try to implement the policies of our government at that particular time on those particular things. If it was to upgrade this or upgrade that, I didn't ask why."[84] Sheltered by a bureaucratic division of labor that protected him from the horrific consequences of his activities, Longan did not have to "think big" in order to perpetuate terror, as Hannah Arendt described Adolf Eichmann's inability to see the larger universe of his actions.[85]

Yet assessments that focus on the dry, modern rationality of institutional repression miss the viscous passions that motivated many U.S. officials. Not only did the United States repeatedly empower darker, reactionary forces, execute or condone barbaric acts, and fuel febrile obsessions, its agents engaged in tactics and expressed opinions seemingly straight out of the counter-Enlightenment. The way the United States fought the Cold War on the ground was anything but liberal or democratic.

Most U.S. Embassy officials in Latin America continued to believe, or at least publicly state, that a clear line separated their goals and actions from domestic "white terror," yet occasional glimpses reveal murkier sentiments at work. Viron Vaky, second-in-command of the U.S. Embassy in Guatemala in the late 1960s, for example, expressed dismay at the terms his underlings used to justify repression: "After all hasn't man been a savage from the beginning of time so let us not be too queasy about terror. I have literally heard these arguments from our people."[86] U.S. agents put to good use their conviction that human beings are driven more by base, unfathomable instincts than by noble reason and that self-interest and doubt would steadily, inexorably corrode social solidarity. Psychological efforts to destabilize Guatemala in 1954, one CIA agent wrote, should avoid intellectual arguments and instead be directed at the "heart, the stomach and the liver (fear)."[87] Twenty years later in Chile, CIA strategies to unseat Allende relied on an unwavering "will to power" to generate dissension. Rumor was to act as a cat's-paw for fear, poisoning commitment and forcing an acceptance of inevitable reaction. The Agency set out to, in its words,

> create the conviction that Allende must be stopped. . . . discredit parliamentary solution as unworkable . . . surface ineluctable conclusion that military coup is the only answer. This is to be carried forward until it takes place. However, we must hold firmly to the outlines or our production will be diffuse, denatured, and ineffective, not leaving the indelible residue in the mind that an accumulation of arsenic does. The key is psych war within Chile. We cannot endeavor to ignite the world if Chile itself is a placid lake. The fuel for the fire must come within Chile. Therefore, the station should employ every stratagem, every ploy, however bizarre, to create this internal resistance.[88]

Will to set the world ablaze, commitment to a universal ideal, faith in the night-side of the soul, contempt for democratic temperance and parliamentary procedure: These qualities are usually attributed to opponents of liberal civility, tolerance, and pluralism—not their defenders.

Throughout the twentieth century, Latin Americans have fought for democracy, in terms of both formal institutional representation and a lived experience of individual freedom, dignity, and solidarity. In Guatemala, forced labor is over, as is overt state-authorized racism. Small cliques of Ladinos no longer control indigenous communities. Despite the dismal conditions in which most Guatemalans today live, this much the war did.[89] Throughout Latin America, the majority of nations now enjoy constitutional rule. Yet for those throughout the continent who gave their lives, the current state of affairs cannot be what they meant by democracy. Poverty is endemic; racism and sexual exploitation continue; wealth inequality is at an all-time high; national armies and security forces seem invulnerable; and most of those responsible for Cold War atrocities continue to enjoy, despite occasional tests, immunity. In some hamlets of Cahabón, including those that won land, the recent rapid fall of international coffee and cardamom prices has led to a nightmare of "unemployment, infectious disease, malnutrition, and extreme misery."[90] Hunger is routine and starvation common.

Yet politics continues, even if under a different name. In the wake of the genocide, Mayan activists, as part of a hemispheric emergence of indigenous movements, have achieved important advances in basic civil and cultural rights. Throughout Latin America, victims of state terrorism and their relatives have patiently, insistently pursued justice, and their at times heroic actions have strengthened national and international legal systems. Every country has a network of feminist activists pushing in different ways for equal treatment, their demands often linked to class and ethnic identities. Despite the devastation visited upon Latin America to install neoliberalism, the continent's social movements and, increasingly, governments lead the global fight against free market orthodoxy. In fall 2003, a mass protest movement in Bolivia led largely by indigenous workers and peasants rebelling against the dictates of the International Monetary Fund and the sale of their nation's natural resources to transnational corporations forced the resignation of a president steadfastly supported by the United States. In Brazil, a left made up of the continent's largest gay rights movement, combative peasant organizations, trade unionists, intellectuals, antiracist associations, indigenous rights advocates, and environmentalists recently overwhelmingly elected the working-class trade unionist Luiz Inácio Lula da Silva as president. In October 2003, Brazil joined with Argentina to produce the "Buenos Aires Consensus"—an answer to the Washington Consensus that insisted on deregulation of capital, open markets, and fiscal austerity.[91] While the pact promises to generate jobs and increase social spending, perhaps its real challenge to the international system comes, as it did during the Cold War, from demands that the promises of development, democracy, and sovereignty offered by that system be realized. Rather than repudiating the principles of free trade and open markets, the agreement is demanding that they be taken seriously and that the United States and Europe should reduce subsidies and tariffs to provide equitable access for Latin American commodities. And, as a reminder that all this activity takes place within a global economic and political regime, Washington and Wall Street are growing increasingly nervous and belligerent at the opposition emerging throughout the continent to more than a decade of failed free market policies.[92]

Over the last decade, scholars have heralded such "new social movements" for mobilizing around culture, community, sexual, and gender identities and interests and for moving away from class analysis and an obsessive focus on the state and economic development.[93] Yet notwithstanding its reputation, in many countries the old, class-based left was, on the ground, more varied and vibrant than its rhetoric often suggested. Despite their inability to incorporate culture and race into their analyses and visions of progress, left political parties and labor organizations in Bolivia, El Salvador, Guatemala, Chile, and Peru, for some examples, drew significant support from rural, often indigenous communities.[94] In fact, in many countries today, movements led by native Americans are the most forceful agents of the kind of democratic socialism that was advanced by the old left. In Mexico, for example, the Zapatistas demand autonomy at the same time as they redeem the ideals of the Mexican Revolution, while in Bolivia the Aymara, who make up one of Latin America's most militant social movements, are fighting for cultural as well as social democratic rights. Likewise, just as recent work in U.S. history has revealed important bridges between the activism of the 1930s and subsequent civil, gay, and women's rights movements, there often exists in Latin America a direct link between the older left and new social movements.[95] In Guatemala, many of the participants in today's Mayan movement can date the beginning of their political careers to their involvement with rebel groups of the 1960s and 1970s, which in turn can trace their roots back to the Agrarian Reform. In Mexico, the Communist Party and fellow-traveler organizations of the 1930s provided apprenticeships for female activists and served as the seedbeds for future independent feminist politics.[96] But more than just a direct connection, many of the identities that drive today's social movements were shaped in the crucible of old left politics.[97] While it would be too much to claim Icó as a precursor to Latin America's modern gay rights movement, his development of a political style not completely encapsulated by family, religion, or community does reflect what many scholars identify as an important condition for the emergence of modern sexuality and the rights claims that come with it.

It would seem that a singular focus on national economic development, the very element of older mass movements most often criticized today for suppressing social and experiential diversity, provided the leverage that allowed marginal groups to press their interests. The importance of the 1952 Agrarian Reform, for example, was that it connected local, indigenous land struggles to elite interests and visions of national progress. The Communist Party designed the reform to advance national capitalism through the extension of democracy in the countryside: its creation of an administrative structure aimed at loosening the ironclad grip planters had over rural life was meant to empower peasants to demand higher salaries for their plantation work. In turn, better wages would, it was hoped, not only transform rural laborers into consumers of national manufactures but force planters addicted to cheap, often free labor and land to invest in new productive technologies and modernize production in order to make a profit. One important point of intersection between local and national ideals was the belief that soil was social, that the value of property rested not only in the profit it gave to individuals but also in the benefit that it accrued to a larger polity, whether it be the community or the country. These ideas were not confined to indigenous peasants or resident plantation workers. Elites drew contradictorily on colonial and positivist conceptions of the common good both to dispossess indigenous communities from their land and to argue for land redistribution. The Agrarian Reform for a brief period allowed many communities to enter into social democratic discourse and to use nationalist visions of progress and development to pursue their own interests.

The 1996 peace accords that finally ended Guatemala's civil war foreclosed on this possibility.[98] By not including even the possibility of a future land reform, they reaffirmed the absolute right of private property inscribed in the military-brokered 1985 constitution.[99] When negotiators for the guerrillas raised the issue of amending the charter to include provisions recognizing the "social use" of land, the state balked and elites threatened to withdraw their support for peace talks. Even worse, the accords called for the execution of a national land survey that when finally completed will once and for all delineate ownership of all existing properties, justified in terms of limiting future conflict. Such a move not only confirms the legitimacy of Guatemala's current property system but undermines the ability of rural workers to make future land claims based on historic, invented or otherwise, injustices. Peasants continue to invade plantations. Alta Verapaz is still one of the departments with the largest number of pending disputes.[100] Yet what no longer exists is an ideological and institutional framework that can align local conflicts with the interests of other groups in a larger oppositional vision of national development.

The point is not to resurrect, albeit with a multicultural twist, an unambiguous heroic or romantic narrative that marked an earlier moment of social history. These revisions do not minimize the diversity between or dissension among the movements that carried forth postwar democracy. Peru's Alianza Popular Revolucionaria Americana and Communist Party seemed to hate each other more than they did the oligarchs. And of course the defining line between revolutionary and counterrevolutionary, democratic and antidemocratic, or liberal and illiberal forces is never fixed. Peronism, for example, contained within itself powerful elements of reform and reaction, and much of its efforts while in power between 1946 and 1955, as Daniel James points out, "can be viewed as an attempt to control the heretical challenge it had unleashed."[101] Neither does an emphasis on the legitimacy of popular liberalism imply a concordance of interests, motives, and visions among the men and women, classes, and groups that joined these movements. In some cases, the diverse interpretation of liberalism described above had the effect of sharpening racism, sexism, and other prejudices, resulting in ideological and political exclusion and sometimes physical repression.[102] By the 1930s in Bolivia and Peru, despite ongoing alliances between urban activists and rural indigenous communities, a focus on "class struggle" had superseded the left's previous concern with racial exploitation.[103] In Mexico, the Communist Party in the early 1930s was the only organization that militantly championed, however fitfully, women's rights, including suffrage (finally enacted in 1953).[104] Yet in 1938 it pushed such issues to the back burner after aligning with the ruling party in the name of fighting fascism. The fact that the left, to use the term in the broadest sense possible, often repressed or silenced democratic ideals when they were advanced by groups that did not easily fit into its conception of history or progress does not make those beliefs and visions any less meaningful, or historically consequential in terms of the reaction they elicited, for those who advanced them.[105] In the years leading up to and following World War II, an array of organizations, movements, and coalitions tapped into popular demands for state-administered economic justice, individual liberties, equal treatment, and national inclusion that had been manifestly visible since at least World War I but had roots going back to the nineteenth century. The postwar period honed such challenges and linked them to prevailing, optimistic notions of national development. While urban and elite reformers repeatedly subsumed diverse local struggles, identities, and experiences into a larger national narrative of progress, it was just that diversity that injected abstract concepts such as equality, democracy, and freedom with a renovating spirit.

The success of the Latin American counterrevolution resided not just in its repressive capacity but in its incorporation of elements of the challenge it sought to contain. In Guatemala, anti-communists were able to connect with disaffected individuals, organizing them into vigilante groups that although often repressive also allowed certain sectors of the local population to assert their interests. In the 1980s, the military established civil patrols and development committees at the community level that mimicked the guerrillas' organizational structures. While such associations allowed the army to establish its authority in the countryside, they also helped undermine Ladino control of the local economy and polity.[106] In many countries, military and civilian governments, prompted by the Alliance for Progress, promoted economic development through political, fiscal, and agrarian reform.[107] In Brazil, the post-1964 military regime adopted many of the cultural elements of the left, including the promotion of a folk nationalism, although in depoliticized form.[108] And when Uruguay's long-standing social welfare tradition collapsed in the late 1960s, leading to the militancy of its primary beneficiary, the urban middle class, the army responded not only with violence but by creating its own welfare system for the families of military recruits, most of whom came from marginal, previously excluded sectors of society.[109]

Counterinsurgent states replaced one moral model with another. One of the threats of mid-twentieth-century democracy was that it offered a venue in which individuality and solidarity could be imagined as existing in sustaining relation to one another through collective politics directed at the state to demand justice. In many places, the practice and philosophy of radical Catholicism was a high expression of this ideal, promoting a notion of individual human dignity nurtured by a larger ethical and historical order. Local political struggles related to other global conflicts and historical events allowed many to experience the world not in its illusionary static present but as evolving, as susceptible to change through action. Yet a closer attention to history not only provided hope that things could change but also imposed on many a duty to bring that change about. As Pope Paul VI wrote in his 1967 encyclical *On the Development of Peoples,* one of liberation theology's foundational texts, "each man is a member of society. . . . We have inherited from past generations, and we have benefited from the work of our contemporaries: for this reason we have obligations towards all, and we cannot refuse to interest ourselves in those who will come after us to enlarge the human family. The reality of human solidarity, which is a benefit for us, also imposes a duty. . . . Social conflicts have taken on world dimensions."[110]

Cold War terror destroyed this vision of a social and historical commons. Violence had the effect of dissolving the affiliation between individual activists and their wider social network, especially when that relationship constituted a challenge to the status quo. Many fled, hid, and went into exile. In Chile and Uruguay, for example, where extrajudicial executions were relatively fewer than in Central America and Argentina, large numbers of citizens left their countries. In Guatemala, the genocide drove nearly 70 percent of the population of some areas from their communities. The widespread practice of torture literally had the effect of "unmaking" people's worlds.[111] Victims had to choose between submitting to unrelenting physical pain—the singular experience of which would make it impossible to feel anything outside of themselves—and informing on and therefore hastening the destruction of the political networks that sustained them. Repression severed alliances between reforming elites and popular classes, disaggregated powerful collective movements into individual survival strategies, extracted leaders from their communities, and redefined the relationship between human beings and society. But activists extracted from the political and social webs that shaped and sustained them were not left in a state of suspended isolation. The key to counterinsurgent triumph lay in the creation of a new way of thinking.[112] Terror trained citizens to turn their political passions inward, to receive sustenance from their families, to focus on personal pursuits, and to draw strength from faiths less concerned with history and politics. Such conversions were the routine manifestations of the larger reinterpretation of democracy discussed in the preface: the idea, widely held in different forms at the end of World War II, that freedom and equality are mutually fulfilling has been replaced by a more vigilant definition, one that stresses personal liberties and free markets and sees any attempt to achieve social equity as leading to at best declining productivity and at worst political turmoil.

This age of astrictive neoliberalism and the destruction of social democratic political subjects was not of course only the work of terror states. Ecuador, Costa Rica, Panama, and Mexico have all abandoned state developmentalism without experiencing anywhere near the levels of repression that afflicted other Latin American countries. In Bolivia, the left emerged from the repressive Hugo Banzer dictatorship (1971–78) strong, only to implode in the 1980s in a relatively open political environment.[113] A staggering debt crisis rendered national developmental models unworkable; deindustrialization and diluted labor legislation weakened worker leverage; pressure applied by international markets, financial institutions, and the United States forced states to open up their economies, privatize their industries, and roll back their social services. Nonetheless, in many countries, unrelenting repression directed at collective projects bloodily demarcated the limits to what would be allowed and proved indispensable for the installation of free market policies. Today demands for economic justice are restrained in less wrathful ways, through the private pleasures of consumption, the dictates of a labor market, the removal of economic decision making from democratic control through central banks and supranational treaties, and the discipline of a competitive global economy. But such suasions are also backed up by more directly coercive relations, new surveillance technologies, and a militarized international regime dominated by the United States, which now proclaims the goal of its preemptive foreign policy as the defense of freedom defined as free enterprise.[114]

Throughout the Latin American Cold War, individuals often had to choose between survival and solidarity, and yet the severity of the violence allowed no choice at all. Blanca Ester Valderas, a Chilean peasant, used the Socialist Party to escape the restraints of family life and to become active in civil affairs, eventually being appointed mayor of her small village.[115] Poorly educated, she learned how to lobby the national government for schools, health centers, and other social services: "I used my head, and that is what people should do. . . .when I was mayor, I knew what had to be done." Yet the September 11, 1973, coup closed politics as an avenue of upward mobility. Security forces executed Valderas's husband, nearly killed her, and kidnapped and tortured her son. She had to change her name and go into hiding, switching jobs, avoiding her family, moving often so as not to be recognized—"always alone, because I didn't trust anyone." In thousands—perhaps hundreds of thousands—of cases such as this, government violence targeting political action had the effect of isolating individual leaders, wrenching them out of their larger political and ethical universe. This divorce between self and solidarity—two qualities that are, after all, the defining essences of liberal democracy and socialism—was the fundamental requirement of Latin America's neoliberal regimes. Democracy is now but a shade of its former substance. This is Cold War terror's most important legacy.

Acknowledgments

It would take another book to list the contributions of friends and colleagues, as well as the individuals willing to share their history with a stranger, that made this work possible. So without rhyme, reason, or comment, I want to thank Arturo Taracena, Efraín Reyes Maaz, Luis Solano, Vicente Tec, Noel López, Pedro Taracena, Carlos Figueroa Ibarra, Carlota McAllister, Sarah Hill (for crucial help with the Icó material), Marcie Mersky, Liz Oglesby, Ana Bela Castro, Luis Merida, Marlon García, Jeff Gould, Piero Gleijeses, Geoff Eley, Tomás Chitic Ren, Marilyn Young, Sinclair Thomson, Ada Ferrer, Alfredo Tzí, Hugo de la Parra, Adela Tziboy, Inocente Tec, Alfonso Huet, Ariel Adams, Niki Adams, Richard Wilson, Erwin Rabanales, Federico Velásquez, Leslye Rivera, Clara Arenas, Rachel Sieder, Tani Adams, Alvaro Pop, Matilde González, Adolfo Tzí, Daniel Wilkinson, Corey Robin, Diane Nelson, Enrique Corral, Gil Joseph, Abigail Adams, Kate Doyle, César Macías, members of the Maquin family, Kathi Weeks, Valia Garzón, Alberto Cardoza, Rosa Torras, Betsy Konefal, Amanda Pop, Maria Victoria García, Di Paton, Deborah Levenson, Emilia Viotti da Costa, Anna Carla Ericastilla, Jan French, Linda Gordon, Patricia Mathews, Thelma Porres Morfín, Gordon Lafer, Molly Nolan, Kieko Matteson, Allen Hunter, Paula Worby, Michael Hardt, Susan Kemp, Ceferino de Paz González, Mark Healey, Kully Kaur, Marisol de la Cadena, Irma Tzí Yat, Charlie Hale, Michelle Chase, Frank Goldman, Antonio Argueta, Miguel Angel Albizurez, John French, Florencia Mallon, Danny James, Robert Perkinson, Paul Seils, Gerardo Rénique, Gustavo Palma, Doug Mitchell, Timothy McGovern, José García, Mario Alfonso Bravo, Arno Mayer, Richard Adams, Marcela Echeverri, Tomás Caal, Fernando Bances, Tannia Goswami, Debbie Poole, Elvin Ramírez, Julio Pinto, Peter Winn, Sonia Alvarez, Susan Thorne, Rebecca Karl, Jolie Olcott, Jim Green, and, most importantly and dearly, Manu Goswami. I received financial support and encouragement from Duke University's Center for Latin American and Caribbean Studies and from New York University's Center for Latin American and Caribbean Studies and International Center for Advanced Studies.

APPENDIX

List of the Dead from Operación Limpieza and the Panzós Massacre*

OPERACIÓN LIMPIEZA, 1966

Enrique Chacon
Fernando Arce Behrens
Francisco Macías Mayora
Leonardo Castillo Flores
Leonardo García Benavente
Víctor Manuel Gutiérrez Garbín
Víctor Manuel Palacios Maldonado
Yolanda Carvajal Mercado
Carlos Edmundo Barrillas
Roberto Augusto Valle Peña
Agustín Martínez
Antonio Poc Alvarado
Balbino Sosa
Carlos Enrique Galindo
César Augusto Salguero Gómez
David Aguilar Mora
Dionisio Alvarez
Emilio Márquez Coroy
Emilio Vásquez
Emma Judith Amezquita
Eunice Campirán de Aguilar Mora
Humberto Pineda Aldana
José León Meda
José de Jesús Alonzo Solís
Juan de Dios Castillo
Juan Estrada Alvarado
Julián Meza
Marco Tulio Molina Licona
Ricardo Berganza Bocaletti
Transito Monterroso Pérez
Iris Yon Cerna
Melvin Galeano Polanco
Francisco Amado Granados
Antonio Morales Zavaleta
José Vicente Guzmán Franco

PANZÓS MASSACRE, 29 MAY 1978

Abelardo Ac Caal
Adelina Caal Caal
Alfredo Choca
Andrés Chub
Andrés Rax
Antonio Sub
Apolonio Tux
Bartolomé Chub Chun
Bartolomé Chun Chub
Bartolomé Sacul Chun
Domingo Cac
Domingo Coc Pérez
Domingo Cuc
Félix Caal Seb
Félix Caal Xo
Francisco Choc
Francisco Coc
Francisco Seb Ché

* As listed in CEH, *Memoria del silencio,* 6:98, 6:22–23; both lists are incomplete.

Francisco Tzalam
Hilario Choc Pop
José Chen Ac
José Coc Pop
José Maquin
José Xol Coc
José Yat Chun
Juan Ché
Juan Cuz
Juan Meza
Lorenzo Choc Cuz
Manuel Cabral Tzí
Marcelino Cuz Choc
María Luisa Cabnal
Marcos Choc
Mena Chun
Miguel Cahuec
Miguel Quib
Norberto Chub Choc
Pablo Caal Chun
Pablo Cuz Mo
Pablo Rax
Paulino Cuz Mo
Pedro Caal
Pedro Maqui
Ricardo Bac Chub
Roberto Ical Choc
Sabina Tuc Xo
Sabino Cuz Coc
Santiago Choc
Santiago Ché
Santiago Seb Caal
Santiago Seb Ché
Tomás Chen Quib
Tomás Coc

Glossary

SPANISH TERMS

alcalde auxiliar: Local agent of municipal government.
campesino: Peasant.
cofradía: Religious brotherhood, or saint cult, members of which are called *cofrades.*
finca: Plantation.
finquero: Planter.
Ladino: The general term used to describe Guatemalans not considered Mayan, composing approximately half of the country's total population.
mozo, or mozo colono: Plantation resident worker, usually indentured but at times in a sharecropper arrangement.
Q'eqchi': One of the largest Mayan linguistic groups in Guatemala, occupying the northern highlands, principally in the department of Alta Verapaz, but also El Petén, Izabal, Baja Verapaz, and into Belize.

ACRONYMS AND POLITICAL FIGURES AND TERMS

Arbenz, Jacobo: Second president of the October Revolution (1951–54).
Arévalo, Juan José: First president of the October Revolution (1945–50).
CAL: Comité Agrario Local, the basic administrative structure of the Agrarian Reform.
CEUA: The Comité de Estudiantes Universitarios Anticomunistas, working with the CIA, led the campaign against Arbenz.
CGTG: Created in 1951 from existing federations, the Confederación General de Trabajadores de Guatemala, headed by Víctor Manuel Gutiérrez, was closely allied with the PGT.
CNCG: Organized in 1950 and led by Leonardo Castillo Flores, the peasant Confederación Nacional Campesina de Guatemala often competed in the countryside with the CGTG.
Comunidad Agraria: Legalized after 1944, *comunidades agrarias,* at times referred to as *comunidades indígenas* or *comunidades campesinas,* served as a cross between peasant unions and mutual aid societies. After 1954, the term *"comunidad,"*

whether legally incorporated or not, often described a collective association of peasants joined together to pursue land or other claims.

CTG: Confederación de Trabajadores Guatemaltecos, an early labor federation during the October Revolution.

CUC: Formed in the mid-1970s, the Comité de Unidad Campesina was the first national peasant organization led by Mayans; closely allied with the EGP.

Decreto 900: Congressional legislation mandating Guatemala's 1952–54 land reform.

EGP: Established in the mid-1970s, the Ejército Guerrillero de los Pobres, or Guerrilla Army of the Poor, became Guatemala's most formidable armed insurgent organization.

FAR: Nominally the armed wing of the PGT, the Fuerzas Armadas Rebeldes was organized in the early 1960s by remnants of the 1960 military uprising and young PGT members. Impatient with the party's reform strategies, the FAR broke with the PGT in the mid-1960s. During its first incarnation, the FAR operated principally in Guatemala's east, along the Sierra de las Minas, the mountain range south of the Polochic Valley, but also in the western coffee region of San Marcos.

FASGUA: By the 1960s, the PGT had effectively taken control of the Federación Autónoma Sindical de Guatemala, an anti-communist labor federation permitted to function following the 1954 coup. Throughout the 1960s and 1970s, FASGUA served as an important legal advisor to peasant communities in their land conflicts.

FPL: The Frente Popular Libertador was one of the first, cautiously moderate, political parties to emerge following the October Revolution.

INTA: Established in 1961 under the impetus of the Alliance for Progress with the stated goal of modernizing Guatemala's agrarian property structure, the Instituto Nacional de Transformación Agraria allowed individuals and collective entities to petition for title to unused land. INTA quickly became a military-controlled bureaucracy whose inefficiency and corruption catalyzed peasant militancy.

JPT: The Juventud Patriótica de Trabajo was the youth section of the PGT, from which many New Left dissidents emerged.

MLN: Organized by the anti-communist activists who led the domestic campaign against Arbenz, the Movimiento de Liberación Nacional (called the Movimiento Democrático Nacionalista during its first years) starting in the 1960s became the principal organizer of death squads. It was closely allied with, and then brought under the control of, the military.

Operación Limpieza: Operación Limpieza, or Operation Cleanup, was carried out by the combined military and police unit headed by Guatemalan colonel Rafael Arriaga Bosque and trained by U.S. security advisor John Longan. Throughout 1966 it executed Latin America's first sustained campaign of counterinsurgent "disappearances," including the March 1966 capture and execution of over thirty activists affiliated with the PGT and the FAR.

PAR: Established during the early phase of the October Revolution, the Partido de Acción Revolucionaria became the most aggressive agent of reform; from within its ranks, activists organized the PGT, the Communist Party, in the late 1940s.

Partido Unionista: Bringing together artisans, laborers, intellectuals, and middle-class and provincial professionals, the Partido Unionista best represented the democratic and reformist impulse of the 1920s.

PGT: Partido Guatemalteco de Trabajo, Guatemala's Communist Party.

PR: Founded in the late 1950s and led mostly by the non-PGT wing of Arbenz's coalition, the Partido Revolucionario, along with the Christian Democrats, was the only consequential reform party allowed to operate in the repressive climate of the 1960s. Although its leadership grew increasingly conservative and anti-communist, there continued to be great overlap at the grassroots level between the PR and the PGT.

Notes

THE FOLLOWING ABBREVIATIONS HAVE BEEN USED THROUGHOUT THE NOTES:

ACG: Archivo del Congreso de Guatemala, Guatemala City
AGCA: Archivo General de Centro América, Guatemala City
AEA: Archivo Eclesiástico de Arzobispado de Guatemala, Guatemala City
AH de CIRMA: Archivo Histórico del Centro de Investigaciones Regional de Mesoamérica, Antigua, Guatemala
AMG: Archives of the Ministerio de Gobernación, Ministerio de Gobernación, Guatemala City
DDRS-US: Declassified Documents Reference System. While most declassified U.S. material can be found at the National Security Archive at Georgetown University in Washington, when a document can also be found online at <www.ddrs.psmedia.com>, in the World Government Documents Archive's Declassified Documents Reference System, I used this citation to reference the source.
INTA: Archives of the defunct Instituto Nacional de Transformación Agraria
LC-GDC: Guatemalan Document Collection, Library of Congress, Washington, D.C.
NSA: National Security Archive, George Washington University, Washington, D.C.
PGT-USAC: Partido Guatemalteco de Trabajo Collection of the Centro de Estudios Urbanos y Regionales, Universidad de San Carlos, Guatemala City
PGT-Tulane: Collection of PGT manifestos, reports, and position papers dating from the late 1950s, Special Collections Division, Tulane University Library, New Orleans.
RP: Registro de Propiedad, Guatemala City
SPCMA: San Pedro Carchá Municipal Archives, San Pedro Carchá, Guatemala

PREFACE

1. "Americans Must Now Feel What the Rest of Us Have Known," *The Independent*, October 3, 2001.

2. For a few examples see Americas Watch, *With Friends Like These: The Americas Watch Report on Human Rights and U.S. Policy in Latin America* (New York: Pantheon Books, 1985); John Gerassi, *The Great Fear: The Reconquest of Latin America* (New York: Macmillan, 1963); Martha K. Huggins, *Political Policing: The United States and*

Latin America (Durham: Duke University Press, 1998); Lars Schoultz, *National Security and United States Policy toward Latin America* (Princeton: Princeton University Press, 1987); John Dinges, *The Condor Years: How Pinochet and His Allies Brought Terrorism to Three Continents* (New York: New Press, 2004); Mark Danner, *The Massacre at El Mozote: A Parable of the Cold War* (New York: Vintage, 1994).

3. The preeminent Cold War historian John Lewis Gaddis, in *We Now Know: Rethinking Cold War History* (New York: Oxford University Press, 1998), condones the excesses of U.S. policy in the third world by emphasizing the misperceptions held by U.S. officials as to Soviet intentions and power: "It is easy now to sit back and say that the United States and its allies never had much to worry about in the 'third world,'" Gaddis writes; "But the failure of fears to materialize does not establish their immateriality. . . . Nightmares always seem real at the time—even if, in the clear light of dawn, a little ridiculous."

4. See, for instance, T. H. Marshall, *Citizenship and Social Class* (Concord, Mass.: Pluto Press, 1991); Karl Polanyi, *The Great Transformation: The Political and Economic Origins of Our Time* (Boston: Beacon, 2001 [1944]); John Rawls, *A Theory of Justice* (Cambridge: Harvard University Press, 1971).

5. Ho Chi Minh, *Selected Works*, vol. 3 (Hanoi: Foreign Languages Publishing House, 1960–62), pp. 17–21; Fidel Castro, *La historia me absolverá* (Havana: Editorial de Ciencias Sociales, 1975).

6. One of the most important assaults on the belief that individual freedom and socialism were mutually reinforcing is of course Friedrich von Hayek's influential *The Road to Serfdom* (London: Routledge, 1944). See also Milton Friedman (with Rose Friedman), *Capitalism and Freedom* (Chicago: University of Chicago Press, 1982). It is this urge to isolate liberalism from socialism that motivates many of the recent exposés of the espionage and authoritarian nature of the Communist Party, U.S.A. See for examples Harvey Klehr, John Earl Haynes, and Fridrikh Igorevich Firsov, eds., *The Secret World of American Communism* (New Haven: Yale University Press, 1995); Harvey Klehr, John Earl Haynes, and Kyrill Mikhailovich Anderson, eds., *The Soviet World of American Communism* (New Haven: Yale University Press, 1998); and John E. Haynes and Harvey Klehr, *Venona: Decoding Soviet Espionage in America* (New Haven: Yale University Press, 1999). See also the recent attack mounted by Ronald Radosh, Grigory Sevostianov, and Mary Habeck, eds., *Spain Betrayed: The Soviet Union in the Spanish Civil War* (New Haven: Yale University Press, 2001), on the last great bastion of popular-front mythology, the Spanish Civil War.

7. For examples see François Furet, *The Passing of an Illusion: The Idea of Communism in the Twentieth Century*, trans. Deborah Furet (Chicago: University of Chicago Press, 1999), and Mark Lilla, *The Reckless Mind: Intellectuals in Politics* (New York: New York Review Books, 2001).

8. http://www.whitehouse.gov/nsc/nssintro.html, emphasis mine.

9. The quote comes from Martin Malia, *The Soviet Tragedy: A History of Socialism in Russia, 1917–1991* (New York: Free Press, 1994), p. 518. For a brief moment, the demise of Soviet Marxism was taken as proof that liberal capitalist democracy more

closely corresponded to human nature and desire than did other forms of government and therefore required less violence to enforce. Gaddis, for example, in *We Now Know*, p. 285, argues that because the promise of liberal democracy had great resonance among women and men in Western Europe and Japan, the United States enjoyed a "strong base of popular support, confirmed repeatedly [by] free elections" that kept allies of the United States in power. The Soviet Union, he goes on, "never won such acceptance" and therefore resorted to bloody repression to maintain its empire. This tautology is overt in Francis Fukuyama's *The End of History and the Last Man* (New York: Free Press, 1992). See also Michael Mandelbaum, *The Ideas That Conquered the World: Peace, Democracy and Free Markets in the Twentieth Century* (New York: Public Affairs, 2002). In response to apparently growing global unrest and criticism directed at free market policies, a number of policy intellectuals are now elaborating a preemptive argument, blaming the instability of self-rule in third world countries for the failure of Western capital investment, thus justifying a renewed colonialism. Fareed Zakaria in *The Future of Freedom: Illiberal Democracy at Home and Abroad* (New York: W.W. Norton, 2003), separates "freedom" (constitutional and institutional protections) from "democracy" (universal suffrage), arguing that when the United States intervenes to overthrow failed or rogue states, it needs to defer, as long as need be, implementation of multiparty elections.

10. Michael Ignatieff, "The Burden," *New York Times Magazine*, January 5, 2003, p. 54. See also Paul Berman, *Terror and Liberalism* (New York: W.W. Norton, 2003); Jean Bethke Elshtain, *Just War against Terror: The Burden of American Power in a Violent World* (New York: Basic Books, 2003).

11. Interview on C-Span, *Washington Journal*, March 28, 2003, www.c-span.org.

12. This seems to be the default position of many liberal thinkers, such as Michael Walzer, who write for *Dissent* magazine toward U.S. global power. See Walzer's "Can There Be a Decent Left?" *Dissent*, Spring 2002. See also Jeffrey Isaac, "Hannah Arendt on Human Rights and the Limits of Exposure, or Why Noam Chomsky Is Wrong about the Meaning of Kosovo," *Social Research* 69, no. 2 (Summer 2002).

13. For one repentant Cold War warrior who now acknowledges the "costs and consequences" of U.S. foreign policy, see Chalmers Johnson, *Blowback: The Costs and Consequences of American Empire* (New York: Henry Holt, 2000).

INTRODUCTION

1. The massacre and the history leading up to it are described in detail in chapter 5.

2. The UN-administered Guatemalan truth commission report, the Comisión para el Esclarecimiento Histórico (hereafter CEH), *Guatemala: Memoria del silencio* (Guatemala City: United Nations Operating Projects Services, 1999), 6:18, estimates a total of fifty-three people died and forty-seven were wounded.

3. For Carchá's 1865 protest and reaction, see Archivo General de Central América (hereafter cited as AGCA) B 28500 75, B 28500 134, B 28576 147, B 28577 84, B 28601 151, B 28601 223, B 28601 226, B 28602 268, B 28602 275, B 28605 144, B 28576 147, B 28601

223, B 28606 117, B 28618 117, B 28743 638 (in citations, "A" indicates colonial and "B" postindependence holdings; the first number corresponds to *legajo,* or packet, and the second to *expediente,* or file. When relevant, a third number corresponds to folio). *El Norte,* January 10, 1935, provides an account seventy years after the event.

4. For patterns of indigenous resistance to colonial rule, see Severo Martínez Peláez, *Motines de Indios: La violencia colonial en Centroamérica y Chiapas* (Puebla: Universidad Autónoma de Puebla, 1985), and Greg Grandin, *The Blood of Guatemala: A History of Race and Nation* (Durham: Duke University Press, 2000), chap. 2.

5. The following description of Latin America's postwar democratic opening owes greatly to Leslie Bethell and Ian Roxborough, eds., *Latin America between the Second World War and the Cold War, 1944–1948* (Cambridge: Cambridge University Press, 1992), as well as their essay "The Impact of the Cold War on Latin America," in *Origins of the Cold War: An International History,* ed. Melvyn Leffler and David Painter (New York: Routledge, 1994).

6. Daniel James, *Resistance and Integration: Peronism and the Argentine Working Class, 1946–1976* (Cambridge: Cambridge University Press, 1988), offers an extraordinary study on the socialization of liberal rights in Argentina. Emilia Viotti da Costa's "Liberalism: Theory and Practice," in her *The Brazilian Empire: Myths and Histories* (Chicago: University of Chicago Press, 1985), is the classic analysis of the contradictory interpretations and consequences of Brazilian liberalism.

7. By "popular front" I am referring to both the specific policy emanating from Moscow directing Communist parties to align with liberals, democratic nationalists, and social democrats against Nazism and a more generalized antifascist wartime coalition stretching into the 1940s that transformed and invigorated the Left. See Geoff Eley, "International Communism in the Heyday of Stalin," *New Left Review,* May–June 1986, 157. Michael Denning's *The Cultural Front: The Laboring of American Culture in the Twentieth Century* (New York: Verso, 1998) argues that the power of the U.S. popular front—defined both as an alliance between the Communist Party and democratic parties and as a broader, more general political and cultural consensus—resided in its combination of democracy and socialism.

8. Perry Anderson, *Conversation on Western Marxism* (London: Verso, 1979), p. 37.

9. Bethell and Roxborough, "Conclusion: The Postwar Conjuncture in Latin America and Its Consequences," in their edited *Latin America between the Second World War and the Cold War,* pp. 327–28.

10. Juan José Arévalo, *Escritos Políticos* (Guatemala City: Tipografía Nacional, 1945), p. 146.

11. See Mary Ann Glendon, *A World Made New: Eleanor Roosevelt and the Universal Declaration of Human Rights* (New York: Random House, 2001); Paolo Carozza, "From Conquest to Constitutions: Retrieving a Latin American Tradition of the Idea of Human Rights," *Human Rights Quarterly* 25 (2003): 281–313.

12. James, *Resistance and Integration,* p. 34.

13. David Green, *The Containment of Latin America: A History of the Myths and Realities of the Good Neighbor Policy* (Chicago: Quadrangle, 1971), p. 291.

14. See David Harvey, *The New Imperialism* (Oxford: Oxford University Press, 2003), pp. 49–62, and Perry Anderson, "Force and Consent," *New Left Review* 17 (September–October 2002): 5–30.

15. In Bethell and Roxborough, "Conclusion: The Postwar Conjuncture in Latin America and its Consequences," p. 332.

16. Brian Loveman and Thomas M. Davis, eds., *Politics of Anti-Politics: The Military in Latin America* (Lincoln: University of Nebraska Press, 1989), describes Latin American military officers' positioning of themselves as above politics and as a bulwark against divisive pluralism.

17. Louis Pérez, *On Becoming Cuban: Identity, Nationality, and Culture* (Chapel Hill: University of North Carolina Press, 1999), p. 487.

18. Pedro Mir, *Countersong to Walt Whitman and other Poems*, trans. Jonathan Cohen and Donald D. Walsh (Washington, DC: Azul Editions, 1993), p. 97.

19. Library of Congress Guatemalan Document Collections (hereafter cited as LC-GDC), reel 5, frame 8004-P, June 23, 1953.

20. Victor Alba, "The Stages of Militarism in Latin America," in *The Role of the Military in Underdeveloped Countries*, ed. John Johnson (Princeton: Princeton University Press, 1962).

21. For fascism in Chile and Argentina, see Sandra McGee Deutsch, *Las Derechas: The Extreme Right in Argentina, Brazil, Chile, 1890–1939* (Stanford: Stanford University Press, 1999), pp. 141–247.

22. This process of radicalization was complex and distinct according to country. James, *Resistance and Integration*, p. 210, describes the emergence of a Peronist armed left among activists frustrated by the "demobilisation of the mass movement in the early 1960s" and critical of an "accommodationist union bureaucracy."

23. George Lukács, *The Historical Novel* (New York: Penguin, 1962), p. 25, makes this point in relation to the restoration that took place after the French Revolution, when Enlightenment thought, in the face of strong reaction, took on the veneer of "historical necessity."

24. In Deborah Levenson-Estrada, *Trade Unionists against Terror: Guatemala City, 1954–1985*(Chapel Hill: University of North Carolina Press, 1994), p. 136.

25. See Capitán Leopoldo Pimental, "La integración del Indígena al desarrollo nacional," *Revista Militar* 3, no. 19 (January–March 1979): 51–62. One military analyst wrote in 1982 that "the existence of diverse ethnic groups, with different languages and dialects demonstrates the partial nature of national integration due to a lack of a common identity." Another counterinsurgent strategist wrote that same year that Mayans "have joined the guerrilla due to a lack of communication with the state." Both in CEH, *Memoria del silencio*, 3:322.

26. Jennifer Schirmer, *The Guatemalan Military Project: A Violence Called Democracy* (Philadelphia: University of Pennsylvania Press, 1998), p. 64.

27. Throughout Latin America, the transition to free market policies took place in a variety of manners. In some cases, as in Chile, military regimes imposed restructuring; in other cases, such as Brazil, military governments continued national

industrialization policies and neoliberalism was implemented by their civilian successors. For two classic studies of the rise of postwar authoritarianism, see Fernando Henrique Cardoso, *Autoritarismo e democratização* (Rio de Janeiro: Paz e Terra, 1975), and Guillermo O'Donnell, *Modernization and Bureaucratic-Authoritarianism* (Berkeley: University of California Press, 1973). For three decades, O'Donnell's work has set the terms of the debate regarding the relationship of economic development and dictatorship. It argued that by the 1960s, the old import-substitution path to national development had exhausted itself, failing to attract or generate enough capital to move beyond the light industrialization stage. As a result, states increasingly found themselves incapable of containing popular mobilization, ensuring political stability, and protecting capital accumulation, thus leading to the authoritarian military regimes of the 1970s. Much subsequent social science literature has questioned the general applicability of O'Donnell's observations. If economic growth is correlated to dictatorships, some asked, then why have Venezuela, Costa Rica, and Colombia managed to maintain at least some form of democracy? Others noted that while Brazil and Argentina possibly had reached the limits of import-substitution development, Chile and Uruguay, which likewise suffered dictatorships, had not. Many of these questions, however, focus nearly exclusively on trying to isolate specific causal economic variables and ignore the larger historical context argued for here. See for examples Jaime Serra, "Three Mistaken Theses Regarding the Connection between Industrialization and Authoritarian Regimes," and Albert Hirschman, "The Turn to Authoritarianism in Latin America and the Search for Its Economic Determinants," both in *The New Authoritarianism in Latin America,* ed. David Collier and Fernando Henrique Cardoso (Princeton: Princeton University Press, 1979). See the discussion in Eduardo Silva, "Authoritarianism, Democracy, and Development," in *Latin America Transformed: Globalization and Modernity,* ed. Robert Gwynne and Cristobal Kay (New York: Oxford University Press, 1999), pp. 42–43, 49.

28. From a 1975 speech reproduced in Loveman and Davis, *Politics of Anti-Politics,* pp. 244, 247. Cf. *El pensamiento conservador en Chile,* ed. Renato Cristo and Carlos Ruiz (Santiago: Editorial Universitaria, 1992).

29. In Patricia Politzer, *Fear in Chile: Lives under Pinochet* (New York: New Press, 2001), p. 205. Many of the Pinochet supporters interviewed in Politzer's book combine a similar appreciation of both individual liberty and order.

30. In Marguerite Feitlowitz, *A Lexicon of Terror: Argentina and the Legacies of Torture* (New York: Oxford University Press, 1998), p. 19.

31. See Patricio Silva, "Modernization, Consumerism and Politics in Chile," in *Neo-liberalism with a Human Face? The Politics and Economics of the Chilean Model,* ed. David Hojman (Liverpool: University of Liverpool, 1995); and José Joaquín Brunner, *El espejo trizado* (Santiago: FLACSO, 1988).

32. Tomás Moulian, "A Time of Forgetting: The Myths of the Chilean Transition," NACLA *Report on the Americas* 32 (September/October 1998): 20. See also Moulian's *El consumo me consume,* Santiago: LOM, 1998.

33. Sidney Almond and Gabriel Verba, *The Civic Culture: Political Attitudes and*

Democracy in Five Nations (Princeton: Princeton University Press, 1963), p. 343, and Samuel Huntington, Michael Crozier, and Joji Watanuki, *The Crisis of Democracy: Report on the Governability of Democracies to the Trilateral Commission* (New York: New York University Press, 1975), are early views that a successful democratic transition needs to create a "relatively passive, uninvolved" and "deferential" citizenry. For a more recent prescription, see Gretchen Casper and Michelle Taylor, *Negotiating Democracy: Transitions from Authoritarian Rule* (Pittsburgh: University of Pittsburgh Press, 1996). Guillermo O'Donnell, Philippe Schmitter, and Laurence Whitehead, *Transitions from Authoritarian Rule* (Baltimore: Johns Hopkins University Press, 1986), made a series of similar recommendations to help guide political elites in their transitions to democracy.

34. Jorge Castañeda, *Utopia Unarmed: The Latin American Left after the Cold War* (New York: Vintage Books, 1994), is the most influential and comprehensively argued example of this position. A more vulgar version of this argument motivated David Stoll's exposé of Rigoberta Menchú's life story; see especially the counterfactual assertions made in the conclusion to *Rigoberta Menchú and the Story of All Poor Guatemalans* (Boulder: Westview, 1999).

35. Castañeda, *Utopia Unarmed*, p. 476.

36. Richard Rorty, "The End of Leninism: Havel and Social Hope," *Truth and Progress*, vol. 3: *Philosophical Papers* (Cambridge: Cambridge University Press, 1998). Rorty's position notably echoes Daniel Bell's *The End of Ideology: On the Exhaustion of Political Ideas in the 1950s* (New York: Free Press, 1962). Published on the eve of the political upheavals of the 1960s, Bell's book describes a dry, procedural liberalism that was thought to have dampened the ideological fires of the 1930s and 1940s.

37. Geoff Eley, *Forging Democracy: The History of the Left in Europe, 1850–2000* (Oxford: Oxford University Press, 2002), p. 4.

38. See the discussion in Susan Buck-Morss, *Dreamworld and Catastrophe: The Passing of Mass Utopia in East and West* (Cambridge: MIT Press, 2000).

39. See Arno J. Mayer, *Dynamics of Counterrevolution in Europe, 1870–1956: An Analytical Framework* (New York: Harper and Row, 1971), p. 9, for the phrase "international civil war."

CHAPTER 1. A SEDITIOUS LIFE

1. San Pedro Carchá, municipal registry, Libro de Defunciones, no. 43, folio 203, November 15, 1950.

2. In addition to archival sources, most information on José Angel Icó's life, unless otherwise cited, comes from a series of interviews with his associates and members of his family in San Pedro Carchá and Guatemala City conducted June–July 2000, June–August 2001, and November 2001.

3. Parroquia San Pedro Carchá, Libro de Bautismos, no. 33, folio 17v, lists Icó's baptismal registry. *Compadrazgo* (godparenthood) was an important formal kin institution in Q'eqchi' culture, entailing a series of obligations and restrictions that would

apply for life. That Icó had no godfather at his baptism and that his godmother was a Ladina suggest a weakening of the institution as described by Arden King in *Cobán and the Verapaz: History and Cultural Process in Northern Guatemala* (New Orleans: Tulane University, Middle American Research Institute, 1974), p. 61.

4. Archivo General de Centro América, Sección de Tierras, Alta Verapaz (hereafter cited as AGCA ST-AV) 3 13 (in citations, the first number indicates *paquete*, or packet, and the second *expediente*, or file). Two years later, Icó's two maternal uncles claimed 1,900 acres in the next village over; AGCA ST-AV 7 12. Icó and his four siblings inherited their father's land and remained throughout the 1920s Chitaña's largest landholders. See San Pedro Carchá Municipal Archives (hereafter cited as SPCMA), "nómina de milperos," 1923.

5. There are two lists of Icó's resident workers in Alta Verapaz's *jefatura política* collection in the AGCA (hereafter cited as AGCA JP-AV), April 5 and June 30, 1925. The first lists eighty-two names, and the second contains Icó's request, which is granted, for exemption from military service for fifty peons.

6. A nephew's recollection that Icó began his day by reading newspapers calls to mind Hegel's comment that "reading the newspaper in early morning is a kind of realistic morning prayer. One orients one's attitude against the world and toward God [in one case], or toward that which the world is [in the other]. The former gives the same security as the latter, in that one knows where one stands." Cited in Susan Buck-Morss, "Hegel and the Haiti," *Critical Inquiry* 26, no. 4 (Summer 2000): 844.

7. The Partido de Acción Revolucionaria's *El Libertador,* May 4, 1945, ran such a story on concentration camps.

8. See Archivo General de Centro América Juicios–Alta Verapaz, index 105 29C 8 (hereafter cited as AGCA J-AV, followed by numbers indicating index, legajo, and expediente).

9. AGCA J-AV, index 104 22B 33.

10. AGCA B 29462, September 9, 1920.

11. David McCreery, *Rural Guatemala: 1760–1940* (Stanford: Stanford University Press, 1994); Lowell Gudmunson and Hector Lindo-Fuentos, *Central America, 1821–1871: Liberalism before Liberals* (Tuscaloosa: University of Alabama Press, 1995); and Julio Castellanos Cambranes, *Café y campesinos en Guatemala, 1853–1897* (Guatemala City: University of San Carlos, 1985), describe in detail the political and economic transformation to coffee production.

12. Kalman Silvert, *A Study in Government: Guatemala* (New Orleans: Tulane University, Middle American Research Institute, 1954), pp. 63–68. For Carchá, see AGCA JP-AV, December 11, 1924 (but found in the bundle marked 1925).

13. AGCA JP-AV, "estadísticas agrícolas," May 1879.

14. McCreery, *Rural Guatemala*, pp. 195–257, discusses the workings of liberal land legislation. For Alta Verapaz, see Guillermo Náñez Falcón, "Erwin Paul Dieseldorff: Guatemala Entrepreneur in the Alta Verapaz of Guatemala, 1889–1937" (Ph.D. diss., Tulane University, 1970), pp. 102–5.

15. Wade Kit, "*Costumbre,* Conflict, and Consensus: Kekchí-Finquero Discourse in

the Alta Verapaz, Guatemala, 1880–1930" (Ph.D. diss., Tulane University, 1998), p. 81; see also Náñez Falcón, "Erwin Paul Dieseldorff," chaps. 2 and 3.

16. Called in Spanish *caseríos* and in Q'eqchi' *calebales,* discussed in Antonio Goubaud Carrera, Juan de Díos Rosales, and Sol Tax, "Reconnaissance of Northern Guatemala, 1944," Microfilm Collection of Manuscripts on Middle American Cultural Anthropology, no. 17, University of Chicago, 1947, p. 124.

17. Kit, "*Costumbre,* Conflict, and Consensus," p. 34. The department of Alta Verapaz well into the 1960s had the highest number of resident peons; Dirección General de Estadística, *II Censo Agropecuario 1964,* vol. 4 (Guatemala City: Dirección General de Estadística, 1969), p. 346. Karl Sapper, the German ethnographer and historian, mentions two events that furthered debt peonage: First, Guatemala's switch to paper money and the gold standard in 1897 led to a precipitous drop in the price of silver and impoverished many rural families who had much of their wealth in silver necklaces; second, a 1902 volcano eruption destroyed corn crops, driving many Q'eqchi's onto plantations for survival; in King, *Cobán and the Verapaz,* pp. 31, 35. AGCA JP-AV, "Comisión conciliadora en las cuestiones que surgen entre jornaleros y patrones," July 23, 1877, and Alta Verapaz's Ministerio de Gobernación collection of the AGCA 28584 (hereafter cited as MG-AV followed by legajo number), describes pre-1871 state-administered labor drafts.

18. Karl Sapper, *Die Alta Verapaz* (Hamburg: Friederichsen, 1902), p. 133. By the end of the nineteenth century, in Latin America only the south of Brazil was as dominated by Germans as was Alta Verapaz; Náñez Falcón, "Erwin Paul Dieseldorff."

19. See King, *Cobán and the Verapaz,* p. 93, and Regina Wagner, *Los Alemanes en Guatemala, 1828–1944* (Guatemala City: Afanes, 1996), p. 174. The first wave of German planters were more willing than their Ladino counterparts to engage with indigenous culture, writing extensively on Q'eqchi' history, language, archaeology, and culture to produce some of the most detailed studies yet available. The acquisition of local knowledge by Germans was not solely academic as settler-scholars used soil analysis and geographic surveying to stake their land claims. Others, such as Erwin Dieseldorff, who by the end of his life enjoyed the sobriquet *el viejo Maya* (the Old Maya), employed his Q'eqchi' cultural and linguistic fluency to manage his workers; in Kit, "*Costumbre,* Conflict, and Consensus," chap. 5. For other examples, see David Sapper, "Costumbres y creencias religiosas de los indios Queckchí," in *Anales de la Sociedad de Geografía y Historia* 2, no. 2 (December 1925): 189–97, and the "Dieseldorff Collection," Tulane University Library, Special Collections Division, which holds many of Erwin Paul Dieseldorff's unpublished scholarly papers.

20. King, *Cobán and the Verapaz,* p. 93.

21. AGCA B 99342 6806.

22. King, *Cobán and the Verapaz,* p. 38.

23. AGCA MG-AV 31402 1938.

24. McCreery, *Rural Guatemala,* p. 243, notes that in the 1870s Q'eqchi' community leaders in Cobán successfully titled holdings under the new laws. Also see AGCA ST-AV 4 2 and 8, 6 1, 10 4, and 13 10.

25. Náñez Falcón, "Erwin Paul Dieseldorff," p. 99.

26. Ibid., pp. 87–97.

27. King, *Cobán and the Verapaz*, p. 299.

28. Susan Buck-Morss, *Dreamworld and Catastrophe: The Passing of Mass Utopia in East and West* (Cambridge: MIT Press, 2000), p. 3, uses the term "wild zone" of power to highlight the permeability between constructions of legitimate and illegitimate violence, a "blind spot, a zone in which power is above the law and thus, at least potentially, a terrain of terror." For my purposes here, I stress the distinction, however notional, between private and public violence to capture the historical consequences of popular demand for state intervention.

29. Karl Marx, *Capital* (New York: International Publishers, 1967), 1:538.

30. In the Libro de Protocolos collection of the AGCA (hereafter cited as AGCA LP, followed by the name of the lawyer or notary and date), Rafael Nuila, March 15, 1898, and January 10, 1897.

31. AGCA JP-AV, "Mozos de Finca El Valle de la Cieba," 1903.

32. *El Norte*, April 25, 1922. Kit, "*Costumbre*, Conflict, and Consensus," p. 161, describes Erwin Paul Dieseldorff's purchase of a farm and its population.

33. See Joseph A. Pitti, "Jorge Ubico and Guatemalan Politics in the 1920s" (Ph.D. diss., University of New Mexico, 1975), pp. 20–29, for opposition to Estrada Cabrera. McCreery, *Rural Guatemala*, pp. 222–23, documents planter dissatisfaction with Estrada Cabrera. For the central role played by artisans and a growing working class, see Asociación de Investigación y Estudios Sociales, ed., *Más de 100 años del movimiento obrero urbano en Guatemala: Artesanos y obreros en el periodo liberal, 1877–1944*, vol. 1 (Guatemala City: Asociación de Investigación y Estudios Sociales, 1991), pp. 64–118, and Carlos Figueroa Ibarra, "Contenido de clase y participación obrera en el movimiento antidictatorial de 1920," *Política y sociedad* 4, no. 5 (1974).

34. In 1917 an earthquake that devastated Guatemala City underscored the political upheavals of that year's Russian Revolution and Mexico's new constitution, which guaranteed social welfare, labor rights, and land to all citizens. In 1921, delegates to the founding meeting of the Central American Workers' Congress called on their countries to follow Mexico's example, while the Guatemalan Communist newspaper reporter Federico Alvarado linked Russia's political upheaval to his own country's recent natural disaster: "the fall of the Russian monarch was like a universal earthquake that shook the foundation and awoke the sleeping. . . . We are now in contact not only with our brothers in Latin America but with those of the whole world." In Federación Obrera de Guatemala para la Protección Legal del Trabajo, *Memorias del Congreso del Trabajo Centroamericano, celebrado en la ciudad de Guatemala en septiembre de 1921* (Guatemala City: Imprenta Nacional, 1922), p. 77.

35. Quoted in Wade Kit, "Precursor of Change: Failed Reform and the Guatemalan Coffee Elite, 1918–1926" (master's thesis, University of Saskatchewan, 1987), p. 32.

36. McCreery, *Rural Guatemala*, pp. 296–97; Arturo Taracena Arriola, "La Confederación Obrera Centroaméricana (COCA): 1921–1926," *Anuario de Estudios Centroamericanos* 10 (1984): 81–93; and Arturo Taracena Arriola "Presencia anarquista en

Guatemala," *Mesoamérica* 9, no. 15 (1988). The 1925 decree establishing the Department of Labor is reprinted in the *Revista de Trabajo,* January 1926, pp. 145–146. During this decade, Guatemala ratified the International Labour Organization's convention calling for a forty-eight-hour workweek, established a savings and loan bank for workers, and mandated an eight-hour workday; see Ralph Lee Woodward, "Communist Infiltration of the Guatemalan Urban Labor Movement, 1920–1954" (master's thesis, Tulane University, 1959), p. 9. For the "generation of 1920," see Epaminondas Quintana, *Historia de la generación de 1920* (Guatemala City: Tipografía Nacional, 1971). For John Stuart Mill, see *El Imparcial,* June 24, 1922. *El Unionista,* June 17 and 18, 1920, carries articles debating women's suffrage.

37. By the end of 1920, the Partido Unionista had organized branches in most department capitals and large municipalities. Its labor affiliate, La Liga Obrera, likewise established offices in Huehuetenango, Quetzaltenango, Sololá, and on the southern coast; see *El Unionista,* June 2, 12, and 14, 1920, February 26, 1921, May 6, 1921, July 29, 1921, August 4, 20, and 23, 1921.

38. McCreery, *Rural Guatemala,* pp. 296–300.

39. *New York Herald,* January 15, 1920; *El Excelsior,* September 1, 1921; and *El Unionista,* March 4, 1920. *El Excelsior,* August 17, 1921, blames a deadly land conflict on the Partido Unionista. *El Excelsior,* September 2 and October 11, 1921, carries reports of more rural unrest, including a supposed plot by conservatives to spark a "*revolución de indios*" to counter their liberal rivals.

40. AGCA B 29466, April 3, 1920.

41. Sapper, "Costumbres y Creencias." As early as 1849, indigenous communities along the Polochic River protested against Ladinos who had taken their land, leading to a minor uprising headed by a Poqomchi' Maya named Feliciano María; in Archivo Eclesiástico de Arzobispado de Guatemala (hereafter cited as AEA), Vicaría: Verapaz, 1844–1854, February 15, 1949. In the 1850s, guerrillas roamed the Sierra Santa Cruz and harassed foreign settlers and government officials; AEA, Vicaría: Verapaz, 1844–1854, June 15, 1852. For the Carchá riots, see the discussion in the introduction as well as *El Demócrata,* July 25 and November 7, 1886, and Karl Sapper, *Mittelamerikanische Reisen und Studien aus den Jahren 1888 bis 1900* (Braunschweig: Vieweg und Sohn, 1902), pp. 194–95. AGCA JP-AV, 1877, contains information on an 1877 violent protest in Cahabón. AGCA B 28579 160159 has one of the first complaints against coffee cultivation in 1859.

42. Cited in Michaela Schmölz-Häberlein, "Continuity and Change in a Guatemalan Indian Community: San Cristóbal-Verapaz, 1870–1940," *Hispanic American Historical Review* 76, no. 2 (1996): 244. Eric Foner, *The Story of American Freedom* (New York: W.W. Norton, 1998), and Judith Shklar, *American Citizenship* (Cambridge: Harvard University Press, 1991), discuss the slavery-freedom dichotomy in U.S. history. Jeffrey L. Gould, *To Die in This Way: Nicaraguan Indians and the Myth of Mestizaje, 1880–1965* (Durham: Duke University Press, 1998), p. 141, analyzes a similar opposition in Nicaragua.

43. AGCA JP-AV, "Tomás Pop, Domingo Tut, José Cuz, Ignacio Ycal, y compañeros

al Jefe Político," May 18, 1902. Some other examples: "They treat us badly, like slaves," complained 123 Poqomchi's from Tucurú in 1917, in AGCA JP-AV, June 23, 1917; "They have established a true system of slavery with us Indians," said seven Q'eqchi's in 1903 to the minister of development, in AGCA JP-AV, August 21, 1903; "We are not slaves but citizens," wrote 138 Q'eqchi's to the president in 1907, found in SPCMA, December 12, 1907; and "The constitution guarantees the complete liberty of all individuals, rich and poor, Ladinos and Indígenas. . . . The arbitrary practice [of forced labor] in Carchá against us of the *clase indígena* can not be more illegal," AGCA JP-AV, February 11, 1925.

44. See the discussion in chapter 1 of Glendon, *World Made New.*

45. Lukács, *Historical Novel,* p. 20.

46. For example: AGCA JP-AV, "Acta Levantada por la municipal de San Juan Chamelco proclamado como su único candidato a la presidencia de la republica . . . Señor Licenciado Manuel Estrada Cabrera," June 15, 1915 (but found in the bundle marked 1925).

47. AGCA B 29468, August 15, 1920.

48. After five days of balloting designed to allow those who lived in remote areas time to get to the polls, Herrera won 239,510 votes while his two main rivals garnered a total of a little over 13,000; *El Unionista,* August 30, 1920. For the sympathetic prefect *(jefe político),* see AGCA J-AV, index 104 22B 33.

49. AGCA J-AV, index 104 22B 33.

50. AGCA B 29462, September 9, 1920. Máximo Kring complains in AGCA J-AV, index 104 22B 33, of Icó's "reckless mouth."

51. AGCA B 29462, September 9, 1920.

52. AGCA J-AV, index 104 22B 33.

53. Ibid.

54. SPCMA, January 10, 1921.

55. SPCMA, January 15, 1921.

56. In Kit, "*Costumbre,* Conflict, and Consensus" p. 210. See also AGCA JP-AV, March 7, 1925, and AGCA J-AV, index 104 26B 29.

57. AGCA J-AV, index 104 26B 29.

58. AGCA MG-AV 30507 40; AGCA MG-AV 30792 12.

59. AGCA J-AV, index 105 28B 21.

60. AGCA MG-AV 30506, December 4, 1931.

61. AGCA J-AV, index 105 29C 8.

62. AGCA J-AV, index 105 31B 13; AGCA MG-AV 30507 27.

63. Gould, *To Die in This Way,* chap. 4, provides a close analysis of elite male sexual conquest, as well as the gendered language that infuses relations of rule and domination in highland Nicaragua. Roger Lancaster describes the "intimacies of power" in urban Nicaragua in *Life Is Hard: Machismo, Danger, and the Intimacy of Power in Nicaragua* (Berkeley: University of California Press, 1992).

64. In Alta Verapaz's Departamento Agrario Nacional— the agency charged with carrying out Guatemala's 1952–54 Agrarian Reform—collection of the AGCA

(hereafter cited as AGCA DAN-AV, followed by numbers indicating packet and file) 1B 11.

65. Reports on Icó's sexuality come from a series of interviews with Eliseo Ax Burmester in July 2000 and August 2001 in San Pedro Carchá. Ax, an eighty-six-year-old man who considers himself Q'eqchi' (he is the extramarital son of a Q'eqchi' woman and a German man), was a founding member of Icó's 1944 Frente Popular Libertador de Indígenas. Icó's nephew, Alfredo Cucul, remembers that once while he was in Cahabón around 1945, one of his uncle's political opponents alluded to his homosexuality, but Cucul insists that this was a common insult against supporters of Juan José Arévalo since most of Arévalo's supporters were young men. Much of the following discussion on the historical importance of Icó's remembered sexuality owes greatly to anthropologist Sarah Hill, with whom I conducted much of the relevant archival research and interviews.

66. King, *Cobán and the Verapaz*, chap. 7, discusses sexual innuendo. Anthropologist Antonio Goubaud Carrera, writing in the 1940s, reports on the ridicule leveled at promiscuous Q'eqchi' men and women in "Notes on San Juan Chamelco, Alta Verapaz," Microfilm Collection of Manuscripts on Middle American Cultural Anthropology, no. 23, University of Chicago, 1949, p. 26. Women who found themselves in sexual disputes with men or women often had to fend off rumors of prostitution, pregnancy, or abortion. Jealous rivalry, for example, apparently drove Cristina Max in 1963 to spread the rumor that Macaria Yat Coy visited the doctor not for parasites but to "remove" her baby, and in 1939 "street gossip" accused Marta Maaz of abortion; AGCA J-AV, index 106 69D 356; AGCA MG-AV 31557 1939.

67. The attack on Chisec is in Karl Sapper, *Alta Verapaz*, p. 24; for the 1865 riot, see the discussion in the introduction.

68. Municipality of Cahabón, "Datos Monográficos del Municipio de Santa María Cahabón," 1990, unpublished monograph in author's possession.

69. AGCA MG-AV 30506, December 4, 1931.

70. AGCA B 29462, September 9, 1920.

71. AGCA J-AV, index 105 29C 8; AGCA JP-AV, "Informe Mensual de Carchá," 1946, and SPCMA, May 24, 1932.

72. In Náñez Falcón, "Erwin Paul Dieseldorff," p. 344.

73. Joaquín Noval, comp., "Socio-económica de la región kekchi," unpublished manuscript compiled by the Instituto Indigenista Nacional, 1950–52, located at Tulane's Latin American Library; and James Kitchen, "Municipal Government in Guatemala" (Ph.D. diss., University of California, Los Angeles, 1955). Also documents detailing the 1865 riot discussed in the introduction provide information on the network of municipal authority. AGCA JP-AV, "Comisión conciliadora en las cuestiones que surgen entre jornaleros y patrones," July 23, 1877, describes cofradía responsibility in supplying labor for early coffee production.

74. The 1879 decree is found in SPCMA. Also SPCMA, "Correspondencia de la jefatura política," January 29, 1918, lists 75 alcaldes auxiliares and 525 subordinates to the alcaldes auxiliares covering the whole Carchá municipality.

75. During the first decades of coffee, for example, cofradías were responsible for supplying workers to the plantations; AGCA JP-AV, "Comisión conciliadora en las cuestiones que surgen entre jornaleros y patrones," July 23, 1877.

76. SPCMA, January 20, 1921.

77. AGCA J-AV, index 105 29C 8.

78. SPCMA, "Santiago Cucul Tuil, mayor de edad, casado, agricultor sin instrucción, originario y vecino de Carchá," October 15, 1945.

79. AGCA MG-AV 32578 37.

80. *El Libertador,* December 9, 1944.

81. Richard Adams [Newbold Stokes, pseud.], "Receptivity to Communist Fomented Agitation in Rural Guatemala," *Economic Development and Cultural Change* 5, no. 1 (October 1956): 360.

82. See *El Libertador,* August 27, 1947. See Kitchen, "Municipal Government," pp. 55–58, for the legislation granting municipal autonomy. Silvert, *Study in Government,* takes Cobán and Carchá as case studies.

83. Cited in Jim Handy, *Revolution in the Countryside: Rural Conflict and Agrarian Reform in Guatemala, 1944–1954* (Chapel Hill: University of North Carolina Press, 1994), p. 10.

84. See McCreery, *Rural Guatemala,* pp. 316–22, for a discussion of Ubico's vagrancy law.

85. The 1945 constitution is in Silvert, *Study in Government,* pp. 207–39.

86. A 1946 circular issued by the national government clarified who was subject to the vagrancy laws: "any individual who did not have a receipt or a work card from the previous year or the first two months of this agricultural year," in SPCMA, May 26, 1946. See also 1945's congressional decree 118, which defines vagrants and sets a prison term of thirty days. In *Recopilación de las leyes de la República de Guatemala* (Guatemala City: Tipografía Nacional, 1947), vol. 66.

87. AGCA JP-AV, "Informe Mensual de Carchá," 1946; SPCMA, "Informes del juzgado de paz," 1946.

88. SPCMA, November 10, 1947.

89. In the Ministerio de Trabajo collection of the AGCA 48750, April 11, 1947 (hereafter cited as AGCA MT followed by legajo number and, when available, date).

90. SPCMA, April 29, 1947.

91. SPCMA, December 19, 1949.

92. As did the Partido Unionista before them, most post-1944 revolutionary parties had auxiliary indigenous sections. Although Icó's organization was often referred to as the Partido de Acción Revolucionaria de Indígenas, it was the only manifestation of the PAR in Carchá. To the degree that it could be considered an auxiliary of the PAR, it was to the Cobán branch of the PAR.

93. Handy, *Revolution in the Countryside,* pp. 149–50 and Archer C. Bush, "Organized Labor in Guatemala: A Case Study of an Adolescent Labor Movement in an Underdeveloped Country," Colgate University Area Studies Latin American Seminar

Reports, no. 2 (Hamilton, N.Y., 1950), part 3, pp. 20–23, discuss *comunidades.* In an interview found in the Robert Alexander Collection at Rutgers University and dated August 11, 1948, Miguel Mármol, the famous Salvadoran Communist who worked as an advisor to the CTG, gives an idea of the new confederation's relationship to indigenous leaders like Icó. As transcribed by Alexander, Mármol reported that organizers of the "CTG go out from Guatemala City into the countryside, many of them practically abandoning their families and going out to do organization work, gaining nothing for their work, and hardly knowing where their next meal is coming. But this is all now beginning to bear fruits, though the Confederation is only three years old. The Indians now come into the capital and look up the headquarters of the Confederation. They will come in delegations, usually led by a 'cacique,' and he will usually be their spokesman. He many times will not be able to talk Spanish, and the people in the office don't know the Indian languages, so Marmol has developed the technique of drawing pictures to represent what he wants to say to them. When the cacique understands what the idea is, he turns around and tells his companeros *[sic]*, and then turns back to continue the conversation. There are now growing up a group of leaders among the Indians in the countryside, who are propagandizing the ideas of the C.T.G. and organizing the Indians. They of course speak in the Indian languages, and don't have these problems just mentioned."

94. *El Imparcial,* September 9, 1946.

95. Ibid.

96. Vivian Gornick, *The Romance of American Communism* (New York: Basic Books, 1977), p. 8.

97. AGCA J-AV, index 106 47G 17. One witness testified that Icó admonished peasants to take good care of their livestock so that they would not be accused of being "*huevones*" (lazy), suggesting that Icó functioned as a disciplinarian to his peasant followers, disseminating certain normative practices and values associated with work and production.

98. SPCMA, April 29, 1947.

99. AGCA MT 48750, April 11, 1947.

100. SPCMA, July 23, 1947.

101. AGCA J-AV, index 105 29C 8.

102. In Gilda Liliana Ochaita de Escaler, "Pervivencia de las Cofradías Indígenas en Rabinal, Guatemala" (*licenciatura* thesis, Universidad Rafael Landivar, Facultad de Humanidades, 1974), p. 100. LC-GDC, reel 2, frame 531, contains a telegram from Tecú describing Rabinal's 1952 May Day parade. *El Imparcial,* May 6, 11, and 20 and June 1, 1945, describes a 1945 protest that resulted in a military occupation of the town to forestall a feared uprising. See also my "The Strange Case of 'La Mancha Negra': Maya-State Relations in Nineteenth-Century Guatemala," *Hispanic American Historical Review* 77, no. 2 (1997): 211–43, which discusses the Cantel leader Antonio Colop Estrada.

103. *Diario de Centro América,* May 22, 1950.

104. SPCMA, January 25, 1947.

105. The national labor federation's bulletin, *Acción Campesina,* June 1, 1951, reports that Cucul, now as leader of Icó's Comunidad Agraria, was still trying to end the application of the vagrancy laws in Carchá and uncompensated public work.

106. Family memories are supported by a 1951 interview with Alfredo Cucul, Icó's great-nephew, found in "Datos sacados del diario del campo de Rosalío Saquic C," section K, p. 4, of the unpublished manuscript "Socio-económica de la región kekchi," cited above.

CHAPTER 2. AN UNCORRUPTED LIFE

1. All information and quotations unless otherwise noted concerning Alfredo Cucul and Manuela Caal de Cucul come from a series of interviews conducted July 2000, June–August 2001, and November 2001 in Guatemala City.

2. The labor code and the social security system were actually implemented by Arévalo; both were amended and extended by Arbenz's government.

3. Piero Gleijeses, *Shattered Hope: The Guatemalan Revolution and the United States, 1944–1954* (Princeton: Princeton University Press, 1991), pp. 8–29; Cindy Forster, *The Time of Freedom: Campesino Workers in Guatemala's October Revolution* (Pittsburgh: University of Pittsburgh Press, 2001), pp. 12–34.

4. Immediately after the triumph of the October Revolution, the new minister of agriculture sent a circular to all municipalities ensuring that all existing debts and laws would continue to be respected; in SPCMA, October 29, 1944. Likewise, the first incarnation of the labor code required that 60 percent of the membership of peasant unions be literate, which proved a great obstacle. In response to growing agrarian unrest, Arévalo prohibited labor organizing until the code was adopted (although evidence suggests he quietly continued to support it); see Edwin Warren Bishop, "The Guatemalan Labor Movement, 1944–1959" (Ph.D. diss., University of Wisconsin, 1959), pp. 25–26.

5. *Diario de Centro América,* February 25 and 26, 1947, reports on the labor code. See also Gleijeses, *Shattered Hope,* pp. 41–43, 94–95; Bishop, "Guatemalan Labor Movement," pp. 43–50; and Bush, "Organized Labor in Guatemala," pp. 41–43.

6. The 1877 forced labor law, for example, mandated that workplace disputes be mediated by either department precepts *(jefes políticos)* or municipal authorities and not by the regular court system; see McCreery, *Rural Guatemala,* p. 188.

7. Interview, Edgar Champney, November 2001.

8. Bishop, "Guatemalan Labor Movement," p. 51, describes the functioning of the ministry of labor and labor courts.

9. AGCA MT 48762 1948.

10. AGCA MT 48832 1953.

11. AGCA MT 48778, November 8, 1950; AGCA MT 48769 1949.

12. AGCA MT 48825 1953.

13. AGCA MT 48806 1951.

14. AGCA MT 48804 1950.

15. AGCA MT 48805 1951.

16. AGCA MT 48768, July 2, 1949.

17. AGCA MT 48825 1953.

18. Arturo Taracena Arriola, *Les origines du mouvement ouvrier au Guatemala, 1878–1932* (Paris, 1982), describes the beginning of the Guatemalan labor movement. Bush, "Organized Labor in Guatemala," part 2, discusses the spread of organized workers' associations into nearly every corner of Guatemalan life.

19. For examples, see AGCA MT, legajos 48754, 48803, 48807, 48800, 48802, and 48824.

20. See AGCA MT 48754 1948 for the slogan; Bush, "Organized Labor in Guatemala," for the candy makers' union. In Alta Verapaz, shoe factory workers organized the department's first nonagricultural union. AGCA AV-MG 1944 51 and AGCA AV-MP, papers, 1944, describe an early labor conflict at the Calzado Cobán, which employed over two hundred workers and was owned by Bernardo Burmester, "German subject" and Eliseo Ax Burmester's father (see chapter 1). The government declared the strike illegal.

21. Total union membership, as well as the number of peasant unions—1,785—comes from Neale J. Pearson, "The *Confederación Nacional Campesina de Guatemala* (SNCG) and Peasant Unionism in Guatemala, 1944–1954" (master's thesis, Georgetown University, 1964), p. 43. Voting population of 415,000 is from U.S. Department of State, *Intervention of International Communism in Guatemala* (Washington, D.C.: U.S. Government Printing Office, 1954), p. 75.

22. AGCA MT 48753.

23. AGCA MT 48753, January 3, 1948.

24. AGCA MT 48762 1948

25. AGCA MT 48733.

26. Gleijeses, *Shattered Hope*, pp. 94–95

27. Interview, Alfonso Bauer Paiz, June 2001. According to Bauer Paiz, who was the minister of labor, the remoteness of Alta Verapaz and its rural plantations made labor inspection practically impossible in the zone. AGCA MT 48807 describes the shortage of labor inspectors.

28. Bishop, "Guatemalan Labor Movement," pp. 76–77, and Pearson, "*Confederación*," pp. 45–46, discuss the difficulty of organizing peasant unions prior to the reform.

29. John Lewis Gaddis, *We Now Know*, p. 178.

30. Gleijeses responds to a particularly opportunistic reading of *Shattered Hope* in "Afterword: The Culture of Fear," in Nick Cullather's *Secret History: The CIA's Classified Account of Its Operations in Guatemala, 1952–1954* (Stanford: Stanford University Press, 1999), pp. xxviii–xxix, xxxii.

31. Many of the older Communists released from Ubico's prisons played only a peripheral role in the new party, gravitating instead to the short-lived Partido Revolucionario Obrero de Guatemala. Founded by Víctor Manuel Gutiérrez, the PROG was

an effort to form a Marxist political party led by workers and union members as opposed to the "nucleus of petty bourgeois intellectuals," as Fortuny described himself and his PGT-cofounders; see Marco Antonio Flores, ed., *Fortuny: Un comunista guatemalteco* (Guatemala City: Universidad de San Carlos, 1994), p. 172. See also Antonio Obando Sánchez, *Memorias* (Guatemala City: Editorial Universitaria, 1978), pp. 114–36; and Gleijeses, *Shattered Hope*, p. 77. Gutiérrez dissolved the PROG in 1952 and joined the PGT. Robert Alexander, *Communism in Latin America* (New Brunswick: Rutgers University Press 1957); Graciela García, *Páginas de lucha revolucionaria en Centroamérica* (Mexico City: Ediciones Linterna, 1971); Huberto Alvarado Arellano, *Apuntes para la historia del Partido Guatemalteco de Trabajo* (Guatemala City: Ediciones PGT, 1975), provide detailed histories of the PGT.

32. Fortuny at thirty-four was the oldest of the PGT founders; the median age of the 1953 congress was thirty-five; see Ronald Schneider, *Communism in Guatemala, 1944–1954* (New York: Praeger, 1958), p. 39. Gleijeses, *Shattered Hope*, pp. 186–87, documents the PGT's autonomy from the Soviet Union and isolation from other Latin American Communist parties. Bishop, "Guatemalan Labor Movement," pp. 130–35, 145–49, and Pearson, "*Confederación*," p. 121, are two anti-communist sources that confirm the dishonesty, pettiness, and lack of vision of the non-Communist labor unions and acknowledge the commitment to reform of Communists.

33. Schneider, *Communism in Guatemala*, pp. 94–96.

34. Gleijeses, *Shattered Hope*, p. 193.

35. *Diario de Centro América*, May 22, 1950.

36. Gleijeses, *Shattered Hope*, pp. 189–96. The PGT had only four congressional deputies, but they sat on all the most important committees.

37. The first draft of Decreto 900, the Agrarian Reform legislation, for example, was written by Fortuny, and the final version was composed by a PGT-dominated committee that included Fortuny, Gutiérrez, and one non-Communist, the national peasants' association's Castillo Flores.

38. Interview, Alfonso Bauer Paiz, June 2001: "It wasn't a requirement that inspectors be members of the PAR or the PGT, but many were." Neale Pearson, supportive of reform but hostile to the PGT, writes, "very little the Communists did in Guatemala was sensational or extraordinary. They merely organized closely where others organized loosely. They worked devotedly for their group's interest while others worked for their interest. They did the dreary, menial jobs while others sought the glamorous jobs. The Communists, though a numerically small part of the population, captured the slogans and influenced the machinery of other parties"; Pearson, "*Confederación*," p. 121. AGCA MT 48805 1951 contains planter complaints of labor inspectors returning at night to the plantation to try to "win adepts to the party to which they belong."

39. The 1954 overthrow of Arbenz greatly restricted the space available for political activity, and many PGT members opted to join the Partido Revolucionario (PR), the successor to the PAR and the only reform party allowed to operate legally. Some, such as Leonardo Castillo Flores and Marcelino Xol, radicalized by the coup, moved in the opposite direction and joined the PGT, which many now saw as the only legitimate

heir to the October Revolution. Other PAR members passed to the PR but continued to work, as they had prior to 1954, with the PGT. (See discussion in chapter 3.)

40. Flores, *Fortuny*, p. 187.

41. Ibid., p. 189. As to the speeches, Fortuny writes that "we did all that we could to avoid language that could be taken as Communist. . . . when we talked about the need to liquidate feudalism, we didn't use this language. Instead, we talked about the need to break with our colonial past. . . . Nobody said these were speeches written by Communists. This was kept between Arbenz and my *compañeros* on the central committee of the party" (p. 191).

42. There is unanimous agreement among historians that the Agrarian Reform did, in the majority of cases, what it was designed to do: expropriate idle land from large plantations and absentee landlords. Under its provisions, the uncultivated portion of plantations larger than 672 acres, as well as properties between 274 and 672 acres if more than two-thirds of their land was not planted, was subject to confiscation. In compensation, affected owners would receive government-issued bonds worth the equivalent of the expropriated land's value as listed in tax declarations. Gleijeses, *Shattered Hope*, pp. 149–64; Handy, *Revolution in the Countryside*, pp. 86–100; Pablo Schneider, Hugo Maul, and Luis Mauricio Membreño, *El mito de la reforma agraria: 40 años de experimentación en Guatemala* (Guatemala City: Centro de Investigaciones Económicas Nacionales, 1989), pp. 13–16; José Luis Paredes Moreira, *Reforma agraria: Una experiencia en Guatemala* (Guatemala City: Imprenta Universitaria, 1963).

43. CALS were inserted into the land reform bill through the initiative of the PGT; see Gleijeses, *Shattered Hope*, p. 152. The PGT also included in the final legislation the controversial provision of granting land to peasants in life tenure rather than as private property. This measure was taken both to prevent peasants from selling their grants and, according to Fortuny, to lay the groundwork for a future collective society. Since the Agrarian Reform was short-lived, this provision was inconsequential except that it served as a rallying point for the growing anti-communist movement, which claimed it was in favor of a land reform based on private property. Gustavo Porras writes that at the Revolution's end, there existed over three thousand CALS. Porras, "Análisis estructural y recomposición clasista de la sociedad guatemalteca de 1954–1980," Centro de Estudios Integrados de Desarrollo Comunal, ed., *Seminario Estado, Clases Sociales y Cuestión Etnico-Nacional* (Mexico City: Editorial Praxis, 1992), remains the most insightful discussion of the CALS. Bishop, "Guatemalan Labor Movement," p. 158, and Department of State, *Intervention of International Communism in Guatemala*, p. 70, single out the CALS for criticism.

44. The Comité Agrario Departamental also had five members, one each appointed by the landowners association, the department governor, the reform's national oversight board , the national labor federation, and the national peasant federation.

45. SPCMA, July 21, 1952.

46. SPCMA, August 18, 1952.

47. In Carchá, Cucul worked with Miguel Guzmán, a PGT member from Jutiapa and public school teacher. In Rabinal, Tomás Tecú and José María López Valdizón, PGT member, delegate to the national labor federation's executive committee, and author of the social realist novel *Sudor y protesta* (Guatemala City: Editorial del Ministerio de Educación Pública, 1953), organized for the PGT. In Cahabón and Senahú, Francisco Curley, Federico García, and Marcelino Xol worked together. Prior to the October Revolution, in rural Guatemala where there were commercial plantations, agrarian radicals, many of them influenced by the Mexican Revolution or exiles from El Salvador, forged ties with local rural workers; see Forster, *Time of Freedom*, pp. 76–81. Carlos Figueroa Ibarra, "El 'bolchevique mexicano' de la Centroamérica de los veinte," in *Memoria* 4, no. 31 (September–October 1990): 213–25, contains an interview with Jorge Fernández Anaya, a member of the Mexican Communist Party who clandestinely organized K'iche' plantation workers in Totonicapán in the late 1920s.

48. The court case in AGCA J-AV, index 107 61J 2788, details Hernández's 1954 arrest and gives a good snapshot of the valley's Arbencista network.

49. In Cobán, the PGT drew support mostly among the teachers and students of the Instituto Normalista. Among the members of Cobán's PGT's youth group, Juventud Democrática, were Hans Overdick, who would join the FAR and be killed in combat, and his brother Walter, who was mayor of Panzós at the time of the 1978 massacre.

50. The number of Alta Verapaz unions comes from Pearson, "*Confederación*," p. 42. Basic information on 118 of these unions is located in the box labeled "Comunidades—Alta Verapaz" in the archives of Guatemala's Ministerio de Gobernación.

51. Mariano Rossell y Arellano, *Tactics and Works of Communism* (Des Moines: National Catholic Rural Life Conference, 1955), p. 8.

52. The following account comes from *Acción Campesina*, June 20, 1952, and interviews with Alfredo Cucul.

53. *Diario de Centro América*, June 2, 1952, describes the remarks of other indigenous activists. In his comments Fortuny said that the days of the planters, "spiritual descendants of the conquistadors and the stockade," were numbered; Manuel Galich, head of the FPL, told the crowd that neither the labor code nor the social security program would have any real effect "as long as campesinos had no land"; and Gutiérrez cautioned rural activists to "protect their leaders" because violence in the countryside was on the rise. *Acción Campesina* carried reports of harassment against agrarian leaders, including an article on the "first martyr" of the Agrarian Reform, Alberto Recinos of Chiqumula, killed by anti-communist "*terratenientes feudales*" (June 20, 1952). See also *Acción Campesina*, August 1, 1953.

54. In 1954 the U.S. anthropologist Richard Adams conducted a survey among jailed rural supporters of Arbenz to determine the sociological factors that contributed to peasant "receptivity to communist fomented agitation," as the published report was subsequently titled. Despite being greatly shaped by the Cold War and limited, as the author admits, by a geographically skewed sample group, the report is fascinating. Among some of its more interesting conclusions are: (1) the sample group had a higher literacy rate than the country as a whole; (2) while members of the unions

and CALs were not religiously active, there was a "strong correlation between activity in political parties and activity in religious associations. This was probably due to the fact that on the community level, both are means to local power" (p. v); (3) poverty and landlessness were not characteristic of the sample population, since 43 percent were "economically adequate" and 36 percent had been landowners prior to the Agrarian Reform. In short, Adams's research corresponds with many of the observations made here about the diversity and depth of support for the Agrarian Reform: "It may be said that these people were being led like sheep in that they did what the Communists wanted; on the other hand, they were doing things which they too wished to do. . . . Communism, as it worked on the rural population through the Arbenz government, offered different things to different people. The members of the rural population who followed Arbenz did not all do it for the same reason" (p. v). That the report likewise takes all jailed peasants as being receptive to "communist agitation" and does not separate out members of anti-communist yet reformist unions and political parties likewise supports the argument that Guatemalan Communism was but one part of a larger environment of reform. Adams, "Receptivity," p. 360. Quotations are from a longer draft of the article located in the Centro de Investigaciones Regionales de Mesoamérica, in Antigua, Guatemala. Many *agrarista* supporters of the Revolution were sincere anti-communists. Amor Velasco can perhaps be considered the department of San Marcos's counterpart to Cucul (or Icó). A relatively well-off tenant farmer, Velasco was strongly influenced by the Mexican Revolution, and, as Cindy Forster describes in *Time of Freedom*, pp. 76–81, had commenced organizing well before the fall of Ubico, building up a peasant network comparable to Icó's and Cucul's. He was, however, at least according to the State Department, expelled from his position as secretary of organization of the national peasant federation for opposing PGT efforts to influence that organization; in U.S. Department of State, *Intervention of International Communism in Guatemala*, pp. 63–64. Gleijeses, *Shattered Hope*, p. 195, reports that in August 1950, the PGT's membership included 50 percent agricultural and industrial workers, 29 percent peasants, and 21 percent middle class, noting that the pressures and time commitments of being in effect the ruling party led the PGT to drop its membership requirements to allow all who sought to join to do so, providing little in the way of political education.

55. *Diario de Centro América*, June 2, 1952, reports that peasants throughout the republic were listening to the speeches on community radios.

56. Under Icó, the Comunidad had been affiliated with the early CTG, but it was now part of the Gutiérrez-led Confederación General de Trabajadores de Guatemala (CGTG), the national labor federation (created in 1951 from the merger of the CTG and another labor federation). Because the CGTG was formed from existing union federations, it already had a head start in the countryside against the Castillo Flores–led peasant federation, the Confederación Nacional Campesina de Guatemala (CNCG), which was organized in 1950.

57. According to records found in the archives of the Ministerio de Gobernación (hereafter cited as AMG), "Comunidades–Alta Verapaz," Carchá rural workers

organized unions in the villages and national plantations of Seabas, Chilté, Canabaj, Sesalché, Ulpan, Chriquin, Chijotón, Cojaj, Sechaj, Chipetón, Sacsí, San Vicente, Chimó, Chinaté, Sacoyou, Xicacao, Chiacám, and Campur. Cucul's co-organizer Miguel Guzmán was a member of the Sindicato de Trabajadores de Educación Guatemalteco (STEG), Guatemala's teachers union, which was led by Víctor Manuel Gutiérrez, who was also a teacher. While the number of teachers committed to reform should not be overestimated (STEG's executive committee complained of the prejudice of many teachers), many infused their pedagogy with social activism, and some, like Guzmán, became active members of the PAR and the PGT. Gutiérrez pushed STEG, which was the only union that had affiliations in all of Guatemala's municipalities, to be the "tutor of the labor movement." Many of its members carried out the literacy campaign that accompanied the land reform. See Bishop, "Guatemalan Labor Movement," pp. 92–94, for Gutiérrez's remark. See also LC-GDC, box 63, "Informe del comité ejecutivo nacional de STEG en el primer tercio de su año de labores," October 25, 1946.

58. The private plantations expropriated in Carchá under the Agrarian Reform tended to be in the municipality's lowlands, in the direction of the Petén or Lanquín; AGCA DAN-AV 2 12, 2 13, and 5 1. For distribution of national plantations, see AGCA DAN-AV *(fincas nacionales)* 17 1, 17 4, 17 10, 17 11, 17 13, 17 14, 17 16, 17 21, and 17 26.

59. See Gleijeses, *Shattered Hope*, p. 52, for the IGSS; Leo Suslow, "Social Security in Guatemala" (Ph.D. diss., University of Connecticut, 1954). In Alta Verapaz, during the Arévalo and Arbenz administrations, IGSS applied only to government employees and national plantations, yet planters still opposed it.

60. For the tanners, see LC-GDC, reel 3, frame 2163, September 25, 1952. Pearson, "*Confederación*," pp. 49–54, describes the reliance of CNCG organizers on government salaries and supplies to conduct their work.

61. LC-GDC, reel 7, frame 4074, contains the complaint of "reactionaries disguised as PRG*istas.*"

62. This equalization paralleled efforts by the new national director of the Guardia Civil, Rogelio Cruz Wer, a PGT ally, to curtail the harassment of peasants by local police chiefs acting on behalf of planters. In February 1953 Cruz issued a memo demanding that chiefs "put an end to such abuses immediately. It is of utmost importance to avoid friction between the policemen and the peasants; otherwise the latter will think of the police . . . with the same revulsion they felt for them during the dictatorship of Ubico . . . . your subordinates . . . must absolutely avoid insulting or abusing the peasants"; quoted in Gleijeses, *Shattered Hope*, p. 163.

63. In Alta Verapaz, the 1953 municipal elections mark a turning point of sorts for the Revolution. Nationally, according to a number of PAR activists, a deal was struck between the PRG and the PAR to split equally the mayoralty of Alta Verapaz's sixteen municipalities. This deal, supposedly brokered by Arbenz, was made to allay the fears of the more moderate PRG that the revolution was getting out of hand. In the new political climate that allowed for fairer voting, the PAR overwhelmingly won fifteen of the sixteen races and reneged on the deal, deepening divisions between pro- and antigovernment forces.

64. Gleijeses, *Shattered Hope*, pp. 155–56. If expropriations from United Fruit are excluded, the department of Verapaz had the most transferred property; Handy, *Revolution in the Countryside*, p. 94. The average size of expropriation—3,507 acres—was also the highest in the republic.

65. LC-GDC, folder "CNCG III Congress, 1954," box 11, February 1954, pp. 1–2.

66. Noval, "Socio-económica de la región kekchi," section K, p. 4, contains a 1950 interview with Alfredo Cucul.

67. Some planters such as Erwin Dieseldorff went further in their efforts to cultivate worker loyalty, financially supporting yearly feasts, making available cheap products such as machetes and cloth to their workers, and working through "traditional" power structures to manage their workforce. Dieseldorff yearly asked for and received exemption from military service for over eight hundred of his plantation's mozos; AGCA JP-AV, May 28, 1925. Q'eqchi's themselves often cited their plantation obligations in order to exempt themselves from public projects. In 1925 the foreman in charge of repairing the road to the Petén complained that "these Indians do not want to work . . . they claim they are plantation peons and therefore are not required to provide labor"; SPCMA, October 23, 1925.

68. AGCA J-AV, index 83 4A 3.

69. All information and quotations, unless otherwise noted, on Saquil's murder come from AGCA J-AV, index 107 59 1770 and from interviews with Alfredo Cucul. LC-GDC, reel 7, frame 3077, contains Cucul's original telegraph to the labor federation's national headquarters informing of Saquil's killing. LC-GDC, reel 7, frame 4173, documents Cucul's request for help from the federation in lobbying the government to capture Alvarado. Also, reel 7, frame 4174, contains a letter from Saquil's wife and son, most likely written by Cucul, to the head of the national judiciary asking for a fairer judge to be appointed: "the superior authorities make laws for the social and collective benefit, but when they start to show results, one or another becomes a victim of the reactionaries and the landlords."

70. *El Impacto*, September 12, 1954; *El Sulfato*, September 21, 1954.

71. LC-GDC, reel 5, frame 1049.

72. Again the conclusions reached by Richard Adams in his prison survey correspond with many of the arguments made here: During the October Revolution "an awakening of profound import did take place for many of the members of this sample . . . for it amounted to a realization that certain of the previously accepted roles and statuses within the social system were no longer bounded by the same rules, and that new channels were suddenly opened for the expression of and satisfaction of needs. The heretofore established series of relationships between political leader and countryman, between employer and laborer, between Indian and Ladino, were not suddenly changed, but it abruptly became possible to introduce some change into them." "Receptivity to Communist Fomented Agitation," p. 360.

73. SPCMA, April 29, 1947.

74. Information on Francisco Curley García comes primarily from interviews with his sister and his brother, July 2001.

75. AMG, "Comunidades–Alta Verapaz," documents Curley's organization of Alta Verapaz peasant unions.

76. AGCA J-AV, index 107 59M 1787.

77. Aside from the accusations in the above court case, see the complaints in LC-GDC, reel 4, frame 375, and reel 4, frame 1166. Curley and his Q'eqchi' allies denied the charges, insisting that the money was for legal and office expenses, such as the purchase of a new typewriter for Cahabón's CAL, and for union dues. Federico García, who today enjoys a more honest reputation than Curley, testified that Leonardo Castillo Flores, head of the national peasant federation, gave them permission to ask for money to offset the cost of distributing the cattle.

78. LC-GDC, reel 6, frame 1964, July 25, 1953. At the same time, Curley "expelled" Cucul and Miguel Guzmán from Alta Verapaz's regional peasant federation; LC-GDC, reel 6, frame 1964/1, July 7, 1953.

79. LC-GDC, July 30, 1953, folder "CNCG Relations with the CGTG," box 13. Curley organized an anti-communist peasant protest during the national labor federation's 1953 departmental assembly, which had on its agenda the expulsion of Curley and García. See also GDC folder "CNCG 1953," box 11. Accusations of "Communism" and "anti-Communism" often flew in jurisdictional disputes between the national peasant federation, the CNCG, which was originally organized by non-Communist agrarian activists, and the PGT-influenced national labor federation, the CGTG. The already established labor CGTG opposed Leonardo Castillo Flores's formation of a separate peasant federation, insisting that it would fracture class unity. In the years prior to the Agrarian Reform, the CNCG and CGTG traded "Communist" and "anti-communist" charges. On a national level, Leonardo Castillo Flores and the CNCG had by 1953 aligned themselves with Gutiérrez's PGT-influenced CGTG. The rapprochement was brought about by the CNCG's need for Arbenz's approval and the strength of the landed class in blocking the Agrarian Reform, which not only led the PGT and CGTG to accept the existence of a separate peasant federation but also radicalized many of the CNCG's formally anti-communist leadership. Yet jurisdictional squabbles over resources and members continued locally. In Alta Verapaz, the CGTG had affiliated peasant unions in Carchá, Panzós, and the Poqomchí communities of Tucurú and Tamahú. The labor federation, which gained its first foothold in the Verapaces in Carchá with Icó's Comunidad Agraria, organized unions, mostly with the help of PGT activists, throughout the Polochic Valley, including plantations in Panzós, Tucurú, Tamahú, Cobán's shoe factory Calzado Cobán, Carchá's tanning workshops and mines, and on Alta Verapaz's railroad, which operated along a short twenty-nine-mile stretch along the Polochic River. The CNCG, through the work of Curley and García, had affiliated unions in Senahú and Cahabón and fought attempts by the CGTG to expand. Bishop, "Guatemalan Labor Movement," pp. 15–20, describes early struggles between Communists and anti-communists in the labor movement. Fighting between Gutiérrez and Castillo Flores, head of the CNCG, is described in Bishop, "Guatemalan Labor Movement," pp. 84–89, and Pearson, "*Confederación,*" pp. 34–40, 78–

80. AMG, "Comunidades–Alta Verapaz," and Bush, "Organized Labor in Guatemala," part 2, pp. 119–20, contains information on the Verapaz railroad workers union.

80. Daniel James, *Red Design for the Americas: Guatemalan Prelude* (New York: John Day, 1954), pp. 123–39, criticizes the Agrarian Reform's application in the southern coast department of Escuintla. Alfonso Bauer Paiz and Ivan Carpio, *Memorias de Alfonso Bauer Paiz: Historia no oficial de Guatemala* (Guatemala City: Rusticatio Ediciones, 1996), pp. 139–41, admits that there was abuse and corruption in its application.

81. Gleijeses, *Shattered Hope*, pp. 150, 162.

82. The PGT-agrarian organizer in Escuintla, Carlos Manuel Pellecer, could perhaps be Curley's Communist equivalent in that he earned an infamous reputation for his high-handed organizing style. Daniel James, *Red Design*, pp. 152–54, describes Pellecer as the "virtual czar" of Escuintla.

83. Curley and García challenged planter power not only in the realm of politics and economics but in the cultural arena as well: in their defense against charges of extortion, they said that some of the money they collected from peasants went to support the campaign of the Red Cross's candidate in the department's beauty pageant against the growers association's contestant. Curley's audacity not only undermined planter authority but bypassed bureaucratic lethargy. He and García, for example, distributed cattle from national plantations before receiving any such orders from Alta Verapaz's governor, thus making the expropriation a fait accompli. AGCA J-AV, index 107 59H 1588, contains more legal charges against Curley. LC-GDC, reel 5, frames 1132, 1137, and 1139, contains telegrams from Curley and García describing their distribution of land from national plantations, which took place in April and May 1953.

84. CEH, *Memoria del silencio*, 1:100–101.

85. AGCA J-AV, index 107 58D 1038; interview, Eliseo Ax Burmester, August 2001.

86. Counterrevolutionary violence will be discussed in greater detail in the following chapter, but see Forster, *Time of Freedom*, pp. 197–213, for "elite backlash and revenge" in San Marcos and the southern coast.

87. Barrington Moore, *Injustice: The Social Bases of Obedience and Revolt* (White Plains, N.Y.: M. E. Sharpe, 1978), p. 459.

88. Pearson, "*Confederación*," pp. 208–10, documents telegrams from peasant committees throughout the country declaring their willingness to defend Arbenz, to die on "the altar of the *patria*" as one put it.

89. When Colonel Carlos Paz Tejada tried to organize four hundred PAR members, mostly workers and campesinos, who had gathered at the Maya Golf Club, he was stymied by the "indifference and passive resistance" of the military officers charged with training them; Figueroa Ibarra, *Paz Tejada*, pp. 263–65.

90. Gleijeses, *Shattered Hope*, p. 344.

91. Interview with José Alberto Cardoza, June 2001.

92. LC-GDC, reel 9, frame 7589, May 31, 1954.

93. This committee, which functioned for eighteen months before being converted

into the General Office of Security, was the beginning of the institutionalization of anti-communism as state ideology, codified by a series of laws and a new constitution in 1956 and executed by a purged judiciary and state bureaucracy. The list was compiled by the chief of national security, who coordinated information gathered from the CIA, local anti-communist groups, and the director of the national census; CEH, *Memoria del silencio,* 1:108–13. For the list, see *El Imparcial,* November 20, 1954; Stephen Streeter, *Managing the Counterrevolution: The United States and Guatemala, 1954–1961* (Athens: Ohio University Press, 2000), p. 39; David Atlee Phillips, *The Night Watch: Twenty-five Years of Peculiar Service* (New York: Atheneum, 1977), pp. 51–52; and a document that explains the ranking of those to be purged found in the personal papers of Eduardo Taracena, which also contains lists that indicate that the anti-communist movement had begun to compile information on Communists and "*filocomunistas*" before the fall of Arbenz.

94. Streeter, *Managing the Counterrevolution,* p. 39.

95. Ibid., pp. 30–32; Handy, *Revolution in the Countryside,* p. 194; and Carlos Figueroa Ibarra, "Violencia y revolución en Guatemala: 1954–1972" (Ph.D. diss., Universidad Nacional Autónoma de Mexico, 2000), pp. 82–92, provide descriptions of the violence and estimations of its toll based on diverse sources, as does the Catholic Church's truth commission report, Proyecto Interdiocesano de Recuperación de la Memoria Histórica (hereafter cited as REMHI), *Guatemala: Nunca Más,* vol. 3 (Guatemala City: Oficina de Derechos Humanos del Arzobispado de Guatemala, 1998), pp. 15–19, and Edelberto Torres-Rivas and Gregorio Selser, *El Guatemalazo: La primera guerra sucia* (Buenos Aires: Editorial Iguazú, 1961). Also Oficina Internacional del Trabajo-OIT, *Boletín Oficial* (Geneva) 38, no. 1 (1955): 51, lists a charge filed by a Belgian union related to the execution of forty-five United Fruit union members. Most murders were not legally processed, although some were.

96. Figueroa Ibarra, "Violencia y revolución," p. 84; Daniel James, the anti-communist writer, in an interview with Robert Alexander, March 8, 1955, found in Alexander's personal papers at Rutgers University Library, mentions a January 1955 rural revolt in six areas. REMHI, *Nunca más,* 3:16, describes a clash between *liberacionistas* and indigenous *Arbencistas* in San Juan Sacatepéquez that left seventeen of the latter dead.

97. Figueroa Ibarra, "Violencia y revolución," p. 84; Forster, *Time of Freedom,* p. 204, for the Jocotán massacre.

98. Streeter, *Managing the Counterrevolution,* p. 30, cites a memo from the *New York Times* archive on the CIA's relationship with the paper; see also Harrison Salisbury, *Without Fear or Favor: The New York Times and Its Times* (New York, 1980), p. 486, and Homer Bigart, "How to Cover a War in Guatemala: It's Best Done from a Bar in Honduras," *New York Herald Tribune,* June 26, 1954. REMHI, *Nunca más,* 3:17, documents the wretched prison conditions on the southern coast that also led to the deaths of many captives.

99. Handy, *Revolution in the Countryside,* pp. 194–202, describes the uneven repeal of the Agrarian Reform. Also an August 19, 1954, interview with U.S. Embassy official William Krieg, found in the papers of Robert Alexander, mentions that landlords were

ignoring the new government's promise not to return land until the current crop was harvested.

100. REMHI, *Nunca más*, 3:17, estimates that ten thousand Guatemalans were held captive on the southern coast alone.

101. AGCA J-AV, index 107 60H 2108.

102. AGCA J-AV, index 107 61 2788 and 60H 2111, describes other interrogations and prosecutions under the anti-communist law.

103. LC-GDC, reel 9, frame 7005, April 21, 1954, contains Cucul's telegram to the CGTG's headquarters complaining of the increased attacks on the part of the "reaction."

CHAPTER 3. UNFINISHED LIVES

1. "John P. Longan Memoir," 2 vols., Institute of Inter-American Affairs Collection, Columbia University, 1986, 1:19.

2. Longan worked in the United States' Overseas Internal Security Program, established in 1957 under the jurisdiction of the National Security Council. According to Martha Huggins, OISP was a "top secret internal security program" that combined "police assistance with a variety of strategies to coordinate internal security planning more carefully by integrating military and police assistance with judicial reform." See Martha K. Huggins, *Political Policing: The United States and Latin America* (Durham, Duke University Press, 1998), p. 80.

3. Throughout its "dirty war" the Argentine Navy conducted weekly "death flights," throwing the bodies of the "disappeared," sometimes drugged but still alive, into the sea. Feitlowitz, *Lexicon of Terror*, pp. 26, 193.

4. Aside from the CEH and REMHI reports, cited throughout, see Patrick Ball, Paul Kobrak, and Herbert Spirer, *State Violence in Guatemala, 1960–1996: A Quantitative Reflection* (Washington, D.C.: American Association for the Advancement of Science, 1999).

5. See Patricia Weiss Fagen, "Repression and State Security," in *Fear at the Edge: State Terror and Resistance in Latin America*, ed. Juan E. Corradi, Patricia Weiss Fagen, and Manuel Antonio Garretón (Berkeley: University of California Press, 1992), p. 57, for pre-1964 Brazilian "death squads" run by the police that killed "petty criminals among the so-called marginal population." Martha Huggins, *Political Policing*, pp. 119–40, analyzes the implementation in Brazil of Operação Limpeza between 1964 and 1966, which, like the subsequent Guatemalan edition, entailed U.S. Public Safety advisors working with Brazilian security forces to rationalize intelligence communication, coordinate police and military operations, and execute "broad searches, seizures, and mass arrests" of as many as fifty thousand Brazilians. The operation was aimed at neutralizing supporters of the recently deposed reformist president João Goulart. Executions and disappearances of political activists, however, did not start in a systematic manner until after 1968.

6. Nancy Caro Hollander, *Love in the Time of Hate: Liberation Psychology in Latin*

America (New Brunswick: Rutgers University Press, 1997), p. 102. See also Sofia Salimovich, Elizabeth Lira, and Eugenia Weinstein, "Victims of Fear: The Social Psychology of Repression," in Corradi, Fagen, and Garretón, *Fear at the Edge.*

7. Huggins, *Political Policing,* chaps. 4 and 5.

8. For El Salvador, see National Security Archive, *El Salvador: The Making of US Policy, 1977–1984* (Alexandria, Va.: Chadwick-Healey, 1989), p. 73; for Uruguay, see the declassified U.S. documents located on the National Security Archive web page, http://www.gwu.edu/~nsarchiv. Although the military turned Uruguay into a prison state in 1973, U.S. counterinsurgency aid to the country continued until 1977. For Chile, likewise see the documents on the NSA web page. For Operation Condor, see John Dinges, *The Condor Years: How Pinochet and His Allies Brought Terrorism to Three Continents* (New York: New Press, 2004). For training manuals used at the U.S. School of the Americas, see http://www.soawne.org/SOAManuals.html. For a list of Latin American officers who graduated from the School of the Americas, see http://www.soaw.org/soag.html. For Brazil, see Huggins, *Political Policing,* which also provides the most detailed historical description of U.S. involvement with a Latin American security force.

9. Throughout Guatemala's nineteenth- and early-twentieth-century history, participation in militias, whether in defense of conservative or liberal regimes, has served as a venue of participatory citizenship. See in particular Robert Carmack, *Rebels of Highland Guatemala: The Quiché-Mayas of Momostenango* (Norman: University of Oklahoma Press, 1995), and Hazel Ingersoll, "The War of the Mountain: A Study in Reactionary Peasant Insurgency in Guatemala, 1837–1873" (Ph.D. diss., George Washington University, 1972).

10. For "white terror," see DDRS-US, Department of State, "Guatemala: A Counter-Insurgency Running Wild," October 23, 1967.

11. "The government of Guatemala has also on occasion engaged in tactics with which we are not in agreement and in conversations with Guatemalan officials we have made our disagreement clear. These practices have included the illegal detention of suspected terrorists and the elimination of individuals the government believed to be deeply involved in terrorist activity either as 'intellectual leaders' or as combatants. . . . While as noted above, we in no way condone the illegal tactics, we should also note that the Guatemalan Government believes itself to be in a situation akin to civil war." In NSA, Department of State, "Sub-Committee Hearings on Guatemala Public Safety Program," September 2, 1971.

12. Unless otherwise indicated, the following analysis of U.S. sponsorship of Arbenz's overthrow comes from the two most comprehensive sources currently available. Piero Gleijeses's *Shattered Hope,* pp. 208–360, is based on declassified U.S. documents and extensive interviews with many of the event's protagonists. Nick Cullather originally wrote his *Secret History* as a CIA in-house report based on still classified information. It was subsequently declassified by the Agency and published by Stanford University Press. See also Stephen Schlesinger and Stephen Kinzer, *Bitter Fruit: The Untold Story of the American Coup in Guatemala* (New York: Doubleday,

1982), and Richard Immerman, *The CIA in Guatemala: The Foreign Policy of Intervention* (Austin: University of Texas Press, 1982). For personal accounts from three CIA agents, see E. Howard Hunt, *Undercover: Memoirs of an American Secret Agent* (New York: Berkeley, 1974); Philip C. Roettinger, "The Company, Then and Now," *Progressive,* July 1986, p. 50; and Phillips, *Night Watch.* In May 2003, the Department of State released 287 documents detailing U.S. involvement in the operation to unseat Arbenz, found online at http://www.state.gov/r/pa/ho/frus/ike/guat/.

13. Cullather, *Secret History,* p. 43.

14. See, for example, *El Impacto,* May 31, 1952.

15. U.S. Department of State, *Intervention of International Communism in Guatemala,* p. 85.

16. Gleijeses, *Shattered Hope,* p. 217.

17. Conflict with the United Fruit Company started immediately after 1944 but worsened when the company complained that the 1947 Labor Code was discriminatory because it exempted smaller plantations from many of its requirements and protections. By the late 1940s, United Fruit had launched simultaneous campaigns to smear Guatemala in the U.S. press and to lobby Harry Truman's State Department for intervention. The Truman administration, in turn, dropped an antitrust suit against UFCO in exchange for the company's taking a hard line in Guatemala and threatening to shut down its operations unless Arévalo curbed his economic nationalism. See Cullather, *Secret History,* pp. 15–19; and Gleijeses, *Shattered Hope,* pp. 91–94.

18. Cullather, *Secret History,* pp. 33–34.

19. Kermit Roosevelt, *Countercoup: The Struggle for Control of Iran* (New York: McGraw Hill, 1979).

20. Cullather, *Secret History,* p. 82

21. Cullather, *Secret History,* p. 75; see also Phillips, *Night Watch,* p. 53.

22. Cullather, *Secret History,* p. 40.

23. Arbenz opponents were good at saying what they "were against," said the *New York Times,* February 24, 1953, but not at showing that "they stood in favor of something."

24. Gleijeses, *Shattered Hope,* pp. 332–33.

25. Jose Luis Chea, *Guatemala: La cruz fragmentada* (San José, Costa Rica: Departamento Ecuménico de Investigaciones, 1988), p. 70.

26. See *Acción Social Cristiana,* March 1, 1945; see also Chea, *Cruz fragmentada,* p. 76.

27. Mariano Rossell y Arellano, *Exhortación pastoral con motivo del día de Pentecostés* (Guatemala City: Sánchez y de Guise, 1944), p. 1; Anita Frankel, "Political Development in Guatemala: The Impact of Foreign, Military, and Religious Elites" (Ph.D. diss., University of Connecticut, 1969), p. 191.

28. Iglesia Católica de Guatemala, *Carta pastoral colectiva del episcopado de Guatemala sobre la amenaza comunista en nuestra patria* (Guatemala City: Sánchez y de Guise, 1945), pp. 3–4. This letter is attributed to a collective authorship, but its tone reflects Rossell y Arellano's style.

29. Rossell y Arellano, *Tactics and Works,* p. 3. See also Douglass Sullivan-González,

Piety, Power, and Politics: Religion and Nation Formation in Guatemala, 1821–1871 (Pittsburgh: University of Pittsburgh Press, 1998), for the Church's defense of peasant communities.

30. See for example, Mariano Rossell y Arellano, *Carta circular . . . con ocasión de los atentados contra la Iglesia en Yugoslavia* (Guatemala City: n.p., 1946).

31. Arévalo, *Escritos políticos*, p. 187.

32. Rossell y Arellano, *Tactics and Works*, p. 4.

33. Mariano Rossell y Arellano, *Mensaje a las clases laborante y patronal* (Guatemala City: Hispana, 1946); Rossell y Arellano, *Alocución en la Catedral Metropolitana* (Guatemala City: Unión Tipográfica, 1954).

34. Mariano Rossell y Arellano, *Carta pastoral sobre la Acción Católica* (Guatemala City: Sánchez y de Guise, 1946), p. 5; Rossell y Arellano, *Instrucción pastoral al pueblo católico de Guatemala sobre el deber y condiciones del sufragio* (Guatemala City: Sánchez y de Guise, 1948), pp. 7–8.

35. In *Acción Social Cristiana*, May 29, 1947, p. 7; Ricardo Bendaña Perdomo, *La Iglesia en Guatemala: Síntesis histórica del catolicismo* (Guatemala City: Librerías Artemis-Edinter, 1996), p. 122.

36. Rossell y Arellano, *Carta pastoral sobre la Acción Católica.*

37. Rossell y Arellano, *Tactics and Works*, p. 1.

38. See the paid ads in *El Imparcial*, May 19, 1952, p. 12; June 10, 1952, p. 10.

39. Rossell y Arellano, *Tactics and Works*, p. 8.

40. Ibid., p. 5.

41. *Amanecer*, May 15, 1938.

42. In 1938, for example, the episcopate celebrated a highly ritualized mass for the victims of Spanish Republicans that brought state and Church hierarchs together along with delegates from the Hitler Youth and the Falange party and the German and Italian ambassadors; in *Amanecer*, May 15, 1938. Rossell y Arellano was not yet named archbishop, but he too shared Ubico's sympathies and actively supported and attended Falange activities. See *Amanecer*, August 15, 1938, pp. 16–17, and Frankel, "Political Development," pp. 188–89. The Church offered aid to Franco's insurgency, and its newspapers provided sympathetic coverage of Franco's rebellion. See *Revista Eclesiástica* 8, no. 70 (July–August 1937) and 8, no. 71 (September–October 1937), and *Verbum*, October 11, 1942.

43. Mariano Rossell y Arellano, *Carta pastoral con ocasión del segundo centenario de la sede Arzobispal de Guatemala* (Guatemala City: Sánchez y de Guise, 1943).

44. Cited in REMHI, *Nunca más*, 3:12.

45. In some communities, leaders of religious brotherhoods *(cofradías)* at first welcomed the Revolution, using political parties and unions to fight for specific issues or to wrest municipal power from Ladinos. At times this support continued throughout the Revolution's course. Yet in some towns, such as Rabinal and Carchá, cofradías began to oppose the secularization and proliferation of new associations that undercut their authority, particularly the raising up of new leaders outside of established channels. Cucul speaks with ambivalence of Carchá's cofradías, recounting how they at

first supported his uncle and the union but then threw their support to the PRG, the principal venue for Arbenz opponents. Informants in Ochaita de Escaler, "Pervivencia de las Cofradías Indígenas," p. 100, say that initial cofradía support for Tecú evaporated as the Revolution radicalized. See also Handy, *Revolution in the Countryside,* p. 142, and Manning Nash, *Machine Age Maya: The Industrialization of a Guatemalan Community* (Chicago: University of Chicago Press, 1967), pp. 130–36, for conflicts between revolutionary organizations and cofradías. At times, planters cultivated cofradía loyalty through the provision of fireworks, food, electric lights, and alcohol for the cult's annual saint's festival; see *El Norte,* April 14, 1946. Throughout the Cold War, counterinsurgent theorists debated whether or not local "culture" was an insurgent threat or a counterinsurgent bulwark. See the discussion in Ron Robin, *The Making of the Cold War Enemy: Culture and Politics in the Military-Intellectual Complex* (Princeton: Princeton University Press, 2001), chap. 9. See Juan Fernando Cifuentes, "Operación Ixil: Plan de Asuntos Civiles," *Revista Militar,* September–December 1982, for a Guatemalan army strategist's argument that traditional Mayan culture could serve as an effective social base of the counterinsurgency.

46. Douglass Sullivan-González, "Where Did Jesus Go? The Black Christ of Esquipulas," paper presented at the Latin American Studies Conference, September 1998, Chicago.

47. Rossell y Arellano, *Tactics and Works,* p. 10. For the Black Christ's entrance into Alta Verapaz, see *El Tactic,* September 5, 1953.

48. Rossell y Arellano, *Tactics and Works,* p. 10.

49. For Ubico, see Mary Holleran, *Church and State in Guatemala* (New York: Colombia University Press, 1949), p. 211.

50. Bush, "Organized Labor in Guatemala," part 4, p. 3.

51. For the Salesians in Carchá, see Luis de León, *Carcha: Una misión en Guatemala entre los Kekchíes de Alta Verapaz* (Guatemala City: Instituto Técnico Ricaldone, 1985).

52. Interview, Father Sebastian Buccellato, April 2002, New York.

53. Kay Warren, *The Symbols of Subordination: Indian Identity in a Guatemalan Town* (Austin: University of Texas Press, 1978), pp. 96–97, describes the slow start of Catholic Action in San Andrés Semetabaj.

54. See the various comments by CIA and embassy officials in Gleijeses, *Shattered Hope,* p. 214.

55. Mariano Rossell y Arellano, *Carta pastoral sobre los avances del comunismo en Guatemala* (Guatemala City: Sánchez y de Guise, 1954), p. 3.

56. Cullather, *Secret History,* p, 64.

57. According to information in the private papers of Eduardo Taracena, anticommunist students came equally from the university's medical, humanities, law, economics, and engineering schools. In 1950, they managed to win the directorate of the Asociación de Estudiantes Universitarios, but they were voted out the following year.

58. Private papers of Eduardo Taracena, "Ideas sobre la ejecución de un programa de propaganda," November 7, 1953.

59. Ibid.

60. Bombings took place against PGT locations and public utilities. Eduardo Taracena, a leader in the movement, admits that he participated in a number of bombing missions. See a May 23, 1974, interview found in Taracena's personal papers. In this collection are a number of manuals with instructions on how to plan and execute bombing, sabotage, and psychological warfare compiled by the CIA and titled "Sabotage *[sic]* para la Liberación de Guatemala: Preparación plan de treinta días," n.d., and "Sabotage *[sic]* para la Liberación de Guatemala: Ejecución," n.d. Judging from the number and nature of grammatical errors—such as the repeated spelling throughout of *sabotage* with a *g*—it is clear that these instruction manuals were written by a native English speaker, most likely someone affiliated with the CIA. Not only do the manuals instruct, with diagrams, how to make and deploy a range of explosives such as tube bombs, remote fuses, chemical bombs, time bombs, nitroglycerin, and dynamite, but they morally justify terrorism and exhort Guatemalans to embrace it: "Like all things in life, sabotage is either good or bad depending on whether it is used for good or bad purposes . . . damage against the enemy is the beginning of the reconstruction of the country and from the ashes of today's fires . . . will emerge a new Guatemala, free and fertile." For the quote, see private papers of Eduardo Taracena, "Ideas sobre la ejecución de un programa de propaganda," November 7, 1953.

61. Rossell y Arellano, *Tactics and Works*, p. 9.

62. Bendaña Perdomo, *La Iglesia*, pp. 123–24.

63. His death is described in detail in Gleijeses, *Shattered Hope*, pp. 50–71.

64. Schneider, *Communism in Guatemala*, p. 32.

65. "The Minutemen of Guatemala," *Reporter* 3, no. 9 (October 24, 1950): 33, 35.

66. Schneider, *Communism in Guatemala*, p. 304, and Flores, *Fortuny*, pp. 195–96. See untitled and undated history of the CEUA found in the private papers of Eduardo Taracena for a student commission that organized the market women. Taracena's papers also contain an intelligence report given to Arbenz by the head of the Civil Guard that notes that the protest was organized by exiled students in Mexico.

67. Flores, *Fortuny*, p. 195.

68. Arno J. Mayer, *The Furies: Violence and Terror in the French and Russian Revolutions* (Princeton: Princeton University Press, 2000), p. 81.

69. Rossell y Arellano, *Tactics and Works*, p. 5.

70. Despite the proliferation of dissident groups, the antigovernment forces remained dispersed. In the January 1953 elections, 105,000 opposition votes garnered only three congressional seats, while 130,000 votes gave pro-government parties twenty-nine deputies; see Schneider, *Communism in Guatemala*, p. 303.

71. Private papers of Eduardo Taracena, "Ideas sobre la ejecución de un programa de propaganda," November 7, 1953.

72. Ibid.

73. Quoted in Cullather, *Secret History*, p. 66.

74. Private papers of Eduardo Taracena, "Ideas sobre la ejecución de un programa de propaganda," November 7, 1953.

75. Cullather, *Secret History,* pp. 66–67, and the private collection of Eduardo Taracena, miscellaneous papers, for the activities described in this paragraph.

76. Private papers of Eduardo Taracena, "Versión taquigráfica de la tercera gran asamblea del Movimiento Democrático Nacionalista," 1957. The MLN at first went by the name Movimiento Democrático Nacionalista.

77. Francisco Villagrán Kramer, *Biografía política de Guatemala: Los Pactos políticos de 1944–1979* (Guatemala City: FLACSO, 1993), p. 286.

78. "I am a fascist," Sandoval Alarcón once reportedly remarked, "and I have tried to model my party after the Spanish Falange"; in George Black, *Garrison Guatemala* (New York: Monthly Review Press, 1984), pp. 17, 22.

79. Like Rossell y Arellano, the MLN likewise sought to defend the particularity of Guatemala's indigenous communities against the supposed coercive universalism of the left. Its 1958 party platform states that "one of the most sure roads of achieving social reconstruction is the adaptation of the indigenous class to the modern environment, but under the concept that it is done through education and never through violence against their nature and customs"; in personal papers of Eduardo Taracena. For another effort to define democratic anti-communism, see the essay "Por Qué Soy Anticomunista" by the novelist Virgilio Rodríguez Macal, an MLN leader who grew up in Franco's Spain, in *El Imparcial,* November 10, 1959. According to miscellaneous telegrams in the personal papers of Eduardo Taracena, the MLN, upon finding itself in charge of local municipalities after the sudden collapse of the Arbenz government, implemented in some areas programs of potable water, electricity, health, and roads, and promoted peasant committees. At its founding in June 1955, the MLN (then called the Movimiento Democrático Nacionalista) claimed over three thousand registered members, mostly middle-class professionals, shopkeepers, and military officers from the capital but also a number of Ladinos and a few Indians from plantation zones where the Agrarian Reform had its largest impact. See "Inscripción de Afiliados al Movimiento Democrático Nacionalista," June 17, 1955, in the personal papers of Eduardo Taracena. For peasant committees see Rosendo Girón's letter to Mario Sandoval Alarcón, dated May 30, 1955, where the writer claims to have organized three thousand peasants in Chimaltenango and on the southern coast in MLN land committees; also in the personal papers of Eduardo Taracena.

80. For the embassy's installation of Castillo Armas, see Gleijeses, *Shattered Hope,* pp. 351–60, and Cullather, *Secret History,* pp. 101–4.

81. Villagrán Kramer, *Biografía,* pp. 208–10, and Susanne Jonas and David Tobis, *Guatemala* (New York: North American Congress on Latin America, 1981), pp. 65, 82–84, describes this post-1954 economic coalition. See Streeter, *Managing the Counterrevolution,* pp. 109–36, for the relationship between the U.S. "Guatemala lobby" and U.S. foreign policy and p. 72 for financial contributions from U.S. corporations to post-1954 Guatemalan anti-communist politicians.

82. For the rollback of Agrarian Reform, see Handy, *Revolution in the Countryside,* pp. 194–202; Foster, *Time of Freedom,* pp. 177–96. Streeter, *Managing the Counterrevolution,* p. 41, quotes the *New York Times* as reporting that planters are taking "justice

in their hands and intimidating the peasants" because they "feel the change in Government took place to protect their interests and free them of the Agrarian Law." Hundreds of unionists were jailed or fired (many employers used a provision in the 1947 labor code to dismiss workers who did not report to their jobs in the days following Arbenz's resignation speech). The new government dismantled the Agrarian Reform and disbanded unions and federations until they proved they had purged suspected Communists and petitioned for recertification. In August 1954, even the MLN-dominated National Committee for Union Reorganization complained of how difficult it was to "fight the fear and terror of workers" and convince them to file for recertification since they knew that "in the street hunger and misery awaits. . . .We respect the fight against Communism, a fight in which we took part, but you do not fight Communism with massive firings of workers or with dissolving unions." For the full scope of workplace restructuring, see the documents in AGCA MT, 1954–56, legajos 48737–48750; see AGCA MT 48739, August 1954 for the quote. See Streeter, *Managing the Counterrevolution*, pp. 51–53, for mixed U.S. reaction to labor repression. See Levenson-Estrada, *Trade Unionists against Terror*, for the "discreet reconstruction" of the labor movement.

83. Figueroa Ibarra, "Violencia y revolución," pp. 172–73. See Norman LaCharite, "Political Violence in Guatemala, 1963–1967: Its Social, Economic, Political, and Historical Origins, and Its Patterns and Sequences" (Ph.D. diss., American University, 1973), p. 151, for Lorenzana's involvement in setting up Mano Blanca.

84. On September 1, 1954, a presidential decree transformed the duty of military commissioners from enforcing conscription to "exercising control and vigilance over the population" and helping to "maintain order and security." For information on military commissioners, see Michael McClintock, *The American Connection: State Terror and Popular Resistance in Guatemala* (London: Zed Books, 1985), p. 66, and John Durston, "Power Structure in a Rural Region of Guatemala: The Department of Jutiapa" (masters thesis, University of Texas–Austin, 1966), p. 84. A report conducted by the Rand Corporation in the mid-1960s states that in Zacapa there were two thousand military commissioners operating under the orders of the local military base; in McClintock, *American Connection*, p. 116.

85. Richard Adams, *Crucifixion by Power: Essays on Guatemalan National Social Structure, 1944–1966* (Austin: University of Texas Press, 1970), pp. 271–72.

86. For an earlier U.S. assessment that Ydígoras intended to create a "counter-military force of campesinos along with a part of the military" in order to stay in power, see NSA, Department of State, "US Interests and the Guatemalan Political Scene," March 31, 1962.

87. DDRS-US, Department of State, "Guatemala: Vigilantism Poses Threat to Stability," October 23, 1967. DDRS-US, Department of State, "Guatemala: A Counter-Insurgency Running Wild?" October 23, 1967, writes that "Civilian counter-insurgency groups armed and organized by the military are also active in rural Guatemala—particularly in the jurisdiction of Colonel Carlos Arana, commander of the Zacapa Military Brigade. Most of these groups are recruited from among . . . the

. . . MLN. The Army says it has approximately 1,800 armed civilians under its control." See also DDRS-US, Central Intelligence Agency, "The Military and the Right in Guatemala," November 6, 1968.

88. CEH, *Memoria del silencio,* 1:141.

89. DDRS-US, Department of State, "Guatemala: A Counter-Insurgency Running Wild?" October 23, 1967. For the relationship between the Guatemalan military, intelligence, and death squads, see ibid. For planter contributions, see LaCharite, "Political Violence in Guatemala," p. 151.

90. NSA, Department of State, "Public Safety Monthly Report, January 1967," February 17, 1967. See also Durston, "Power Structure," for the MLN's destruction of the PR in Jutiapa.

91. See CEH, *Memoria del silencio,* 6:291–96. Likewise in central and southern Quiché the oligarch Herrera family after 1954 voluntarily gave land to a number of its rural workers who in turn provided support for the labor contractors, merchants, and landowners who headed the MLN; personal communication with Elizabeth Oglesby. See also AGCA DAN-Quiché 16 10.

92. Norman Gall, *Correo de Guatemala,* no. 13 (September 1971); Carlos Cáceres, *Aproximación a Guatemala* (Mexico City: Universidad Autónoma de Sinaloa, 1980), p. 112. See also *El Día* (Mexico City), March 6, 1982.

93. Figueroa Ibarra, "Violencia y revolución," p. 111; Alvarado Arellano, *Apuntes,* p. 25.

94. See Gleijeses, *Shattered Hope,* pp. 186–87, and Cullather, *Secret History,* pp. 106–7, for discussions on the weak ties between the PGT and the USSR.

95. See Figueroa Ibarra, "Violencia y revolución," pp. 123–24. The "*autocrítica*" entered Guatemala in 1955 disguised as a small pamphlet with ads for Philips Milk of Magnesia on the cover. It is known in party lore as the "magnesia document."

96. For examples, see Alfonso Bauer Paiz, *Como opera el capital yanqui en Centroamérica (El caso de Guatemala)* (Mexico City: Editorial Iberoamericana, 1956); Luis Cardoza y Aragón, *La revolución Guatemalteca* (Guatemala City: Editorial Pensativo, 1994 [1955]); Manuel Galich, *Por qué lucha Guatemala* (Guatemala City: Editorial Cultura del Ministerio de Cultura y Deportes de Guatemala, 1994 [1955]); Guillermo Toriello Garrido, *La batalla de Guatemala* (Mexico City: Cuadernos Americanos, 1955), and *Tras la cortina de banano* (Mexico City: Fondo de Cultura Económica, 1976); and Jaime Díaz Rozzotto, *El carácter de la revolución Guatemalteca: Ocaso de la revolución democrática-burguesa corriente* (Mexico City: Ediciones Revista Horizonte, 1958). See Figueroa Ibarra's discussion of these works in "Violencia y revolución," pp. 113–14.

97. Lukács, *Historical Novel,* p. 25.

98. Huberto Alvarado Arellano, "Walt Whitman: Poeta nacional, democrático, y realista," in *Cuadernos del Guayas* (Ecuador) 6 (1955): 1, 5, 20.

99. See Figueroa Ibarra, "Violencia y revolución," p. 128.

100. Ibid., p. 129.

101. See Figueroa Ibarra, "Violencia y revolución," pp. 238–40. Fortuny, who had little influence in the post-1954 PGT, was always hostile to the idea of armed revolution. See

Flores, *Fortuny,* pp. 257–66. The CIA observed in 1965 that the "actions of the strongly anti-communist military regime" had led "many of the younger party leaders to become more and more attracted to the idea of armed struggle and resentful of the old guard's subservience to the Russian line of coexistence." See DDRS-US, Central Intelligence Agency, "Special Report: Guatemalan Communists Take Hard Line As Insurgency Continues," August 6, 1965.

102. Figueroa Ibarra, "Violencia y revolución," p. 239.

103. Ibid., p. 199. See DDRS-US, Central Intelligence Agency, "Special Report: Guatemalan Communist Take Hard Line As Insurgency Continues," August 6, 1965, for the influence of the Chinese Revolution on Guatemala's new generation of revolutionaries as well.

104. Figueroa Ibarra, "Violencia y revolución," p. 164.

105. Ibid., pp. 158–59, 164.

106. Ibid., pp. 161–63; Alvarado Arellano, *Apuntes,* pp. 38–39.

107. Figueroa Ibarra, "Violencia y revolución," p. 163.

108. See NSA, Department of State, "Marco Antonio Yon Sosa," February 7, 1962, for ongoing guerrilla activities.

109. Alvarado Arellano, *Apuntes,* pp. 57–62.

110. Levenson-Estrada, *Trade Unionists against Terror,* pp. 39–40.

111. For the formation of the FAR, see Figueroa Ibarra, "Violencia y revolución"; Alvarado Arellano, *Apuntes,* pp. 43–62; Julio César Macías, *La guerrilla fue mi camino: Epitafio para César Montes* (Guatemala City: Piedra Santa, 1997), pp. 25–28; Mario Robles, "Concepciones ideológicas y políticas en FAR," unpublished monograph in author's possession, pp. 19-22; and Orlando Fernández [Ricardo Ramírez], *Luis Augusto Turcios Lima: Biografía* (n.p., n.d.).

112. Figueroa Ibarra, "Violencia y revolución," p. 285; interview, César Macías, July 2001; and Flores, *Fortuny,* pp. 295–96.

113. Edgar Ruano, "Los cincuenta años de los comunistas guatemaltecos," *La Ermita* 4, no. 16 (October–December 1999): 38–44, argues that the PGT could never reconcile its Leninist, urban party structure with a rural guerrilla command structure.

114. Guillermo Toriello Garrido, *Guatemala: Más de 20 años de Traición, 1954–1979* (Guatemala City: Editorial Universitaria, 1979), p. 55, describes FAR leader Luis Turcios Lima's disgust with PGT foot-dragging.

115. Interview, César Macías, July 2001.

116. Alberto Cardoza, one of the original founders of the PGT, recalls that during a trip to Russia following the PGT's adoption of its 1960 resolution he was told by a high-ranking member of the Soviet Communist Party that "the Soviet Union does not support these experiences born from the enthusiasm that the Cuban Revolution is provoking. Guatemala does not have the conditions stipulated by Marxism-Leninism to make a revolution through armed struggle and what is more this struggle is going to have costs that the USSR is not able to pay, especially if the Revolution triumphs;" in Figueroa Ibarra, "Violencia y revolución," p. 131.

117. Figueroa Ibarra, "Violencia y revolución," p. 240.

118. Founded in the late 1950s by non-Communist Arbencistas, the PR fashioned its own critique of the October Revolution's failure, blaming it on the activities and excesses of the PGT, which provoked a backlash. For the PR, see the interview with Francisco Villagrán Kramer, July 3, 1967, in the papers of Robert Alexander.

119. For the PR's mildly reformist platform, see the series of editorials written in *La Hora* by Clemente Marroquín Rojas throughout January and February 1966.

120. *La Hora,* January 3, 1966. Gutiérrez was not naive; in this opinion piece he admitted that Guatemala's recent history did not bode well for electoral politics but insisted that a great many Guatemalans "sincerely believed that the solution for Guatemala . . . lies in the electoral political struggle," a belief that, according to Gutiérrez, had to be respected. See also Figueroa Ibarra, "Violencia y revolución," p. 329.

121. Interview, José Alberto Cardoza, June 2001.

122. Figueroa Ibarra, "Violencia y revolución," p. 331; see also César Macías, *La guerrilla,* pp. 113–14. As with the social base of the PAR and the PGT during the October Revolution, there existed much overlap in the countryside between supporters of the PGT, the FAR, and the PR. Immediately after Méndez Montenegro's March triumph, rumors started circulating in San Marcos and Tecpán that Arbenz would soon return and that plantation land would be distributed to workers. See *La Hora,* March 18, 1966.

123. As represented by Régis Debray's polemical essay *Revolución en la revolución?* (Havana: Casa de las Américas, 1967). Ricardo Ramírez, a member of the FAR who became friends with Che Guevara while they were both asylum seekers in the Argentine Embassy after 1954 and would break with the FAR to form the EGP, had already come to the conclusion that "the party is not only not necessary but an obstacle." See Figueroa Ibarra, "Violencia y revolución," p. 333. The revolutionary movement was further divided by a Trotskyist split, which pulled the Izabal front out of the FAR.

124. For a retrospective critique of the PGT's support for Méndez Montenegro—"the bloody Yankee puppet"—as well as a general attack on the party by the founder of the EGP, see Fernández (pseud. Ricardo Ramírez), *Luis Augusto Turcios Lima.*

125. A number of memoirs have been published in recent years by revolutionaries who came of age in the 1960s and were influenced by the Cuban Revolution. See César Macías, *La guerrilla;* Yolanda Colom, *Mujeres en la alborada* (Guatemala City: Artemis, 1998); Miguel Angel Sandoval, *Los años de la resistencia* (Guatemala City: Editorial Oscar de León Palacios, 1999); Chiqui Ramírez, *La guerra de los 36 año: Vista con ojos de mujer de izquierda* (Guatemala City: Editorial Oscar de León Palacios, 2001)—the last two describe in detail the importance of 1962's urban uprising. For memoirs from the older left on the 1960s, see Carlos Figueroa Ibarra, *Paz Tejada: Militar y revolucionario* (Guatemala City: Universidad de San Carlos, 2001), pp. 317–404; Flores, *Fortuny,* pp. 249–66; and Bauer Paiz and Carpio, *Memorias de Alfonso Bauer Paiz,* pp. 206–14.

126. Interview, José Alberto Cardoza, June 2001.

127. See Figueroa Ibarra, "Violencia y revolución," pp. 333–34; César Macías, *La guerrilla*, pp. 112–15. Interviews with César Macías, July 2001, and José Alberto Cardoza, June 2001, were also helpful.

128. César Macías, *La guerrilla*, p. 115.

129. See Streeter, *Managing the Counterrevolution*, p. 225; Cáceres, *Aproximación*, p. 21; Torriello Garrido, *Más de 20 años*, p. 44.

130. For the Ydígoras regime's immediate evocation of Castro, see DDRS-US, Department of State, outgoing embassy telegram, November 4, 1960. See NSA, Central Intelligence Agency, "Intelligence Note: Revolutionary Outbreaks in Central America," November 4, 1960, for evidence that U.S. officials knew the 1960 military revolt was not led by the PGT. See NSA, Department of State, "Guatemalan Defense Minister Requests Assistance in Securing Military Equipment," October 16, 1961, where Ydígoras's defense minister noted that even if Castro was not involved in the November 1960 revolt, he was still its "spiritual instigator."

131. Streeter, *Managing the Counterrevolution*, p. 233.

132. For Eisenhower, see Streeter, *Managing the Counterrevolution*, p. 237. In 1962 the chief public safety advisor to Guatemala complained of a "lack of a government willingness to develop an intelligence capability, perhaps because it does not feel a need for it. The fact is, however, that no intelligence mechanisms now exist"; see DDRS-US, Department of State, "Technician Interview #50," September 25, 1962. The advisor went on to complain that "the complete lack of intelligence capabilities on the part of the police forces is the more serious because of the comparable complete lack of intelligence capabilities on the part of the military forces. The army G-2 has no knowledge of what is going on." See also NSA, Department of State, "Internal Security Situation and Needs," May 22, 1961, and NSA, Department of State, "Internal Defense Plan," September 15, 1962, which complains that Guatemala's military intelligence system "cannot be regarded as effective" and that "uncoordinated rumors serve in lieu of professional intelligence." See also DDRS-US, Department of State, "Internal Defense Plan for Guatemala," March 9, 1964, and DDRS-US, White House, Interdepartmental Survey Team for Venezuela and Guatemala, "Report to the President on Guatemala," October 12, 1962. Martha Huggins notes that many Latin American countries at first resisted U.S. offers to improve intelligence capabilities. The National Security Council complained in 1959 that "most Latin America governments . . . believe that the United States overemphasizes communism as a threat to the Western hemisphere"; *Political Policing*, p. 81.

133. NSA, Department of State, "Use of Firearms by the National Police of Guatemala," March 28, 1962, describes the head of the special investigations unit of the police as a "common thug and assassin" and blames him for the murder of protesters. Both NSA, Department of State, "The Current Guatemalan Situation and Outlook," March 1962, and NSA, Department of State, "US Interests and the Guatemalan Political Scene," March 31, 1962, reveal U.S. displeasure with the way Ydígoras handled the 1962 protests.

134. DDRS-US, Department of State, "Briefing for Mr. Edwin W. Martin, Assistant Secretary of State for Inter-American Affairs," July 4, 1962.

135. NSA, Department of State, "State, Policy and Operational Guidance for US Activities in Guatemala," October 17, 1962. The U.S. ambassador's opposition to Arévalo is expressed in DDRS-US Department of State, untitled memo (no issue date but declassified on May 31, 1994), where he writes that it is "entirely conceivable, that Juan Jose Arevalo could be elected in a free election, and a peaceful transfer of administration achieved. If this occurred, political power in Guatemala would be in the hands of a man not only passionately and pathologically antagonistic to the United States and all its works, but a man who certainly paved the way for the accession of Communism into power in Guatemala during the Arbenz regime. In my opinion the coming of Arevalo again into power would be most likely to set into motion again a chain of events leading toward a seizure of power by the Communists. A close review of Guatemalan history certainly supports the contention that Arevalo paved the way for Communist control; if he did not realize he was doing so, he is dangerously stupid; if he did realize the logical results of his acts, he must be assumed to have intended or to have accepted those results. In either case, it is hardly credible that the nature of the man has changed. He was nearly 50 years old at that time; he was no misguided, well-meaning youthful reformer."

136. The plotters approached the U.S. Embassy to ask for permission before they acted. DDRS-US, Department of State, untitled cable, March 13, 1963.

137. See McClintock, *American Connection,* p. 69; Arturo Taracena Ariolla, "Orígenes y primera etapa del conflicto armado interno en Guatemala, 1954–1971," unpublished manuscript in author's possession, pp. 67–74; and Villagrán Kramer, *Biografía,* pp. 379–83.

138. NSA, Department of State, "Internal Defense Plan: Progress Report (Comments of the Inter Departmental Working Group)," May 28, 1963. See also NSA, Department of State, "Guatemala Internal Defense Plan—Progress Report," September 25, 1963, where Assistant Secretary of State for Inter-American Affairs Edwin Martin writes that after "exasperating delays, there is now some encouraging progress toward establishment of an effective counter-subversive intelligence apparatus."

139. NSA, Department of State, "Internal Defense Plan," September 15, 1962, called for the establishment of "effective professional intelligence channels within the military forces" and an intensification of "intelligence security and training." In 1955, the United States had ten advisors abroad and civil police training programs in three countries—two in Asia and Guatemala. By 1958, the numbers had risen to 115 advisors in twenty-four countries. See Huggins, *Political Policing,* pp. 77–97.

140. Between 1956 and 1961, over six hundred Guatemalan military officers were trained either in the United States or at Fort Glick in the Canal Zone; see NSA, Department of State, "Internal Security Situation and Needs," May 21, 1961. NSA, Agency for International Development, "Termination Phase-Out Study: Public Safety Project, Guatemala," July 1974, provides information on police training between 1957 and

1973. See also NSA, Department of Defense, "MTTs Deployed by Country and Year," c. September 1973, for number and duty of military training teams that arrived in Guatemala between 1962 and 1973; NSA, Department of State, "Internal Defense Plan Progress Report: The Status of the Central American Defense Council," 1964, describes a plan to coordinate counterinsurgent activity throughout Central America. See also DDRS-US, Department of State, "Proposed Central American International Security Telecommunications Network," March 23, 1964. Schirmer, *Guatemalan Military Project,* pp. 157–58, provides information on the 1964 establishment of the presidential intelligence agency, the Centro Regional de Telecomunicaciones, or la Regional, and the 1965 establishment of Comando Seis, a special unit in the national police, all of which would become important elements in the state-military death squad apparatus.

141. See for examples DDRS-US, Department of State, "Guatemala: Vigilantism Poses Threat to Stability," October 23, 1967; DDRS-US, Department of State, "Guatemala: A Counter-Insurgency Running Wild?" October 23, 1967; and NSA Department of State, "Ojo por Ojo," May 19, 1970.

142. DDRS-US, Department of State, "Guatemala: Vigilantism Poses Threat to Stability," October 23, 1967; NSA, Department of State, "The Democratic Left," March 22, 1971. In addition to being housed in the National Security Archive, most of the documents pertaining to Operación Limpieza, including the untitled and undated CIA reports, have been reprinted in my *Denegado en su totalidad: Documentos estadounidenses liberados* (Guatemala City: Asociación para el Avance de las Ciencias Sociales en Guatemala, 2001).

143. NSA, Department of State, memo from John Longan to Byron Engle, January 4, 1966.

144. See Sandoval, *Los años de la resistencia,* in particular the interview in the appendix with Arnaldo Vásquez Rivera, one of the leaders of the Urban Resistance, pp. 135–55.

145. NSA, Department of Defense, "US Army Mission to Guatemala: Program Report," January 15, 1965. See also NSA, Department of Defense, "US Army Mission to Guatemala: Program Report," July 15, 1964; NSA, Department of State, "Guatemala Internal Defense Plan—Progress Report," March 1964; NSA, Department of State, "Briefing Papers on Guatemalan Problems," November 1964; and NSA, Department of State, "Report on Guatemala: Public Safety Program," June 2, 1965. See also DDRS-US, Department of State, "Memorandum for Mr. Bundy," June 12, 1965, which, in the face of growing rebel activity, recommended that the United States "1. Continue to push for an expanded Public Safety program to enable the police to deal more effectively with insurgency problems, with primary emphasis on urban areas but also including rural activities. 2. Consider the creation of a special group within the police force to deal with counter-insurgency."

146. NSA, Department of State, "Operation Resume of Terrorist Kidnappings and Guatemala Police Effort to Counter," December 17, 1965; NSA, Department of State, memo from John Longan to Byron Engle, January 4, 1966.

147. NSA, Department of State, memo from John Longan to Byron Engle, January

4, 1966; NSA, Department of State, "No Evidence State of Siege under Active Consideration," December 11, 1965.

148. NSA, Department of State, "No Evidence State of Siege under Active Consideration," December 11, 1965.

149. NSA, Department of State, "Operation Resume of Terrorist Kidnappings and Guatemala Police Effort to Counter," December 17, 1965.

150. Ibid.

151. See the two untitled embassy cables in NSA dated January 5, 1966, and March 1, 1966.

152. See NSA, Central Intelligence Agency, untitled, March 1966 (declassified in February 1998): "Acting on information obtained from communists and guerrillas captured in Retalhuleu by Guatemalan troops on March 3, Guatemalan judicial police raided a private house . . ."

153. This crime has historically gone by the name "los 28," but both the Catholic Church's REMHI report and the United Nations' truth commission identified over thirty fatal victims. See CEH, *Memoria del silencio,* 6:89–98, and REMHI, *Nunca más,* 3:45–48, for a detailed description of the executions. The names of the dead are reproduced here in the appendix. Carlos Figueroa Ibarra, *Los que siempre estarán en ninguna parte: La desaparición forzada en Guatemala* (Guatemala City: Grupo de Apoyo Mutuo, 1999), pp. 46–56, provides the testimony of Raúl Díaz Ramírez, a captured, tortured, yet released PGT member. See also Cáceres, *Aproximación,* pp. 104–9. César Macías, *La guerrilla,* has an account of an escape by other high-level leaders of the PGT and the FAR from the raid that captured Gutiérrez.

154. See the two undated and untitled March 1966 CIA documents found in NSA which provide detailed information of intelligence information gathered from their interrogation, suggesting that CIA agents were probably present at the questioning. In an interview, Viron Vaky, the deputy chief of the U.S. mission in Guatemala at the time of the executions, reports that there was a separation between the analytical and operations divisions of Embassy CIA agents, with the former often not knowing what the latter was doing. When asked if it were possible that CIA agents were present at the interrogation, he answered: "I don't know that they would have gone that far. They would have been aware of it, but present I'm not sure. It depends." The U.S. Embassy had previously urged Guatemala to be thorough in its interrogation techniques, as suggested by a telegram from the embassy to the State Department stating that in "addition to identification of weapons assume Embassy is urging Guatemalan authorities to conduct thorough interrogation of captured guerrillas"; see NSA, Department of State, untitled telegram, October 22, 1964. César Macías in his memoir *La guerrilla,* p. 115, reports that years after the murders a government minister confessed, while he was a prisoner of the EGP, that the U.S. Embassy ordered the executions.

155. "John P. Longan Memoir," 1:19.

156. For the newspaper report, see *El Gráfico,* July 19, 1966. This informer seems to be Julio Ruano Pinzón, the same source mentioned by Eduardo Galeano in *Guatemala: País ocupado* (Mexico City: Nuestro Tiempo, 1967), p. 60, although Galeano

identifies him as a deserter from the army. According to Galeano, Ruano fled the military after three other soldiers who had participated in the capture, murder, and packing of the bodies in sacks died under mysterious violent circumstances.

157. NSA, Department of State, "Public Safety Monthly Report—March, 1966," April 13, 1966.

158. See DDRS-US, Central Intelligence Agency, Report, "Guatemala on the Eve of the Elections," March 5, 1966. According to the date, this document was written on the eve of the March 1966 murders. Unfortunately, the three pages following the concern that the PGT would publicly support Méndez Montenegro are completely excised, concealing what remedies the CIA may have suggested. This document was originally declassified through the Lyndon Baines Johnson Presidential Library. When I requested the document directly from the CIA through a Freedom of Information Act request, the same sections were expunged.

159. Villagrán Kramer, *Biografía*, pp. 458–62, contains the text of the pact.

160. CEH, *Memoria del silencio*, 1:74–146, and REMHI, *Nunca más*, 2:65–112, analyze the growth of Guatemala's intelligence system and its centrality in state repression.

161. DDRS-US, Central Intelligence Agency, Report, "The Danger of a Military Coup in Guatemala," September 28, 1966.

162. REMHI, *Nunca más*, 2:74, gives the eight thousand figure.

163. DDRS-US, Central Intelligence Agency, "The Military and the Right in Guatemala," November 6, 1968, reports that "[t]he army began a counterinsurgency program in late 1966 that soon degenerated into counter terrorism. Military strategists armed and fielded various clandestine terrorist groups, including some 3000 dedicated anti communist civilians with ties to the MLN. . . . Mano Blanca was formed by rightists but later taken over by the military. . . . Personnel, weapons, funds, and operation instructions were supplied [to death squads] by the armed forces. The death toll mounted." See also NSA, Department of State, "Guatemala's Counter-insurgency: Problems of Ends and Means," March 8, 1968, and DDRS-US, Department of State, "Guatemala: A Counter-Insurgency Running Wild?" October 23, 1967, for Arriaga Bosque's centralization of MLN vigilante groups and death squads.

164. Cáceres, *Aproximación*, p. 185; *El Gráfico*, October 5, 1972; CEH, *Memoria del silencio*, 6:183–91.

165. CIA analysts were quite astute at recognizing the political consequences of state violence. Eight months prior to the March 1966 disappearances, the Agency acknowledged that the influence of the "soft-liners" in the PGT had been greatly weakened as a result of state repression. It also believed that the "exclusion of all but those partisan groups considered 'safe' by the incumbent government represents to both extreme and moderate liberals a commitment to an intolerable status quo. It has been clear to most of the Liberal parties for some time that they have no early opportunity to achieve power through legal means. Most of the moderate groups, while recognizing that subversion is the only path open at this time, have feared to engage in serious plotting in the face of the relative efficiency of the security apparatus. The government, on the other hand, may have painted itself into a corner. Renewed restriction of

civil liberties under martial law . . . might well turn usually moderate groups to violence"; in DDRS-US, Central Intelligence Agency, "Special Report: Guatemalan Communist Take Hard Line as Insurgency Continues," August 6, 1965.

166. In NSA, Department of State, untitled memo, April 12, 1968.

167. NSA, Department of State, "Public Safety Program Monthly Report," February 1963. See also *Verdad,* February 23, 1963.

168. *El Imparcial,* May 20, 1966; *Prensa Libre,* June 23, 1966.

169. NSA, Department of State, "Guatemala's Disappeared," March 28, 1986.

170. Schneider, *Communism in Guatemala,* pp. 94–96; James, *Red Design,* p. 112.

171. Cáceres, *Aproximación,* pp. 66–67, gives a partial list of his numerous small books and pamphlets.

172. See Alvarado Arellano, *Apuntes,* pp. 58–60.

173. DDRS-US, Department of State, "Attacks upon US Installations in Latin America, January–March 1968," May 28, 1968.

174. REMHI, *Nunca más,* 3:66.

175. DDRS-US, Department of State, "Guatemala: A Counter-Insurgency Running Wild?" October 23, 1967.

CHAPTER 4. CLANDESTINE LIVES

1. Unless otherwise noted, all information on and quotations from Efraín Reyes Maaz come from four interviews conducted during the summers of 2000 and 2001.

2. Gornick, *Romance of American Communism,* pp. 15, 17. For the classic on the loss of self to ideology, see Hannah Arendt, *The Origins of Totalitarianism* (London: Andre Deutsch, 1986).

3. For the forging of "ideological armour" during periods of reaction, see Lukács, *Historical Novel,* p. 25.

4. In the 1999 presidential elections, for example, the left candidate, who came in third nationally, beat the candidate who won the general election. That year, left candidates, including two former members of the FAR, won the mayoralty in Cahabón, Chahal, and Fray Bartolomé de las Casas. Also the "yes" vote in 1999's *consulta popular,* generally considered a referendum on the social, cultural, and political reforms of the peace process, lost nationally but won in Cahabón by over 75 percent. See Tribunal Supremo Electoral, *Memoria: Consulta popular 1999* (Guatemala City: Tribunal Supremo Electoral, 2000), p. 291.

5. In addition to cited archival sources, information throughout this chapter on Sepacuité and the Champney family unless otherwise noted comes mostly from interviews in July and November 2001 with its chief administrator in the 1950s and 1960s and with Champney family members, including Benjamin's daughter Erika Champney and son Edgar Champney.

6. For land granted to Champney by successive presidents, see also the national Registro de Propiedad (hereafter cited as RP), finca 1878, folio 231, libro 28, first series; and RP, finca 268, folio 27, libro 13, 14, and 15, first series.

7. For folklore surrounding the arrival of these two hundred Jamaican workers, see Mario de la Cruz Torres, "Monografía del municipio de Senahú," *Guatemala Indígena* 17, nos. 3/4 (1982): 56.

8. See ibid. for faded photographs of this colonial life. See also Elin Danien, "Send Me Mr. Burkitt, Some Whisky and Wine: Early Archaeology in Central America," *Expedition* 27, no. 3 (1985), for a description of the strange career of Robert Burkitt, a freelance archaeologist and linguist from the United States who spent most of his later life living at Sepacuité.

9. For Kensett Champney's foreclosure on Curley's plantation in 1933, see RP, finca 45, folio 49, libro 14, first series.

10. Unless otherwise cited, all information on the Agrarian Reform's expropriation of Sepacuité comes from AGCA DAN-AV 1B 15. In Cahabón seven other land claims resulted in the expropriation of 20,240 acres. All were returned after 1954. See AGCA DAN-AV 5A 7, 1B 10, 1 3, 6 3, 8 7, 10 5, and 5 8. In 1955, according to Jorge del Valle Matheu, *Guía sociogeográfica de Guatemala* (Guatemala City: Tipografía Nacional, 1956), p. 276, nearly 96 percent of Cahabón's 13,249 residents were Q'eqchi'; 95.6 were illiterate.

11. See Edgar Champney's complaint that his resident peons were refusing to work, corroborated in a number of interviews, in AGCA DAN-AV 1B 15.

12. For the plantation's value, see RP, Dirección de la Rentas, December 23, 1960.

13. RP, finca 45, folio 50, libro 14, first series. See RP, finca 44, folio 49, libro 14, first series for Erika Champney losing land to lawyers, and RP, finca 268, folio 27, libro 13, 14, 15, first series, for Erika losing the remainder to Jaime.

14. AGCA DAN-AV 1B 15.

15. The files marked "*comunidades,*" "*asociaciones,*" and "*comités*" in the archives of the Ministerio de Gobernación list the large number of peasant organizations organized in the 1960s and 1970s.

16. See for example *Estatuto Agrario: Emitido por el Gobierno de la República,* Decree 559 (Guatemala City: Imprenta Liberación, March 1, 1956). See Handy, *Revolution in the Countryside,* pp. 194–201, for the fitful application of early post-1954 land decrees.

17. Congreso de la República, *Ley de transformación Agraria,* Decreto 1151 (Guatemala City: Tipografía Nacional, 1962). The stated goal of INTA was to "transform" Guatemala's agrarian structure, making it more productive and increasing the consuming power of peasants. It had three primary functions: First, it sought to rationalize Guatemala's land tax system by applying a high rate for idle land yet allowing successive deductions for water sources, pastures, forests, and croplands. Second, it aimed to encourage peasant colonization of the northern lowlands of Alta Verapaz, Quiché, and the Petén. Finally, it established a series of mechanisms by which individuals or communities could solicit land that was already claimed by an individual or a corporation if it was not used or its ownership was in dispute. A number of these functions were defined by successive laws and amendments. Upon its inception, INTA immediately received thousands of petitions for land from individual peasants and

communities. An article in *El Imparcial,* October 10, 1966, claims that INTA in its first four years provided 150,000 peasants with land and had pending on the southern coast alone more than 20,000 land petitions.

18. Héctor Ramos, a Cobán lawyer and member of the PGT under Arbenz, joined the Partido Revolucionario after 1954 but continued to serve as the PGT's primary legal advisor in the Polochic Valley throughout the 1960s and 1970s, providing counsel and notary services for successive conflicts. His 1979 murder by the military is listed in CEH, *Memoria del silencio,* 8:23. Information on the Partido Revolucionario in Cahabón as well as its relationship with the PGT is drawn from interviews in June 2000 and July 2001 with a number of former activists from both parties.

19. The 1956 constitution once again made it a point to say that "vagrancy is punishable," as did the 1963 *Carta Guatemalteca de Trabajo,* Decreto Ley no. 1, and the 1965 *Constitución de la República de Guatemala* (Guatemala City: Tipografía Nacional, 1965). The 1985 constitution finally dropped all references to vagrancy. The 1963 "Libro de Sentencias Económicas," in Cahabón's municipal archives, lists fines levied against vagrants. A number of Q'eqchi' Cahaboneros report that forced or unpaid labor continued throughout the 1970s. A 1974 description of a university delegation to Cahabón confirms the persistence of forced labor, reporting that a small number of Ladinos forced Q'eqchi's to work one week a month "without any monetary compensation" in exchange for the right to cultivate crops on their plantations. The study also goes on to say that "children under ten have to also work free . . . doing domestic work like sweeping, running errands, husking corn, pasturing animals" and that there "are cases when the landlords carry to their homes workers" to work as servants; Universidad de San Carlos, Facultad de Ciencias Jurídicas y Sociales, "Visita al Municipio de Santa María Cahabón," October 1974, unpublished manuscript in author's possession.

20. The PGT's 1970 platform remarked on the relationship of reform and revolution, noting that the "party will work for immediate reforms, for the concrete demands of the diverse popular sectors—urban and rural workers, peasants, students, intellectuals, artisans, and small and medium property holders, industrialists, and merchants—but in order to make Guatemalans see that their legitimate interests and rights . . . can never be achieved through reform, whose stability is subject to the arbitrariness of imperialism and of the bourgeois-landlord oligarchy. The fight for immediate reforms is part of a permanent struggle that will unite and organize the people and advance toward objectives more important"; PGT-Tulane, box 1, folder 2, 1970. To that end, the party mostly strived to create a "broad front," working with activists to "politically and ideologically develop the periphery that surrounds us"; PGT-Tulane, box 1, folder 14, June 28, 1977.

21. Max Weber, "Politics as Vocation," *From Max Weber: Essays in Sociology,* ed. H. H. Gerth and C. W. Mills (New York: Oxford University Press, 1946), p. 128.

22. Interview with Xol's daughter, July 2001. See also Xol's entry in the civil registry of the Municipality of Cahabón, "Libros de Cédulas," no. 1, cédula 91, folio 46.

23. AGCA J-AV, index 107 57D 563.

24. AGCA J-AV, index 107 62 D 3074 contains bootlegging charges against Xol during the town's saint day.

25. RP, finca 1656A, folio 117, libro 20; Alta Verapaz. *El Norte*, January 21, 1967, also reports the transaction.

26. *El Norte*, March 11, 1967. See also *El Norte*, August 28, 1965, for an earlier conflict.

27. The 1974 university delegation report cited above makes reference to this expulsion. *El Norte*, March 11, 1967, reports that Curley accused Edgar Champney of threatening to burn down the homes of those against the sale.

28. There have been a number of studies exploring customary law in Guatemala in relationship to the current breakdown of the state legal system in the countryside in the wake of the civil war. See Misión de Verificación de las Naciones Unidas en Guatemala, *Los linchamientos: Un flagelo contra la dignidad humana* (Guatemala City: MINUGUA, 2000), and Rachel Sieder, "Customary Law and Local Power in Guatemala," in *Guatemala after the Peace Accords*, ed. Rachel Sieder (London: Institute for Latin American Studies, 1998). Historians tend to agree that the extension of a modern legal system in Guatemala had little or negative impact on local social relations, yet evidence from Alta Verapaz's court records provides an important corrective. Despite the legal system's racism, corruption, and disdain, indigenous peasants by the 1930s at times eagerly used the courts to gain advantage in their dealings with other peasants and to seek justice. Whether or not one would seek petition for state-administered justice depended on one's social standing in the community, as it was often those most vulnerable to the disruptions of capitalism, particularly women, who sought help from courts. Furthermore, long before the civil war, violence and retribution played a central role in local conceptions of justice and should not be considered in opposition to state jurisprudence, which often did not so much displace rough justice as act as its first circuit of appeal. For historical work on the relationship of the state legal system to community life, particularly in terms of gender relations, see Forster, *Time of Freedom*, pp. 63–73. See also Carmack, *Rebels of Highland Guatemala.*

29. AGCA J-AV, index 105 35D 69.

30. AGCA J-AV, index 105 35D 22. See also AGCA J-AV, index 107 75A 5250, and AGCA J-AV, index 107 3556, for fire fights between Q'eqchi' small landholders over land.

31. See the cases contained in legajos 27D 29E 30D 31C 32B 33E 34D 35D 36F 37F 38G 39H 40J 41M 42I and 43K in AGCA J-AV, index 105.

32. AGCA J-AV, index 107 69A 92.

33. AGCA J-AV, index 107 69F 4411. See also the municipal archives of Panzós, "Libro de Actas General," May 31, 1963. This case also provides another example of the quick resurgence of PGT peasant organizing after the fall of Arbenz.

34. AGCA J-AV, index 107 69A 143 and 69B 205.

35. AGCA J-AV, index 107 72 4780.

36. The valley straddles a number of strategically important areas including the Petén lowlands and the Sierra de las Minas and connects the Atlantic coast to the western highlands. In 1971 the army upgraded its detachment in Cobán from a garrison to

a base. At the same time, it strengthened other garrisons throughout the region, particularly in Panzós. The military carried out some of its first civic action programs in the valley, funneling development funds and technologies to the area. See U.S. Major José Morales, "Acción Cívica: El Desarrollo de los Ciudadanos," *Revista Militar,* no. 70 (October–December 1971): 17–22; *Diario de Centro América,* April 3 and 28, 1964, March 17, 1965; and *Revista Militar,* no. 59 (December 1968): 112–15. See also *Diario de Centro América,* December 5 and 18, 1964, which singles out Alta Verapaz for civic action because of its dense indigenous population.

37. *El Norte,* August 28, 1965, defends Fratz while alluding to accusations that were "repulsive to read."

38. Stories of Jaime Champney's brutality are numerous. For documented acts of repression carried out on his plantation, see CEH, *Memoria del silencio,* 8:22, 28.

39. Federación Autónoma Sindical de Guatemala (FASGUA), "Análisis y origines de los hechos acaecidos en Panzós," June 27, 1978, unpublished manuscript in author's possession from the personal papers of Antonio Argueta.

40. Ibid.

41. CEH, *Memoria del silencio,* 8:22.

42. After 1973 selective violence intensified although still not always to deadly effect. Marcelino Xol was executed in 1972, yet a year later military commissioners kidnapped and tortured but then released PGT members Juan Pop Cuc, Mateo Chun, and Marcos Pachán; CEH, *Memoria del silencio,* 8:114–115. The following year, Tomás Caal, along with four other PGT members, suffered the same, as did six more activists in 1979; ibid., 8:87. After 1980 the chances of returning alive from a torture session shortened. In 1980, a military commissioner executed a cooperative leader; ibid., 8:105. That same year, Salac's military commissioners tortured and killed Joaquín Chen Cucul as well as an indeterminate number of other victims; ibid., 8:111. Ibid., 8:87, lists more executions.

43. Located just north of Sepacuité's coffee fields, these villages led the original land claim under Arbenz. Workers from these communities were subject to the intensification of labor demands that began when Benjamin Champney inherited the plantation in 1939 yet were far enough removed to have escaped some of the paternalistic incentives and surveillances that bound residents from communities closer to the plantation house.

44. A party document in PGT-Tulane, box 1, folder 15, July 21, 1977, distinguishes between *militante* (member), *activista* ("militant that stands out due to his or her initiative" yet without much experience or leadership responsibilities); *cuadro* (local, sectional, or regional leader); and *simpatizante* (sympathizer). PGT-USAC, September 22, 1982, lists party enrollment in the Polochic Valley as 205 *militantes;* 85 members of the party's youth section, the JPT; and three to five thousand *simpatizantes.* These figures reflect the worst months of the counterinsurgency and are probably lower than those of previous periods.

45. Mario Payeras, *Days of the Jungle: The Testimony of a Guatemalan Guerrillero, 1972–1976* (New York: Monthly Review Press, 1983), pp. 39–40. See Nicolás Anderson,

Guatemala: Escuela revolucionaria de nuevos hombres (Mexico City: Editorial Nuestro Tiempo, 1982), p. 26, for an Ixil EGP member commenting on the poor revolutionary consciousness of Q'eqchi's. Interviews with a number of FAR and EGP members repeat these characterizations. In many accounts of indigenous support for the FAR or the EGP, Achís from Rabinal are mistakenly described as Cakchiquel.

46. For Emilio Rax Pop's murder, see CEH, *Memoria del silencio,* 8:22, where his surnames are erroneously reversed.

47. According to some accounts, throughout the early 1960s, between 200 and 250 Q'eqchi's, including Reyes Maaz, traveled to Cuba for political and military training.

48. Timothy Tyson, *Radio Free Dixie: Robert F. Williams and the Roots of Black Power* (Chapel Hill: University of North Carolina Press, 1999), pp. 287–89, describes African American activist Robert Williams's fifty-thousand-watt jazz and political radio broadcast from Havana into the southern United States in 1963.

49. Parishes in northern and western Alta Verapaz, particularly in Cobán's northern *parroquia calvario,* where the EGP did garner support, became more socially active than parishes to the east. Interview, Catholic catechist, July 2000. See Richard Wilson, *Maya Resurgence in Guatemala: Q'eqchi' Experiences* (Norman: University of Oklahoma Press, 1995).

50. Wilson, *Maya Resurgence,* pp. 180–81, 214.

51. CEH, *Memoria del silencio,* 8:87.

52. Interview, ex-catechist and PGT member from Cahabón, July 2000. Quote in Wilson, *Maya Resurgence,* p. 215.

53. According to a catechist who in 1966 formed part of the first group of twelve Q'eqchi' youth to be educated by the Centro San Benito de Promoción Humana, nearly every intellectual and head of every development organization, from the Penny Foundation to USAID, came to speak to them: "We had sixteen professors for twelve students!" After two years, the group began to develop its social agenda: bilingual education; savings and loan coops; a Cobán branch of the national university; and a Q'eqchi' radio program. The Centro trained an average of forty Q'eqchi's a year from 1971 to 1974. Father Juan Gerardi, who would be murdered in 1998 for his work with the Catholic Church's inquiry into state repression, took over the diocese in 1973. While supportive of social activism, Gerardi was more inclined toward evangelicalism: "80 percent evangelical, from Moses to Jesus," according to one catechist, "with about 20 percent social work." In Cobán, he says, "they didn't even hear of liberation theology, they didn't do anything with Paulo Freire."

54. The PGT's *El Camino de la revolución guatemalteca* (Mexico City: Ediciones de Cultura Popular, 1972), pp. 29–36, reveals the poor attention paid by the party to racism. See also the PGT's 1970 "Programa de la revolución popular," PGT-Tulane, box 2, folder 1. For a high-handed attack on PGT racism by a young leftist, see Fernández (pseudonym for Ricardo Ramírez, one of the founders of the EGP), *Luis Augusto Turcios Lima,* p. 19. See Richard Adams, *Joaquín Noval como indigenista, antropólogo y revolucionario* (Guatemala City: Editorial Universitaria, 2000), for the conflicts at the

national university between older intellectuals, represented by Noval, and a new generation led by Carlos Guzmán Böckler, Julio Quan, and Jean-Loup Herbert.

55. Böckler, who was from Guatemala yet received his doctorate in France, and Herbert, who was French but taught in Guatemala at the national university, were coauthors of *Guatemala: Una interpretación histórico-social* (Mexico: Siglo Veintiuno, 1970). Both were influenced by the anticolonialist writings of Frantz Fanon and Albert Memmi. For two examples of Noval's criticisms of Böckler and Herbert, see "El estado y la violencia," *Revista de la Facultad de Ciencias Jurídicas y Sociales de Guatemala* 9, no. 4 (1977): 10–20, and "Acerca de la lucha ideológica," *ibid.*, 9, no.1 (1976): 22–23. See Adams, *Joaquín Noval*, pp. 36–40, for a discussion of these debates and Noval's bibliography.

56. See Noval's "Notas sobre la cuestión indígena en Guatemala," written in 1960 but published in the national university's *7 Días en la USAC* 2, no. 31 (June 4–10, 1979): 4–5.

57. For the quotes, see pp. 30–31 of the section on the "Indian Question" in the PGT's *El Camino de la revolución guatemalteca*, which was probably written by Noval. Noval and other PGT intellectuals argued that Mayan culture was susceptible to manipulation by the dominant classes, but this analysis did not translate in any concrete form into PGT policy. On the contrary, it seems to have led the PGT to avoid the question altogether. For the opinions of the different insurgent groups in regard to the relationship between indigenous culture and revolutionary consciousness, see the collected position papers in Centro de Estudios Integrados de Desarrollo Comunal, ed., *Guatemala: Seminario sobre la realidad étnica* (Mexico City: Editorial Praxis, 1990). See CEH, *Memoria del silencio*, 1:178–83, for a discussion of the relationship of these positions to revolutionary strategy and violence.

58. Interview, November 2002.

59. Compare this quote with V. I. Lenin, *Collected Works*, 4th English ed. (Moscow: Progress Publishers, 1972), 38:360–61: "The condition for the knowledge of all processes of the world in their *self-movement*, in their spontaneous development, in their real life, is the knowledge of them as a unity of opposites. Development is the 'struggle' of opposites. . . . Such must also be the method of exposition (or study) of dialectics in general. . . . To begin with what is the simplest, most ordinary, common, etc., with any *proposition:* the leaves of a tree are green; John is a man; Fido is a dog, etc. Here already we have dialectics (as Hegel's genius recognised): the individual is the universal." See also Friedrich Engels, *Dialectics of Nature* (Moscow: Foreign Languages Publishing House, 1954), chap. 2, for the "law of the transformation of quantity into quality and *vice versa*."

60. Where this clash did take place, such as in Carchá, the Salesian "modernizers" tended to be politically conservative. See Wilson, *Maya Resurgence*, pp. 180–81.

61. While always constantly evolving, in the wake of the war Q'eqchi' religious beliefs and rituals are undergoing an accelerated process of transformation. The description given here is a reconstruction of where things stood in the 1960s and 1970s

in Cahabón's PGT communities based on information mostly drawn from the local leaders of those communities. See Wilson, *Maya Resurgence,* for a discussion of transformation in Q'eqchi's religious worldviews. See also Jon Schackt, "The Tzuultaq'a: Religious Lore and Cultural Processes among the Kekchi," *Belizean Studies* 12, no. 5 (1984): 16–29; Luis Pacheco, *La religiosidad Maya-Kekchi alrededor de maíz* (San José, Costa Rica: Editorial Escuela para todos, 1985); Carlos Cabarrús, *La cosmovisión K'ekchi' en proceso de cambio* (San Salvador: Universidad Centroamericana, 1979); and Ruth Carlson and Francis Eachus, "El mundo espiritual de los kekchies," *Guatemala Indígena* 8, nos. 1–2 (1978): 40–73.

62. Wilson, *Maya Resurgence,* p. 53.

63. Ibid., p. 68.

64. Instituto Nacional de Transformación Agraria (hereafter cited as INTA), "Expediente general: Sillab, Seasir, Salac, Setzacpec, Chiacach, Chiax."

65. See Wilson, *Maya Resurgence,* p. 77, for a similar observation.

66. Ibid., p. 66.

67. FASGUA, "Análisis y origines de los hechos acaecidos en Panzós."

68. *El Gráfico,* July 7, 8, and 11, 1977; *La Nación,* July 10, 1977; *Prensa Libre,* July 9 and 21, 1977; and *El Impacto,* May 29 and July 8, 1977.

69. *La Nación,* July 20, 1977.

70. INTA, "Epediente general de las Comunidades de Santa María de Cahabón."

71. See INTA, "Expediente general: Sillab, Seasir, Salac, Setzacpec, Chiacach, Chiax."

72. The vice president of INTA admitted that the cost of the paperwork was prohibitively high for many peasant families. Ibid.

73. Ibid.

74. Ibid. mentions conflicts in Balamté, Chicach, and Chiax. Informants report some degree of discord in all six communities.

75. The following is a partial list of land conflicts reported in Guatemala's national press between 1973 and 1978: Los Liros, Masagua, Escuintla, *La Tarde,* May 19 and 28, 1976; Tabuexco, Mazatenango, Suchitepéquez, *Prensa Libre,* July 2, 1977; Todos Santos, *La Nación,* October 29, 1976; Las Cruces, Escuintla, *El Impacto,* June 21, 1978; San Antonio Suchitepéquez, *La Nación,* July 7, 1977; Concepción Chiquistepéque, Suchitepéquez, July 21, 1977; Florida, Escuintla, *La Tarde,* March 18, 1975; Semuy, Alta Verapaz, *Prensa Libre,* June 22 and 23, 1978, and *La Nación,* September 14, 1978; Chisec, Alta Verapaz, *Prensa Libre,* January 17, 24, and 27, 1976; Soledad, Panzós, Alta Verapaz, *La Nación,* July 28, 1975; Sebol, Alta Verapaz, *El Impacto,* November 15, 1973, and *Prensa Libre,* April 1, 1975; Chitinibal, Sacatepéquez, *La Nación,* June 24, 1978; and La Esperanza, Tucurú, *La Tarde,* June 28, 1978. For conflicts in the department of El Petén, see *El Impacto,* November 15, 1975; for Izabal, *El Impacto,* August 12, 1975. See also the paid ad in *El Impacto,* May 20, 1978, which lists disputes in Izabal and Chimaltenango and in Guatemala's eastern departments. Also see *El Imparcial* May 28, 1973, for the deaths of fifteen peasants in Sansirisay, Jalapa.

76. In Alta Verapaz by 1984 INTA had distributed over 656,000 acres to 18,535 ben-

eficiaries in 148 communities. See Instituto Nacional de Transformación Agraria, *Asentamientos agrarios localizados en el departamento de Alta Verapaz* (Guatemala City: INTA, 1984).

77. *Prensa Libre,* July 2, 1977. See also *La Tarde,* March 18, 1975, for more homicidal violence against south coast peasant leaders.

78. *El Impacto,* June 21, 1978. For other evictions, see *La Tarde,* May 28, 1976, July 13, 1976, and June 28, 1978; *La Nación,* May 29, 1976; *El Impacto,* August 12, 1975, July 8, 1977, and June 21, 1978; *Prensa Libre,* June 14, 1976, and February 14, 1979; and *La Hora,* February 13, 1979.

79. *Prensa Libre,* July 7, 1977.

80. *La Nación,* July 7, 1977; *El Gráfico,* July 7, 1977. For other land invasions, see *El Imparcial,* May 12, 1976; *Inforpress,* no. 177 (May 29, 1976); and *Prensa Libre,* October 17, 1980.

81. *El Impacto,* May 29, 1977, and July 8, 1977.

82. Margaret Popkin, *Las patrullas civiles y su legado: Superar la militarización y polarización del campo guatemalteco* (Washington, D.C.: Robert F. Kennedy Memorial Center for Human Rights, 1996); Joel Solomon, *Violencia institucional: Las patrullas de autodefensa civil en Guatemala, 1993–1994* (Washington, D.C.: Robert F. Kennedy Memorial Center for Human Rights, 1994); and CEH, *Memoria del silencio,* 2:181–234, analyze the civil patrols.

83. David Stoll, *Between Two Armies in the Ixil Towns of Guatemala* (New York: Columbia University Press, 1995), p. 115.

84. INTA, "Expediente general: Sillab, Seasir, Salac, Setzacpec, Chiacach, Chiax," contains a letter from families from Setzacpec complaining of Curley.

85. See CEH, *Memoria del silencio,* 8:21–137, for the large number of victims from Cahabón who were heads of land committees. In 1981, for example, Sebastián Choc Cholón, a catechist, and Manuel Tec Caal, a PGT member, were disappeared. That year, military commissioners kidnapped and tortured Ventura Chub and civil patrollers executed Gerardo Maaz, Santiago Coc, and Santos Sacal (ibid., 8:69, 72, 87, 115, 116, and 117). Planters used the military's counterinsurgency to eliminate troublesome workers; see ibid., 8:60, 106, 132, and 133. Others used the crisis to settle accounts: in early 1984 in Cahabón a military commissioner informed the army that two merchants to whom he owed money were guerrillas; the merchants were executed and their bodies fed to dogs (ibid., 8:43).

86. See *La Nación,* January 16, 20, and 24, 1979; *Prensa Libre,* January 15, 17, and 20, 1979; *El Gráfico,* January 15 and 16, 1979; *Nuevo Diario,* January 16, 1979; and *El Imparcial,* January 15, 1979.

87. The following description of political violence comes from a number of interviews and CEH, *Memoria del silencio,* 8:21–137.

88. Schirmer, *Guatemalan Military Project,* pp. 24, 44, and 47, provides a chronology of operations.

89. CEH, *Memoria del silencio,* 8:52.

90. Fundación de Antropología Forense de Guatemala, *Informe especial de la*

Fundación de Antropología Forense de Guatemala, 1996–1999 (Guatemala City: Fundación de Antropología Forense de Guatemala, 2001), p. 94.

91. CEH, *Memoria del silencio,* 8:39.

92. Fundación de Antropología Forense de Guatemala, *Informe especial,* p. 94.

93. CEH, *Memoria del silencio,* 8:62.

94. For one case of mass rape conducted by civil patrollers in Marichaj, see ibid., 8:120.

95. Ibid., 8:90.

96. Ibid., 8:110.

97. Ibid., 8:112.

98. Information on the PGT's attempt to establish an armed front comes from a number of interviews with participants conducted in July and August 2001.

99. PGT-USAC, c. November 1982.

100. See RP, finca 268, folio 27, libro 13, 14, 15, first series, for Jamie Champney's mortgage of his property in 1970, which he lost in 1983. See RP, finca 1878, folio 231, libro 28, first series for Edgar Champney's default on a loan to the Banco de Ejército, which resulted in the foreclosure of part of his plantation.

101. See INTA, "Expediente general: Sillab, Seasir, Salac, Setzacpec, Chiacach, Chiax," and INTA, "Expediente general de las comunidades de Santa María Cahabón: Pinares; Tzalantun; Panla; Chicanoz; Chinatal; Chivite; Santo Domingo; Chipoc y Chicanuz."

102. Information on the payments comes from the Guatemalan state agency Fondo de Tierras, Dirección de Regularización, Guatemala City.

103. Marx, *Capital,* 1:669.

104. See especially Carmack, *Rebels of Highland Guatemala.*

105. Schirmer, *Guatemalan Military Project,* pp. 235–57, discusses the political and military logic of this plan.

CHAPTER 5. AN UNSETTLED LIFE

1. PGT-Tulane, box 1, folder 2, 1970.

2. Anthropologist Richard Wilson reports, in a personal communication, that until Protestant Evangelicalism and Catholic catechists weakened the practice, polygamy was common in Cobán and Cahabón, but not in Carchá.

3. PGT-USAC, "Descripción de la reunión especial con las mujeres," July 23, 1982.

4. Ibid.

5. See for examples King, *Cobán and the Verapaz,* chap. 7, and Goubaud Carrera, *Notes on San Juan Chamelco.*

6. Mary Kay Vaughn, "Modernizing Patriarchy: State Policies, Rural Households, and Women in Mexico, 1930–1940," and Maxine Molyneux, "Twentieth-Century State Formations in Latin America," both in *Hidden Histories of Gender and the State in Latin America,* ed. Elizabeth Dore and Maxine Molyneux (Durham: Duke Univer-

sity Press, 2000), describe state-directed attempts to reorganize and institutionalize gender inequalities.

7. AGCA AV-MG 30792 12. For essays on the ongoing resonance of the public/private split, see Joan Landes, ed., *Feminism: The Public and the Private* (New York: Oxford University Press, 1997).

8. See Molyneux, "Twentieth-Century State Formations," for the ambiguous effects of liberal state formation on women.

9. In addition to the cases mentioned below, see AGCA J-AV, index 107 70 4477, for a 1964 Chamelco case of adultery.

10. AGCA J-AV, index 107 69D 355. For infanticides and abortions, see AGCA J-AV, index 105 45 48, 69a 134, 69D 356, 69D 355, 70B 4509, 45 27, and 72 4800.

11. AGCA J-AV, index 105 27D 12 contains a 1926 case of a woman accusing a man of infanticide. AGCA J-AV, index 107 41 29 is an accusation against a man for female child rape. For male child rape see AGCA J-AV, index 107 72A 1645. For adult rape, see AGCA J-AV, index 107 69E 545.

12. AGCA J-AV, index 105 35D 1.

13. AGCA J-AV, index 106 49J 11. Also see AGCA J-AV, index 107 72 4776.

14. AGCA J-AV, index 107 69D 77.

15. AGCA J-AV, index 107 69 8.

16. AGCA J-AV, index 107 70D 4559.

17. AGCA J-AV, index 107 69 1.

18. Municipal archives of Cahabón, "Libros de Cédulas," vol. 8, folio 395, January 21, 1954; municipal archives of Panzós, "Libro de Cédulas," vol. 21, folio 256, August 12, 1977.

19. See Rebecca Earle, "Rape and the Anxious Republic: Revolutionary Colombia, 1810–1830," in Dore and Molyneux, *Hidden Histories of Gender,* for women's involvement in Colombia's war for independence.

20. Ibid., pp. 140–42, describes the Colombian republican government's domestication of women's militancy during the war of independence in order to promote the image of a sanctified family as an icon of the new nation.

21. For accounts that stress the importance of narrative in constructing a sense of the self, see Hannah Arendt, *The Human Condition,* 2nd ed. (Chicago: University of Chicago Press, 1998), and Lewis Hinchman and Sandra Hinchman, *Memory, Identity, Community: The Idea of Narrative in the Human Sciences* (New York: State University of New York Press, 1997).

22. For an example, see the comments made at the February 25, 1999, presentation of the UN-administered Guatemalan truth commission report by Otilia Lux de Cotí, a Mayan member of the commission, found at http://www.c.net.gt/ceg/doctos/lux0225.html. Lux insisted on denying indigenous participation in the civil war, despite her own report's overwhelming evidence to the contrary.

23. "Levantamiento de Indios en San Agustín," *El Excelsior,* August 17, 1921; "Turba de 2 Mil Campesinos Atacó el Destacamento Militar de Panzós," *Diario de Centro*

América, May 31, 1978. *El Imparcial,* May 6, 11, and 20 and June 1, 1945, describes Achí mobilization in Rabinal. *El Norte,* January 10, 1935, recounts the 1865 indigenous protest in Carchá discussed in the introduction, elevating the number of protesters—"la chusma indígena," as the article puts it—from a few hundred to five thousand. See also Richard Adams, "Ethnic Images and Strategies in 1944," in *Guatemalan Indians and the State, 1540–1988,* ed. Carol A. Smith (Austin: University of Texas Press, 1990).

24. See the British Agricultural Company's map in AGCA Sección de Cartografía, 1.1.11B.

25. AGCA A 76 1515, A 2296 16828, A 590 11700 200V, A 382 7942, A 382 7943–44, A 382 7946, and A 132 2621.

26. AEA, Vicaria 1844–1854, Verapaz T7, December 15, 1849, and July 2, 1851.

27. See AGCA ST-AV 39 11, 45 9, 47 5, 54 8, 55 2, 74 12, 77 8, 78 4, 79 9, 80 12 82 2, 82 3, 83 4, 83 5, 84 5, 84 11, 87 7, 88 2, 89 12, 90 1, 90 2, 94 4, 94 11, 94 12, 96 9, 95 12, 96 9, 99 4, 99 12, 101 1, 107 5, and 111 4.

28. *El Norte,* April 8, 1922; AGCA B 28865 358–261; and AGCA MG-AV 32744 10 list peasant complaints against this land grab.

29. AGCA ST-AV 54 8.

30. AGCA ST-AV 99 9.

31. Peasant protests are scattered through AGCA JP-AV, papers, 1877. See also the complaint in AGCA DAN-AV 1A 9.

32. AGCA JP-AV, December 21, 1879.

33. AGCA ST-AV 54 8.

34. AGCA MG-AV 31887.

35. *Polochic,* May 4, 1895, reports on Guillermo Dieseldorff's travels to Germany to raise money for the project. This citation also contains a list of the principal German holders of the company. *El Progreso Nacional,* September 11, 1894, lists government land and tax concessions made to the company.

36. *Tactic,* February 13, 1954.

37. For examples, see AGCA B 28599 132; AGCA ST-AV 54 8; *El Norte,* October 24, 1936. AGCA J-AV, index 107 28 7732 describes the 1927 poisoning of Englishman William Taylor, by either his lover or his Jamaican assistant.

38. By the early 1920s, the first wave of speculation had led to a concentration of land in the form of eight large plantations that cultivated corn, coffee, sugar, cacao, cattle, and rice, along with some rubber and tobacco. Three of the eight were owned by a German corporation and one by Minor Keith, whose enormous 165,000-acre plantation Las Tinajas would be converted in 1922 into a branch of the United Fruit Company. Three plantations were owned by Federico Gerlach, the head of perhaps the largest German-owned agricultural corporation operating in Guatemala; Marroquín hermanos, ed., *Directorio oficial y guía general de la Republica de Guatemala* (Guatemala City: Marroquín hermanos, 1915), pp. 221–22, and Wagner, *Los Alemanes,* pp. 146–47.

39. *Verapaz,* December 1969. The article in the magazine *Panzós,* August 1979, pro-

vides a useful summary of landownership in the region that focuses on the rise of new "pioneers."

40. *Verapaz*, December 1969. Carlos Díaz Molina, "Que fluya la verdad," *Crónica*, July 10, 1998, says that Monzón arrived in 1922.

41. Carlos Díaz Molina, "Que fluya la verdad," *Crónica*, July 10, 1998.

42. Both the PGT and the PAR during the October Revolution, and later the FAR in the 1960s, had significant support among a number of provincial merchant and small-business-owning Ladino families throughout the Polochic Valley. In Panzós, PGT members Marcela Lemus, a schoolteacher and ticket agent for Taca Airlines, and her lover Herculano Hernández owned a "well-stocked" dry goods store and informal restaurant where "peasants of different ages and sexes come to make their purchases." The two were part of a regional association of activists that included families in Purulhá, Tactic, Cahabón, and Senahú. See the 1954 accusation that Lemus and Hernández used their store and restaurant as a site to politicize peasants, in AGCA J-AV, index 107 61J 2788.

43. *El Norte*, January 1, 1915, and April 8, 1922, relates complaints of monopolization and high prices of corn, salt, lard, pork, and sugar. For protests against the high cost and bad service of train transport, see *El Norte*, April 8, 1922, and July 5, 1922; AGCA ST-AV 54 8; and AGCA Formato 22188, 1929.

44. For Panama disease, see AGCA 22188 1937 and *Panzós*, August 1979.

45. In 1952 Las Tinajas, by then owned by the Compañía Agraria Tinajas, comprised roughly 132,000 acres divided into two main portions, the first approximately 88,000 acres and centered on the village Pueblo Viejo and the second about 44,000 acres and centered on the community Cahaboncito. The first was completely nationalized while the second had 5,500 acres appropriated and parceled out to seventy-two Q'eqchi' families. For the Agrarian Reform in Panzós, see AGCA DAN-AV 2B 10, 9A 5, 1A 9, 2B 10, 2 1, 7B 5; and AGCA DAN-AV, finca nacionales, 23 13. The file AGCA DAN-AV 3 2 is listed in the AGCA's DAN index but is missing from its holdings. There is also a file that never made it to the AGCA, located in INTA's warehouse, detailing the expropriation of 3,000 acres from the plantation Sepur.

46. See AGCA J-AV, index 107 60H 2122 and 61J 2788, for arrests and trials. The municipal archives of Panzós, "Libro de Actas," vol. 4, July 16, 1954, folio 238, and October 19, 1954, folio 251, describes Monzón's appointment as mayor.

47. Dirección General de Estadística, *II Censo Agropecuario 1964*, vol. 4 (Guatemala City: Dirección General de Estadística, 1969), p. 346, describes the skewed municipal land distribution that forced peasants to either seek out sharecropping arrangements or settle on unclaimed national land.

48. Most of the thirty communities and 3,867 families that had received collective title to land in Panzós by 1984 had initiated their petitions between the early 1960s and the early 1970s; Instituto Nacional de Transformación Agraria, *Asentamientos*.

49. *La Nación*, June 21, 1978, reports that within the boundaries of what was Las Tinajas there existed "overlapping and badly measured properties . . . superimpositions,

overlays, and contradictory information yielding a series of incongruent data" as to who owned what. *Diario de Centro América,* June 22, 1978, relates another history of Las Tinajas's perplexing boundaries.

50. By the early 1970s Flavio Monzón had become owner of large tracts of property throughout Panzós; Díaz Molina, "Que fluya la verdad."

51. This 1964 swindle is widely remembered in Panzós, as reported in CEH, *Memoria del silencio,* 6:14.

52. AGCA B 28605 144; AGCA MG-AV 29483 5.

53. In 1887 Alta Verapaz's prefect complained that Q'eqchi's had migrated to the banks of the Polochic "out of the control" of the local authorities; AGCA B 28743 638.

54. *El Norte,* September 7, 1963. AGCA MG-AV 30654 documents two attempts in 1930 and 1934 by planters to claim riverbank land from Q'eqchi' peasants.

55. AGCA A 182 3740; AGCA B 28577 84.

56. AGCA JP-AV, November 6, 1868.

57. Gabriel Aguilera Peralta, *La matanza de Panzós y el desarrollo capitalista de Guatemala* (Mexico City: Universidad Iberoamericana, 1980), places the massacre at the intersection of international capitalism, military developmentalism, and government corruption.

58. For the FAR in Panzós, see DDRS-US, Department of State, untitled cable, November 4, 1964. *Diario de Centro América,* December 5 and 18, 1964, singles out the department of Alta Verapaz because of its dense indigenous population for military "civic action" work. For civic action in Panzós, see *Diario de Centro América,* April 3 and 28, 1964 and March 17, 1965.

59. See *El Imparcial,* November 27, 1964, for the decree establishing the Proyecto Nacional de Desarrollo a la Comunidad.

60. For the Servicio de Fomento Económico Indígena, see *Diario de Centro América,* January 3, April 3, and May 12, 1964. For the Secretaria de Bienestar Social, see *Diario de Centro América,* November 12 and December 5, 1964, and *El Imparcial,* April 15, 1966. For the Programa de Desarrollo de la Comunidad, see *Diario de Centro América,* December 5, 1964, and *El Imparcial,* November 27, 1964. These institutions supplemented already established entities such as the Instituto Indigenista Nacional and the Seminario de Integración Social de Guatemala. The Consejo Nacional de Planificación Económica, *Plan de desarrollo 1975–1979* (Guatemala City: Consejo Nacional de Planificación Económica, 1974), p. 4, describes Panzós as an "agricultural sector in expansion." The government also encouraged private, large-scale industries in rural areas. Guatemala in 1965 generously granted Canada's International Nickel Company a forty-year concession to begin mining operations on the northern shore of Lake Izabal between El Estor and Panzós.

61. The families who solicited land were all migrants from Senahú, Carchá, Cahabón, Salamá, and Zacapá; INTA, "Expediente general: La Soledad."

62. Ibid.

63. Ibid.

64. Ibid. *Alerta,* July 26, 1975, briefly describes the ceremony in which the provisional titles were granted.

65. For Cahaboncito, see *La Nación,* July 28, 1975.

66. "Datos en relación a los hechos de Panzós," July 24, 1978, is a summary of testimony presented to the national university's free legal clinic by Soledad residents allied with the Maquins; copy in author's possession from the personal papers of Antonio Argueta.

67. Each of the sixty families were to make a yearly payment of 96 quetzals for a total sum of 6,336.00, or 10 percent of the land's assessed value. INTA, "Expediente general: La Soledad." See also *Alerta,* July 26, 1975.

68. INTA, "Expediente general: La Soledad."

69. Today, Adelina Caal's oldest son's testimony corresponds with complaints filed by FASGUA prior to the massacre, as well as with a post-massacre summary of events leading to the killings. See a letter to Walter Overdick, mayor of Panzós, from FASGUA dated April 7, 1978, copy in author's possession from the personal papers of Antonio Argueta, and "Datos en relación a los hechos de Panzós."

70. "Datos en relación a los hechos de Panzós."

71. César Macías recalls that in 1963, when he was a rising FAR militant about to enter the region to scout out potential insurgent support, Joaquin Noval gave him the names of a number of possible supporters, including the Maquin family. Interview, César Macías, July 2001. See also his *La Guerrilla,* pp. 45–47, 64–65. According to César Macías, FAR rebels carried out a number of operations in Panzós, the most notable being in 1964 when, on the twentieth anniversary of the October Revolution, guerrillas took over Las Tinajas and held a political rally that included singing the national anthem and making a speech in Q'eqchi' promising Arbenz's return and the reinstitution of the Agrarian Reform. The rebels replayed the event in plantations down the Polochic Valley until they reached Panzós, where they held a large meeting. See also "Guerrilleros Atacan en Panzos," in *El Norte,* October 24, 1964.

72. *La Nación,* June 2, 1978. *El Gráfico,* June 2, 1978, and *La Tarde,* July 20, 1978, give Overdick's conflicted accounts of the causes of the massacre. Peasants involved in the struggle interpreted Overdick's vacillations and inability to address their grievances as evidence of his complicity. Some even report that he tricked the Maquins into organizing the May 29 protest. Prior to the massacre, Q'eqchi' witnesses say that Overdick "tried to pass himself off as *un compañero más*" and that he twice came to Soledad, on May 16 and 19, saying, "You are revolutionaries, I am one too, I'm here to help. When you want to come to the town to talk about your problems, come, and bring everybody to the municipality, I will help you"; in "Datos en relación a los hechos de Panzós," cited above. A series of post-massacre letters from Panzós peasants dated August 12 and October 22 and 23 directed to the president of the national university ask for help and complain of Overdick's alliance with a military commissioner who allegedly extorted money from the community on behalf of Overdick; copies in author's possession from the personal papers of Antonio Argueta. *La Tarde,* July 20, 1978, gives

Overdick's complaint against INTA. "Análisis y orígenes de los hechos acaecidos en Panzós," FASGUA press release, June 27, 1978, copy in author's possession from the personal papers of Antonio Argueta, conveys more frustration with INTA corruption and inefficiency.

73. Fundación de Antropología Forense de Guatemala, *Informe especial,* p. 89.

74. In the unpublished manuscript on which the above Fundación de Antropología Forense de Guatemala's *Informe especial* is based, "Informe del peritaje antropológico forense del cementerio clandestino ubicado en Panzós AV con referencia al proceso penal #2636–97," p. 19, located in the Office of the Fundación de Antropología Forense de Guatemala, Guatemala City.

75. Conflicts broke out in Cahaboncito, El Corozal, Carabajal, Caguachá, Rubetzul, Jolomix, Concepción, Tampur, Palestina, San Vicente, San Antonio, Esperanza, San Marcos, San Juan, San José, Sacoy, Polomijich, Río Chiquito, Manga Vieja, Salac, Sacsuha, Río Zarco, Semococh, Canguaxa, Sepacay, and the plantation Moyagua. This list is culled from a number of interviews and documentary sources, including INTA files; newspapers; the personal papers of Antonio Argueta; the Archivo del Congreso de Guatemala (hereafter cited as ACG), "Diario de las Sesiones," August 24, 1978; and *La Tarde,* July 20, 1978, and August 21, 1978.

76. See the results of the investigation carried out by the national university's Cobán branch, the Centro Universitario del Norte, May 30, 1978, located in the Archivo Histórico del Centro de Investigaciones Regionales de Mesoamérica (hereafter cited as AH de CIRMA), "Conflictos: Panzós."

77. *La Nación,* June 2, 1978.

78. Testimonies given after the massacre by Ladinos, soldiers, and planters remark on the swirl of rumors of a Q'eqchi' plot to burn the town down or attack the military base. See the investigation carried out by the Catholic Church and published as a paid advertisment in *La Nación,* June 4, 1978, "Sacerdotes y religiosas de la diocesis de la Verapaz hacen el siguiente comunicado en relación a los hechos de Panzós."

79. Municipal archives of Panzós, "Libro de Actas Varias," vol. 9, May 3, 1978, folio 2.

80. Quoted in CEH, *Memoria del silencio,* 6:14, from a document found in the office of Alta Verapaz's governor, "acta de audiencia," May 5, 1978.

81. For the rifles, see *Newsweek,* June 19, 1978. Estimates of the number of soldiers ranged at the time between 40 and 150; CEH, *Memoria del silencio,* 6:14, gives the lower number, and Centro de Investigaciones de Historia Social, *Panzós: Testimonio* (Guatemala City: n.p., 1979), p. 32, provides the higher figure. There also are discrepancies in accounts as to whether the troops arrived three, four, or five days prior to the massacre. Walter Overdick reports that thirty soldiers arrived three days earlier, on Saturday, while his municipal office was closed. As to whether the troops were from Cobán or Zacapa, denunciations at the time insist that the troops were from Zacapa, perhaps as a way to link the event to that department's notorious military zone, which executed the 1966–68 counterinsurgency against the FAR and was closely linked to the MLN. Yet all the officials involved were stationed at the base in Cobán, and it was to

Cobán's governor that Monzón made his request for reinforcements. Evidence does suggest that planters used the Zacapa base's infamous reputation as a threat; some survivors said that planters "threatened to turn the Zacapa military base on them if they continued to demand their land rights"; in *La Tarde,* May 31, 1978.

82. FASGUA, "Análisis y orígenes de los hechos acaecidos en Panzós."

83. CEH, *Memoria del silencio,* 6:15 n. 20. Fundación de Antropología Forense de Guatemala, *Informe especial,* p. 89, reports the rapes.

84. *La Nación,* June 2, 1978. *El Gráfico,* June 7, 1978, provides more government accusations against *"la familia Maquin."*

85. *El Grafico,* June 2, 1978.

86. "Datos en relación a los hechos de Panzós."

87. Municipal archives of Panzós, "Libro de Defunciones," no. 26, May 31, 1978, registers the death by *"arma blanca"* of Pedro Cuc, twenty-three, in Soledad on May 27, 1978.

88. "Informe del peritaje antropológico forense del cementerio clandestino ubicado en Panzós," p. 19.

89. Dated May 26, 1978, the letter announced that a FASGUA delegation would arrive June 7; copy in author's possession from the personal papers of Antonio Argueta.

90. "Datos en relación a los hechos de Panzós."

91. *Newsweek,* June 19, 1978.

92. *El Impacto,* May 31, 1978.

93. Centro de Investigaciones de Historia Social, *Panzós,* p. 32.

94. CEH, *Memoria del silencio,* 6:16.

95. *El Impacto,* May 31, 1978.

96. For the government and military's distribution of blame, see *Diario de Centro América,* May 31, 1978; *El Imparcial,* May 29, 1978; *El Gráfico,* June 1, 1978; *Prensa Libre,* June 1 and 2, 1978; *Excelsior de Mexico,* June 2, 1978; and *El Impacto,* June 7, 1978. The paid advertisement from Polochic planters in *Prensa Libre,* June 7, 1978, thanks the army and blames the protesters.

97. *El Gráfico,* June 1, 1978, observes that the three soldiers were not allowed to give unsupervised interviews and did not suffer bullet wounds.

98. *El Gráfico,* June 1, 1978.

99. *El Gráfico,* June 2, 1978. Fundación de Antropología Forense de Guatemala, *Informe especial,* p. 90, reports a scuffle. Another witness testifies that the scuffle broke out when a soldier spoke "strong words" in Spanish and a Q'eqchi' protester, "believing himself offended because he did not understand Spanish, attacked the soldier, who fell wounded"; in the Catholic Church investigation "Sacerdotes y religiosas de la diocesis de la Verapaz hacen el siguiente comunicado en relación a los hechos de Panzós," published as a paid ad in *La Nación,* June 4, 1978.

100. *El Gráfico,* June 2, 1978.

101. Recounted in Centro de Investigaciones de Historia Social, *Panzós,* p. 32. See also his account in *El Impacto,* June 2, 1978.

102. "Datos en relación a los hechos de Panzós" reports that protesters came from

the communities of Soledad, Panzós, Cahaboncito, El Corozal, Carabajal, Caaguachá, and Senahú. Fundación de Antropología Forense de Guatemala, *Informe especial,* p. 88, states that others came from Semococh, Canguaxa, Sepacay, and the plantation Moyagua.

103. *La Nación,* June 2, 1978.

104. *El Gráfico,* May 31, 1978, and *La Nación,* June 2, 1978.

105. See the report from the Centro Universitario del Norte, May 30, 1978, located in AH de CIRMA, "Conflictos: Panzós," and *La Nación,* June 2, 1978. The Catholic Church's investigation, published in *La Nación,* June 3, 1978, states that the protesters carried sticks and machetes because some planned to go to work in the fields after the protest.

106. "Informe del peritaje antropológico forense del cementerio clandestino ubicado en Panzós," p. 16, contains descriptions from witnesses that the protesters showed up *"animados," "alegre,"* and *"enojados."*

107. Fundación de Antropología Forense de Guatemala, *Informe especial,* p. 89.

108. *El Gráfico,* June 2, 1978.

109. Ibid.

110. Fundación de Antropología Forense de Guatemala, *Informe especial,* p. 89; see also the description in *El Gráfico,* June 2, 1978.

111. *Washington Post,* June 24, 1978.

112. *La Tarde,* June 3, 1978, reports twenty-five wounded in a local health clinic, three of them women, and twelve by "projectiles." Others were treated for bullet wounds and broken bones; CEH, *Memoria del silencio,* 6:16–18; and Fundación Antropología Forense de Guatemala, *Informe especial,* pp. 89–91.

113. "Informe del peritaje antropológico forense del cementerio clandestino ubicado en Panzós," p. 18.

114. Fundación de Antropología Forense de Guatemala, *Informe especial,* p. 93. CEH, *Memoria del silencio,* 6:22–23, provides an incomplete list of the victims, which is reproduced here in the appendix.

115. Municipal archives of Panzós, "Libro de Defunciones," vol. 9, acts 27 to 58.

116. Centro de Investigaciones de Historia Social, *Panzós,* p. 32. *La Tarde,* May 31, 1978, gives the names of other planters accused of organizing the killing. See also *El Imparcial,* May 31, 1978. FASGUA, "Análisis y orígenes de los hechos acaecidos en Panzós," reports that the troops were from Zacapa. The MLN denies involvement in *El Impacto,* June 3, 1978. After the massacre, Panzós mayor Walter Overdick told reporters that planters had requested help from the military, in *La Nación,* June 2, 1978.

117. FASGUA, "Análisis y orígenes de los hechos acaecidos en Panzós," and "Datos en relación a los hechos de Panzós" accuse Monzón. Monzón's remark about doing away with *"indios"* seems to have been reported by Sebastian Maquin, in Centro de Investigaciones de Historia Social, *Panzós,* p. 33, and *La Nación,* May 31, 1978. Laugerud's threat to bring charges of libel against Monzón for implying that he authorized the killing is in *El Imparcial,* June 1, 1978. Monzón took out a paid ad in *La Nación,* June 2, 1978, denying all responsibility.

118. Overdick made a number of statements to the press in the days immediately after the massacre highly critical of INTA, the planters, and the military, and today insists that the military forced him to resign. See Comisión Nacional de Solidaridad con Panzós, "Boletín de Prensa no. 4," copy in author's possession from the personal papers of Antonio Argueta; *La Nación,* June 2 and July 19, 1978; *El Gráfico,* June 2, 1978; and *La Tarde,* July 20, 1978. Municipal archives of Panzós, "Libro de Actas de Sesiones Municipales," no. 9, July 30, 1978, folio 511, registers Overdick's resignation as mayor. *Prensa Libre,* May 28, 1996, reports on Arturo de la Cruz's accusation that Overdick was responsible for the massacre. To support charges against Overdick, de la Cruz, in *Prensa Libre,* May 29, 1996, referenced a study conducted by the military on the massacre. "It must be in the ministry of defense," said de la Cruz, "it is an enormous volume." Guatemala's defense ministry has ignored my repeated requests to review it.

119. The United Nations–administered truth commission, the CEH, concludes that the military "arbitrarily executed fifty-three people and attempted to do so with forty-seven others" and blames both planters and the government for maintaining "terror over the population, whose effects lasted almost two decades." CEH, *Memoria del silencio,* 6:21–22.

120. *La Nación,* June 1, 1978, and *El Impacto,* June 1, 1978.

121. *Newsweek,* June 19, 1978.

122. *La Nación,* June 9, 1978. Levenson-Estrada, *Trade Unionists against Terror,* pp. 139–40, describes the discussion among workers that went into the making of a banner that read "Guatemala, '78, Headquarters of the World Tournament of Murders. We Repudiate the Massacre at Panzós, Union of Workers at TACASA." These demonstrations foreshadowed the 1980 May Day parade when popular organizations linked to the EGP would call for the overthrow of the government.

123. *La Nación,* June 9, 1978.

124. For scores of paid advertisements from all sectors of Guatemalan society, see Centro de Investigaciones de Historia Social, *Panzós,* pp. 47–81.

125. *El Gráfico,* June 21, 1978.

126. ACG, "Diario de las Sesiones," June 6, 1978, June 13, 1978, June 15, 1978, August 24, 1978, August 25, 1978.

127. Ibid., June 15, 1978.

128. Ibid., June 13, 1978.

129. Ibid., June 13, 1978.

130. Ibid., July 19, 1978.

131. Ibid., August 30, 1978.

132. See ibid., June 22, 1978, and August 24, 1978. ACG, "punto resolutivo," July 28, 1978, describes the Congress's rejection of a motion to send five members along with a commission convened by nongovernmental agencies to investigate events.

133. ACG, "Diario de las Sesiones," June 22, 1978.

134. Jim Handy, *Gift of the Devil: A History of Guatemala* (Boston: South End Press, 1984), p. 178.

135. See *Prensa Libre,* June 14, 1979, for a paid ad on the anniversary of their deaths.

The *Washington Post*, June 24, 1978, reports that the number of soldiers killed was seventeen. It also notes that it was the EGP that took the revenge, yet informants say that it was actually members of the PGT who joined the EGP after the bombing.

136. PGT-Tulane, box 1, folder 24, "Declaración de la Comisión Política del CC, PGT," June 17, 1978.

137. For the expulsion of members who "cultivated militarism," see PGT-Tulane, box 1, folder 27, August 28, 1978, and box 1, folder 28, "Documento para el estudio interno. Comisión política del comité central del PGT," December 1978.

138. Miguel Angel Albizúres, *Tiempo de sudor y lucha* (Guatemala City [?]: Edición Local, 1987).

139. Levenson-Estrada, *Trade Unionists against Terror,* pp. 134–135.

140. While it did not take its name until 1978, the CUC has roots that go back to the 1967 creation of the Sindicato de Trabajadores Agrícolas Independientes in Chichicastenango. Influenced by liberation theology, local peasant committees organized against the abuses of contract labor, the exploitation of migrant plantation work, conscription, prohibitions against cutting down trees, delinquency, land and water expropriation, and cultural discrimination. As it began to take shape in 1977, its leaders had some political connection with the EGP, but it was neither structured nor formal. The EGP, reacting to the failed militarism of the guerrillas in the 1960s, saw the CUC as an important allied social movement. For the CUC, see REMHI, *Nunca más,* 3:123–25; CEH, *Memoria del silencio,* 1:169–70; José Manuel Fernández Fernández, *El Comité de Unidad Campesina: Orígen y desarrollo* (Guatemala City: Centro de Estudios Rurales Centroamericanos, 1988); Greg Grandin, "To End with All These Evils: Ethnic Transformation and Community Mobilization in Guatemala's Western Highlands, 1954–1980," *Latin American Perspectives* 24, no.2 (1997): 7–33; María del Pilar Hoyos de Asig, *Fernando Hoyos, ¿dónde estás?* (Guatemala City: Centroamérica: Fondo de Cultura Editorial, 1997); and CEH, *Memoria del silencio,* 1:169–71. *Diario de Centro América,* February 7 and 12, May 4, and December 10, 1964, and *El Imparcial,* January 8 and October 19, 1964, report on early cooperatives in the indigenous western highlands. *Diario de Centro América,* November 28, 1966, and December 22, 1966, and *El Imparcial,* September 27, 1966, and November 12, 1966, describe peasant leagues.

141. Interviews with a number of EGP and CUC leaders and cadres related the importance of the Panzós massacre to their political work.

142. Composed June 1, 1978, published in *La Nación,* June 4, 1978.

143. As part of a CUC presentation to a national-university-sponsored roundtable that took place on June 20, 1978, reproduced in Centro de Investigaciones de Historia Social, *Panzós,* pp. 87–88. A flyer also circulated by an entity called "Grupos indígenas de Guatemala" that linked the massacre to rural violence elsewhere: "from colonial times they have used the Indian as a beast of burden or an instrument of work and now as a machine of death, since now in the military there are Indians dehumanized by diverse methods to be turned into instruments at the service of the powerful"; in AH de CIRMA "Conflictos: Panzós," June 1978. *Cha'b'l Tinamit,* June 23, 1978, an in-

digenous newspaper run out of San Juan Sacatepéquez, also condemned the government. Betsy Konefal's forthcoming doctoral dissertation documents how the Panzós massacre radicalized indigenous beauty contestants throughout the highlands.

144. Aside from the demands for justice in Panzós, peasants throughout Guatemala continued to invade plantations, while a group of thirty Ixil-Mayan women complained to the press and national and international organizations that their husbands had been disappeared. For land invasions, see *La Hora,* June 5, 1978; for the Ixil women, see *El Gráfico,* June 21, 1978, and *El Imparcial,* June 15, 1978. For international criticism, see *Le Monde* (France), June 9, 1978.

145. For attacks against the Catholic Church, see *La Tarde,* June 14, 1978, and *El Impacto,* June 7, 1978.

146. *El Gráfico,* June 3, 1978.

147. *El Gráfico,* June 8 and 14, 1978.

148. Municipal archives of Panzós, "Libro de Actas Varias," no. 9, July 5, 1978, folio 11.

149. Asociación para el Avance de las Ciencias Sociales en Guatemala (AVANCSO), *La Política de desarrollo del estado guatemalteco, 1986–1988* (Guatemala City: AVANCSO, 1988); AVANCSO, *Política exterior y estabilidad estatal* (Guatemala City: AVANCSO, 1989), and Schirmer, *Guatemalan Military Project.*

150. Municipal archives of Panzós, "Libro de Actas Varias," no. 9, July 5, 1978, folio 20.

151. *Prensa Libre,* August 22, 1978.

152. In September, peasants from Telemán complained to the national university's free legal clinic that Fidel Augusto Ponce had sent other peasants to invade their land. See letter addressed to Fidel Augusto Ponce, dated September 25, 1978, copy in author's possession from the personal papers of Antonio Argueta.

153. See the three press releases by the CNT in AH de CIRMA, "Conflicts: Panzós," dated January 3, 1979, May 14, 1979, and January 26, 1980. See also *La Nación,* April 19, 1980.

154. See *El Imparcial*, May 31 and June 5, 1978; *El Gráfico,* June 2 and 7, 1978.

155. Centro de Investigaciones de Historia Social, *Panzós,* p. 37

156. INTA, "Expediente general: La Soledad."

157. Although the military did commit a number of massacres in the community of San Marcos where the PGT maintained some support; CEH, *Memoria del silencio,* 8:90, 93; pp. 62–64 describes the military's August 1982 campaign of rape and murder in a number of organized plantations in southern Senahú.

158. See the entries for these communities in CEH, *Memoria del silencio,* 8:26–136.

159. Ibid., 8:135.

160. Ibid., 8:104. For more violence against labor organizers on the plantation Miramar, see *La Nación-Norte,* May 1, 1979. *La Nación,* April 12, 1979; *Nuevo Diario,* January 6, 1979; and *Prensa Libre,* October 9, 1978, describe post-massacre selective violence in Panzós. *Nuevo Diario,* June 20, 1978, relates the disappearance of Napoleón Torres, leader of a Carchá peasant league. Torres was arrested in a sweep of activists

immediately after the massacre and upon his release was kidnapped off a Cobán street by a group of heavily armed men.

161. CEH, *Memoria del silencio,* 8:132.

162. See ibid., 8:28, 30, 27, 74, 75, 78, 80, 81, and 86.

163. Fundación de Antropología Forense de Guatemala, *Informe especial,* p. 92.

164. In "Informe del peritaje antropológico forense del cementerio clandestino ubicado en Panzós," p. 18.

165. Ibid., p. 17.

166. See the discussion in Seyla Benhabib, *Situating the Self: Gender, Community and Postmodernism in Contemporary Ethics* (New York: Routledge, 1992), p. 243.

167. See Luce Irigaray, "Equal to Whom?" *differences* 1 (Summer 1989).

168. Joan Wallach Scott, *Only Paradoxes to Offer: French Feminists and the Rights of Man* (Cambridge: Harvard University Press, 1996), p. 7. Lynn Hunt also argues that the belief in human rights entails the dual process of individuation and difference, yet stresses the importance of empathy with others—rather than their subordination—to the emergence of universal notions of equality and justice. See "The Paradoxical Origins of Human Rights," in *Human Rights and Revolutions,* ed. Jeffrey N. Wasserstrom, Lynn Hunt, and Marilyn B. Young (Lanham, Md.: Rowman and Littlefield, 2000).

169. Diana Taylor, *Disappearing Acts: Spectacles of Gender and Nationalism in Argentina's "Dirty War"* (Durham: Duke University Press, 1997), pp. 203, 205.

CONCLUSION

1. Gabriel García Márquez, "La soledad de América Latina," 1982, found online at http://sololiteratura.com/marquezdislasoledad.htm.

2. Gabriel García Márquez, *One Hundred Years of Solitude,* trans. Gregory Rabassa (New York: Harper and Row, 1970), p. 383.

3. Eduardo Posada-Carbó, "Fiction as History: The *Bananeras* and Gabriel García Márquez's *One Hundred Years of Solitude,*" *Journal of Latin American Studies* 30 (1998): 395–414.

4. Catherine LeGrand identifies *One Hundred Years of Solitude,* with its tales of erased memory and shattered communities, as the cultural correlate to dependency theory. The arrival of the foreign fruit company in Macondo "spells the end of the familiar world, and it destroys the capacity of communities to draw on their past so as to create new visions of what the future should be." LeGrand, however, describes a society that was neither created nor eradicated by foreign capital, one with complex social relations and cultural identities that creatively engaged with the challenges and opportunities brought by a deepening insertion in a world economy; Catherine C. LeGrand, "Living in Macondo: Economy and Culture in a United Fruit Company Banana Enclave in Colombia," in *Close Encounters of Empire: Writing the Cultural History of U.S.-Latin American Relations,* ed. Gilbert M. Joseph, Catherine LeGrand, and Ricardo D. Salvatore (Durham: Duke University Press, 1998), p. 333.

5. See also the comparison between the Mocando killing and the 1968 Tlatelolco massacre in Mexico in Greg Grandin, "Chronicles of a Guatemalan Genocide Foretold: Violence, Trauma, and the Limits to Historical Inquiry," *Nepantla: Views from South* 1, no. 2 (2000): 391–412.

6. Mario de la Cruz Torres, "Monografía del Municipio de San Antonio Senahú, Alta Verapaz," *Guatemala Indígena* 17, nos. 3/4 (1982): 52.

7. CEH, *Memoria del silencio,* 6:19.

8. Hannah Arendt, *On Revolution* (New York: Penguin Books, 1963), p. 20.

9. Mayer, *Furies,* p. 75.

10. Pablo Neruda, *Canto General* (Berkeley: University of California Press, 1991), p. 200.

11. See the discussion in Miguel A. Centeno, "The Peaceful Continent: War in Latin America," in *Latin America: An Interdisciplinary Approach,* ed. Gladys Varona-Lacey and Julio López-Arias (New York: Peter Lang, 1999).

12. Edelberto Torres-Rivas, "Epilogue: Notes on Terror, Violence, Fear and Democracy," in *Societies of Fear: The Legacy of Civil War, Violence and Terror in Latin America,* ed. Kees Koonings and Dirk Kruijt (London, Zed Books, 1999), p. 285.

13. For her part, Diana Taylor sees terror as transcending both history and politics, arguing that Argentine state violence emerged from a set of gendered "performative traditions deeper than any explicit political position." *Disappearing Acts,* p. 34.

14. Linda Green, *Fear as a Way of Life: Mayan Widows in Rural Guatemala* (New York: Columbia University Press, 1999), p. 172.

15. Work done in disciplines other than history tends to reinforce the timeless nature of Latin American state violence. Liberal legal theorists shy away from social analyses of political violence, nervous that historical judgments will serve only to inflame political passions. In Argentina, Raúl Alfonsín's government studiously refused to attach historical import to the repression conducted by the previous military regime apart from the belief that political violence is a symptom of illiberal intolerance. Jaime Malamud-Goti, an advisor to Alfonsín, has written that Argentine political violence erupts from a "dictatorial mind" chronic to Argentine history. See *Game without End: State Terror and the Politics of Justice* (Norman: University of Oklahoma Press, 1996), p. 83.

16. See Mayer, *Dynamics of Counterrevolution in Europe,* p. 47, for the quote. See also Charles Tilly, *From Mobilization to Revolution* (Reading, Mass: Addison-Wesley, 1978), p. 193.

17. Eric D. Weitz, "The Modernity of Genocide: War, Race, and Revolution in the Twentieth Century," in *The Specter of Genocide: Mass Murder in Historical Perspective,* ed. Ben Kiernan and Robert Gellately (Cambridge: Cambridge University Press, 2003).

18. Ibid.

19. Mayer, *Furies.*

20. Such a dynamic is what propelled Cuban foreign policy through the 1960s and 1970s not only in Latin America but in Africa as well. Piero Gleijeses, *Conflicting*

Missions: Havana, Washington, and Africa, 1959–1976 (Chapel Hill: University of North Carolina Press, 2002).

21. Recent work on the Cuban Revolution, such as Thomas G. Paterson, *Contesting Castro: The United States and the Triumph of the Cuban Revolution* (New York: Oxford University Press, 1994), which examines the immediate revolutionary conjuncture, and Jules R. Benjamin, *The United States and the Origins of the Cuban Revolution: An Empire of Liberty in an Age of National Liberation* (Princeton: Princeton University Press, 1990), which places the breakdown of relations within a larger century-long history, attributes the lion's share of responsibility for its radicalization to the intransigence of the United States.

22. Dan Michael, "Chile and the Shadows of the Cold War," paper presented at the Annual Spring Graduate Student Conference, April 19–20, 2002, George Washington University.

23. Allende's defeat had global repercussions: The general secretary of Italy's Communist Party—which with its independence from the Soviet Union and its own form of Marxist pluralism was gaining in popularity—took from the Chilean example the lesson that his party would never be allowed to take power even if it won free elections. Mario del Pero, "Kissinger e la politica estera americana nel Mediterraneo: il caso portoghese" [Kissinger and American foreign policy in the Mediterranean: The Portuguese case], *Studi Storici*, no. 42 (October–December 2001): 973–88.

24. Peter Winn, "The Furies of the Andes: Violence and Terror in the Chilean Revolution and Counterrevolution of 1970–1973," paper given at the conference Rethinking Latin America's Century of Revolutionary Violence, May 15–17, 2003, Yale University. The following discussion is greatly indebted to observations made at this conference, especially by Carlota McAllister, Deborah Levenson, Peter Winn, Gerardo Rénique, and Jeffrey Gould, on the remarkably restrained response by the left to state and right-wing violence.

25. A number of the essays in Steve Stern, ed., *Peru's Shining and Other Paths: War and Society in Peru, 1980–1995* (Durham: Duke University Press, 1998), emphasize the "deep frustrations" of the Maoist Left with political repression and compromise, as Florencia Mallon puts it in her essay "Chronicle of a Path Foretold?: Velasco's Revolution, Vanguardia Revolucionaria, and 'Shining Omens' in the Indigenous Communities of Andahuaylas," p. 85.

26. Winn, "Furies of the Andes."

27. This paragraph is largely drawn from the collected essays in Bethell and Roxborough's *Latin America between the Second World War and the Cold War.*

28. Jeremy Adelman's "Andean Impasses," *New Left Review* 18 (November–December 2002): 52, argues that because the central and northern Andean countries of Venezuela, Peru, and Colombia did not experience the kind of mid-century populist movements that occurred in other Latin American nations, they were spared the "wave of brutal military dictatorships that swept the rest of the continent."

29. See Ada Ferrer, *Insurgent Cuba: Race, Nation, and Revolution, 1868–1898* (Chapel Hill: University of North Carolina Press, 1999).

30. See John Coatsworth, "Measuring Influence: The United States and the Mexican Peasantry," in *Rural Revolt in Mexico: U.S. Intervention and the Domain of Subaltern Politics,* ed. Daniel Nugent (Durham: Duke University Press, 1998).

31. In Rabinal, Emilio Roman López was a Communist Party member who after the fall of Arbenz and ensuing theft of municipal elections by the MLN organized other Achí-Mayans into a guerrilla front. After his assassination in 1968, a number of his indigenous followers were among the first group of rebels that crossed into Guatemala from Mexico to form the EGP. Figueroa Ibarra, "Revolución y violencia," pp. 284–85; César Macías, *La Guerrilla,* p. 107–8, 121–23; Régis Debray and Ricardo Ramírez, "Guatemala," in Debray, *Las pruebas de fuego* (Mexico City: Siglo Veintiuno, 1975), p. 265. See also Ceferino de Paz González, "El valiente muere cuando el cobarde lo decide," unpublished manuscript in author's possession, for the capture and torture of Rabinal's Achí PGT general secretary, Lorenzo de Paz Cuquej, in 1954. Paz's son Ceferino became a member of the PGT in the 1960s at the age of fourteen and joined the FAR rebels three years later. As of this writing he is mayor of Fray Bartolomé de las Casas, Alta Verapaz. Daniel Wilkinson, *Silence on the Mountain: Stories of Terror, Betrayal, and Forgetting in Guatemala* (New York: Houghton Mifflin, 2002), describes how on the coffee plantations of San Marcos, first the FAR in the 1960s and then the Organización Revolucionaria del Pueblo en Armas, an armed rebel group, in the 1970s and 1980s found support among plantation workers through the social networks created by the CALs and unions during the October Revolution. Another example: Juan Coc's father was the president of the CAL on plantation El Tesoro in San Miguel Uspantán, Quiché. Forced to flee after 1954, his family migrated to the Ixcán lowlands, and Coc became a leader of the region's cooperative movement, which was destroyed by the military in the late 1970s; Pilar Yoldi, *Don Juan Coc: Príncipe Q'eqchí, 1945–1995* (Guatemala City: Piedra Santa, 1996).

32. Grandin, "The Strange Case of 'La Mancha Negra,'" discusses the 1982 rejection of the civil patrol.

33. Interview with David Ordóñez Colop's son, June 1995.

34. See Charles Berguist, *Labor in Latin America: Comparative Essays on Chile, Argentina, Venezuela and Colombia* (Stanford: Stanford University Press, 1986), and Ruth Berins Collier and David Collier, *Shaping the Political Arena: Critical Junctures, the Labor Movement, and Regime Dynamics in Latin America* (Princeton: Princeton University Press, 1991).

35. Steve Stern, "Between Tragedy and Promise: The Politics of Writing Latin American History in the Late Twentieth Century," in *Reclaiming the Political in Latin American History: Essays from the North,* ed. Gilbert Joseph (Durham: Duke University Press, 2001), pp. 44–45, discusses the hostile reactions to Florencia Mallon's first suggestion of the possibility of "peasant nationalism," made in chapter 3 of *The Defense of Community in Peru's Central Highlands: Peasant Struggle and Capitalist Transition, 1860–1940* (Princeton: Princeton University Press, 1983), and later developed more fully in *Peasant and Nation: The Making of Postcolonial Mexico and Peru* (Berkeley: University of California Press, 1995). Even historians who had initially

emphasized the importance of popular mobilization and political culture in the forging of national identity and state formation turned sour, as did John Womack whose 1969 book on Emiliano Zapata's peasant army continues to inspire new generations of historians. By the late 1980s, Womack was describing the Mexican Revolution as little more than a "bourgeois civil war" that resulted in the creation of a decidedly unpopular, leviathan state. John Womack, "The Mexican Revolution, 1910–1920," in *Mexico since Independence*, ed. Leslie Bethell (Cambridge: Cambridge University Press, 1991), p. 128.

36. For histories of the Latin American left, see Castañeda, *Utopia Unarmed;* Timothy Wickham-Crowley, *Guerrillas and Revolutions in Latin America: A Comparative Study of Insurgents and Regimes since 1956* (Princeton: Princeton University Press, 1992); and Barry Carr and Steve Ellner, eds., *The Latin American Left: From the Fall of Allende to Perestroika* (Boulder: Westview Press, 1993).

37. This new scholarship on mid-twentieth-century social movements is complemented by a similar rethinking of nineteenth-century rural politics, which now emphasizes the power that "popular liberalism" had in posing a "haunting challenge" by demanding that the "ideals of post-Enlightenment liberal nation-states" be taken seriously, as Peter Guardino, *Peasants, Politics, and the Formation of Mexico's National State: Guerrero, 1800–1857* (Stanford: Stanford University Press, 1996), p. 220, puts it for the case of Mexico. See also David Nugent, *Modernity at the Edge of Empire: State, Individual, and Nation in the Northern Peruvian Andes, 1885–1935* (Stanford: Stanford University Press, 1997); Guy P. Thomson with David G. LaFrance, *Patriotism, Politics, and Popular Liberalism in Nineteenth Century Mexico: Juan Francisco Lucas and the Puebla Sierra* (Wilmington: Scholarly Resources, 1999); and my *Blood of Guatemala.*

38. James, *Resistance and Integration,* p. 263. For Chile, see Thomas Miller Klubock, *Contested Communities: Class, Gender, and Politics in Chile's El Teniente Copper Mine, 1904–1951* (Durham: Duke University Press, 1998), p. 289. For Nicaragua, see Jeffrey Gould, *To Lead as Equals: Rural Protest and Political Consciousness in Chinandega, Nicaragua, 1912–1979* (Chapel Hill: University of North Carolina Press, 1990). For Brazil, see John French, *The Brazilian Workers' ABC: Class Conflict and Alliances in Modern São Paulo* (Chapel Hill: University of North Carolina Press, 1992).

39. By highlighting the broad political overlap and social affinity between the Colombian Communist Party and Gaitán's left liberalism (despite the bitter, destructive rivalry of its leadership), Green argues against an earlier interpretation that excluded Gaitanism from the left. As occurred in Argentina, the moderate, foreign-focused popular front policies of the Communist Party hamstrung its efforts to adequately represent the interests of workers, opening the way for a populist willing to confront the oligarchy. See W. John Green, "Sibling Rivalry on the Left and Labor Struggles in Colombia during the 1940s," *Latin American Research Review* 35, no.1 (2000): 85–117.

40. Brooke Larson, "Capturing Indian Bodies, Hearths and Minds: '*El hogar campesino*' and Rural School Reform in Bolivia, 1920s–1940s," paper presented at the New York City Latin American History Workshop, New York University, April 26,

2002. See also Jorge Dandler, *El sindicalismo campesino en Bolivia: Los cambios estructurales en Ucureña* (Mexico City: Instituto Indigenista Interamericano, 1969).

41. For this process in Brazil, see Richard Graham, *Patronage and Politics in Nineteenth Century Brazil* (Stanford: Stanford University Press, 1990); in Nicaragua, see Elizabeth Dore, "Land Privatization and the Differentiation of the Peasantry: Nicaragua's Coffee Revolution, 1850–1920," *Journal of Historical Sociology* 8, no. 3 (September 1995): 303–26; in Guatemala, see David McCreery, *Rural Guatemala, 1760–1940* (Stanford: Stanford University Press, 1994); in the Yucatan, Mexico, see Gilbert Joseph, *Revolution from Without: Yucatan, Mexico, and the United States, 1880–1924* (Durham: Duke University Press, 1988); and in Chile, see Brian Loveman, *Struggles in the Countryside: Politics and Rural Labor in Chile, 1919–1973* (Bloomington: Indiana University Press, 1976).

42. Molyneux, "Twentieth-Century State Formations," and Elizabeth Dore, "One Step Forward, Two Steps Back: Gender and the State in the Long Nineteenth Century," in Dore and Molyneux, *Hidden Histories of Gender*, p. 9 for the quote.

43. Since its initial scholarly use in 1965 to describe Latin American mass mobilization, the term "populism" to describe mass political movements in Latin America has generated endless contention. See Ernesto Laclau, "Toward a Theory of Populism," in *Politics and Ideology in Marxist Theory: Capitalism, Fascism, and Populism*, ed. Laclau (London: NLB Books, 1977); and Paul Drake, *Socialism and Populism in Chile, 1932–1952* (Urbana: University of Illinois Press, 1978). Castañeda, *Utopia Unarmed*, pp. 39–45, discusses the relationship of postwar "national-populist" movements to the official left.

44. In his review of Marshall Berman's *All That Is Solid Melts into Air: The Experience of Modernity* (New York: Penguin, 1992), Perry Anderson attributes the political and cultural vitality of much of the third world in the twentieth century to a relatively late commodification of social relations, at least in relation to what happened in Europe and the United States; "Modernity and Revolution," *New Left Review*, no. 144 (March–April 1984): 96–113. My interpretation of the revolutionary vitality of Latin American modernity in the early twentieth century draws on both Anderson and Berman.

45. Arendt, *Origins of Totalitarianism*, p. vii. See also Theodor Adorno et al., *The Authoritarian Personality* (New York: Harpers, 1950), for the view that monopoly capitalism weakened the image of the patriarchal father and destroyed the venue in which ego formation could take place, thus leaving the unanchored self vulnerable to the allure of mass politics, particularly Nazism.

46. Richard Crossman, ed., *The God That Failed* (New York: Harper, 1949), is the classic on this point. The following discussion owes greatly to Corey Robin's *Fear: The History of a Political Idea* (New York: Oxford University Press, 2004).

47. Defining the relationship between modern individualism and social solidarity has long been a major preoccupation of political theorists and philosophers. Hannah Arendt saw the modern separation of society into narrowly defined political, economic, and household spheres as leading to disenfranchisement through the constriction of

the public realm; see her *Human Condition,* pp. 38–49. Most discussions of the rise of individualism and its relationship to liberalism are notably abstract, taking place predominantly on a philosophical level. Individualism comes about by the loss of a unified, moral order–be it rooted in religion or community—that accompanies the development of a secular bureaucratic nation-state and the spread of a market economy. Debates on how best to define and achieve justice and solidarity within such pluralism and dislocation are likewise often ethereal, divorced from the gritty reality of social conflict and elite resistance. This book has attempted to provide such concerns with a historical grounding, examining how individuation was intimately tied to the rise of oppositional mass politics. Such a threat provoked a backlash, in the form of counterinsurgent violence, that reconfigured the individual's relationship to a larger ethical and political community. Thus, in this approach, individualism, anomie, egotism, and alienation are less the products of a functional modernity than the results of political conflict and struggle. My position is therefore also at odds with postmodern interpretations of modern identity— not so much in their analysis of its emergence, which is often perceptive, but in their understanding of its consequences. In many such interpretations, personal sovereignty is a discursive fiction brought into being by a nexus of modern surveillance and disciplinary practices, knowledges, technologies, and institutions that produce a self-regulating (what liberals would call rights-bearing) individual. Thus the rise of individualism is understood to be restrictive, as denying the fundamental instability that defines our psyches. Despite differences, most postmodern approaches see liberation as coming about through an embrace of this instability and the destruction of the pretense of psychic coherence. The history presented here, however, suggests that the rise of individualism was absolutely indispensable to the overthrow or weakening of forced labor, state-enforced racism, sexual subordination, and other forms of domination. That is not of course to say that liberation is at hand but only to insist that historical variations in the methods of rule matter. Jerrold Seigel, "Problematizing the Self," in *Beyond the Cultural Turn: New Directions in the Study of Society and Culture,* ed. Victoria E. Bonnell and Lynn Hunt (Berkeley: University of California Press, 1999), critiques all-or-nothing visions of the self: "Such a vision, simultaneously wrapping the self like a mummy inside a tight [linguistic, grammatical, or disciplinary] web of relations and projecting its escape into a world where no bonds restrain it, hardly seems a promising way to think about the powers and limits of the self" (p. 309). For differing interpretations of individuation, see Charles Taylor, *Sources of the Self: The Making of the Modern Identity* (Cambridge: Cambridge University Press, 1989), and *The Ethics of Authenticity* (Cambridge: Harvard University Press, 1992); Michel Foucault, "The Subject and Power," afterword to Hubert L. Dreyfus and Paul Rabinow, *Michel Foucault: Beyond Structuralism and Hermeneutics* (Chicago: University of Chicago Press, 1983); and Jacques Derrida, "Différance," *The Margins of Philosophy,* trans. Alan Bass (Chicago: University of Chicago Press, 1992).

48. Patricia Seed, *To Love, Honor, and Obey in Colonial Mexico: Conflicts over Marriage Choice, 1574–1821* (Stanford: Stanford University Press, 1998), and Pamela Voekel,

Alone before God: The Religious Origins of Modernity in Mexico (Durham: Duke University Press, 2002), document, respectively, the economic and religious roots of individualism in Latin America during the late eighteenth century. Seed engages with and draws from Albert O. Hirschman's classic *The Passions and the Interests: Political Arguments for Capitalism before its Triumph* (Princeton: Princeton University Press, 1977). More generally, John D'Emilio famously identified the spread of capitalism as central to the emergence of modern gay identity; see "Capitalism and Gay Identity:" in *The Gender/Sexuality Reader: Culture, History, Political Economy*, ed. Roger N. Lancaster and Micaela di Leonardo (New York: Routledge, 1997).

49. Voekel, *Alone before God*, p. 3.

50. See the studies cited in note 39.

51. Jeffrey Gould, in *To Die in This Way*, p. 26, cites Toribio Mendoza, a leader of an indigenous rebellion in Nicaragua in 1881, as saying, "I'm 70 years old and I'm going to live another 50 years so I can go on making revolutions."

52. The most obvious expression of this is of course found in the title of Rigoberta Menchú's autobiography, *Me llamo Rigoberta Menchú y así me nació la conciencia* (Mexico City: Siglo Veintiuno, 1985). For El Salvador, see Miguel Marmol, *Miguel Marmol*, ed. Roque Dalton, trans. Kathleen Ross and Richard Shaaf (Willimantic, Conn.: Curbstone Press, 1987), and Claribel Alegría (with D. J. Flakoll), *No me agarran viva: la mujer salvadoreña en la lucha* (Mexico City: Ediciones Era, 1983).

53. Daniel James, *Doña María's Story: Life History, Memory, and Political Identity* (Durham: Duke University Press, 2000), p. 33.

54. Chico Mendes, *Chico Mendes in His Own Words: Fight for the Forest* (London: Latin American Bureau, 1989), p. 16.

55. See Ranahit Guha's "On Some Aspects of the Historiography of Colonial India," in *Selected Subaltern Studies*, ed. Guha and G. C. Spivak (New York: Oxford University Press, 1998), for an account of vertical popular mobilization that emphasizes more than I do here the autonomy of subaltern politics.

56. Deutsch, *Las Derechas*, especially pp. 81–83.

57. Department of State, embassy telegram, Santiago 3741, "The Communists Take Over Chile," September 17, 1970, on http://www.dwu.edu/~nsarchiv/nsaebb/nsaebb8/ch19–01.

58. See Frederick B. Pike, *Hispanismo 1898–1936: Spanish Conservatives and Liberals and the Relations with Spanish America* (Notre Dame: University of Notre Dame Press, 1971).

59. Mayer, *Furies*, chap. 2, and *Dynamics of Counterrevolution in Europe*, chap. 3, describes in detail the vital nature of counterrevolution. The literature on conservative and right-wing practice and ideas in Latin America, already considerable, is growing. For examples from which the following discussion is drawn, see Pike, *Hispanismo 1898–1936;* Margaret Power, *Right-Wing Women in Chile: Feminine Power and the Struggle against Allende, 1964–1973* (University Park: Pennsylvania State University Press, 2002); Sandra McGee Deutsch, *Counterrevolution in Argentina, 1900–1932: The Argentine Patriotic League* (Lincoln: University of Nebraska Press, 1986), and *Las*

Derechas, as well as Sandra McGee Deutsch and Ronald H. Dolkart, eds., *The Argentine Right: Its History and Intellectual Origins, 1910 to the Present* (Wilmington: Scholarly Resources, 1993).

60. Deutsch, *Las Derechas,* pp. 143–247.

61. See Tina Rosenberg, *Children of Cain: Violence and the Violent in Latin America* (New York: Penguin, 1992), particularly the chapters on Chile and Argentina.

62. See Power, *Right-Wing Women in Chile.*

63. Aside from the death squads and paramilitaries discussed in chapter 3, during the overthrow of Arbenz in 1954, the CIA, with the help of its Guatemalan assets, organized "shock troops" and "five man HORNET teams" to generate internal disruptions and preempt possible organized support for the government; Central Intelligence Agency, "Memorandum from Operation PBSUCCESS Headquarters in Florida to the Chief of Station in Guatemala," June 9, 1954, located at Department of State, Office of the Historian, http://www.state.gov/r/pa/ho/frus/ike/guat/20180.htm.

64. Huggins, *Political Policing,* pp. 135–36.

65. Ibid., pp. 20–22.

66. Michelle Chase, "The Cuban Trials," paper presented at the conference Rethinking Latin America's Century of Revolutionary Violence, May 15–17, 2003, Yale University.

67. Three hundred and twenty Chileans were condemned and executed by military tribunals within two months of the September 11, 1973, coup against Allende. This figure does not include other forms of state-administered "extrajudicial" killings; in Department of State, Briefing Memorandum, "Chilean Executions," November 16, 1973, on http://www.gwu.edu/~nsarchiv/NSAEBB/NSAEBB8/ch10-01.htm.

68. Lynn Horton, *Peasants in Arms: War and Peace in the Mountains of Nicaragua, 1979–1994* (Athens: Ohio University Center for International Studies, 1998).

69. Department of State, Briefing Memorandum, "Chilean Executions," cited above.

70. Feitlowitz, *Lexicon of Terror,* pp. 19–62.

71. For the continuation of U.S. aid despite Carter's restrictions, see Tanya Broder and Bernard D. Lambek, "Military Aid to Guatemala: The Failure of U.S. Human Rights Legislation," *Yale Journal of International Law* 13, no.1 (1988): 114–45; "U.S. Military Aid for Guatemala Continuing despite Official Curbs," *New York Times,* December 19, 1982, and United States General Accounting Office, National Security and International Affairs Division, *Military Sales: The United States Continuing Munition Supply Relationship with Guatemala* (Washington, D.C.: U.S. General Accounting Office, 1986).

72. NSA, Department of State, "US-Guatemalan Relations-Arms Sales," November 26, 1982. For the pattern of rationalization that repeatedly appears in declassified embassy and State Department documents defending the Guatemalan government and military during the genocide, see my *Denegado en su totalidad: Documentos estadounidenses liberados* (Guatemala City: Asociación para el Avance de las Ciencias So-

ciales en Guatemala, 2001). For the El Mozote massacre, see Mark Danner, *The Massacre at El Mozote: A Parable of the Cold War* (New York: Vintage. 1994). For the United States in Central America, see John Coatsworth, *Central America and the United States: The Clients and the Colossus* (New York: Twayne, 1994); William LeoGrande, *Our Own Backyard: The United States in Central America, 1977–1992* (Chapel Hill: University of North Carolina Press, 1998); Walter LaFeber, *Inevitable Revolutions: The United States in Central America* (New York: Norton, 1993).

73. "Reagan Denounces Threats to Peace in Latin America," *New York Times*, December 5, 1982. See also Schirmer, *Guatemalan Military Project*, pp. 170–73, for the CIA's support for the military modernizers of the 1980s, which, as in the 1960s, again entailed professionalizing the intelligence system.

74. Chase, "Cuban Trials"; Department of State, Briefing Memorandum, "Chilean Executions," cited above.

75. Huggins, *Political Policing*, provides a detailed account of the central role of the United States in the construction of Brazil's counterinsurgent state. For El Salvador, Chile, Argentina, and Uruguay, see the sources cited in chapter 3, note 8.

76. Schirmer, *Guatemalan Military Project*, p. 44.

77. As one intelligence manual put it in 1972 (a year before the EGP entered Guatemala's western highlands to organize indigenous peasants), "the enemy has the same sociological traits as the inhabitants of our highlands"; CEH, *Memoria del silencio*, 3:322.

78. Feitlowitz, *Lexicon of Terror*, pp. 42–43, discusses the public relations campaign; see Hollander, *Love in the Time of Hate*, p. 93, for the anti-Semitic quote.

79. Robert Jay Lifton, "Beyond Atrocity," in *Crimes of War: A Legal, Political-Documentary, and Psychological Inquiry into the Responsibility of Leaders, Citizens, and Soldiers for Criminal Acts in Wars*, ed. Richard Falk, Gabriel Kolko, and Robert Jay Lifton (New York: Vintage Books, 1971), p. 25.

80. Gabriel Kolko, "On the Avoidance of Reality," in Falk, Kolko, and Lifton, *Crimes of War*, p. 13.

81. Ibid., p. 15.

82. Noam Chomsky, *American Power and the New Mandarins* (New York: Pantheon Books, 1967), pp. 6–7. Chomsky here is quoting from the 1917 essay by Randolph Bourne, "The Twilight of the Idols," found in *The World of Randolph Bourne*, ed. Lillian Schlissel (New York: E. P. Dutton, 1965), pp. 198–99.

83. See NSA, Department of State, "The Democratic Left," March 22, 1971.

84. "John P. Longan Memoir," 1:22.

85. Hannah Arendt, *Eichmann in Jerusalem: A Report on the Banality of Evil* (New York: Viking Press, 1963), p. 143.

86. In NSA, Department of State, "Terror and Counter-Terror," March 29, 1968.

87. Quoted in Cullather, *Secret History*, p. 66.

88. Reprinted in *Harper's Magazine*, April 2001.

89. "Central America's Cities Grow Bigger, and Poorer," *New York Times*, March 17,

2002, p. 3; "Malnourished to Get Help in Guatemala," *New York Times,* March 20, 2002, p. 3; United Nations' 2000 human development report for Guatemala, "Guatemala: La fuerza incluyente del desarrollo humano," found at http://www.onu.org.gt/indh2000/; and Douglas Chalmers et al., eds., *The New Politics of Inequality in Latin America: Rethinking Participation and Representation* (New York: Oxford University Press, 1997).

90. *Prensa Libre,* May 2, 2003, "Cahabón en la miseria y olvido."

91. "Argentina and Brazil Align to Fight U.S. Trade Policy," *New York Times,* October 21, 2003.

92. Richard Lapper, "Latin America's Leftwingers Give Washington the Jitters," *Financial Times,* October 23, 2002.

93. For "new social movements" in Latin America, see Tilman Evers, "Identity: The Hidden Side of New Social Movements in Latin America," in *New Social Movements and the State in Latin America,* ed. David Slater (Amsterdam: CEDLA Workshop Papers, 1985), pp. 43–71; Judith Aldler Hellman, "The Riddle of New Social Movements: Who They Are and What They Do," in *Capital, Power and Inequality in Latin America,* ed. Sandor Halebski and Richard L. Harris (Boulder: Westview Press, 1995); Arturo Escobar, "Culture, Practice and Politics: Anthropology and the Study of Social Movements," *Critique of Anthropology* 12, no. 4 (1992): 395–432; and Sonia Alvarez, Evelina Dagnino, and Arturo Escobar, "Introduction: The Cultural and the Political in Latin American Social Movements," in their edited *Cultures of Politics, Politics of Cultures: Re-visioning Latin American Social Movements* (Boulder: Westview Press, 1998). Yet see the critical discussion in the introduction to Mark Edelman, *Peasants against Globalization: Rural Social Movements in Costa Rica* (Stanford: Stanford University Press, 1999).

94. For El Salvador, see Jeffrey L. Gould, "Revolutionary Nationalism and Local Memories in El Salvador," in *Reclaiming the Political: Essays from the North,* ed. Gilbert Joseph (Durham: Duke University Press, 2001); for Bolivia, Forrest Hylton, "Common Ground: Urban Radicals, Indian Caciques, and the Chayanta Rebellion," a work in progress based on a master's thesis, University of Pittsburgh, Department of History; for Peru, see the essays in Stern, *Peru's Shining and Other Paths,* and for Chile, see Rosa Isolde Reuque Paillalef, *When a Flower Is Reborn: The Life and Times of a Mapuche Feminist,* ed. and trans. Florencia Mallon (Durham: Duke University Press, 2002).

95. See, for examples, John D'Emilio, *Sexual Politics, Sexual Communities: The Making of a Homosexual Minority in the United States, 1940–1970* (Chicago: University of Chicago Press, 1983); Daniel Horowitz, *Betty Friedan and the Making of the Feminine Mystique: The American Left, the Cold War, and Modern Feminism* (Amherst: University of Massachusetts Press, 1998); Robin D. G. Kelley, *Hammer and Hoe. Alabama Communists during the Great Depression* (Chapel Hill: University of North Carolina Press, 1990); and Gerda Lerner, *Fireweed: A Political Autobiography* (Philadelphia: Temple University Press, 2002). Paul Berman, *A Tale of Two Utopias: The Political Journey of the Generation of 1968* (New York: Norton, 1997), argues that the au-

thoritarian, moralistic nature of the New Left was a key factor in the politicization of personal relations, which proved to be a precondition for the takeoff of identity politics. While he is right to identify an attention to sexual and women's rights as an indispensable extension of democracy, his account uncannily parallels many of the assumptions of modernization theory: it is overly mechanistic; deemphasizes the importance of politics and activism; downplays the fierce resistance against the New Left's humanistic and democratic elements (that is, the elements he would deem acceptable and worthy); interprets increased radicalization, authoritarianism, and militancy not in relation to this resistance but as an already existing ideological flaw within the movement; and posits that radicalization, authoritarianism, and militancy as an aberration, albeit a somewhat useful one, in the transition to liberal democracy.

96. Jocelyn Olcott, "Las Hijas de la Malinche: Gender and State Formation in Post-Revolutionary Mexico, 1934–1940" (Ph.D. diss., Yale University, 2000).

97. Craig Calhoun, "New Social Movements of the Early Nineteenth Century," in *Repertoires and Cycles of Collective Action*, ed. Mark Traugott (Durham: Duke University Press, 1995), argues that in Europe participation in working-class politics had long been based on diverse identities.

98. While the accords at least raised the issue of human development, they also took other concerns off the agenda. Whereas in El Salvador the FMLN was able to wrest significant reforms, including some land redistribution, in Guatemala the 1996 settlement reached by an enervated guerrilla leadership and a powerful, emboldened military was hollow. Emphasizing "participation," "dialogue," and "consensus-building," it read more like a page taken from a corporate human relations manual than a blueprint for creating a redistributive state; see Susanne Jonas, *Of Centaurs and Doves: Guatemala's Peace Process* (Boulder: Westview Press, 2000), p. 78.

99. Rosalinda Hernández Alarcón, *The Land Issue in the Peace Accords: A Summary of the Government's Response* (Guatemala City: Inforpress Centroamericana, 1998), provides a detailed discussion.

100. Ibid., p. 22, states that as of 1996, there existed 338 property disputes in fifteen of the country's twenty-two departments, with the most land occupations occurring in Alta Verapaz, Quiché, Izabal, and San Marcos.

101. James, *Resistance and Integration*, p. 34.

102. The point is not simply that unfortunate attitudes and practices persisted in otherwise noble movements. As Thomas Klubock in *Contested Communities*, Heidi Tinsman in *Partners in Conflict: The Politics of Gender, Sexuality, and Labor in the Chilean Agrarian Reform, 1950–1973* (Durham: Duke University Press, 2002), and I here, in chapters 2 and 5, have tried to show, these divisions and internal hierarchies and ideologies were essential to subaltern militancy.

103. For Peru, see Marisol de la Cadena, "From Race to Class: Insurgent Intellectuals *de provincia* in Peru, 1910–1970," in Stern, *Peru's Shining and Other Paths*, p. 42; for Bolivia, see Hylton's "Common Ground." See also Gould's work on the historical consequences of discursive violence and exclusion in "Revolutionary Nationalism and Local Memories in El Salvador."

104. Olcott, "Las Hijas de la Malinche," corrects the standard interpretation that held that the Mexican left opposed women's suffrage because it feared that franchised women would support the Catholic Church. While the left leadership of the ruling party opposed granting women the vote, the Mexican Communist Party actively promoted women's political rights, including funding and organizing the 1937 test campaign to elect Maria del Refugio García as Michoacán's congressional deputy.

105. Ferrer, *Insurgent Cuba,* p. 199, makes a similar argument in terms of Cuba's nineteenth-century antiracist nationalism.

106. The use of local militias to check revolutionary threats long predates the Cold War. In Namiquipa, Mexico, in 1916, for instance, U.S. General Pershing encouraged the establishment of civil patrols to undermine the support of Francisco Villa. As in Guatemala seven decades later, the patrols were an impressive success. Segments of the local population used them to establish political stability, advance their own interests, and speak in the name of the community as a whole. See Ana Maria Alonso, "U.S. Military Intervention, Revolutionary Mobilization, and Popular Ideology in the Chihuahuan Sierra, 1916–1917," in *Rural Revolt in Mexico: U.S. Intervention and the Domain of Subaltern Politics,* ed. Daniel Nugent (Durham: Duke University Press, 1998), p. 208.

107. Loveman and Thomas, introduction to their *Politics of Anti-Politics,* p. 8, notes that while since at least the 1920s Latin American military officers saw the link between national security and economic development, it was during the Cold War, especially during the Alliance for Progress years, that the two became "synonymous."

108. Idelber Avelar, *The Untimely Present: Postdictatorial Latin American Fiction and the Task of Mourning* (Durham: Duke University Press, 1999), pp. 41–44.

109. Juan Rial, "Makers and Guardians of Fear: Controlled Terror in Uruguay," in Corradi, Fagen, and Garretón, *Fear at the Edge,* pp. 92–93.

110. Pope Paul VI, *Encyclical Letter of His Holiness Pope Paul VI on the Development of Peoples* (New York: Paulist Press, 1967).

111. Elaine Scarry's *The Body in Pain: The Making and Unmaking of the World* (New York: Oxford University Press, 1987), chap. 1.

112. For Argentina, see Inés Izaguirre, *Los desaparecidos: Recuperación de una identidad expropiada* (Buenos Aires: Centro de América Latina, Instituto de Investigaciones de la Facultad de Ciencias Sociales de la Universidad de Buenos Aires, 1994).

113. James Dunkerley, "The Crisis of Bolivian Radicalism" in Carr and Ellner, *Latin American Left.*

114. http://www.whitehouse.gov/nsc/nssintro.html.

115. Politzer, *Fear in Chile,* pp. 9–10, 15.

Bibliography

ARCHIVES

Archivo del Congreso de Guatemala (ACG), Guatemala City.
Archivo General de Centro América (AGCA), Guatemala City.
Archivo Eclesiástico de Arzobispado de Guatemala (AEA), Guatemala City.
Archivo Histórico del Centro de Investigaciones Regional de Mesoamerica (AH de CIRMA), Antigua, Guatemala.
Archives of the Ministerio de Gobernación (AMG), Eighteenth Street and Seventh Avenue, zone 1, Guatemala City.
Archives of the Instituto Nacional de Transformación Agraria (INTA), eighteen kilometers out of Guatemala City, on the road to Escuintla.
Guatemalan Document Collection, Library of Congress (LC-GDC), Washington, D.C.
National Security Archive (NSA), George Washington University, Washington, D.C.
Partido Guatemalteco de Trabajo Collection of the Centro de Estudios Urbanos y Regionales (PGT-USAC), Universidad de San Carlos, Guatemala City.
Partido Guatemalteco de Trabajo Collection, Tulane University Library Special Collections Division (PGT-Tulane), New Orleans, La.
Registro de Propiedad (RP), Guatemala City.
San Pedro Carchá Municipal Archives (SPCMA), San Pedro Carchá, Guatemala.

OTHER WORKS

Adams, Richard. *Crucifixion by Power: Essays on Guatemalan National Social Structure, 1944–1966.* Austin: University of Texas Press, 1970.
———. "Ethnic Images and Strategies in 1944." In *Guatemalan Indians and the State, 1540–1988,* ed. Carol. A. Smith. Austin: University of Texas Press, 1990.
———. *Joaquín Noval como indigenista. antropólogo y revolucionario.* Guatemala City: Editorial Universitaria, 2000.
——— [Newbold Stokes, pseud.]. "Receptivity to Communist Fomented Agitation in Rural Guatemala." *Economic Development and Cultural Change* 5, no. 1 (October 1956): 338–61.

Adelman, Jeremy. "Andean Impasses." *New Left Review* 18 (November–December 2002): 41–72.

Adorno, Theodor, et al. *The Authoritarian Personality.* New York: Harpers, 1950.

Aguilera Peralta, Gabriel. *La matanza de Panzós y el desarrollo capitalista de Guatemala.* Mexico City: Universidad Iberoamericana, 1980.

Alba, Victor. "The Stages of Militarism in Latin America." In *The Role of the Military in Underdeveloped Countries,* ed. John Johnson. Princeton: Princeton University Press, 1962.

Albizúres, Miguel Angel. *Tiempo de sudor y lucha.* Guatemala City [?]: Edición Local, 1987.

Alegría, Claribel, with D. J. Flakoll. *No me agarran viva: la mujer salvadoreña en la lucha.* Mexico City: Ediciones Era, 1983.

Alexander, Robert. *Communism in Latin America.* New Brunswick: Rutgers University Press, 1957.

Almond, Sidney, and Gabriel Verba. *The Civic Culture: Political Attitudes and Democracy in Five Nations.* Princeton: Princeton University Press, 1963.

Alonso, Ana Maria. "U.S. Military Intervention, Revolutionary Mobilization, and Popular Ideology in the Chihuahuan Sierra, 1916–1917." In *Rural Revolt in Mexico: U.S. Intervention and the Domain of Subaltern Politics,* ed. Daniel Nugent. Durham: Duke University Press, 1998.

Alvarado Arellano, Huberto. *Apuntes para la historia del Partido Guatemalteco de Trabajo.* Guatemala City: Ediciones PGT, 1975.

——— "Walt Whitman: Poeta nacional, democrático, y realista." *Cuadernos del Guayas* (Ecuador) 6 (1955): 1, 5, 20.

Alvarez, Sonia, Evelina Dagnino, and Arturo Escobar. "Introduction: The Cultural and the Political in Latin American Social Movements." In *Cultures of Politics, Politics of Cultures: Re-visioning Latin American Social Movements,* ed. Alvarez, Dagnino, and Escobar. Boulder: Westview Press, 1998.

Americas Watch. *With Friends like These: The Americas Watch Report on Human Rights and U.S. Policy in Latin America.* New York: Pantheon Books, 1985.

Anderson, Nicolás. *Guatemala: Escuela revolucionaria de nuevos hombres. Mexico* City: Editorial Nuestro Tiempo, 1982.

Anderson, Perry. *Conversation on Western Marxism.* London: Verso, 1979.

———. "Modernity and Revolution." *New Left Review,* no. 144 (March–April 1984): 96–113.

Arendt, Hannah. *Eichmann in Jerusalem: A Report on the Banality of Evil.* New York: Viking Press, 1963.

———. *The Human Condition.* 2nd ed. Chicago: University of Chicago Press, 1998 [1958].

———. *On Revolution.* New York: Penguin Books, 1963.

———. *The Origins of Totalitarianism.* London: Andre Deutsch, 1986.

Arévalo, Juan José. *Escritos políticos.* Guatemala City: Tipografía Nacional, 1945.

Asociación de Investigación y Estudios Sociales, ed. *Más de 100 años del movimiento obrero urbano en Guatemala: Artesanos y obreros en el periodo liberal, 1877–1944.* Vol. 1. Guatemala City: Asociación de Investigación y Estudios Sociales, 1991.

Asociación para el Avance de las Ciencias Sociales en Guatemala (AVANCSO). *La política de desarrollo del estado guatemalteco, 1986–1988.* Guatemala City: AVANCSO, 1988.

———. *Política exterior y estabilidad estatal.* Guatemala City: AVANCSO, 1989.

Avelar, Idelber. *The Untimely Present: Postdictatorial Latin American Fiction and the Task of Mourning.* Durham: Duke University Press, 1999.

Ball, Patrick, Paul Kobrak, and Herbert Spirer. *State Violence in Guatemala, 1960–1996: A Quantitative Reflection.* Washington, D.C.: American Association for the Advancement of Science, 1999.

Bauer Paiz, Alfonso. *Como opera el capital yanqui en Centroamérica (El caso de Guatemala).* Mexico City: Editorial Iberoamericana, 1956.

———, and Ivan Carpio. *Memorias de Alfonso Bauer Paiz: Historia no oficial de Guatemala.* Guatemala City: Rusticatio Ediciones, 1996.

Bell, Daniel. *The End of Ideology: On the Exhaustion of Political Ideas in the 1950s.* New York: Free Press, 1962.

Bendaña Perdomo, Ricardo. *La Iglesia en Guatemala: Síntesis histórica del catolicismo.* Guatemala City: Librerías Artemis-Edinter, 1996.

Benhabib, Seyla. *Situating the Self: Gender, Community and Postmodernism in Contemporary Ethics.* New York: Routledge, 1992.

Benjamin, Jules R. *The United States and the Origins of the Cuban Revolution: An Empire of Liberty in an Age of National Liberation.* Princeton: Princeton University Press, 1990.

Berguist, Charles. *Labor in Latin America: Comparative Essays on Chile, Argentina, Venezuela and Colombia.* Stanford: Stanford University Press, 1986.

Berman, Marshall. *All That Is Solid Melts into Air: The Experience of Modernity.* New York: Penguin, 1992.

Berman, Paul. *A Tale of Two Utopias: The Political Journey of the Generation of 1968.* New York: Norton, 1997.

———. *Terror and Liberalism.* New York: W.W. Norton, 2003.

Bethell, Leslie, and Ian Roxborough. "Conclusion: The Postwar Conjuncture in Latin America and Its Consequences." In Bethell and Roxborough, *Latin America between the Second World War and the Cold War.*

———. "The Impact of the Cold War on Latin America." In *Origins of the Cold War: An International History,* ed. Melvyn Leffler and David Painter. New York: Routledge, 1994.

———, eds. *Latin America between the Second World War and the Cold War, 1944–1948.* Cambridge: Cambridge University Press, 1992.

Bishop, Edwin. "The Guatemalan Labor Movement, 1944–1959." Ph.D. diss., University of Wisconsin, 1959.

Black, George. *Garrison Guatemala.* New York: Monthly Review Press, 1984.
Bourne, Randolph. "The Twilight of the Idols." In *The World of Randolph Bourne,* ed. Lillian Schlissel. New York: E. P. Dutton, 1965.
Broder, Tanya, and Bernard D. Lambek. "Military Aid to Guatemala: The Failure of U.S. Human Rights Legislation." *Yale Journal of International Law* 13, no.1 (1988): 111–45.
Brunner, José Joaquín. *El espejo trizado.* Santiago: FLACSO, 1988.
Buck-Morss, Susan. *Dreamworld and Catastrophe: The Passing of Mass Utopia in East and West.* Cambridge: MIT Press, 2000.
———. "Hegel and the Haiti." *Critical Inquiry* 26, no. 4 (Summer 2000): 821–65.
Bush, Archer. "Organized Labor in Guatemala: A Case Study of an Adolescent Labor Movement in an Underdeveloped Country." Colgate University Area Studies Latin American Seminar Reports, no. 2. Hamilton, N.Y., 1950.
Cabarrús, Carlos. *La cosmovisión K'ekchi' en proceso de cambio.* San Salvador: Universidad Centroamericana, 1979.
Cáceres, Carlos. *Aproximación a Guatemala.* Mexico City: Universidad Autónoma de Sinaloa, 1980.
Calhoun, Craig. "New Social Movements of the Early Nineteenth Century." In *Repertoires and Cycles of Collective Action,* ed. Mark Traugott. Durham: Duke University Press, 1995.
Cardoso, Fernando Henrique. *Autoritarismo e democratização.* Rio de Janeiro: Paz e Terra, 1975.
Cardoza y Aragón, Luis. *La revolución Guatemalteca.* Guatemala City: Editorial Pensativo, 1994 [1955].
Carlson, Ruth, and Francis Eachus. "El mundo espiritual de los kekchies." *Guatemala Indígena* 8, nos. 1–2 (1978): 40–73.
Carmack, Robert. *Rebels of Highland Guatemala: The Quiché-Mayas of Momostenango.* Norman: University of Oklahoma Press, 1995.
Carozza, Paolo. "From Conquest to Constitutions: Retrieving a Latin American Tradition of the Idea of Human Rights." *Human Rights Quarterly* 25 (2003): 281–313.
Carr, Barry, and Steve Ellner, eds. *The Latin American Left: From the Fall of Allende to Perestroika.* Boulder: Westview Press, 1993.
Casper, Gretchen, and Michelle Taylor. *Negotiating Democracy: Transitions from Authoritarian Rule.* Pittsburgh: University of Pittsburgh Press, 1996.
Castañeda, Jorge. *Utopia Unarmed: The Latin American Left after the Cold War.* New York: Vintage Books, 1994.
Castellanos Cambranes, Julio. *Café y campesinos en Guatemala, 1853–1897.* Guatemala City: University of San Carlos, 1985.
Castro, Fidel. *La historia me absolverá.* Havana: Editorial de Ciencias Sociales, 1975.
Centeno, Miguel A. "The Peaceful Continent: War in Latin America." In *Latin America: An Interdisciplinary Approach,* ed. Gladys Varona-Lacey and Julio López-Arias. New York: Peter Lang, 1999.

Centro de Estudios Integrados de Desarrollo Comunal, ed. *Guatemala: Seminario sobre la realidad étnica.* Mexico City: Editorial Praxis, 1990.

Centro de Investigaciones de Historia Social. *Panzós: Testimonio.* Guatemala City: n.p., 1979.

Chalmers, Douglas, et al., eds. *The New Politics of Inequality in Latin America: Rethinking Participation and Representation.* New York: Oxford University Press, 1997.

Chase, Michelle. "The Cuban Trials." Paper given at the conference Rethinking Latin America's Century of Revolutionary Violence, Yale University, May 15–17, 2003.

Chea, José Luis. *Guatemala: La cruz fragmentada.* San José, Costa Rica: Departamento Ecuménico de Investigaciones, 1988.

Chomsky, Noam. *American Power and the New Mandarins.* New York: Pantheon Books, 1967.

Cifuentes, Juan Fernando. "Operación Ixil: Plan de Asuntos Civiles." *Revista Militar* 27 (September–December 1982): 25–72.

Coatsworth, John. *Central America and the United States: The Clients and the Colossus.* New York: Twayne, 1994.

———. "Measuring Influence: The United States and the Mexican Peasantry." In *Rural Revolt in Mexico: U.S. Intervention and the Domain of Subaltern Politics,* ed. Daniel Nugent. Durham: Duke University Press, 1998.

Collier, Ruth Berins, and David Collier. *Shaping the Political Arena: Critical Junctures, the Labor Movement, and Regime Dynamics in Latin America.* Princeton: Princeton University Press, 1991.

Colom, Yolanda. *Mujeres en la alborada.* Guatemala City: Artemis, 1998.

Comisión Nacional de Solidaridad con Panzós. "Boletín de Prensa, no. 4." Press release, 1978.

Comisión para el Esclarecimiento Histórico (CEH). *Guatemala: Memoria del silencio.* Guatemala City: United Nations Operating Projects Services, 1999.

Consejo Nacional de Planificación Económica. Plan de desarrollo, 1975–1979. Guatemala City: Consejo Nacional de Planificación Económica, 1974.

Cristo, Renato. "Estado nacional y pensamiento conservador en la obra madura de Mario Góngora." In *El pensamiento conservador en Chile,* ed. Renato Cristo and Carlos Ruiz. Santiago: Editorial Universitaria, 1992.

Crossman, Richard, ed. *The God That Failed.* New York: Harper, 1949.

Cullather, Nick. *Secret History: The CIA's Classified Account of Its Operations in Guatemala, 1952–1954.* Stanford: Stanford University Press, 1999.

Dandler, Jorge. *El sindicalismo campesino en Bolivia: Los cambios estructurales en Ucureña.* Mexico City: Instituto Indigenista Interamericano, 1969.

Danien, Elin. "Send Me Mr. Burkitt, Some Whisky and Wine: Early Archaeology in Central America." *Expedition* 27, no. 3 (1985): n.p.

Danner, Mark. *The Massacre at El Mozote: A Parable of the Cold War.* New York: Vintage, 1994.

"Datos en relación a los hechos de Panzós." Unpublished manuscript. 1978.
"Datos Monográficos del Municipio de Santa María Cahabón." Unpublished manuscript. 1990.
Debray, Régis. *Revolución en la revolución?* Havana: Casa de las Américas, 1967.
———, and Ricardo Ramírez. "Guatemala." In *Las pruebas de fuego.* Régis Debray Mexico City: Siglo Veintiuno, 1975.
De la Cadena, Marisol. "From Race to Class: Insurgent Intellectuals *de provincia* in Peru, 1910–1970." In *Peru's Shining and Other Paths: War and Society in Peru, 1980–1995,* ed. Steve Stern. Durham: Duke University Press, 1998.
De la Cruz Torres, Mario. "Monografía del Municipio de San Antonio Senahú, Alta Verapaz." *Guatemala Indígena* 17, nos. 3/4 (1982): 1–176.
De León, Luis. Carchá: Una misión en Guatemala entre los Kekchíes de Alta Verapaz. Guatemala City: Instituto Técnico Ricaldone, 1985.
Del Pero, Mario. "Kissinger e la politica estera americana nel Mediterraneo: il caso portoghese" [Kissinger and American foreign policy in the Mediterranean: The Portuguese case], *Studi Storici,* no. 42 (October–December 2001): 973–88.
Del Valle Matheu, Jorge. *Guía sociogeográfica de Guatemala.* Guatemala City: Tipografía Nacional, 1956.
D'Emilio, John. "Capitalism and Gay Identity." *The Gender/Sexuality Reader: Culture, History, Political Economy,* ed. Roger N. Lancaster and Micaela di Leonardo. New York: Routledge, 1997.
———. *Sexual Politics, Sexual Communities: The Making of a Homosexual Minority in the United States, 1940–1970.* Chicago: University of Chicago Press, 1983.
Denning, Michael. *The Cultural Front: The Laboring of American Culture in the Twentieth Century.* New York: Verso, 1998.
De Paz González, Ceferino. "El valiente muere cuando el cobarde lo decide." Unpublished manuscript.
Derrida, Jacques. "Différance." *The Margins of Philosophy,* trans. Alan Bass. Chicago: University of Chicago Press, 1992.
Deutsch, Sandra McGee. *Counterrevolution in Argentina, 1900–1932: The Argentine Patriotic League.* Lincoln: University of Nebraska Press, 1986.
———. *Las Derechas: The Extreme Right in Argentina, Brazil, Chile, 1890–1939.* Stanford: Stanford University Press, 1999.
———, and Ronald H. Dolkart, eds. *The Argentine Right: Its History and Intellectual Origins, 1910 to the Present.* Wilmington: Scholarly Resources, 1993.
Díaz Molina, Carlos. "Que fluya la verdad." *Crónica,* July 10, 1998.
Díaz Rozzotto, Jaime. *El carácter de la revolución Guatemalteca: Ocaso de la revolución democrática-burguesa corriente.* Mexico City: Ediciones Revista Horizonte, 1958.
Dinges, John. *The Condor Years: How Pinochet and His Allies Brought Terrorism to Three Continents.* New York: New Press, 2004.
Dirección General de Estadística. *II Censo Agropecuario 1964.* Vol. 4. Guatemala City: Dirección General de Estadística, 1969.

Dore, Elizabeth. "Land Privatization and the Differentiation of the Peasantry: Nicaragua's Coffee Revolution, 1850–1920." *Journal of Historical Sociology* 8, no. 3 (September 1995): 303–26.

———. "One Step Forward, Two Steps Back: Gender and the State in the Long Nineteenth Century." In *Hidden Histories of Gender and the State in Latin America,* ed. Elizabeth Dore and Maxine Molyneux. Durham: Duke University Press, 2000.

Drake, Paul. *Socialism and Populism in Chile, 1932–1952.* Urbana: University of Illinois Press, 1978.

Draper, Theodore. "The Minutemen of Guatemala." *Reporter* 3, no. 9 (October 24, 1950).

Dunkerley, James. "The Crisis of Bolivian Radicalism." In *The Latin American Left: From the Fall of Allende to Perestroika,* ed. Barry Carr and Steve Ellner. Boulder: Westview Press, 1993.

Durston, John. "Power Structure in a Rural Region of Guatemala: The Department of Jutiapa." Masters thesis, University of Texas at Austin, 1966.

Earle, Rebecca. "Rape and the Anxious Republic: Revolutionary Colombia, 1810–1830." In *Hidden Histories of Gender and the State in Latin America,* ed. Elizabeth Dore and Maxine Molyneux. Durham: Duke University Press, 2000.

Edelman, Mark. *Peasants against Globalization: Rural Social Movements in Costa Rica.* Stanford: Stanford University Press, 1999.

Eley, Geoff. *Forging Democracy: The History of the Left in Europe, 1850–2000.* Oxford: Oxford University Press, 2002.

———. "International Communism in the Heyday of Stalin." *New Left Review,* no. 157 (May–June 1986): 90–100.

Elshtain, Jean Bethke. *Just War against Terror: The Burden of American Power in a Violent World.* New York: Basic Books, 2003.

Engels, Friedrich. *Dialectics of Nature.* Moscow: Foreign Languages Publishing House, 1954.

Escobar, Arturo. "Culture, Practice and Politics: Anthropology and the Study of Social Movements." *Critique of Anthropology* 12, no. 4 (1992): 395–432.

Evers, Tilman. "Identity: The Hidden Side of New Social Movements in Latin America." In *New Social Movements and the State in Latin America,* ed. David Slater. Amsterdam: CEDLA Workshop Papers, 1985.

Fagen, Patricia Weiss. "Repression and State Security." In *Fear at the Edge: State Terror and Resistance in Latin America,* ed. Juan E. Corradi, Patrica Weiss Fagen, and Manuel Antonio Garretón. Berkeley: University of California Press, 1992.

Falk, Richard, Gabriel Kolko, and Robert Jay Lifton, eds. *Crimes of War: A Legal, Political-Documentary, and Psychological Inquiry into the Responsibility of Leaders, Citizens, and Soldiers for Criminal Acts in Wars.* New York: Vintage Books, 1971.

Federación Autónoma Sindical de Guatemala (FASGUA). "Análisis y orígenes de los hechos acaecidos en Panzós." Press release. 1978.

———. "Análisis y origines de los hechos acaecidos en Panzós." Unpublished manuscript. 1978.

Federación Obrera de Guatemala para la Protección Legal del Trabajo. *Memorias del Congreso del Trabajo Centroamericano celebrado en la ciudad de Guatemala en septiembre de 1921.* Guatemala City: Imprenta Nacional, 1922.

Feitlowitz, Marguerite. *A Lexicon of Terror: Argentina and the Legacies of Torture.* New York: Oxford University Press, 1998.

Fernández, Orlando [Ricardo Ramírez]. *Luis Augusto Turcios Lima: Biografía.* N.p., n.d.

Fernández Fernández, José Manuel. *El Comité de Unidad Campesina: Orígen y desarrollo.* Guatemala City: Centro de Estudios Rurales Centroamericanos, 1988.

Ferrer, Ada. *Insurgent Cuba: Race. Nation. and Revolution, 1868–1898.* Chapel Hill: University of North Carolina Press, 1999.

Figueroa Ibarra, Carlos. "El 'bolchevique mexicano' de la Centroamérica de los veinte." *Memoria* 4, no. 31 (September–October 1990): 213–25.

———. "Contenido de clase y participación obrera en el movimiento antidictatorial de 1920." *Política y Sociedad* 4, no. 5 (1974): 5–51.

———. *Paz Tejada: Militar y revolucionario.* Guatemala City: Universidad de San Carlos, 2001.

———. "Violencia y revolución en Guatemala: 1954–1972." Ph.D. diss., Universidad Nacional Autónoma de Mexico, 2000.

Flores, Marco Antonio, ed. *Fortuny: Un comunista guatemalteco.* Guatemala City: Universidad de San Carlos, 1994.

Foner, Eric. *The Story of American Freedom.* New York: W.W. Norton, 1998.

Forster, Cindy. *The Time of Freedom: Campesino Workers in Guatemala's October Revolution.* Pittsburgh: University of Pittsburgh Press, 2001.

Foucault, Michel. "The Subject and Power." In *Michel Foucault: Beyond Structuralism and Hermeneutics,* by Hubert L. Dreyfus and Paul Rabinow. Chicago: University of Chicago Press, 1983.

Frankel, Anita. "Political Development in Guatemala: The Impact of Foreign, Military, and Religious Elites." Ph.D. diss., University of Connecticut, 1969.

French, John. *The Brazilian Workers' ABC: Class Conflict and Alliances in Modern São Paulo.* Chapel Hill: University of North Carolina Press, 1992.

Friedman, Milton, with Rose Friedman. *Capitalism and Freedom.* Chicago: University of Chicago Press, 1982.

Fukuyama, Francis. *The End of History and the Last Man.* New York: Free Press, 1992.

Fundación de Antropología Forense de Guatemala. "Informe del peritaje antropológico forense del cementerio clandestino ubicado en Panzós AV con referencia al proceso penal #2636–97." Unpublished manuscript. 1998.

———. *Informe especial de la Fundación de Antropología Forense de Guatemala, 1996–1999.* Guatemala City: Fundación de Antropología Forense de Guatemala, 2001.

Furet, François. *The Passing of an Illusion: The Idea of Communism in the Twentieth Century.* Trans. Deborah Furet. Chicago: University of Chicago Press, 1999.

Gaddis, John Lewis. *We Now Know: Rethinking Cold War History.* New York: Oxford University Press, 1998.

Galeano, Eduardo. *Guatemala: País ocupado.* Mexico City: Nuestro Tiempo, 1967.
Galich, Manuel. *Por qué lucha Guatemala.* Guatemala City: Editorial Cultura del Ministerio de Cultura y Deportes de Guatemala, 1994 [1955].
García, Graciela. *Páginas de lucha revolucionaria en Centroamérica.* Mexico City: Ediciones Linterna, 1971.
Gerassi, John. *The Great Fear: The Reconquest of Latin America.* New York: Macmillan, 1963.
Gleijeses, Piero. "Afterword: The Culture of Fear." In Cullather, *Secret History.*
———. *Conflicting Missions: Havana, Washington, and Africa, 1959–1976.* Chapel Hill: University of North Carolina Press, 2002.
———. *Shattered Hope: The Guatemalan Revolution and the United States, 1944–1954.* Princeton: Princeton University Press, 1991.
Glendon, Mary Ann. *A World Made New: Eleanor Roosevelt and the Universal Declaration of Human Rights.* New York: Random House, 2001.
Gornick, Vivian. *The Romance of American Communism.* New York: Basic Books, 1977.
Goubaud Carrera, Antonio, Juan de Díos Rosales and Sol Tax. "Reconnaissance of Northern Guatemala, 1944." Microfilm Collection of Manuscripts on Middle American Cultural Anthropology, no. 17. University of Chicago, 1947.
Gould, Jeffrey L. "Revolutionary Nationalism and Local Memories in El Salvador." In *Reclaiming the Political: Essays from the North,* ed. Gilbert Joseph. Durham: Duke University Press, 2001.
———. *To Die in This Way: Nicaraguan Indians and the Myth of Mestizaje, 1880–1965.* Durham: Duke University Press, 1998.
———. *To Lead as Equals: Rural Protest and Political Consciousness in Chinandega, Nicaragua, 1912–1979.* Chapel Hill: University of North Carolina Press, 1990.
Graham, Richard. *Patronage and Politics in Nineteenth Century Brazil.* Stanford: Stanford University Press, 1990.
Grandin, Greg. *The Blood of Guatemala: A History of Race and Nation.* Durham: Duke University Press, 2000.
———. "Chronicles of a Guatemalan Genocide Foretold: Violence, Trauma, and the Limits to Historical Inquiry." *Nepantla: Views from South* 1, no. 2 (2000): 391–412.
———. *Denegado en su totalidad: Documentos estadounidenses liberados.* Guatemala City: Asociación para el Avance de las Ciencias Sociales en Guatemala, 2001.
———. "The Strange Case of 'La Mancha Negra': Maya-State Relations in Nineteenth-Century Guatemala." *Hispanic American Historical Review* 77, no. 2 (1997): 211–43.
———. "To End with All These Evils: Ethnic Transformation and Community Mobilization in Guatemala's Western Highlands, 1954–1980." *Latin American Perspectives* 24, no. 2 (1997): 7–33.
Green, David. *The Containment of Latin America: A History of the Myths and Realities of the Good Neighbor Policy.* Chicago: Quadrangle, 1971.
Green, Linda. *Fear as a Way of Life: Mayan Widows in Rural Guatemala.* New York: Columbia University Press, 1999.

Green, W. John. "Sibling Rivalry on the Left and Labor Struggles in Colombia during the 1940s." *Latin American Research Review* 35, no. 1 (2000): 85–117.

Guardino, Peter. *Peasants, Politics, and the Formation of Mexico's National State: Guerrero, 1800–1857.* Stanford: Stanford University Press, 1996.

Gudmunson, Lowell, and Hector Lindo-Fuentos. *Central America, 1821–1871: Liberalism before Liberals.* Tuscaloosa: University of Alabama Press, 1995.

Guha, Ranahit. "On Some Aspects of the Historiography of Colonial India." In *Selected Subaltern Studies,* ed. Guha and G. C. Spivak. New York: Oxford University Press, 1998.

Guzmán Böckler, Carlos, and Jean-Loup Herbert. *Guatemala: Una interpretación historico-social.* Mexico City: Siglo Veintiuno, 1970.

Handy, Jim. *Gift of the Devil: A History of Guatemala.* Boston: South End Press, 1984.

———. *Revolution in the Countryside: Rural Conflict and Agrarian Reform in Guatemala, 1944–1954.* Chapel Hill: University of North Carolina Press, 1994.

Hayek, Friedrich von. *The Road to Serfdom.* London: Routledge, 1944.

Hellman, Judith Aldler. "The Riddle of New Social Movements: Who They Are and What They Do." In *Capital. Power and Inequality in Latin America,* ed. Sandor Halebski and Richard L. Harris. Boulder: Westview Press, 1995.

Hernández Alarcón, Rosalinda. *The Land Issue in the Peace Accords: A Summary of the Government's Response.* Guatemala City: Inforpress Centroamericana, 1998.

Hinchman, Lewis, and Sandra Hinchman. *Memory, Identity, Community: The Idea of Narrative in the Human Sciences.* New York: State University of New York Press, 1997.

Hirschman, Albert O. *The Passions and the Interests: Political Arguments for Capitalism before Its Triumph.* Princeton: Princeton University Press, 1977.

———. "The Turn to Authoritarianism in Latin America and the Search for Its Economic Determinants." In *The New Authoritarianism in Latin America,* ed. David Collier and Fernando Henrique Cardoso. Princeton: Princeton University Press, 1979.

Ho Chi Minh. *Selected Works.* Vol. 3. Hanoi: Foreign Languages Publishing House, 1960–62.

Hollander, Nancy Caro. *Love in the Time of Hate: Liberation Psychology in Latin America.* New Brunswick: Rutgers University Press, 1997.

Holleran, Mary. *Church and State in Guatemala.* New York: Colombia University Press, 1949.

Horowitz, Daniel. *Betty Friedan and the Making of the Feminine Mystique: The American Left, the Cold War, and Modern Feminism.* Amherst: University of Massachusetts Press, 1998.

Horton, Lynn. *Peasants in Arms: War and Peace in the Mountains of Nicaragua, 1979–1994.* Athens: Ohio University Center for International Studies, 1998.

Hoyos de Asig, María del Pilar. *Fernando Hoyos, ¿dónde estás?* Guatemala City: Centroamérica: Fondo de Cultura Editorial, 1997.

Huggins, Martha K. *Political Policing: The United States and Latin America.* Durham: Duke University Press, 1998.

Hunt, E. Howard. *Undercover: Memoirs of an American Secret Agent.* New York: Berkeley, 1974.

Hunt, Lynn. "The Paradoxical Origins of Human Rights." In *Human Rights and Revolutions,* ed. Jeffrey N. Wasserstrom, Lynn Hunt, and Marilyn B. Young. Lanham, Md.: Rowman and Littlefield, 2000.

Huntington, Samuel, Michael Crozier, and Joji Watanuki. *The Crisis of Democracy: Report on the Governability of Democracies to the Trilateral Commission.* New York: New York University Press, 1975.

Hylton, Forrest. "Common Ground: Urban Radicals, Indian Caciques, and the Chayanta Rebellion." Unpublished manuscript. 2002.

Iglesia Católica de Guatemala. *Carta pastoral colectiva del episcopado de Guatemala sobre la amenaza comunista en nuestra patria.* Guatemala City: Sánchez y de Guise, 1945.

Ignatieff, Michael. "The Burden." *New York Times Magazine,* January 5, 2003.

Immerman, Richard. *The CIA in Guatemala: The Foreign Policy of Intervention.* Austin: University of Texas Press, 1982.

Ingersoll, Hazel. "The War of the Mountain: A Study in Reactionary Peasant Insurgency in Guatemala, 1837–1873." Ph.D. diss., George Washington University, 1972.

Instituto Nacional de Transformación Agraria. *Asentamientos Agrarios localizados en el departamento de Alta Verapaz.* Guatemala City: Instituto Nacional de Transformación Agraria, 1984.

Irigaray, Luce. "Equal to Whom?" *differences* 1 (Summer 1989): 58–76.

Isaac, Jeffrey. "Hannah Arendt on Human Rights and the Limits of Exposure, or Why Noam Chomsky Is Wrong about the Meaning of Kosovo." *Social Research* 69, no. 2 (Summer 2002): 263–95.

Izaguirre, Inés. *Los desaparecidos: Recuperación de una identidad expropiada.* Buenos Aires: Centro de América Latina, Instituto de Investigaciones de la Facultad de Ciencias Sociales de la Universidad de Buenos Aires, 1994.

James, Daniel. *Doña María's Story: Life History, Memory, and Political Identity.* Durham: Duke University Press, 2000.

———. *Resistance and Integration: Peronism and the Argentine Working Class, 1946–1976.* Cambridge: Cambridge University Press, 1988.

James, Daniel. *Red Design for the Americas: Guatemalan Prelude.* New York: John Day, 1954.

Johnson, Chalmers. *Blowback: The Costs and Consequences of American Empire.* New York: Henry Holt, 2000.

Jonas, Susanne. *Of Centaurs and Doves: Guatemala's Peace Process.* Boulder: Westview Press, 2000.

———, and David Tobis. *Guatemala.* New York: North American Congress on Latin America, 1981.

Joseph, Gilbert. *Revolution from Without: Yucatan, Mexico, and the United States, 1880–1924.* Durham: Duke University Press, 1988.

Kelley, Robin D. G. *Hammer and Hoe: Alabama Communists during the Great Depression.* Chapel Hill: University of North Carolina Press, 1990.

King, Arden. *Cobán and the Verapaz: History and Cultural Process in Northern Guatemala.* New Orleans: Tulane University, Middle American Research Institute, 1974.

Kit, Wade. "*Costumbre,* Conflict, and Consensus: Kekchí-Finquero Discourse in the Alta Verapaz, Guatemala, 1880–1930." Ph.D. diss., Tulane University, 1998.

———. "Precursor of Change: Failed Reform and the Guatemalan Coffee Elite, 1918–1926." Master's thesis, University of Saskatchewan, 1987.

Kitchen, James. "Municipal Government in Guatemala." Ph.D. diss., University of California, Los Angeles, 1955.

Klehr, Harvey, and John E. Haynes. *Venona: Decoding Soviet Espionage in America.* New Haven: Yale University Press, 1999.

Klehr, Harvey, John E. Haynes, and Fridrikh Igorevich Firsov, eds. *The Secret World of American Communism.* New Haven: Yale University Press, 1995.

Klehr, Harvey, John E. Haynes, and Kyrill Mikhailovich Anderson, eds. *The Soviet World of American Communism.* New Haven: Yale University Press, 1998.

Klubock, Thomas Miller. *Contested Communities: Class, Gender, and Politics in Chile's El Teniente Copper Mine, 1904–1951.* Durham: Duke University Press, 1998.

Kolko, Gabriel. "On the Avoidance of Reality." In Falk, Kolko, and Lifton, *Crimes of War.*

LaCharite, Norman. "Political Violence in Guatemala, 1963–1967: Its Social, Economic, Political, and Historical Origins, and Its Patterns and Sequences." Ph.D. diss., American University, 1973.

Laclau, Ernesto. "Toward a Theory of Populism." In *Politics and Ideology in Marxist Theory: Capitalism, Fascism, and Populism,* ed. Laclau. London: NLB Books, 1977.

LaFeber, Walter. *Inevitable Revolutions: The United States in Central America.* New York: Norton, 1993.

Lancaster, Roger. *Life Is Hard: Machismo, Danger, and the Intimacy of Power in Nicaragua.* Berkeley: University of California Press, 1992.

Landes, Joan, ed. *Feminism: The Public and the Private.* New York: Oxford University Press, 1997.

Larson, Brooke. "Capturing Indian Bodies, Hearths, and Minds: '*El hogar campesino*' and Rural School Reform in Bolivia, 1920s–1940s." Paper presented at New York City Latin American History Workshop, New York University, April 26, 2002.

LeGrand, Catherine. "Living in Macondo: Economy and Culture in a United Fruit Company Banana Enclave in Colombia." In *Close Encounters of Empire: Writing the Cultural History of U.S.-Latin American Relations,* ed. Gilbert M. Joseph, Catherine LeGrand, and Ricardo D. Salvatore. Durham: Duke University Press, 1998.

Lenin, V. I. *Collected Works.* 4th English ed. Vol. 38. Moscow: Progress Publishers, 1972.

LeoGrande, William. *Our Own Backyard: The United States in Central America, 1977–1992.* Chapel Hill: University of North Carolina Press, 1998.

Lerner, Gerda. *Fireweed: A Political Autobiography.* Philadelphia: Temple University Press, 2002.

Levenson-Estrada, Deborah. *Trade Unionists against Terror: Guatemala City, 1954–1985.* Chapel Hill: University of North Carolina Press, 1994.

Lifton, Robert Jay. "Beyond Atrocity." In Falk, Kolko, and Lifton, *Crimes of War.*

Lilla, Mark. *The Reckless Mind: Intellectuals in Politics.* New York: New York Review Books, 2001.

López Valdizón, José María. *Sudor y protesta.* Guatemala City: Editorial del Ministerio de Educación Pública, 1953.

Loveman, Brian. *Struggles in the Countryside: Politics and Rural Labor in Chile, 1919–1973.* Bloomington: Indiana University Press, 1976.

———, and Thomas M. Davis, eds. *Politics of Anti-Politics: The Military in Latin America.* Lincoln: University of Nebraska Press, 1989.

Lukács, George. *The Historical Novel.* New York: Penguin, 1962.

Macías, Julio César. *La Guerrilla fue mi camino: Epitafio para César Montes.* Guatemala City: Piedra Santa, 1997.

Malamud-Goti, Jaime. *Game without End: State Terror and the Politics of Justice.* Norman: University of Oklahoma Press, 1996.

Malia, Martin. *The Soviet Tragedy: A History of Socialism in Russia, 1917–1991.* New York: Free Press, 1994.

Mallon, Florencia. "Chronicle of a Path Foretold?: Velasco's Revolution, Vanguardia Revolucionaria, and 'Shining Omens' in the Indigenous Communities of Andahuaylas." In Stern, *Peru's Shining and Other Paths.*

———. *The Defense of Community in Peru's Central Highlands: Peasant Struggle and Capitalist Transition, 1860–1940.* Princeton. Princeton University Press, 1983.

———. *Peasant and Nation: The Making of Postcolonial Mexico and Peru.* Berkeley: University of California Press, 1995.

Mandelbaum, Michael. *The Ideas That Conquered the World: Peace, Democracy, and Free Markets in the Twentieth-Century.* New York: Public Affairs, 2002.

Mármol, Miguel. *Miguel Marmol.* Ed. Roque Dalton. Trans. Kathleen Ross and Richard Shaaf. Willimantic, Conn.: Curbstone Press, 1987.

Marshall, T. H. *Citizenship and Social Class.* Concord, Mass.: Pluto Press, 1991.

Martínez Peláez, Severo. *Motines de Indios: La violencia colonial en Centroamérica y Chiapas.* Puebla: Universidad Autónoma de Puebla, 1985.

Marx, Karl. *Capital.* Vol. 1. New York: International Publishers, 1967.

Mayer, Arno J. *Dynamics of Counterrevolution in Europe, 1870–1956: An Analytical Framework.* New York: Harper and Row, 1971.

———. *The Furies: Violence and Terror in the French and Russian Revolutions.* Princeton: Princeton University Press, 2000.

McClintock, Michael. *The American Connection: State Terror and Popular Resistance in Guatemala.* London: Zed Books, 1985.

McCreery, David. *Rural Guatemala: 1760–1940.* Stanford: Stanford University Press, 1994.

Menchú, Rigoberta. *Me llamo Rigoberta Menchú y así me nació la conciencia.* Mexico City: Siglo Veintiuno, 1985.

Mendes, Chico. *Chico Mendes in His Own Words: Fight for the Forest.* London: Latin American Bureau, 1989.
Michael, Dan. "Chile and the Shadows of the Cold War." Paper presented at the Annual Spring Graduate Student Conference, George Washington University, April 19–20, 2002.
Mir, Pedro. *Countersong to Walt Whitman, and Other Poems.* Trans. Jonathan Cohen and Donald D. Walsh. Washington, D.C.: Azul, 1993.
Misión de Verificación de las Naciones Unidas en Guatemala. *Los linchamientos: Un flagelo contra la dignidad humana.* Guatemala City: MINUGUA, 2000.
Molyneux, Maxine. "Twentieth-Century State Formations in Latin America." In *Hidden Histories of Gender and the State in Latin America,* ed. Elizabeth Dore and Maxine Molyneux. Durham: Duke University Press, 2000.
Moore, Barrington. *Injustice: The Social Bases of Obedience and Revolt.* White Plains: M. E. Sharpe, 1978.
Morales, José. "Acción civica: El desarrollo de los ciudadanos." *Revista Militar,* no. 70 (October–December 1971): 17–22.
Moulian, Tomás. *El consumo me consume.* Santiago: LOM, 1998.
———. "A Time of Forgetting: The Myths of the Chilean Transition." NACLA Report on the Americas, 32 (September/October 1998): 16–22.
Náñez Falcón, Guillermo. "Erwin Paul Dieseldorff: Guatemala Entrepreneur in the Alta Verapaz of Guatemala, 1889–1937." Ph.D. diss., Tulane University, 1970.
Nash, Manning. *Machine Age Maya: The Industrialization of a Guatemalan Community.* Chicago: University of Chicago Press, 1967.
National Security Archive. *El Salvador: The Making of U.S. Policy, 1977–1984.* Alexandria, Va.: Chadwick-Healey, 1989.
Neruda, Pablo. *Canto General.* Berkeley: University of California Press, 1991.
Noval, Joaquín. "Acerca de la lucha ideológica." *Revista de la Facultad de Ciencias Jurídicas y Sociales de Guatemala* 9, no.1 (1976): 22–23.
———. "El estado y la violencia." *Revista de la Facultad de Ciencias Jurídicas y Sociales de Guatemala* 9, no. 4 (1977): 10–20.
———. "Notas sobre la cuestión indígena en Guatemala." *7 Días en la USAC* 2, no. 31 (1979): 4–10.
———, comp. Socio-económica de la región kekchi. Unpublished manuscript compiled by the Instituto Indigenista Nacional. 1950–52.
Nugent, David. *Modernity at the Edge of Empire: State, Individual, and Nation in the Northern Peruvian Andes, 1885–1935.* Stanford: Stanford University Press, 1997.
Obando Sánchez, Antonio. *Memorias.* Guatemala City: Editorial Universitaria, 1978.
Ochaita de Escaler, Gilda Liliana. "Pervivencia de las cofradías indígenas en Rabinal, Guatemala." Licenciatura thesis, Universidad Rafael Landivar, Facultad de Humanidades, 1974.
O'Donnell, Guillermo. *Modernization and Bureaucratic-Authoritarianism.* Berkeley: University of California Press, 1973.

———, Philippe Schmitter, and Laurence Whitehead. *Transitions from Authoritarian Rule.* Baltimore: Johns Hopkins University Press, 1986.

Olcott, Jocelyn. "Las Hijas de la Malinche: Gender and State Formation in Post-Revolutionary Mexico, 1934–1940." Ph.D. diss., Yale University, 2000.

Pacheco, Luis. *La religiosidad Maya-Kekchi alrededor de maíz.* San José, Costa Rica: Editorial Escuela para todos, 1985.

Paredes Moreira, José Luis. *Reforma agraria: Una experiencia en Guatemala.* Guatemala City: Imprenta Universitaria, 1963.

Partido Guatemalteco de Trabajo. *El camino de la revolución guatemalteca.* Mexico City: Ediciones de Cultura Popular, 1972.

Paterson, Thomas G. *Contesting Castro: The United States and the Triumph of the Cuban Revolution.* New York: Oxford University Press, 1994.

Paul VI. *Encyclical Letter of His Holiness Pope Paul VI on the Development of Peoples.* New York: Paulist Press, 1967.

Payeras, Mario. *Days of the Jungle: The Testimony of a Guatemalan Guerrillero, 1972–1976.* New York: Monthly Review Press, 1983.

Pearson, Neale. "The Confederación Nacional Campesina de Guatemala (SNCG) and Peasant Unionism in Guatemala, 1944–1954." Masters thesis, Georgetown University, 1964.

Pérez, Louis. *On Becoming Cuban: Identity, Nationality, and Culture.* Chapel Hill: University of North Carolina Press, 1999.

Phillips, David Atlee. *The Night Watch: Twenty-five Years of Peculiar Service.* New York: Atheneum, 1977.

Pike, Frederick B. *Hispanismo 1898–1936: Spanish Conservatives and Liberals and the Relations with Spanish America.* Notre Dame: University of Notre Dame Press, 1971.

Pimental, Leopoldo. "La integración del Indígena al desarrollo nacional." *Revista Militar* 3, no. 19 (January–March 1979): 51–62.

Pitti, Joseph A. "Jorge Ubico and Guatemalan Politics in the 1920s." Ph.D. diss., University of New Mexico, 1975.

Polanyi, Karl. *The Great Transformation: The Political and Economic Origins of Our Time.* Boston: Beacon, 2001 [1944].

Politzer, Patricia. *Fear in Chile: Lives under Pinochet.* New York: New Press, 2001.

Popkin, Margaret. *Las patrullas civiles y su legado: Superar la militarización y polarización del campo guatemalteco.* Washington, D.C.: Robert F. Kennedy Memorial Center for Human Rights, 1996.

Porras, Gustavo. "Análisis estructural y recomposición clasista de la sociedad guatemalteca de 1954–1980." In *Seminario estado: Clases sociales y cuestión etnico-nacional,* ed. Centro de Estudios Integrados de Desarrollo Comunal. Mexico City: Editorial Praxis, 1992.

Posada-Carbó, Eduardo. "Fiction as History: The *Bananeras* and Gabriel García Márquez's *One Hundred Years of Solitude.*" *Journal of Latin American Studies* 30 (1998): 395–414.

Power, Margaret. *Right-Wing Women in Chile: Feminine Power and the Struggle against Allende, 1964–1973.* University Park: Pennsylvania State University Press, 2002.

Proyecto Interdiocesano de Recuperación de la Memoria Histórica (REMHI). *Guatemala: Nunca Más.* Guatemala City: Oficina de Derechos Humanos del Arzobispado de Guatemala, 1998.

Quintana, Epaminondas. *Historia de la generación de 1920.* Guatemala City: Tipografía Nacional, 1971.

Radosh, Ronald, Grigory Sevostianov, and Mary Habeck, eds. *Spain Betrayed: The Soviet Union in the Spanish Civil War.* New Haven: Yale University Press, 2001.

Ramírez, Chiqui. *La guerra de los 36 año: Vista con ojos de mujer de izquierda.* Guatemala City: Editorial Oscar de León Palacios, 2001.

Rawls, John. *A Theory of Justice.* Cambridge: Harvard University Press, 1971.

Recopilación de las leyes de la República de Guatemala. Vol. 66. Guatemala City: Tipografía Nacional, 1947.

Reuque Paillalef, Rosa Isolde. *When a Flower Is Reborn: The Life and Times of a Mapuche Feminist.* Ed. and trans. Florencia Mallon. Durham: Duke University Press, 2002.

Rial, Juan. "Makers and Guardians of Fear: Controlled Terror in Uruguay." In *Fear at the Edge: State Terror and Resistance in Latin America,* ed. Juan E. Corradi, Patricia Weiss Fagen, and Manuel Antonio Garretón. Berkeley: University of California Press, 1992.

Robin, Corey. *Fear: The History of a Political Idea.* New York: Oxford University Press, 2004.

Robin, Ron. *The Making of the Cold War Enemy: Culture and Politics in the Military-Intellectual Complex.* Princeton: Princeton University Press, 2001.

Robles, Mario. "Concepciones ideológicas y políticas en FAR." Unpublished monograph.

Roettinger, Philip C. "The Company, Then and Now." *Progressive,* July 1986.

Roosevelt, Kermit. *Countercoup: The Struggle for Control of Iran.* New York: McGraw Hill, 1979.

Rorty, Richard. "The End of Leninism: Havel and Social Hope." *Truth and Progress,* vol. 3: *Philosophical Papers.* Cambridge: Cambridge University Press, 1998.

Rosenberg, Tina. *Children of Cain: Violence and the Violent in Latin America.* New York: Penguin, 1992.

Rossell y Arellano, Mariano. *Alocución en la Catedral Metropolitana.* Guatemala City: Unión Tipográfica, 1954.

———. *Carta circular . . . con ocasión de los atentados contra la Iglesia en Yugoslavia.* Guatemala City: n.p., 1946.

———. *Carta pastoral con ocasión del segundo centenario de la sede Arzobispal de Guatemala.* Guatemala City: Sánchez y de Guise, 1943.

———. *Carta pastoral sobre la Acción Católica.* Guatemala City: Sánchez y de Guise, 1946.

———. *Carta pastoral sobre los avances del comunismo en Guatemala.* Guatemala City: Sánchez y de Guise, 1954.

———. *Exhortación pastoral con motivo del día de Pentecostés.* Guatemala City: Sánchez y de Guise, 1944.

———. *Instrucción pastoral al pueblo católico de Guatemala sobre el deber y condiciones del sufragio.* Guatemala City: Sánchez y de Guise, 1948.

———. *Mensaje a las clases laborante y patronal.* Guatemala City: Hispania, 1946.

———. *Tactics and Works of Communism.* Des Moines: National Catholic Rural Life Conference, 1955.

Ruano, Edgar. "Los cincuenta años de los comunistas guatemaltecos." *La Ermita.* 4, no. 16 (October–December 1999): 38–44.

Salimovich, Sofia, Elizabeth Lira, and Eugenia Weinstein. "Victims of Fear: The Social Psychology of Repression." In *Fear at the Edge: State Terror and Resistance in Latin America,* ed. Juan E. Corradi, Patrica Weiss Fagen, and Manuel Antonio Garretón. Berkeley: University of California Press, 1992.

Sandoval, Miguel Angel. *Los años de la resistencia.* Guatemala City: Editorial Oscar de León Palacios, 1999.

Sapper, David. "Costumbres y creencias religiosas de los indios Queckchí." *Anales de la Sociedad de Geografía y Historia* 2, no. 2 (December 1925): 189–97.

Sapper, Karl. *Die Alta Verapaz.* Hamburg: Friederichsen, 1902.

———. *Mittelamerikanische Reisen und Studien aus den Jahren 1888 bis 1900.* Braunschweig: Vieweg und Sohn, 1902.

Scarry, Elaine. *The Body in Pain: The Making and Unmaking of the World.* New York: Oxford University Press, 1987.

Schackt, Jon. "The Tzuultaq'a: Religious Lore and Cultural Processes among the Kekchi." *Belizean Studies* 12, no. 5 (1984): 16–29.

Schirmer, Jennifer. *The Guatemalan Military Project: A Violence Called Democracy.* Philadelphia: University of Pennsylvania Press, 1998.

Schlesinger, Stephen, and Stephen Kinzer. *Bitter Fruit: The Untold Story of the American Coup in Guatemala.* New York: Doubleday, 1982.

Schmölz-Häberlein, Michaela. "Continuity and Change in a Guatemalan Indian Community: San Cristóbal-Verapaz, 1870–1940." *Hispanic American Historical Review* 76, no. 2 (1996): 226–48.

Schneider, Pablo, Hugo Maul, and Luis Mauricio Membreño. *El mito de la reforma agraria: 40 años de experimentación en Guatemala.* Guatemala City: Centro de Investigaciones Económicas Nacionales, 1989.

Schneider, Ronald. *Communism in Guatemala, 1944–1954.* New York: Octagon Books, 1979 [1958].

Schoultz, Lars. *National Security and United States Policy toward Latin America.* Princeton: Princeton University Press, 1987.

Scott, Joan Wallach. *Only Paradoxes to Offer: French Feminists and the Rights of Man.* Cambridge: Harvard University Press, 1996.

Seed, Patricia. *To Love, Honor, and Obey in Colonial Mexico: Conflicts over Marriage Choice, 1574–1821.* Stanford: Stanford University Press, 1998.

Seigel, Jerrold. "Problematizing the Self." In *Beyond the Cultural Turn: New Directions in the Study of Society and Culture,* ed. Victoria E. Bonnell and Lynn Hunt. Berkeley: University of California Press, 1999.

Serra, Jaime. "Three Mistaken Theses regarding the Connection between Industrialization and Authoritarian Regimes." In *The New Authoritarianism in Latin America,* ed. David Collier and Fernando Henrique Cardoso. Princeton: Princeton University Press, 1979.

Shklar, Judith. *American Citizenship.* Cambridge: Harvard University Press, 1991.

Sieder, Rachel. "Customary Law and Local Power in Guatemala." In *Guatemala after the Peace Accords,* ed. Rachel Sieder. London: Institute for Latin American Studies, 1998.

Silva, Eduardo. "Authoritarianism, Democracy, and Development." In *Latin America Transformed: Globalization and Modernity,* ed. Robert Gwynne and Cristobal Kay. New York: Oxford University Press, 1999.

Silva, Patricio. "Modernization, Consumerism, and Politics in Chile." In *Neoliberalism with a Human Face? The Politics and Economics of the Chilean Model,* ed. David Hojman. Liverpool: University of Liverpool, 1995.

Silvert, Kalman. A Study in Government: Guatemala. New Orleans: Tulane University, Middle American Research Institute, 1954. pp. 63–68.

Solomon, Joel. *Violencia institucional: Las patrullas de autodefensa civil en Guatemala, 1993–1994.* Washington, D.C.: Robert F. Kennedy Memorial Center for Human Rights, 1994.

Stern, Steve. "Between Tragedy and Promise: The Politics of Writing Latin American History in the Late Twentieth Century." In *Reclaiming the Political in Latin American History: Essays from the North,* ed. Gilbert Joseph. Durham: Duke University Press, 2001.

———, ed. *Peru's Shining and Other Paths: War and Society in Peru, 1980–1995.* Durham: Duke University Press, 1998.

Stoll, David. *Between Two Armies in the Ixil Towns of Guatemala.* New York: Columbia University Press, 1995.

———. *Rigoberta Menchú and the Story of All Poor Guatemalans.* Boulder: Westview, 1999.

Streeter, Stephen. *Managing the Counterrevolution: The United States and Guatemala, 1954–1961.* Athens: Ohio University Press, 2000.

Sullivan-González, Douglass. *Piety, Power, and Politics: Religion and Nation Formation in Guatemala, 1821–1871.* Pittsburgh: University of Pittsburgh Press, 1998.

———. "Where Did Jesus Go? The Black Christ of Esquipulas." Paper presented at the Latin American Studies Conference, Chicago, September 1998.

Suslow, Leo. "Social Security in Guatemala." Ph.D. diss., University of Connecticut, 1954.

Taracena Arriola, Arturo. "La Confederación Obrera Centroaméricana (COCA): 1921–1926." *Anuario de Estudios Centroamericanos* 10 (1984): 81–93.

———. *Les origines du mouvement ouvrier au Guatemala, 1878–1932.* Paris, 1982.

———. "Presencia anarquista en Guatemala." *Mesoamérica* 9, no. 15 (1988): 1–23.

Taylor, Charles. *The Ethics of Authenticity.* Cambridge: Harvard University Press, 1992.

———. *Sources of the Self: The Making of the Modern Identity.* Cambridge: Cambridge University Press, 1989.

Taylor, Diana. *Disappearing Acts: Spectacles of Gender and Nationalism in Argentina's "Dirty War."* Durham: Duke University Press, 1997.

Thomson, Guy P., with David G. LaFrance. *Patriotism, Politics, and Popular Liberalism in Nineteenth Century Mexico: Juan Francisco Lucas and the Puebla Sierra.* Wilmington: Scholarly Resources, 1999.

Tilly, Charles. *From Mobilization to Revolution.* Reading, Mass: Addison-Wesley, 1978.

Tinsman, Heidi. *Partners in Conflict: The Politics of Gender, Sexuality, and Labor in the Chilean Agrarian Reform, 1950–1973.* Durham: Duke University Press, 2002.

Toriello Garrido, Guillermo. *La batalla de Guatemala.* Mexico: Cuadernos Americanos, 1955.

———. *Guatemala: Más de 20 años de Traición, 1954–1979.* Guatemala City: Editorial Universitaria, 1979.

———. *Tras la cortina de banano.* Mexico City: Fondo de Cultura Económica, 1976.

Torres-Rivas, Edelberto. "Epilogue: Notes on Terror, Violence, Fear and Democracy." In *Societies of Fear: The Legacy of Civil War, Violence and Terror in Latin America,* ed. Kees Koonings and Dirk Kruijt. London: Zed Books, 1999.

———, and Gregorio Selser. *El Guatemalazo: La primera guerra sucia.* Buenos Aires: Editorial Iguazú, 1961.

Tribunal Supremo Electoral. *Memoria: Consulta popular 1999.* Guatemala City: Tribunal Supremo Electoral, 2000.

Tyson, Timothy. *Radio Free Dixie: Robert F. Williams and the Roots of Black Power.* Chapel Hill: University of North Carolina Press, 1999.

United States Department of State. *Intervention of International Communism in Guatemala.* Washington, D.C.: U.S. Government Printing Office, 1954.

United States General Accounting Office, National Security and International Affairs Division. *Military Sales: The United States Continuing Munition Supply Relationship with Guatemala.* Washington, D.C., 1986.

Universidad de San Carlos, Facultad de Ciencias Jurídicas y Sociales. "Visita al Municipio de Santa María Cahabón." Unpublished manuscript. 1974.

Vaughan, Mary Kay. "Modernizing Patriarchy: State Policies, Rural Households, and Women in Mexico, 1930–1940." In *Hidden Histories of Gender and the State in Latin America,* ed. Elizabeth Dore and Maxine Molyneux. Durham: Duke University Press, 2000.

Villagrán Kramer, Francisco. *Biografía política de Guatemala: Los pactos políticos de 1944–1979.* Guatemala City: FLACSO, 1993.

Viotti da Costa, Emilia. *The Brazilian Empire: Myths and Histories.* Chicago: University of Chicago Press, 1985.

Voekel, Pamela. *Alone before God: The Religious Origins of Modernity in Mexico.* Durham: Duke University Press, 2002.

Wagner, Regina. *Los Alemanes en Guatemala, 1828–1944.* Guatemala City: Afanes, 1996.

Walzer, Michael. "Can There Be a Decent Left?" *Dissent,* Spring 2002.

Warren, Kay. The Symbols of Subordination: Indian Identity in a Guatemalan Town. Austin: University of Texas Press, 1978.

Weber, Max. "Politics as Vocation." In *Max Weber: Essays in Sociology,* ed. H. H. Gerth and C. W. Mills. New York: Oxford University Press, 1946.

Weitz, Eric D. "The Modernity of Genocide: War, Race, and Revolution in the Twentieth Century." In *The Specter of Genocide: Mass Murder in Historical Perspective,* ed. Ben Kiernan and Robert Gellately. Cambridge: Cambridge University Press, 2003.

Wickham-Crowley, Timothy. *Guerrillas and Revolutions in Latin America: A Comparative Study of Insurgents and Regimes since 1956.* Princeton: Princeton University Press, 1992.

Wilkinson, Daniel. *Silence on the Mountain: Stories of Terror, Betrayal, and Forgetting in Guatemala.* New York: Houghton Mifflin, 2002.

Wilson, Richard. *Maya Resurgence in Guatemala: Q'eqchi' Experiences.* Norman: University of Oklahoma Press, 1995.

Winn, Peter. "The Furies of the Andes: Violence and Terror in the Chilean Revolution and Counterrevolution of 1970–1973." Paper given at the conference Rethinking Latin America's Century of Revolutionary Violence, Yale University, May 15–17, 2003.

Womack, John. "The Mexican Revolution, 1910–1920." In *Mexico since Independence,* ed. Leslie Bethell. Cambridge: Cambridge University Press, 1991.

Woodward, Ralph Lee. "Communist Infiltration of the Guatemalan Urban Labor Movement, 1920–1954." Masters thesis, Tulane University, 1959.

Yoldi, Pilar. *Don Juan Coc: Príncipe Q'eqchí, 1945–1995.* Guatemala City: Piedra Santa, 1996.

Zakaria, Fareed. *The Future of Freedom: Illiberal Democracy at Home and Abroad.* New York: W. W. Norton, 2003.

Index